The Forgotten Front

After a decade and a half of war in Iraq and Afghanistan, U.S. policymakers are seeking to provide aid and advice to local governments' counterinsurgency campaigns rather than directly intervening with U.S. American forces. This strategy and U.S. counterinsurgency doctrine in general fail to recognize that, despite a shared aim of defeating an insurgency, the United States and its local partner frequently have differing priorities with respect to the conduct of counterinsurgency operations. Without some degree of reform or policy change on the part of the insurgency-plagued government, American support will have a limited impact. Using three detailed case studies – the Hukbalahap Rebellion in the Philippines, Vietnam during the rule of Ngo Dinh Diem, and the Salvadorian Civil War – Ladwig demonstrates that providing significant amounts of aid will not generate sufficient leverage to affect a client's behavior and policies. Instead, Ladwig argues that influence flows from pressure and tight conditions on aid rather than from boundless generosity.

WALTER C. LADWIG III is Assistant Professor of International Relations in the Department of War Studies at King's College London and an Associate Fellow at the Royal United Services Institute. His work has appeared in *International Security*, the *Journal of Strategic Studies*, and *Small Wars & Insurgencies*, as well as the *New York Times* and the *Wall Street Journal*.

The Forgotten Front

Patron-Client Relationships in Counterinsurgency

WALTER C. LADWIG III
King's College London

CAMBRIDGE
UNIVERSITY PRESS

CAMBRIDGE
UNIVERSITY PRESS

University Printing House, Cambridge CB2 8BS, United Kingdom

One Liberty Plaza, 20th Floor, New York, NY 10006, USA

477 Williamstown Road, Port Melbourne, VIC 3207, Australia

4843/24, 2nd Floor, Ansari Road, Daryaganj, Delhi – 110002, India

79 Anson Road, #06–04/06, Singapore 079906

Cambridge University Press is part of the University of Cambridge.

It furthers the University's mission by disseminating knowledge in the pursuit of education, learning, and research at the highest international levels of excellence.

www.cambridge.org
Information on this title: www.cambridge.org/9781107170773
DOI: 10.1017/9781316756805

First published 2017

Printed in the United States of America by Sheridan Books, Inc.

A catalogue record for this publication is available from the British Library.

ISBN 978-1-107-17077-3 Hardback
ISBN 978-1-316-62180-6 Paperback

If we turn down additional aid, we could be helping a Communist guerrilla takeover of the country. But on the other hand, we'll be aiding a government we're not happy with. The bottom line is: which is the lesser of two evils?

– Senator J. James Exon (D-Neb), 1982

Contents

Acknowledgments

The aphorism "He that is taught only by himself has a fool for a master" is variously attributed to Ben Jonson and Hunter S. Thompson. Whatever faults I may have, this is fortunately not one of them, because I have been the beneficiary of teaching by a number of extraordinary scholars during the course of my academic career. I was first exposed to the academic study of international relations at the University of Southern California, where Professors Steve Lamy and John Odell planted the seed for a future career in a San Diegan who had never been out of the country. At Princeton, Richard Ullman, Michael O'Hanlon, and Michael Meese all taught me that rigorous academic scholarship could also inform public policy. I owe a particular note of thanks to my supervisors at Oxford, Hew Strachan and Yuen Foong Khong, for their supportive and patient guidance throughout the writing of this book, which evolved from a vague study of training foreign forces for counterinsurgency to its present form. Working with them demanded rigorous attention to the highest standards of both history and political science, and this book is much improved as a consequence. In their own work, they both have set a standard of scholarship that I can only hope to emulate.

My colleague at DFI International, Dr. Janine Davidson, was the first to recognize that I *needed* to do a Ph.D. I have her to thank (or to blame) for the encouragement that set me off on this path. Such a journey would never have been possible without the generous support from Merton College, Oxford. Their decision to select me as a Domus A scholar not only made my doctoral studies possible but also provided me with a welcoming home across the pond, a stimulating intellectual environment, and a plethora of high-table meals. Oxford is truly a special place, and Merton is a gem within Oxford. As the only person beyond my supervisors and immediate family to read this book cover to cover twice, my Merton colleague Nina Silove deserves particular thanks for her penetrating questions, detailed feedback, and fervent belief that this was a high-quality project. I also benefited from debate and discussion with my fellow Oxonians Janina Dill, Alexander Feldman, Matthew Jenkinson, Michael Sulmeyer, Daniel Twining, Tarun Chhabra, Sandeep Sengupta, and T. X. Hammes.

This research project has been the recipient of generous grants from Merton College, the Cyril Foster Fund, the John Fell Fund of Oxford University Press, and the Smith Richardson Foundation, which made it possible for me to access archives, presidential libraries, and other private repositories of personal papers across the United States, the Philippines, and the United Kingdom. Although it is impossible to name them all here, I would like to thank the many archivists and librarians who helped me during my research. Financial and moral support was also provided by the Miller Center of Public Affairs at the University of Virginia, where I was a predoctoral fellow for a year in the middle of this project. Brian Balogh, Mel Leffler, and Jeff Legro have created a wonderful scholarly environment in which promising graduate students can be nurtured and made to understand that – contrary to the feedback they get from most of the academic world – they are talented and capable. As a result of my association with the Miller Center, I had the good fortune to have Dan Byman of Georgetown – whose own work had inspired this project – serve as my "dream mentor" for a year. I was also fortunate to have the support of a pair of senior scholars and friends in Sumit Ganguly and C. Christine Fair who involved me in a number of their research projects and provided me with opportunities to expand the scope of my scholarly expertise. The idea that a Ph.D. dissertation could be both a rigorous piece of scholarship and policy relevant was inculcated in me at the Summer Workshop on the Analysis of Military Operations and Strategy, and I thank Richard Betts, Stephen Biddle, and Eliot Cohen for the time they gave to this endeavor. The methodological rigor of this project benefited from the curriculum of the Institute for Qualitative Research Methods at Syracuse University and the mentorship of some of the leading scholars in the field. Colin Ellman, Andrew Bennett, Gary Goertz, and their colleagues provide a valuable service to junior scholars, and this book was positively shaped by the feedback I received there as well as through conversations with Stéfanie von Hlatky, Michael Cohen, and Joshua Shifrinson. Todd Greentree, Tim Hoyt, and Sean Sean Lynn-Jones all provided extensive feedback on Chapter 6 of this work. Theo Farrell served as the external examiner for my Ph.D., recommended this book to the editors at Cambridge University Press, and has championed its arguments to multiple audiences.

An edifice is only as solid as its foundations, and I am very fortunate to have had those foundations laid by my parents, Kit and Walt Ladwig. From an early age, they inculcated an interest in politics and foreign affairs and set an example of a lifelong love of learning. My parents have read more draft chapters of this book than I care to recall and continued to be supportive despite their incessant question, "When will this be finished?" Finally, I cannot properly articulate the debt of gratitude that I owe to my wife, Jen. For years she surrendered control of her dining room table to an endless pile of books and gave over whole sections of our living room to enough boxes of archival papers to create a fire hazard. She also accepted the "loss" of her husband for long stretches of time as I became an "absent-minded professor," still mentally absorbed with a fifty-year-old telegram or working out a problem with a chapter despite the fact that we were on a date, out to dinner, at the theater, or on vacation. More important, she was an invaluable source of encouragement and support – having unconditional faith in my abilities when I lacked the same. I could not have done this without her. Thank you for everything.

Archival and Primary Sources

Acheson Papers	Dean G. Acheson Papers, HST
ADST	Association for Diplomatic Studies and Training, Arlington, VA
Bohannan Papers	Charles Bohannan Papers, HIA
CALL	Center for Army Lessons Learned, Fort Leavenworth, KS
CIA	Central Intelligence Agency FOIA Electronic Reading Room
CMH	U.S. Army Center for Military History, Washington, DC
Cowen Papers	Myron M. Cowen Papers, HST
DAM	MacArthur Memorial Library and Archives, Norfolk, VA
DDE	Dwight D. Eisenhower Presidential Library
DDRS	Declassified Documents Reference Service
Dodge Papers	Joseph M. Dodge Papers, DDE
Durbrow Papers	Elbridge Durbrow Papers, HIA
FRUS 1948	*Foreign Relations of the United States 1948*, vol. I, part 2, General
FRUS 1950	*Foreign Relations of the United States 1950*, vol. VI, East Asia and the Pacific
FRUS 1951	*Foreign Relations of the United States 1951*, vol. VI, East Asia and the Pacific
FRUS 1952–1954	*Foreign Relations of the United States 1952–1954*, vol. XIII, Indochina, part 2
FRUS 1955–1957	*Foreign Relations of the United States 1955–1957*, vol. I, Vietnam
FRUS 1958–1960	*Foreign Relations of the United States 1958–1960*, vol. I, Vietnam
FRUS 1961	*Foreign Relations of the United States 1961–1963*, vol. I, Vietnam, 1961

FRUS 1962   *Foreign Relations of the United States 1961–1963*, vol. II, Vietnam, 1962
FRUS 1963/1   *Foreign Relations of the United States 1961–1963*, vol. III, Vietnam, January–August 1963
FRUS 1963/2   *Foreign Relations of the United States 1961–1963*, vol. IV, Vietnam, August–December 1963
FRUS 1964   *Foreign Relations of the United States 1964–1968*, vol. I, Vietnam, 1964
HIA   Hoover Institution Archive, Stanford University
HRA   U.S. Air Force Historical Research Agency, Maxwell, AL
HST   Harry S. Truman Presidential Library
JFK   John F. Kennedy Presidential Library
Lansdale Papers   Edward Lansdale Papers, HIA
LBJ   Lyndon B. Johnson Presidential Library
LOC   El Salvador Human Rights Collection, Library of Congress
Magsaysay Papers   Ramon Magsaysay Papers, RMAF
Melby Papers   John F. Melby Papers, HST
MHI   Military History Institute, Carlisle, PA
NACP   U.S. National Archive at College Park, MD
NAUK   National Archives of the United Kingdom
Nolting Papers   Fredrick Nolting Papers, Alderman Library, University of Virginia
NSA   National Security Archive, George Washington University
Quirino Papers   Elpidio R. Quirino Papers, Filipinas Heritage Library, Manila
RG 59   Records of the U.S. Department of State, NACP
RG 218   Records of the U.S. Joint Chiefs of Staff, NACP
RG 319   Records of the U.S. Army Staff
RG 330   Records of the U.S. Secretary of Defense, NACP
RG 334   Records of Interservice Agencies, NACP
RG 472   Records of the U.S. Forces in Southeast Asia, NACP
RMAF   Ramon Magsaysay Award Foundation, Manila

Roxas Papers	Manuel A. Roxas Papers, University of the Philippines Diliman
RRL	Ronald W. Reagan Presidential Library
Scaff Papers	Alvin Scaff Papers, HIA
STATE	U.S. State Department FOIA Virtual Reading Room
Tannenwold Papers	Theodore Tannenwold, Jr., Papers, HST
VVA	The Virtual Vietnam Archive, Texas Tech University
Williams Papers	Samuel Williams Papers, HIA
Wilson Papers	Wilbur Wilson Papers, MHI

Acronyms and Abbreviations

AFP	Armed Forces of the Philippines
AID	Agency for International Development
ANSESAL	Salvadoran National Security Agency
ARENA	National Republican Alliance
ARVN	Army of the Republic of Vietnam
CG	Civil Guard
CIA	Central Intelligence Agency
DASS	Deputy Assistant Secretary of State
DoD	U.S. Department of Defense
ECA	Economic Cooperation Administration (forerunner of AID)
ESAF	Salvadoran Armed Forces
FDR	Revolutionary Democratic Front, political wing of the FMLN
FMLN	Farabundo Martí National Liberation Front
GoES	Government of El Salvador
GoP	Government of the Philippines
GVN	South Vietnamese Government
Hukbalahap	Hukbong Bayan Laban sa mga Hapon (The People's Army against the Japanese)
ICA	International Cooperation Administration (forerunner of AID)
JCS	Joint Chiefs of Staff
JUSMAG	Joint U.S. Military Assistance Group
MAAG	Military Assistance Advisory Group
MACV	Military Assistance Command, Vietnam
MILGROUP	U.S. Military Advisory Group
MIS	Military Intelligence Service
NAMFREL	National Movement for Free Elections
NIE	National Intelligence Estimate
PC	Philippine Constabulary

PCN	Party of National Conciliation
PDC	Christian Democratic Party
PSC	Salvadoran Public Security Corps: National Guard, Treasury Police and National Police
SDC	Self-Defense Corps
SHP	Strategic Hamlet Program
USAID	U.S. Agency for International Development
VC	Vietcong

1 | *A Recurring Obstacle*

A critical error lies at the heart of American thinking about counterinsurgency (COIN): the assumption that the United States will share common goals and priorities with a local government it is assisting in COIN, which will make it relatively easy to convince that government to implement U.S. counterinsurgency prescriptions. In fact, the historical record suggests that maintaining power is frequently a competing priority for an incumbent regime, which means that many of the standard reform prescriptions for counterinsurgency – streamlining the military chain of command, ending patronage politics, engaging in economic reform, and embracing disaffected minority groups – can appear as threatening to a besieged government and its supporters as the insurgency itself.[1] Therefore, while the United States has provided its local partners with overwhelming amounts of money and materiel to support their counterinsurgency efforts, it has frequently had difficulty convincing them to abide by its counterinsurgency doctrine. This problem is particularly salient because after a decade of inconclusive war in Afghanistan and Iraq between 2003 and 2012, the United States has reoriented its approach to counterinsurgency. Instead of directly intervening in conflicts with American forces, the focus is on supporting local governments' counterinsurgency efforts with aid and advice.[2] If, as the *2009 U.S. Government Counterinsurgency Guide* asserts, "any COIN campaign is only as good as the political strategy which the affected nation adopts," the ability to influence the choices of a partner government is essential to the success of future U.S. efforts to support counterinsurgency.[3]

---

[1] For an example of such prescriptions, see David Kilcullen, *Counterinsurgency* (Oxford: Oxford University Press, 2010), p. 160.

[2] U.S. Department of Defense, *Sustaining U.S. Global Leadership: Priorities for 21st Century Defense* (Washington, D.C.: U.S. Department of Defense, 2012), p. 6.

[3] Department of State, *U.S. Government Counterinsurgency Guide* (Washington, DC: Bureau of Political-Military Affairs, January 2009), p. 29.

The mistaken assumption of a unanimity of interests with a local government was most notable in the 2006 U.S. Army/Marine Corps counterinsurgency field manual, FM 3–24, which shaped American thinking on civil wars for nearly a decade. The manual asserts that "the primary objective of any COIN operation is to foster development of effective governance by a legitimate government."[4] Toward that end, U.S. forces were enjoined to build trust with host-nation authorities and work closely with them to enhance their legitimacy by undertaking reform and responding to popular grievances. No suggestion is made that these goals might not be in the interest of the ruling government.[5]

In American experience since 2003, however, local partners in Iraq, Afghanistan, and Pakistan frequently appeared to actively subvert Washington's counterinsurgency ambitions. An inability to restrain Iraqi prime minister Nouri Maliki's sectarian agenda prevented the military gains from the 2007 surge from being translated into positive political outcomes and laid the foundation for the rise of the Islamic State.[6] In Afghanistan, President Hamid Karzai's use of patronage politics was seen by outsiders as a form of corruption, which undercut public support for the very government that U.S. and NATO forces were trying to assist. Washington's apparent inability to shape the behavior of what many observers believed was a dependent partner led one European diplomat to marvel that "never in history has any superpower spent so much money, sent so many troops to a country, and had so little influence over what its president says and does."[7] Across the border in Pakistan, the United States has supplied Islamabad with more than $30 billion in military and economic assistance since 2001, yet is unable to influence the Pakistani government to cease its support of militant groups that are undermining U.S. objectives in

---

[4] Department of the Army, *Counterinsurgency*, Field Manual (FM) 3–24 (Chicago: University of Chicago Press 2007), p. 37.

[5] Stephen Biddle, "The New U.S. Army/Marine Corps Counterinsurgency Field Manual as Political Science and Political Praxis," *Perspectives on Politics*, 6, no. 2 (June 2008), p. 348.

[6] Peter Beinart, "The Surge Fallacy," *The Atlantic*, September 2015. On the military effects of the surge, see Stephen Biddle, Jeffrey Friedman, and Jacob Shapiro, "Testing the Surge, Why Did Violence Decline in Iraq in 2007?" *International Security* 37, no. 1 (Summer 2012), pp. 7–40.

[7] Rod Nordland et al., "Gulf Widens between U.S. and a More Volatile Karzai," *New York Times*, March 17, 2012.

Afghanistan – even as some of those same groups have turned against the Pakistani state.[8] FM 3–24's assumption of a unanimity of interests between patron and client was clearly misplaced.

Incorporating the experience gained in Iraq and Afghanistan, the 2014 edition of FM 3–24, *Insurgencies and Countering Insurgencies*, briefly acknowledges that the local government's interests may not always coincide with those of the United States.[9] It does not, however, examine in any detail the difficulty of convincing a local government to adopt American counterinsurgency principles.[10] When a host-nation government believes that it is so important to Washington that it cannot be allowed to fail, it is inclined to resist any U.S.-backed reform effort that would challenge the domestic status quo. As a result, the United States has found itself in the paradoxical situation of supporting weak allies in danger of internal collapse, who were highly dependent on external support for their continued survival, yet over whom Washington had little control or influence.

Contrary to the assumptions of the aforementioned U.S. counter-insurgency manual – and much of the classic counterinsurgency litera-ture on which it is based – when supporting counterinsurgency, the relationship between Washington and its local partner is often far from harmonious. Although this has been clearly highlighted by recent events in Iraq and Afghanistan, the challenge of generating sufficient influence over a client state to shape its behavior has plagued American counterinsurgency assistance efforts for decades. Writing in 1963, before the "Americanization" of the Vietnam War, the senior U.S. advisor to the South Vietnamese I Corps presciently warned in his end-of-tour report that "the development of techniques and means to increase U.S. leverage in Vietnam is the single most important problem facing us there and it will be a fundamental problem in any future counterinsurgency effort in which we become involved."[11] Since then, a host of critics have pointed out that while the United States has

[8] Timothy D. Hoyt, "Pakistan, an Ally by Any Other Name," *U.S. Naval Institute Proceedings*, 137/7/1,301 (July 2011); C. Christine Fair and Sumit Ganguly, "An Unworthy Ally," *Foreign Affairs*, 94, no. 5 (September–October 2015), pp. 160–70.

[9] FM 3–24, *Insurgencies and Countering Insurgencies* (Washington, DC: Department of the Army, 2014), pp. 1–8, 10–5.

[10] *Ibid.*, pp. 10–15.

[11] Bryce Denno, Senior Officer Debriefing Reports: Vietnam War, 1962–1972, September 6, 1963, Military History Institute, Carlisle, PA (MHI), p. 7.

provided partner governments with extensive assistance to combat insurgents, an inability to convince them to adopt its counterinsurgency prescriptions or address what Washington sees as the political and economic "root causes" of an insurgency has repeatedly emerged as a major impediment to success.[12] In the absence of sufficient leverage to compel a client regime to address these shortcomings, significant external aid and support can actually reduce its incentives to address domestic discontent or govern inclusively, which can render a supported government less stable than it would have been without U.S. assistance.[13]

As the United States seeks to focus its efforts on supporting local governments' counterinsurgency operations, rather than directly intervening in conflicts, it will have to confront this question of influence head on. Without U.S. troops on the ground capable of independent action, success will depend on the policies and choices of the client government. In these circumstances, achieving desired outcomes can be particularly challenging because the U.S. advisors do not directly control the levers of governance in the host nation.[14] Instead, their role is limited to offering guidance and attempting to influence the local regime's behavior.

Despite the fact that the majority of America's experiences with counterinsurgency – both during the Cold War and today – involve assisting another government in combating an insurgency, the particular challenges of working with or through a partner nation are not widely discussed in the counterinsurgency literature. Indeed, a review of the literature on counterinsurgency, both theoretical and practical, reveals that it has largely failed to integrate issues of alliance behavior into the study of the dynamics of revolutionary and counterrevolutionary war.[15] Even when the role of supporting allies is discussed, the implicit

---

[12] Important works in this vein are Douglas S. Blaufarb, *The Counterinsurgency Era* (New York: Free Press, 1977); D. Michael Shafer, *Deadly Paradigms* (Princeton, NJ: Princeton University Press, 1988); Benjamin C. Schwarz, *American Counterinsurgency Doctrine and El Salvador* (Santa Monica, CA: RAND, 1991); and William E. Odom, *On Internal War* (Durham, NC: Duke University Press, 1992).

[13] Odom, *On Internal War*, p. 9.

[14] Ronald H. Spector, *Advice and Support: The Early Years, 1941–1960* (Washington, DC: Center of Military History, 1985), p. 346.

[15] One notable exception to this neglect is Daniel L. Byman, "Friends Like These: Counterinsurgency and the War on Terrorism," *International Security*, 31, no. 2 (Fall 2006).

assumption is that the counterinsurgent forces are a unitary actor. This problem is compounded by the fact that contemporary counterinsurgency scholarship has drawn a significant number of its insights from the colonial era, particularly the experiences of the British in Malaya and the French in Algeria, which can blind scholars to the challenge of working through an autonomous local government, because in those cases the European power *was* the government.[16] Consequently, this literature frequently fails to recognize the local government's opposition to externally fostered reform and the limits on American leverage to bring about the reforms its doctrine calls for. Although scholars and analysts have spent much time and effort in recent years trying to divine the "key" to counterinsurgency, they have not given the same level of attention to understanding when a local government will be willing to follow American guidance. As Benjamin Schwarz sagely noted, "[I]t is one thing to have the key; it is entirely a different matter to force another to use it to unlock a door through which he does not wish to enter."[17]

Examining efforts to support a local government's counterinsurgency campaign with aid and advice, this book puts the focus on U.S. patron-client relations by asking how a patron can best influence a client state's counterinsurgency strategy and behavior? Finding structural explanations such as power differential, aid dependence, strategic utility, and selectorate theory unable to explain the patterns of influence observed in the interventions examined here, this study employs *agency theory* – which is concerned with the challenges of motivating one party (the agent) to act on behalf of another (the principal) – to examine the patron-client dynamics that arise when assisting counterinsurgency.[18] Drawing on the insights of agency theory, two

---

[16] For example, the work of John Nagl, which achieved prominence in the mid-2000s as the United States grappled with counterinsurgency in Iraq, draws its lessons from the British experience in Malaya and the writings of Robert Thompson. John A. Nagl, *Learning to Eat Soup with a Knife: Counterinsurgency Lessons from Malaya and Vietnam* (London: Praeger, 2002). The writings of David Galula, a French infantry officer who served in the Algerian War, have also been influential in shaping contemporary American counterinsurgency doctrine. Indeed, the authors of the 2006 version of FM 3–24 write that "of the many books that were influential in the writing of [FM] 3–24, perhaps none was as important as David Galula's *Counterinsurgency Warfare: Theory and Practice.*" FM 3–24, *Counterinsurgency*, p. xix.

[17] Schwarz, *American Counterinsurgency Doctrine*, p. 77.

[18] For an overview of agency theory, see Joseph Stiglitz, "Principal and Agent (II)," in *A Dictionary of Economics* (Basingstoke: Palgrave, 2002), pp. 185–90.

archetypical influence strategies are identified: *inducement*, which assumes that the unilateral provision of assistance to a client, coupled with strong public statements of support, will be reciprocated by compliance with a patron's preferred policies; and *conditionality*, which tries to shape the client's behavior by making delivery of assistance contingent on a client's prior implementation of a patron's preferred policies. The relative utility of these strategies is then tested in three historical case studies of the most significant U.S. counterinsurgency support efforts of the Cold War: the Philippines (1946–54), Vietnam (1955–63), and El Salvador (1979–91). By delving deeply into the archival records of these conflicts, this study demonstrates that there were important variations in the degree of influence achieved over the host nation's counterinsurgency policies which correlate with the influence strategy employed: the client government complied with U.S. preferences when the United States attached conditions on aid, but not when it provided inducements.[19]

The cases examined here are ones where the United States provided aid and support to another country's counterinsurgency effort short of the introduction of regular combat troops, what Mi Yung Yoon has termed "indirect military intervention."[20] The focus on the contested relations between the United States and its client states in this book mirrors developments in the "new" historiography of the Cold War which recognize that, far from being puppets, third-world leaders had great latitude to shape their own destinies and often were able to achieve their own policy goals at the expense of their great power patrons.[21]

This book makes several distinctive contributions to the scholarship on counterinsurgency. First, academic knowledge at the intersection of

[19] The topic under examination is the relative utility of inducement and conditionality to influence the behavior of a client state in counterinsurgency. Why a patron chooses one particular influence approach over another and under which conditions these approaches would be more or less effective are extremely important questions for future research, but answering them is beyond the scope of the present research design.

[20] Mi Yung Yoon, "Explaining U.S. Intervention in Third World Internal Wars, 1945–1989," *Journal of Conflict Resolution*, 41, no. 4 (1997).

[21] See, e.g., John Lewis Gaddis, "On Starting All Over Again: A Naive Approach to the Study of the Cold War," in O.A. Westad, ed., *Reviewing the Cold War: Approaches, Interpretations, Theory* (London: Frank Cass, 2000), p. 31; Tony Smith, "New Bottles for New Wine: A Pericentric Framework for the Study of the Cold War," *Diplomatic History*, 24, no. 4 (Fall 2000).

alliance behavior and counterinsurgency, which is currently under-theorized, is advanced by exploring the patron-client dynamics that occur in assisting counterinsurgency. Structural tensions in the patron-client relationship are identified as the "forgotten front" in the conflict that requires as much attention as the battle against the insurgents themselves. Second, this work demonstrates that providing significant amounts of aid will not generate the leverage necessary to affect a client's behavior; influence is more likely to flow from tight conditions on aid than from boundless generosity. In doing so, this book integrates findings from the field of economic development – where a parallel problem of divergent priorities between aid donors and recipients exists – to identify the role that conditioned foreign aid can play in generating interalliance leverage. Third, based on extensive archival research, the study adds to the historical knowledge of the three cases examined here by bringing to light a detailed understanding of the impact and degree of influence the United States had over the local governments' counterinsurgency operations, some of which has been overlooked or misunderstood by previous scholars.[22] Consequently, it identifies and corrects several important errors of causality in the historiography of these conflicts. Finally, this book offers five policy-relevant suggestions for generating influence over the behavior of client states in future interventions.

Studying Patron-Client Relations in Counterinsurgency

The primary research strategy employed in this book is the comparative historical case study.[23] This is the most appropriate method for exploring the causal mechanisms at play when a patron seeks to influence its client's counterinsurgency policies because the detailed studies allow an examination of the intervening steps whereby a presumptive cause

---

[22] For example, compare the findings reported here to Douglas Blaufarb and Michael Shafer's assessment of the degree of American influence exercised during the Huk Rebellion or Benjamin Schwarz' evaluation of the credibility of U.S. threats to withhold aid to the Salvadoran government. Blaufarb, *Counterinsurgency Era*, p. 38; Shafer, *Deadly Paradigms*, pp. 223–6; Schwarz, *American Counterinsurgency Doctrine*, p. vii.

[23] James Mahoney and Dietrich Rueschemeyer, "Comparative Historical Analysis: Achievements and Agendas," in James Mahoney and Dietrich Rueschemeyer, eds., *Comparative Historical Analysis in the Social Sciences* (Cambridge: Cambridge University Press, 2003), pp. 10–15.

(patron influence strategy) leads to an observed outcome (client [in]action).[24] Although formal models can examine the deductive logic of specific hypotheses and econometric analysis can measure causal effects, both of these approaches require the use of case studies to substantiate the actual functioning of mechanisms that link a given cause to a particular outcome.[25] The comparative method allows us to examine U.S. support efforts in context, yet systematically analyze the individual cases to identify recurring patterns of behavior and the associated challenges in dealing with partner governments.

Case studies are particularly useful when dealing with concepts, such as influence, that are difficult to measure. Delving deeply into the historical record allow us to examine the sequences of interaction between the United States and its local ally as the United States attempted to positively shape the host nation's counterinsurgency strategy – recognizing the dynamic nature of this process with moves and countermoves by each party.[26] Since causality can be complicated to demonstrate in such instances, it is important to be explicit about how we will assess the role of the patron's use of rewards or pressure in shaping the client state's behavior. *Congruence*, a within-case tool of causal inference, is employed to assess the relative effectiveness of inducement and conditionality in influencing the degree to which the client state implemented specific political, military, or economic reform measures favored by the United States as part of its counterinsurgency strategy.[27] Across the three cases there were twenty-six discrete influence events.[28] Each of these episodes began with the host nation

---

[24] Alexander L. George and Andrew Bennett, *Case Studies and Theory Development in the Social Sciences* (London: MIT Press, 2005), pp. 205–32.

[25] David Collier and James Mahoney, "Insights and Pitfalls: Selection Bias in Qualitative Research," *World Politics*, 49, no. 1 (1996); George and Bennett, *Case Studies and Theory Development*, p. 23. For a detailed discussion of the complementarity of alternate research methods, see Henry Brady and David Collier, eds., *Rethinking Social Inquiry: Diverse Tools, Shared Standards* (Oxford: Rowman & Littlefield, 2004).

[26] This is similar to the approach taken by Byman and Waxman in their study of coercion. Daniel L. Byman and Matthew Waxman, *The Dynamics of Coercion: American Foreign Policy and the Limits of Military Might* (New York: Cambridge University Press, 2002), p. 37.

[27] George and Bennett, *Case Studies and Theory Development in the Social Sciences*, pp. 181–204.

[28] Thus, although containing three cases, the study is based on significantly more than just three observations. Gary King et al., *Designing Social Inquiry* (Princeton, NJ: Princeton University Press, 1994), pp. 208–30.

actively opposing U.S. entreaties for reform, reorganization, or policy change, so it is clear that compliance was not their preferred course of action. This allows us to surmise that if any subsequent implementation of U.S.-backed measures did occur, the U.S. influence approach played a key role in shaping the client's decisions. To ensure that the observed congruence is not spurious, the studies employ process tracing, alert to any external shocks that could explain the client's changed behavior.[29]

With twenty-six observations, this project is a "medium-n" study, and its findings can be expected to have a reasonable degree of generalizability. At the same time, any theoretical proposition derived from or tested against a small universe of cases can run afoul of omitted variable bias or interaction effects. At a minimum, this analysis can provide circumstantial evidence of the responsiveness of client regimes to a patron's preferences under alternate influence strategies that allows, in David Waldner's phraseology, a "tentative commitment ... for which the reasons for belief outweigh the reasons for disbelief, relative to existing rival hypotheses and open to revision in the face of future challenges."[30]

The three U.S.-support efforts examined in this study are the Philippines during the Hukbalahap Rebellion (1946–54), Vietnam under Ngo Dinh Diem (1955–63), and El Salvador during that country's civil war (1979–91). In terms of their scope and duration, these three episodes were the most significant American counterinsurgency assistance efforts prior to the recent conflicts in Iraq and Afghanistan, which makes them among the most challenging of interventions.

Although the cases are hardly identical in every respect, they do share a number of substantive attributes that are important for a controlled comparison. All three cases

1. Are examples of U.S. support to an indigenous government's counterinsurgency effort;
2. Are instances where the country in question was perceived to be strategically important;

---

[29] John Gerring, "What Is a Case Study and What Is It Good For?" *American Political Science Review*, 98, no. 2 (May 2004), p. 348; George and Bennett, *Case Studies and Theory Development in the Social Sciences*, p. 183.
[30] David Waldner, *State Building and Late Development* (Ithaca, NY: Cornell University Press, 1999), p. 235.

3. Feature governments that were highly dependent on U.S. support for their survival yet reluctant to implement the counterinsurgency plans proposed by the United States; and
4. Occur during the Cold War, ensuring that the interstate dynamics under review all operate in the same geopolitical context.

Importantly, the three cases present varying outcomes in terms of the ability of the United States to shape the behavior of the local government. Vietnam is a clear example of a failure; the Philippines is widely regarded as a success; while in El Salvador the results were mixed, with Washington having helped shepherd through some political and economic reforms yet having achieved less success in influencing the military aspects of the host nation's counterinsurgency approach. By choosing cases with successful, unsuccessful, and ambiguous influence outcomes, the problem of selection bias is minimized.

From a historical standpoint, the cases align themselves around the U.S. experience in Vietnam – which has strongly influenced contemporary American attitudes toward irregular warfare.[31] The Hukbalahap (Huk) Rebellion is an earlier success against a Communist insurgency in Asia, the perceived lessons of which influenced the initial U.S. approach to Vietnam. El Salvador is the successor to Vietnam that gave lie to the notion that the U.S. government was done with counterinsurgency when it left Southeast Asia in 1975.

The history recounted in this book draws on thousands of pages of primary materials from twenty-four different archives, making use of embassy cables, intelligence assessments, internal memoranda, meeting notes, and transcripts of conversations, some of which were declassified for this book and are being referenced for the first time. These sources are supplemented by personal papers, unpublished manuscripts, and oral-history interviews, as well as secondary sources by regional specialists and historians. A key advantage of exploiting multiple sources of evidence in this manner is that they allow a researcher to triangulate findings, thereby providing more convincing conclusions.[32]

---

[31] Robert M. Cassidy, "Back to the Street without Joy: Counterinsurgency Lessons from Vietnam and Other Small Wars," *Parameters*, 34, no. 2 (Summer 2004), p. 74.

[32] Robert K. Yin, *Case Study Research: Design and Methods* (Thousand Oaks, CA: SAGE, 2003), p. 98.

Befitting a study of state-to-state relations between the United States and its clients, the focus is on the highest levels of government: heads of state, government ministers, ambassadors, chiefs of advisory missions, and senior military personnel are the key players. Although some – including the author at the outset of this project – may believe that the appropriate locus of attention for a study of assistance to counter-insurgency should be in the field at the regional, province, or even village level, in examining these cases it quickly becomes clear that, in Douglas Blaufarb's words, "good tactics cannot prevail when embedded in bad strategy."[33] In the absence of "leverage and support from the top" to shape a client's counterinsurgency strategy, prior study of U.S. advisory missions indicates that it is difficult, if not impossible, for advisory personnel at lower levels to render effective assistance to a client state.[34]

Looking Ahead

Chapter 2 briefly surveys literature on internal conflict before turning attention to the difficulty of working with an ally in counterinsurgency. Agency theory is employed to examine the potentially divergent preferences of a local government and its patron as well as the perni-cious effects that external assistance can have on COIN choices if the supporting nation cannot shape its client's behavior. This discussion suggests that the agency tools of monitoring and contracting are the best way to align the interests of the patron and the client.

Chapter 3 examines theories of influence and compares the insights of agency theory to alternative explanations of the influence patterns observed in the three cases. Structural realism, asymmetric interdepen-dence, strategic utility, selectorate theory, as well as the monitoring aspects of agency theory are examined and are all found to be unable to explain the actual influence patterns observed in the three case studies. Focusing instead on the "contract" between the patron and client, two

---

[33] Blaufarb, *Counterinsurgency Era*, p. 310. The U.S. counterinsurgency field manual also concurs that "tactical success guarantees nothing." FM 3–24, *Counterinsurgency*, p. 50. For a similar argument from the recent U.S. experience in Iraq, see Janine Davidson, *Lifting the Fog of Peace* (Ann Arbor: University of Michigan Press, 2010), p. 161.

[34] Robert Ramsey, *Advising Indigenous Forces: American Advisors in Korea, Vietnam and El Salvador* (Fort Leavenworth, KS: Combat Studies Institute, 2006), p. 71. See also Denno, "Debriefing," p. 7.

archetypical influence strategies (inducement and conditionality) are examined, and their observable implications are identified for testing in the case studies.

Chapter 4 examines the U.S. effort to assist the government of the Philippines during the Huk Rebellion (1947–53). Despite active opposition by Philippine leaders to American reform proposals and the expectation that Washington would aid them in their struggle regardless of what they did, a conditionality-based influence strategy resulted in a significant degree of American leverage over the counter-insurgency strategy of the government in Manila.

Chapter 5 focuses on American aid to South Vietnam during the reign of Ngo Dinh Diem (1957–63). In contrast to the Philippine case, the Eisenhower and Kennedy administrations primarily employed *inducement* to cultivate influence over the South Vietnamese government which provided little ability to shape their counterinsurgency policies.

Chapter 6 looks at America's twelve-year involvement in the Salvadoran civil war (1979–92). The United States achieved success in shaping the Salvadoran's counterinsurgency strategy in some areas but had very little impact in others. The observed variation in influence can be explained by the alternate use of *inducement* and *conditionality* by three different administrations. Important reforms and policy changes occurred when strict conditions were attached to aid and not when inducements were given.

Chapter 7 synthesizes the evidence from the three case studies, which provides significantly more support for conditionality than inducement and offers some recommendations for effectively employing conditionality to influence clients in future counterinsurgency assistance efforts.

2 | The Trouble with Allies in Counterinsurgency

Before delving into a discussion of the complexity of assisting an ally in counterinsurgency, it is helpful to quickly survey the literature on internal conflict. This chapter begins by outlining the difficulties facing local governments engaged in counterinsurgency and identifies two archetypical responses, recognizing that, in practice, local governments apply a synthesis of both. A new layer is then added to this analysis by examining the challenges faced by an external power working with a local partner.[1] Through the medium of agency theory, which examines situations in which one party delegates responsibility for execution of a task to another, two persistent problems are identified: understanding the ally's counterinsurgency preferences and appreciating the pernicious effects that external support can have on the ally's incentives to embrace its patron's preferred counterinsurgency strategies. The combination of these two factors highlights the importance of gaining sufficient influence over the local ally to shape its counterinsurgency strategy. Agency theory provides two relevant means of gaining such influence – close monitoring of the agent's behavior and careful contracting that aligns the interests of principal and agent – which are tested against alternative theories of influence in Chapter 3.

Terms of Reference

In order to provide the necessary clarity for discussing issues of insurgency and counterinsurgency, the terms of reference used in this study must be defined. *Insurgency* is considered to be the employment of political, military, and psychological means by an organized movement in order to achieve political aims by eroding the will of a ruling

---

[1] The supporting power is alternately referred to as the *great power* or the *patron*. The local government is called the *partner, host nation, local ally*, or *client*.

government and weakening its legitimacy in the eyes of the broad population. Among the tactics employed by insurgents are subversion, terrorism, and guerilla warfare.

Subversion is a systematic effort, short of the use of armed force, to undermine the political, economic, and military strength of a government. Underground organizations marshal resources, provide intelligence, recruit members, distribute antigovernment propaganda, and establish base areas or safe houses. Scholarly examination of the tactic suggests that the strength of an insurgency's subversive organization and the depth of its penetration of the civilian population are directly correlated with the success of the associated insurgency.[2]

Terrorism is the deliberate use of violence, or the threat of violence, against civilians with the aim of inspiring fear to achieve political ends. Insurgents can employ this tool to call attention to their cause, to surgically eliminate government loyalists and rival rebel movements, or to intimidate uncooperative members of the population into allowing them to operate unhindered in a given area.[3]

Guerrilla warfare is the employment of lightly armed, highly mobile fighters who seek to wear down their opponents over time rather than defeat them in direct combat. Avoiding the force-on-force conflicts of conventional war, guerrillas make use of raids, ambushes, and surprise attacks to exploit superior local intelligence and mobility, concentrating their forces on a single target before melting back into the civilian population.[4] This ability to control the tempo of operations by attacking when they are strong and regrouping when they are weak allows the guerrillas to carry on a protracted struggle.[5] Moreover, their range of potential targets normally outstrips the ability of the security forces to defend them: "disorder . . . is cheap to create and very costly to prevent," David Galula writes. "The insurgent blows up a bridge, so every bridge has to be guarded,

[2] Timothy Wickham-Crowley, *Guerrillas and Revolution in Latin America: A Comparative Study of Insurgents and Regimes since 1956* (Princeton, NJ: Princeton University Press, 1992), pp. 3–18.

[3] James E. Cross, *Conflict in the Shadows: The Nature and Politics of Guerrilla War* (New York: Doubleday, 1963), p. 35; Walter Laqueur, *Guerilla Warfare: A Historical and Critical Study* (New Brunswick, NJ: Transaction, 1998), p. 401.

[4] T. E. Lawrence, *Seven Pillars of Wisdom* (Garden City, NY: Doubleday, 1935), p. 194.

[5] Ernesto Guevara, *On Guerrilla Warfare* (New York: Praeger, 1962), p. 17.

he throws a grenade in a movie theater, so every person entering a public place has to be searched."[6]

Although *the population* or *the people* are frequently cited as the focal point of an internal conflict, assumptions about the characteristics of the population are less frequently identified. As figure 2.1 illustrates, a number of counterinsurgency theorists suggest that in terms of popular support for an insurgency, there will be an active minority for or against a particular cause and a neutral majority.[7] Scholarly examination of the dynamics of internal conflict tends to support this segmentation, with 5 to 7 percent of the population typically expressing strong support for either side.[8] To say that a large portion of the population is neutral is not to suggest that they have no preferences; however, it is frequently a small minority of the aggrieved population that decides to take up armed violence. Fence-sitting is a logical strategy for an individual whose primary goal is survival, particularly if uncommitted members of the populace can "free ride" on the sacrifice of an insurgent group, gaining the benefit of their success without sharing their risks.

Patterns of Insurgency in the Twentieth Century

Root causes of internal conflict typically include some form of societal cleavage along religious, class, race, or linguistic lines, which is often accompanied by economic or political inequality for large portions of a population and a corresponding privileged elite who seek to maintain the status quo.[9] Regardless of their professed ideology, rank-and-file guerrillas and their civilian supporters are frequently motivated by concrete social, economic, or political grievances.[10] This discontent

[6] David Galula, *Counter-Insurgency Warfare: Theory and Practice* (London: Pall Mall Press, 1964), p. 11.

[7] *Ibid.*, pp. 75–6. See also Robert Trinquier, *Modern Warfare: A French View of Counterinsurgency* (New York: Praeger, 1964), p. 109.

[8] Thomas Greene, *Comparative Revolutionary Movements: Search for Theory and Justice* (London: Prentice-Hall International, 1990), p. 75; Mark I. Lichbach, *The Rebel's Dilemma* (Ann Arbor: University of Michigan Press, 1995), p. 18.

[9] Lucian Pye, "Roots of Insurgency," in Harry Eckstein, ed., *Internal War* (New York: Free Press, 1964), p. 163; Fredrick Williams, "Guerrilla Warfare," in Franklin Osanka, ed., *Modern Guerrilla Warfare: Fighting Communist Guerrilla Movements, 1941–1961* (New York: Free Press, 1962), p. 14.

[10] Jack A. Goldstone, "An Analytical Framework," in Jack A. Goldstone, ed., *Revolutions of the Late Twentieth Century* (Boulder, CO: Westview Press, 1991), pp. 37–40; Chalmers A. Johnson, "Civilian Loyalties and Guerrilla

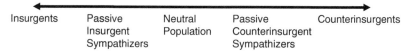

Figure 2.1 Popular support for insurgency and counterinsurgency.

increases the willingness of segments of the population to embrace a belief system that rationalizes armed violence to overturn the status quo and as such is a necessary, but not a sufficient, condition for the outbreak of an insurgency.[11]

For widespread discontent to transform into an active insurgency, proximate causes are also necessary. Two of the most important of which are the presence of revolutionary leadership and the weakness of the state. When one examines the leadership of twentieth-century insurgent movements, including the cases studied here, one finds doctors, lawyers, university professors, and even former politicians waging revolution on behalf of the "exploited masses."[12] The presence of what Theda Skocpol called "marginal political elites," who are willing to seek the power and status denied to them by their society's existing political and social structures through violence, is a key component in the emergence of an armed rebellion.[13]

The combination of mass discontent with frustrated elite leadership can be a powerful force when employed against a fragile government. James Fearon and David Laitin's quantitative analysis of the outbreak

Conflict," *World Politics*, 14, no. 4 (July 1962), p. 657; Bard E. O'Neill, *Insurgency and Terrorism* (Washington, DC: Potomac Books, 2005), pp. 171–2. For evidence of the unimportance of ideology among the rank and file, see Gabriel Almond, *The Appeals of Communism* (Princeton, NJ: Princeton University Press, 1954), p. 65; Stathis Kalyvas, "New and Old Civil Wars: A Valid Distinction?" *World Politics*, 54, no. 1 (October 2001), pp. 106–7. A percentage of insurgents are primarily motivated by the status their position garners them or the opportunity to kill, rape, or steal. Steven Metz, *Rethinking Insurgency* (Carlisle, PA: Strategic Studies Institute, 2007), pp. 10–11.

[11] Ted Gurr, *Why Men Rebel* (Princeton, NJ: Princeton University Press, 1974), pp. 216–17.

[12] High levels of education may correlate with a more serious commitment to the movement's goals. Jeremy Weinstein, "Resources and the Information Problem in Rebel Recruitment," *Journal of Conflict Resolution*, 49, no. 4 (2005), pp. 603–5.

[13] Theda Skocpol, *States and Social Revolutions: A Comparative Analysis of France, Russia, and China* (Cambridge: Cambridge University Press, 1979), p. 112. See also Goldstone, "An Analytical Framework," pp. 37–47.

of 126 internal conflicts since the end of World War II finds that the weakness of a state's security forces and the government's inability to administer a country's rugged, rural hinterlands are highly correlated with the emergence of an insurgency.[14] An failure to maintain law and order, deliver public services, or prevent corruption undermines the credibility of the government. As a regime starts to lose what Max Weber called its "monopoly on legitimate violence," armed groups can fill the vacuum created by weak state authority.[15] In considering the success of iconic insurgent movements in China, Cuba, Nicaragua, Algeria, and Vietnam, one cannot ignore the fact that the governments opposing them were either corrupt and incompetent or in an advanced state of political dissolution or both.[16]

Counterinsurgency Strategies: Iron Fists and Velvet Gloves

In the face of the challenge posed by an insurgent movement, governments have sought to defend and extend their authority over the civilian population while degrading the military capability of the insurgents. For the purposes of this study, civil, political, economic, psychological, and military measures undertaken by the government to defeat an insurgency are *counterinsurgency operations*. From a historical standpoint, a range of coercive and conciliatory measures has been employed – both successfully and unsuccessfully – to respond to the outbreak of internal violence. Contemporary discussions of counterinsurgency theory, in both the governmental and scholarly communities, identify two schools of thought based on the primary focus of their efforts: *enemy-centric* approaches, which see the insurgents as the conflict's center of gravity, and *population-centric* approaches, which give that role to the civilian population.[17] These

---

[14] James Fearon and David Laitin, "Ethnicity, Insurgency and Civil War," *American Political Science Review*, 97, no. 1 (February 2003), pp. 80, 88.

[15] Max Weber, "Politics as a Vocation," in H. H. Gerth and C. Wright Mills, eds., *From Max Weber: Essays in Sociology* (Oxford: Oxford University Press, 1958), p. 78; Galula, *Counter-Insurgency Warfare*, p. 19; Michael Klare, "The Deadly Connection: Paramilitary Bands, Small Arms Diffusion and State Failure," in Robert Rotberg, ed., *When States Fail: Causes and Consequences* (Princeton, NJ: Princeton University Press, 2003), pp. 116–134.

[16] Walter Laqueur, *Guerrilla* (Boston: Little Brown, 1976), p. 402.

[17] For examples of both government publications and scholarly works making use of this formulation, see Department of State, *U.S. Government*

titles can confuse as much as they clarify because population-centric counterinsurgency still recognizes the importance of taking action against the enemy, while enemy-centric strategies still include means for engaging the civilian population. As a result, there can be a degree of overlap in the kinds of tactical operations or programs carried out under the two approaches. The key difference is in their theories of victory.

Enemy-Centric Counterinsurgency

Echoing the imperatives of conventional warfare, advocates of enemy-centric counterinsurgency maintain that the focus of efforts should be on destroying the insurgents' will or ability to fight through military means.[18] The scope of enemy-centric operations can range from surgical strikes against specific guerrilla leaders to the employment of overwhelming military force to annihilate insurgents and their supporters en masse.[19] When it comes to the civilian population, the focus is on deterring support for the insurgents by applying coercion and punishment either selectively to individuals or indiscriminately to large segments of the population so that the fear of reprisals outweighs any desire to aid the guerrillas.[20] "The truth is," the senior American

Counterinsurgency Guide, p. 14; and Mark Moyar, *A Question of Command: Counterinsurgency from the Civil War to Iraq* (New Haven, CT: Yale University Press, 2009), pp. 2–3.

[18] Bernard Finel, "A Substitute for Victory," *Foreign Affairs*, April 8, 2010, available at www.foreignaffairs.com/articles/66189/bernard-finel/a-substitute-for-victory. Examples of scholarly works that examine insurgency primarily through a military lens include Ian Beckett, *The Roots of Counter-Insurgency: Armies and Guerilla Warfare 1900–1945* (London: Blandford, 1988); Ian Beckett and John Pimlott, *Armed Forces and Modern Counter-Insurgency* (London: Croom Helm, 1985); Michael Klare and Peter Kornbluh, *Low Intensity Warfare: Counterinsurgency, Proinsurgency, and Antiterrorism in the Eighties* (New York: Pantheon Books, 1988).

[19] Bartle Breese Bull, "The Wrong Force for the 'Right War,'" *New York Times* August 14, 2008; James Clancy and Chuck Crossett, "Measuring Effectiveness in Irregular Warfare," *Parameters*, 37, no. 2 (Summer 2007), p. 91.

[20] Nathan Leites and Charles Wolf, *Rebellion and Authority: An Analytic Essay on Insurgent Conflicts* (Santa Monica, CA: RAND, 1970), pp. 12–15. Edward N. Luttwak, "Dead End: Counterinsurgency Warfare as Military Malpractice," *Harper's* (February 2007), pp. 33–42; Harry Summers, "A War Is a War Is a War Is a War," in Loren B. Thompson, ed., *Low-Intensity Conflict* (Lexington, MA: Lexington Books, 1989), pp. 37–8. Stathis Kalyvas argues for the effectiveness of the discriminate targeting of civilians in Stathis Kalyvas,

military advisor in Vietnam counseled in 1960, "that the population of South Vietnam, like any other, is more responsive to fear and force than to an improved standard of living."[21] In the language of economics, it is believed that raising the "costs" of being an insurgent or a supporter by imposing fines, collective punishment, forced relocation, or even harsher measures will reduce the overall "supply" of insurgents.[22]

Population-Centric Counterinsurgency

Population-centric counterinsurgency focuses on overcoming the insurgency indirectly by gaining the compliance of the population. Proponents of this school of thought maintain that "without the active assistance of the people, an insurgent force cannot be defeated."[23] Consequently, it is suggested that a major focus of the government's efforts should be on enhancing its legitimacy by first protecting the population from the guerrillas, and then address the grievances driving support for the insurgency by engaging in economic development, civic action, and political reform to drain the guerrillas' base of support.

The *Logic of Violence in Civil War* (Cambridge: Cambridge University Press, 2006), pp. 146–209. For evidence that indiscriminate government violence against civilians can be effective in deterring support to insurgents, see Ivan Arreguin-Toft, "How the Weak Win Wars: A Theory of Asymmetric Conflict," *International Security*, 26, no. 1 (Summer 2001); Jason Lyall, "Does Indiscriminate Violence Incite Insurgent Attacks? Evidence from Chechnya." *Journal of Conflict Resolution*, 53, no. 3 (June 2009), pp. 331–62. Other scholars find that this practice may work in some instances but is largely counterproductive. Alexander Downes, "Draining the Sea by Filling the Graves: Investigating the Effectiveness of Indiscriminate Violence as a Counterinsurgency Strategy," *Civil Wars*, 9, no. 4 (December 2007), pp. 420–44; Kalyvas, *Logic of Violence*, p. 167.

[21] Memorandum, Williams to Durbrow, February 25, 1960, quoted in Spector, *Advice and Support*, p. 335.

[22] Leites and Wolf, *Rebellion and Authority*, pp. 37–8, 76–8; Luttwak, "Dead End," p. 40; Arnold Buss, *The Psychology of Aggression* (New York: Wiley, 1961), pp. 57–9; Douglas A. Hibbs, *Mass Political Violence: A Cross-National Causal Analysis* (New York: Wiley, 1973), pp. 82–93; Edward Muller and Mitchell Seligson, "Inequality and Insurgency," *American Political Science Review*, 81, no. 2 (June 1987); and David Snyder and Charles Tilly, "Hardship and Collective Violence in France, 1830 to 1960," *American Sociological Review*, 37, no. 5 (October 1972), p. 527.

[23] David Hackworth and Julie Sherman, *About Face* (New York: Simon & Schuster, 1989), pp. 556, 613–54.

Reducing political violence to an acceptable level does not always require a fundamental change in the political or economic conditions that fuel the insurgency, but the worst aspects of those conditions must be ameliorated through some type of reform.[24] Where active support from the population is not possible, David Kilcullen contends that self-interested cooperation may suffice: "For your side to win, the people do not have to like you but they must respect you, accept that your actions benefit them, and trust your integrity and ability to deliver on promises."[25] It is presumed that once the civilian population no longer supplies the guerrillas with intelligence, sanctuary, and supplies, the remaining insurgents who have not been co-opted by the state will be vulnerable to the security forces' efforts to capture or kill them.[26]

Despite the focus on reform and economic development, counter-insurgents under a population-centric approach are not strictly aid workers in uniform. Physical control and security of the population are viewed as essential preconditions to enable political reform, economic development, and civic action to take effect, which has led Hew Strachan to describe the approach as giving the populace "the firm smack of government."[27]

Synthesis

In the real world, counterinsurgency campaigns employ a blend of military and political efforts to both punish and persuade in the course of defeating a rebellion and are neither explicitly enemy-centric nor population-centric.[28] Moreover, the particular mix of military and

---

[24] Anthony James Joes, *Resisting Rebellion* (Lexington: University Press of Kentucky, 2004), pp. 30–1; Guy J. Pauker, *Notes on Non-Military Measures in Control of Insurgency* (Santa Monica, CA: RAND, 1962), p. 12.

[25] Kilcullen, *Counterinsurgency*, p. 30.

[26] Robert Thompson, *Defeating Communist Insurgency* (London: Praeger, 1966), p. 118.

[27] Hew Strachan, "British Counter-Insurgency from Malaya to Iraq," *The RUSI Journal*, 152, no. 6 (2007), p. 8. Kalyvas contends that the decision to collaborate with the government or insurgents is primarily driven by which party exerts territorial control. Kalyvas, *Logic of Violence*, pp. 89–91.

[28] David Kilcullen, *The Accidental Guerrilla: Fighting Small Wars in the Midst of a Big One* (Oxford: Oxford University Press, 2009), p. 183; David Kilcullen, "Two Schools of Classical Counterinsurgency," *Small Wars Journal* (January 27, 2007), available at http://smallwarsjournal.com/blog/two-schools-of-classical-counterinsurgency.

political measures employed by a state is hardly static: as John Nagl has demonstrated, the strategies of successful counterinsurgents change and adapt over the course of a conflict.[29]

In practice, there is a reasonable degree of convergence on several key areas between these two schools of thought. Both agree that the legitimacy of the incumbent government is key to its success, though they differ as to whether that legitimacy is best sustained by killing guerrillas or responding to the population's needs. Similarly, both emphasize the need to deny support to the insurgents, again with differences of emphasis on attacking remote base areas versus reducing the population's desire to aid the insurgents. The need for unity of effort and close coordination among the various government agencies involved in the counterinsurgency campaign—which can otherwise result in a lack of clear authority, inadequate intelligence analysis, and military operations that fail to achieve their desired effect—is an imperative recognized by theorists from both schools of thought.[30] Proponents of both approaches recognize that strengthening the administrative capacity of the government "is as much part of counter-insurgency as any military operation" because, as Robert Thompson noted, "without a reasonably efficient government machine, no programs or projects, in the context of counter-insurgency, will produce the desired results."[31] Finally, there is agreement that highly trained security forces possessing superior levels of adaptability and operational initiative are required to move beyond a mere reactive response to insurgent violence.

Counterinsurgency is innately challenging. Success can require not only military prowess but also the willingness and ability to make difficult political and economic changes. Progress in internal conflict is often difficult to measure, and the appearance of success at a tactical level may obscure failings at the strategic level. In a conflict where the first challenge is to find the enemy, counterinsurgents face the paradox that they will need actionable intelligence to make progress against an insurgency, but the population will be unlikely to risk providing such

---

[29] Nagl, *Counterinsurgency Lessons*, pp. 191–208.
[30] For a successful model of unity of command over all elements of the civil government, military, and police involved in a counterinsurgency operation, see Walter C. Ladwig III, "Managing Counterinsurgency: Lessons from Malaya," *Military Review*, 87, no. 3 (May–June 2007), pp. 55-66.
[31] Thompson, *Defeating Communist Insurgency*, p. 51.

information until the counterinsurgents can demonstrate success.[32] While all these difficulties and more confront a government engaged in counterinsurgency, the problems are compounded when an outside power attempts to support a local government's counterinsurgency campaign.[33]

The Dynamics of Intervention

As the preceding section indicated, regardless of the dominant strategy employed, counterinsurgency will require a state to undertake some sort of reform – be it the social, political, and economic measures called for by population-centric theorists or a restructuring of military and intelligence agencies to improve their efficiency pursuant to an enemy-centric approach. While it can be difficult enough for a state to reform itself in peacetime, it is even more challenging for an external power to foster such reform in another state that is conducting a counterinsurgency campaign.

The particular challenges of working with or through a partner nation are not widely recognized in counterinsurgency literature.[34] This is a major omission because the majority of America's experience with counterinsurgency, both during the Cold War and today, involves assisting another nation's effort abroad. When external allies are mentioned, many counterinsurgency theorists treat the host nation government and its supporting power as if they were one and the same, assuming that the interests, preferences, and goals of the two will be so closely aligned that they will operate hand in glove against the insurgency.[35] In this vein, the vaunted 2006 U.S. *Counterinsurgency Field Manual* implicitly presumed that the interests and priorities of the United States and the country it is supporting in counterinsurgency

---

[32] Frank Kitson, *Low Intensity Operations* (London: Faber & Faber, 1971), p. 58; Nagl, *Counterinsurgency Lessons*, p. 3.

[33] Benjamin R. Beede, *Intervention and Counterinsurgency* (New York: Garland, 1985), p. xxxii.

[34] Daniel L. Byman, *Going to War with the Allies You Have: Allies, Counterinsurgency and the War on Terrorism* (Carlisle, PA: Strategic Studies Institute, 2006), p. 3.

[35] For example, see the famed British counterinsurgency theorist Robert Thompson's comments on the subject in Robert Thompson, "Civic Action in Low-Intensity Warfare," in *Proceedings of the Low Intensity Warfare Conference* (Washington, DC: Department of Defense, 1986), p. 74.

would be closely aligned.[36] In reality, the local regime is an independent actor, and the external power supporting it has, at best, only indirect control over its economic policies, political arrangements, and military doctrines.[37] Moreover, the types of reforms called for by COIN theorists are potentially a threat to the interests or stability of a government presiding over a society with a significantly skewed distribution of power or wealth.[38]

In contrast to the assumptions of a unanimity of interests between patron and client, a number of scholars suggest that the divergence in interests, goals, and priorities between the local government and its external patron, and the limited influence the patron has over its client's behavior, have repeatedly emerged as major obstacles to the success of American counterinsurgency assistance efforts.[39] A similar view is also advanced by those who have worked with local militaries in such endeavors: for example, after serving as an advisor to the South Vietnamese Army, Colonel Bryce Denno counseled his superiors in a 1963 memo that

it would be a miraculous coincidence if a host nation in a war of counterinsurgency were to share identical objectives with the U.S. or arrive at identical solutions to problems that arise. Hence, it behooves the U.S. to seek ways in which it can influence the host nation to act in a manner compatible with U.S. interests in a war which we are financing to a large extent and otherwise supporting.[40]

Nevertheless, Benjamin Schwarz points out that for decades U.S. thinking on counterinsurgency has labored under the mistaken

---

[36] For example, it is assumed that the United States and the local government will work together to enhance the legitimacy of the ruling regime by responding to the needs of the population. Moreover, it is also assumed that the local government desires to defend the interests of all of the country's citizens. The idea that the goals and interests of the host nation might significantly diverge from those of the United States is not addressed. FM 3–24, *Counterinsurgency*, pp. 37–9, 66, 134, 153.

[37] Thomas Grant, "Government, Politics, and Low-Intensity Conflict," in Edwin Corr and Stephen Sloan, eds., *Low-Intensity Conflict: Old Threats in a New World* (Boulder, CO: Westview Press, 1992), p. 265.

[38] Douglas North, John Wallis, and Barry Weingast, *Violence and Social Orders: A Conceptual Framework for Interpreting Recorded Human History* (Cambridge: Cambridge University Press, 2009), pp. 19–20.

[39] Blaufarb, *Counterinsurgency Era*, p. 311; Shafer, *Deadly Paradigms*, p. 5; Schwarz, *American Counterinsurgency Doctrine*, p. 77.

[40] Denno, "Debriefing," p. 8.

belief "that it is relatively easy to ensure that an ally does what American policymakers deem necessary to eliminate an insurgency."[41]

To some extent, resistance to American advice is understandable. As Lucian Pye recognized, "[F]ew governments can accept the view that it was their own policy deficiencies which drove people to violence."[42] Given that states facing internal political violence often have weak economies, dilapidated infrastructure, and increasing domestic disorder, it is not necessarily clear that a besieged government will possess either the resources or the administrative capacity to undertake reforms that can improve efficiency or address popular grievances.[43] In a time of crisis, even capable governments may balk at yielding some measure of economic or political power to ethnic groups or factions considered to be of dubious political loyalty. More often than not, however, the reform prescriptions the United States offered partners to rally popular support and undercut the appeal of the insurgency were resisted by the local ally because they struck at the very foundations the regime and endangered the privileges of the ruling elites.[44] "The client sees our advice," Douglas Blaufarb writes, "as forcing him to face unacceptable risks of instability and loss of power, and so he evades and maneuvers to avoid our pressures, satisfying our demands with token adjustments which leave essentials unchanged."[45] As a result, in many cases, the local government was as much an obstacle to the success of U.S. counterinsurgency assistance efforts as the insurgents were.

The difficulties of assisting counterinsurgency are not merely due to the inherent deficiencies of the client state. The very act of intervening can trigger a host of unintended consequences that can skew the incentives and behavior of the local government. If a patron is unable to induce or compel a client government to accept advice that runs contrary to its genuine desires, providing the client government with economic and military aid can actually have a pernicious effect on its

---

[41] Schwarz, *American Counterinsurgency Doctrine*, p. 77.

[42] Lucian Pye, *Aspects of Political Development: An Analytic Study* (Boston: Little Brown, 1966), p. 139.

[43] William J. Olson, "The New World Disorder," in Max G. Manwaring, ed., *Gray Area Phenomena: Confronting the New World Disorder* (Boulder, CO: Westview Press, 1993), p. 11.

[44] Blaufarb, *Counterinsurgency Era*, p. 311; Schwarz, *American Counterinsurgency Doctrine*, p. viii.

[45] Blaufarb, *Counterinsurgency Era*, p. 308.

counterinsurgency efforts by changing its incentive structure.[46] Military assistance can sap the host nation's motivation to defeat insurgents on its own or undertake the measures necessary to enhance its counterinsurgency prowess, while economic aid reduces an allied regime's incentives for fiscal reforms that would grow and strengthen the wartime economy.[47] With a significantly reduced incentive to improve its administration or extend government control across the country in an effort to extend its tax base, external aid can allow the supported government to remain corrupt and inefficient while largely immune to any internal pressures for reform.

Is involvement in foreign counterinsurgency so difficult and fraught with unintended consequences that, as some suggest, the United States "should eschew involvement in internal wars entirely?"[48] From a practical standpoint, the recommendation to avoid all internal conflicts is not likely to be heeded. U.S. policymakers may perceive that important national interests are at stake in a given struggle, or a situation may attract domestic, congressional, or even international pressure to "do something."[49] As a result, even critics of U.S. involvement abroad recognize that Washington cannot completely steer clear of foreign entanglements.[50]

From the perspective of the intervening state, there is evidence to suggest that indirect interventions – providing aid and support short of the deployment of combat forces – can achieve positive results. John Fishel and Max Manwaring's quantitative factor analysis of forty-three post–World War II insurgencies involving a Western power finds that the deployment of a small number of military advisors, coupled with long-term support for the incumbent regime, is one of the best predictors of success in counterinsurgency.[51] This is broadly consistent with the findings of Roy Licklider, who suggests that outside interventions

---

[46] Odom, *On Internal War*, pp. 213–15.   [47] *Ibid.*, pp. 103–4.

[48] *Ibid.*, p. 215.

[49] For a discussion of the high degree of "penetrability" of U.S. foreign policymaking by Congress and public opinion vis-à-vis that of other liberal democracies, see Thomas Risse-Kappen, "Public Opinion, Domestic Structure and Foreign Policy in Liberal Democracies," *World Politics*, 43, no. 4 (July 1991), pp. 487–93.

[50] Stanley Hoffmann, "Restraints and Choices in American Foreign Policy," *Daedelus*, 91 (Fall 1962), p. 678.

[51] John T. Fishel and Max G. Manwaring, *Uncomfortable Wars Revisited* (Norman: University of Oklahoma Press, 2006), p. 253.

affecting the military capabilities of either the government or the rebels provide the opponent with an increased incentive to settle rather than continue fighting.[52] Turning from the general question of external support for counterinsurgency to the specific American experience, Anthony Joes' examination of American involvement in assisting foreign governments challenged by guerrillas concludes that providing aid and support to the incumbent government, without actual combat troops, "both minimizes American vulnerabilities and emphasizes American strengths."[53]

Although there is some scholarly support for the viability of indirect intervention as a strategy, it is also clear that regardless of the quality of the counterinsurgency plan devised or the earnestness and effort of the U.S. personnel sent to provide assistance, the support efforts will not succeed if the host nation's government is not willing to take action. Therefore, it is necessary to explore two key issues in more detail:

1. The character of the supported regime and its preferences, and
2. The effect – for good or ill – that U.S. aid and support can have on the incentive structure and decision making of the supported regime.

A theoretical foundation for understanding both these problems can be found in the economic literature on agency theory.

Principals and Agents, Patrons and Clients

Agency theory examines the challenges and conflicts of interest that commonly arise when one party delegates responsibility for carrying out a task to another in an environment of asymmetric information. The *principal-agent problem*, as it is commonly known, occurs when one actor, the principal, chooses to employ another, the agent, to act on its behalf in situations where the agent can perform a given task more efficiently due to its expert knowledge, superior skill, or other crucial factor. In delegating, the principal is trying to accomplish its task at

---

[52] Roy E. Licklider, "The Consequences of Negotiated Settlements in Civil Wars, 1945–1993," *American Political Science Review*, 89, no. 3 (1995); Roy E. Licklider, "How Civil Wars End: Questions and Methods," in Roy E. Licklider, ed., *Stopping the Killing: How Civil Wars End* (London: New York University Press, 1993).

[53] Anthony James Joes, *America and Guerrilla Warfare* (Lexington: University Press of Kentucky, 2000), p. 326.

a lower cost by employing an agent who is seemingly better equipped to do the job. These relationships exist in all aspects of economic and political life, whether the relationship is between a company (principal) and its traveling salesperson (agent), investors (principal) and a broker charged with managing their money (agent), or congress (principal) and a federal agency charged with implementing legislation (agent). Managers, employees, customers, and virtually every member of modern society have to contend with the thorny challenges created by delegation and agency on a regular basis.[54] The "problem" in principal-agent relationships is that the interests of the agent are not completely aligned with those of the principal. For example, an employer may want his staff to work diligently all day long, while employees may prefer to get paid for shirking – not doing what the employer wants or not in the way he wants – particularly if they know their employer would have a hard time catching them. As strategic actors, agents seek to achieve their own goals, within the restrictions put on them by the principal. Shirking can never be prevented completely; thus the act of delegating carries with it transaction costs known as *agency losses.*[55]

How can the principal get the agent to do what the principal wants rather than what the agent wants? Agents generally have a superior understanding of their own priorities and actual level of effort in carrying out their assigned duties which cannot be easily measured or observed by the principal. This knowledge is referred to as *private information.* The agent's private information comes in two forms: hidden knowledge about its preferences (the case of *adverse selection*) or hidden actions undertaken by the agent (the case of *moral hazard*).[56] This, in turn, requires the principal to either design a reward structure that can motivate an agent to act according to the principal's interests or deploy costly resources to monitor the agent's level of compliance – which it can only do imperfectly – or do both.[57]

---

[54] John Pratt and Richard Zeckhauser, "Principals and Agents: An Overview," in John Pratt and Richard Zeckhauser, eds., *Principals and Agents: The Structure of Business* (Cambridge, MA: Harvard Business School Press, 1985), p. 4.

[55] Roderick Kiewiet and Matthew McCubbins, *The Logic of Delegation: Congressional Parties and the Appropriation Process* (Chicago: University of Chicago Press, 1991), p. 5.

[56] Jean-Jacques Laffont and David Martimort, *The Theory of Incentives: The Principal-Agent Model* (Princeton, NJ: Princeton University Press, 2002), p. 3.

[57] Stephen Ross, "The Economic Theory of Agency: The Principal's Problem," *American Economic Review*, 63, no. 2 (May 1973). Agency theory assumes that

Although the kind of patron-client interaction we are examining in this study is not a pure example of the principal-agent problem in the sense that the agents (the client state) are not hired by the principal (the patron), agency theory can still apply in situations that lack an overt or official delegation of responsibility.[58] The very fact that the patron is attempting to reduce the costs of responding to a specific foreign policy challenge by relying on a client who may not completely share its policy preferences for executing the counterinsurgency campaign, rather than doing it themselves, makes the literature relevant for this discussion. In fact, the anarchical nature of the international system can actually compound the effects of principal-agent-type interactions.[59] Whereas in the domestic sphere principals and agents have recourse to binding contracts and legal adjudication for failure to perform duties, such measures do not carry the same weight in interactions between sovereign states.

Adverse Selection and the Preferences of the Local Regime

Adverse selection, which relates to the counterinsurgency critiques about the patron state not understanding the character and preferences of the local regime, is a product of the "unobservability of the information, beliefs, and values on which the decisions of [the agent] are based."[60] In simple terms, due to the agent's information advantages about its own characteristics and preferences, in certain types of transactions, "bad" agents will overwhelmingly seek to participate. A prototypical example of adverse selection could be found in the U.S. health insurance market, prior to the introduction of "Obamacare," where people buying insurance have a better knowledge about the state of their own health than the underwriter selling them a policy. As a result, the people most likely to seek a policy are those who suspect that they will face significant health problems that would cost more

a principal can observe the general outcome of the agent's actions but cannot determine the degree to which a specific outcome is due to the agent's level of effort or some other random factor such as chance.

[58] Ray Rees, "The Theory of Principal and Agent, Part 1," *Bulletin of Economic Research*, 37, no. 1 (1985), p. 3.

[59] Kenneth N. Waltz, *Theory of International Politics* (London: Addison-Wesley, 1979), p. 89.

[60] Terry Moe, "The New Economics of Organization," *American Journal of Political Science*, 28, no. 4 (November 1984), p. 754.

than the price of insurance to treat. Moreover, such people have a strong incentive to misrepresent either the state of their health or their own beliefs about their future health in order to get a policy. If an insurance company merely insured all customers who sought their services and charged them all the same fixed price, it would bear a disproportionate amount of risk and likely lose money on most of the policies it issued.[61] To mitigate this information asymmetry, insurers will typically require new clients to undergo physical examinations to determine the state of their health and charge higher premiums to those engaged in high-risk behavior such as smoking.

The decision to assist a nation in counterinsurgency frequently involves adverse selection because effective, legitimate governments are rarely conducive to insurgencies. The only governments needing external assistance to combat domestic political opponents are almost by definition flawed in some key respects. Consequently, as Thomas Grant points out, American assistance to counterinsurgency "usually entails U.S. aid and pressure to shore up and reform an inefficient, corrupt, and abusive government; it is rare to have a morally splendid ally in counterinsurgency work, simply because morally pristine, administratively effective governments do not provide the inspiration or excuse for a guerrilla war."[62]

Regardless of the strategy employed, counterinsurgency requires well-trained, well-led, and highly motivated security forces that possess high levels of operational initiative, good intelligence, and the ability to adapt to changing circumstances.[63] Yet, among other failings, the security forces of states beset by political violence are liable to suffer from poor intelligence, inferior leadership, and a lack of initiative. In non-democratic regimes, these deficiencies are often compounded by "coup-proofing" measures undertaken to hobble the armed forces who are not necessarily seen by ruling elites as the country's faithful defenders but as a potential rival base of power. Consequently, political loyalty is favored over competence, and multiple chains of command or

---

[61] Michael Rothschild and Joseph Stiglitz, "Equilibrium in Competitive Insurance Markets," *Quarterly Journal of Economics*, 90, no. 4 (November 1976), pp. 629–49.

[62] Grant, "Government, Politics, and Low-Intensity Conflict," p. 261.

[63] Tactical imperatives of counterinsurgency are discussed in Joseph H. Felter, "Taking Guns to a Knife Fight: A Case for Empirical Study of Counterinsurgency," Ph.D. dissertation, Stanford University, 2005, pp. 13–24.

duplicate security agencies are created to protect the ruling class at the expense of military effectiveness.[64] At an institutional level, the impact of intrigue, distrust, and cronyism on civil-military relations can inhibit information sharing and cooperation across government agencies, which, in turn, hinder the ability to achieve unity of effort in a counterinsurgency campaign. The efficacy of counterinsurgency operations can be further undermined by corruption and the government's perceived lack of legitimacy. Widespread corruption undermines public trust in the state's leadership and can reduce the quality and professionalism of the security forces as soldiers focus on "getting paid" rather than on mastering the skills of their profession. In a similar vein, gaining popular support for a government that is seen to only represent the interests of a narrow segment of society, such as an oligarchic elite or a specific ethnic group, can be difficult. This makes the information-gathering aspects of intelligence work very challenging because few citizens will be willing to risk insurgent reprisal to provide actionable intelligence to authorities they view as oppressive or illegitimate.

As this discussion illustrates, the preferences of the host nation government – as reflected in its pernicious political choices and policies – are not peripheral issues in counterinsurgency assistance efforts – they are a central concern. Contrary to the assumption that the values and interests of a local government and its supporting ally will be aligned, a principal challenge of assisting a nation in counterinsurgency arises from the fact that both the supported and supporting governments possess different goals and priorities. At the broadest level, the United States and its local partner may share a common aim of defeating the insurgency; however, the host nation government typically has competing priorities, such as maintaining power and continuing the domestic social and economic arrangements that benefit its core supporters. Significant divergence between patron and client can lead the parties to pursue differing or even opposing strategies in the context of defeating an insurgency. Under such conditions, a client's compliance with its patron's wishes is far from certain. Thus patron-client politics are a key factor in shaping the effectiveness of counterinsurgency assistance efforts.

---

[64] For an extended discussion on the effects of coup proofing, see James T. Quinlivan, "Coup-Proofing: Its Practice and Consequences in the Middle East," *International Security*, 24, no. 2 (Fall 1999) and Caitlin Talmadge, "Different Threats, Different Militaries: Explaining Organizational Practices in Authoritarian Armies," *Security Studies*, 25, no. 1 (February 2016).

The Patron's Goals

In intervening, the patron is primarily seeking to strengthen its client's military and political capacity so that it has the ability to overcome the threat posed by the insurgency without requiring the patron to deploy its own troops. At the same time, if the insurgency is perceived to be abetted by an outside power, the patron may also be seeking to send a message to third parties about its commitment to defend the client and defeat the insurgency. For example, during the Cold War, the two superpowers frequently supported ideologically aligned regimes against the threat of internal instability, often believing that the other side was instigating the turmoil.[65] Providing needed economic and military assistance can lead the supporting nation to expect to have some degree of influence over its client's policy choices, influence that can be exerted to further the patron's interests or the perceived best interests of the client. Often, however, the client government will be focused primarily on the immediate security and economic situation at hand rather than on the patron's geopolitical concerns and objectives.[66]

Although as Christopher Carney notes "patrons enter into these special relationships to enhance their international prestige, not reduce it," should wanton brutality be the primary counterinsurgency tool employed by the local government, the supporting power could find itself publicly associated with its client's behavior, which could negatively affect its reputation.[67] Alignment with a domestically abusive regime can also pose a foreign policy challenge because it provides sufficient justification for regime opponents to oppose the patron state and its interests. American support for Batista in Cuba, Somoza in Nicaragua, and Pahlavi in Iran, for example, came back to haunt Washington after those regimes were overthrown and replaced by governments with strong anti-American views – harming both America's international prestige and its relations with the successor governments. Both of these circumstances suggest that in order to

---

[65] Christopher Shoemaker and John Spanier, *Patron-Client State Relationships: Multilateral Crises in the Nuclear Age* (New York: Praeger, 1984), pp. 17–19.

[66] *Ibid.*, pp. 21–2; W. Howard Wriggins and Gunnar Adler-Karlsson, *Reducing Global Inequities* (New York: McGraw-Hill, 1978), p. 77.

[67] Christopher Carney, "International Patron-Client Relationships: A Conceptual Framework," *Studies in Comparative International Development*, 24, no. 2 (1989), p. 48.

achieve its objectives, the patron needs to be able to regulate the repressive behavior of its clients.[68]

The Client's Goals

A client state accepts the assistance of a great power in an effort to draw on external sources of strength to pursue its own interests; however, this is more frequently due to necessity than choice.[69] In so doing, the client will try to manipulate the dynamics of the relationship with its patron to maximize the amount of political, economic, or military assistance it receives while simultaneously seeking to avoid surrendering its autonomy. If the patron seeks to pressure its client to take an undesired action, the client may try to reduce its dependence on the patron for certain forms of aid, for example, by enhancing its self-sufficiency or cultivating alternative sources of assistance.[70] Alternately, if the client senses divisions in the patron government, it may seek to play one agency off against another in an attempt to meet its needs. In this vein, the commander of the U.S. Military Assistance Group (MAAG) in Vietnam complained to his superiors that "[f]rankly, the [South Vietnamese government] appears to feel they can get anything they want, regardless of MAAG recommendations, by going through the Ambassador to top American levels."[71]

As Bruce Bueno de Mesquita and Alastair Smith have argued, the behavior of political leaders is based primarily on their desire for political survival: "[D]ecisions are not taken to improve the welfare

---

[68] *Ibid.*

[69] Michael Handel, *Weak States in the International System* (London: Frank Cass, 1990), p. 121; Stanley Hoffmann, *Gulliver's Troubles: The Setting of American Foreign Policy* (New York: McGraw-Hill, 1968), p. 28; William Lewis, "Political Influence: The Diminished Capacity," in Stephanie Neuman and Robert Harkavy, eds., *Arms Transfers in the Modern World* (New York: Praeger, 1979), p. 186; Robert Rothstein, *Alliances and Small Powers* (New York: Columbia University Press, 1968), p. 127.

[70] Klaus Knorr, "International Economic Leverage and Its Uses," in Klaus Knorr and Frank Trager, eds., *Economic Issues and National Security* (Lawrence: University of Kansas Press, 1977), pp. 103–7; Avi Plascov, *Modernization, Political Development and Stability* (London: Gower, 1982), pp. 109–10; J. David Singer, "Inter-Nation Influence: A Formal Model," *American Political Science Review*, 57, no. 2 (June 1963), p. 422.

[71] Letter, McGarr to Lyman Lemnitzer, October 12, 1961, Box 24, MAAG Vietnam, RG 472, p. 10.

of the people unless coincidentally this simultaneously aids survival."[72]
This is particularly true for a government facing an insurgency in which
security of the ruling classes is frequently disconnected from the security of the broader population.[73] Therefore, the priority for a besieged
government is to bolster its position within its domestic society by
tightening control over the security forces and co-opting societal elites
who could pose a threat to the regime, rather than undertaking the
most effective measures to defeat the insurgents. Consequently, Byman
warns that "U.S. COIN doctrine, no matter how well thought out,
cannot succeed without the appropriate political and other reforms
from the host nation, but these regimes are likely to subvert the reforms
that threaten the existing power structure."[74] In the Philippines, for
example, the U.S. ambassador pushed for the removal of the heads of
the Armed Forces and the Philippine Constabulary, who were leading
the government's abusive and ineffective counterinsurgency campaign.
However, President Elpidio Quirino's paranoia about the potential for
a coup led him to forcibly reject the idea of replacing these political
loyalists with more competent men, even though it hurt the progress of
the battle against the insurgents.[75]

Although from the outside, transforming a nation's military into
a competent and effective force would appear to be a key step in overcoming an insurgency, such efforts are likely to be seen as threatening by
a local government that fears its military as a rival power base and
commands loyalty via patronage and payoffs. Advice to increase
popular support by expanding political participation or broadening the
government to include opposition elements is likely to be spurned
because it would undoubtedly reduce the incumbent's power and influence. Increasing economic transparency or undertaking liberalization

---

[72] Bruce Bueno de Mesquita and Alastair Smith, "Foreign Aid and Policy
Concessions," *Journal of Conflict Resolution*, 51, no. 2 (2007), p. 254.

[73] Robin Luckham, "Security and Disarmament in Africa," *Alternatives*, 9, no. 2
(Fall 1983), p. 217.

[74] Byman, "Friends Like These," p. 82. See also Samuel P. Huntington and
Joan M. Nelson, *No Easy Choice: Political Participation in Developing
Countries* (Cambridge, MA: Harvard University Press, 1976), p. 29.

[75] Letter, Cowen to Melby, March 6, 1951, Box 8; Melby Survey Mission,
Embassy Brief, September 18, 1950, Box 12; Letter, Cowen to Melby, April 6,
1951, Box 8, all in John F. Melby Papers, Harry S. Truman Presidential Library
(Melby Papers); Letter, Cowen to Dewey, February 18, 1952, Box 6,
Myron M. Cowen Papers, Harry S. Truman Presidential Library (Cowen
Papers).

may strengthen the client state's economy, but this would reduce the elite's ability to use state funds to pay off key supporters who help them remain in power. Government effectiveness may be increased by reducing patronage in the military or civil service, but this could increase the risk that the government would be overthrown by disaffected officials. As a result, the types of reforms and policy changes often suggested by counterinsurgency theorists could appear to be just as threatening to the ally as the insurgents themselves. A failure to recognize this kind of divergence of preferences can, in turn, lead to great frustration for patrons, as former Assistant Secretary of State for Far Eastern Affairs Roger Hilsman found in Vietnam, where, in his view, the client government resisted well-intentioned advice and appeared to "struggle irrationally against all reform."[76] The nub of the problem, of course, is that from the perspective of the local government, resisting such measures was extremely rational.

The Time-Horizon Dilemma

Differing time horizons between the patron and client can be a second potential source of divergence: Depending on the circumstances, the short-term outlook of the client may not match the long-term interests of the patron or vice versa. Throughout the course of responding to an insurgency, both the local government and the supporting power face tradeoffs that can affect their short- and long-term interests in different ways. For example, employing repression or indiscriminate violence in response to political opposition may result in increased stability in the short term while sowing the seeds for more serious discontent in the longer run. Conversely, although certain types of reforms intended to address popular grievances may contribute to long-term stability, their implementation may be extremely destabilizing in the short run. In South Vietnam, President Diem consistently rebuffed American pressure to broaden his government by including the country's other non-Communist political movements or to delegate authority for counterinsurgency operations to appropriate civil and military leaders. Such steps, he contended would dilute his personal authority and undercut

---

[76] Roger Hilsman, "Internal War: The New Communist Tactic," in
      Thomas Greene, ed., *The Guerilla and How to Fight Him* (New York: Praeger:
      1962), p. 32. For a similarly pessimistic view, see Hans Morgenthau,
      "A Political Theory of Foreign Aid," *American Political Science Review*, 56
      (June 1962).

the government's ability to restore order.[77] Although a local government may be expected to favor short-term concerns over long-term ones, fixation on a particular local rivalry, regional balance of power, or other external threat might prevent it from taking steps that would undermine that particular position – even in the face of an immediate threat posed by an active insurgency.[78] As a case in point, even though the FMLN insurgents nearly captured San Salvador in their 1981 "Final Offensive," continued hostility toward Honduras stemming from their 1969 war made the leaders of the Salvadoran military extremely unwilling to adapt their forces for counterinsurgency in a manner that would retard their ability to fight a conventional war against their larger neighbor.[79]

The supporting power must also manage its potentially divergent short- and long-term interests. In the short term, it is concerned with the security and stability of the particular client government it is assisting. It has a longer-term interest, however, in maintaining a friendly government in the country in question, irrespective of who the particular leader is, as well as in preventing it from falling into the orbit of a hostile power. As the cases studied here illustrate, these interests can come into conflict, particularly if the local government's response to the insurgency appears to aggravate rather than ameliorate internal violence. This can create a problem for the patron's policymakers that Alexander George has termed *value complexity*, which occurs with "the presence of multiple, competing values and interest

---

[77] NSAM 111, November 22, 1961, Meetings and Memos, NSF, JFK Presidential Papers, John F. Kennedy Presidential Library (JFK); Telegram 678, Saigon to State, November 18, 1961, *Foreign Relations of the United States 1961–1963*, vol. I, Vietnam, 1961 (FRUS 1961), pp. 642–4; Telegram 708, Saigon to State, November 25, 1961, FRUS 1961, pp. 666–8.

[78] Andrew Boutton, "U.S. Foreign Aid, Interstate Rivalry, and Incentives for Counterterrorism Cooperation," *Journal of Peace Research*, 51, no. 6 (November 2014), pp. 741–54.

[79] For example, the headquarters of the 4th Brigade in El Paraiso, Chaletenango department was designed to fend off a conventional invasion from Honduras. While building a major military facility in a depression, away from the local civilian population, may reduce its vulnerability to airstrikes, this isolated facility, overlooked by commanding heights, was extremely vulnerable to infiltration by insurgents. Michael Sheehan, "Comparative Counterinsurgency Strategies: Guatemala and El Salvador," *Conflict*, 9, no. 2 (1989), p. 135. See also Wallace Nutting, "Oral History Interview," January 31, 1989, MHI, p. 24; Andrew J. Bacevich et al., *American Military Policy in Small Wars: The Case of El Salvador* (Boston: Potomac Books, 1988), p. 37.

that are embedded in a single issue."[80] Depending on the actions of the local government, the supporting power may have to compel their partner to take steps that appear to threaten or undermine its short-term position – and run the risk of weakening it to the benefit of the insurgents – in the belief that these measures will enhance the local government's long-term stability. In the Philippines, for example, with the Huk insurgents operating on the outskirts of Manila, the United States withheld its military aid to force the unwilling Philippine government to undertake a time-consuming reorganization and retraining of the security forces.[81] Although this ultimately enhanced the effectiveness of Filipino forces, it hindered their ability to take action against the insurgents for months at a critical time in the conflict. Unsurprisingly, some American policymakers have found the challenge of seeking to preserve a local regime against an insurgency, while simultaneously pressing it to change, to be an "unpalatable task" that borders on the insurmountable.[82]

As this section has illustrated, the character of the local regime can have a significant impact on its counterinsurgency prowess. While much of the counterinsurgency literature advocates some degree of reform or government reorganization to respond to political violence, in many instances the local government has logical reasons to resist such measures. Far from the presumed unanimity of interests between the supporting and supported states, significant differences in interests and priorities can emerge that affect each side's preferred counterinsurgency strategies. Asymmetry of information about the host nation's real counterinsurgency preferences can lead an intervening power to support a regime that refuses to implement its patron's counterinsurgency prescriptions and may even seek to "free ride" by forcing the patron to bear the costs of fighting the insurgents.

---

[80] Alexander L. George, *Presidential Decision Making in Foreign Policy* (Boulder, CO: Westview Press, 1980), p. 26.

[81] Telegram 211, Manila to State, July 26, 1950, 796.00/7–2650; Telegram 220, July 27, 1950, 796.00/7–2750, Records of the U.S. Department of State, U.S. National Archive, College Park, MD (RG 59); JUSMAG, "Weekly Summary of Activities," July 29, 1950, Records of the U.S. Army Staff, U.S. National Archive, College Park, MD (RG 319).

[82] See the comments of Secretaries of State Dean Rusk and George Schultz, respectively, in Memorandum of Conversation, Kennedy, Johnson, Rusk et al., January 28, 1961, FRUS 1961, p. 15; and Elaine Sciolino, "Panama's Chief Defies U.S. Powers of Persuasion," *New York Times*, January 17, 1988.

The Moral Hazard of Assisting Counterinsurgency

The second principal-agent problem that a supporting power faces is what economists have termed a *moral hazard*. This is a situation in which possessing insurance against risk inadvertently leads a party to act less carefully than it otherwise would have because it does not bear the full consequences of its actions.[83] By intervening to provide assistance, the patron state is altering the burden of risk in a way that can unintentionally change the behavior of the local government by altering its incentive structure. If a regime believes that an external power is committed to its survival, it might ignore the potential risks of its own actions (or lack thereof), in the belief that the patron will protect it from harm if the situation deteriorates too far.[84] In counterinsurgency, a firm commitment from a great power patron can reduce the local government's incentives to ameliorate the grievances driving support for the rebels. As James Cross warned nearly five decades ago:

The confidence inspired by strong American backing ... may tempt the leaders to defer the very reforms which the American aid was intended to facilitate, the reasoning being that the regime is now so firmly entrenched and backed that those inconvenient and distasteful changes are no longer necessary.[85]

To put it simply, if a superpower proclaims an intent to "pay any price, bear any burden, meet any hardship, support any friend, oppose any foe" on your behalf, why not let it?[86] While a patron may intend to bolster its client's confidence, a strong pledge to assist a local government could actually harm the supported regime if that pledge leads it to ignore the reforms that the patron believes are necessary to overcome the insurgency. Criticizing the Carter and Reagan administrations' support for the Salvadoran Armed Forces on this count, William LeoGrande argued that American aid created a severe moral hazard

---

[83] Yehuda Kotowitz, "Moral Hazard," in John Eatwell, Murray Milgate, and Peter Newman, eds., *The New Palgrave: A Dictionary of Economics* (New York: Norton, 1987), pp. 207–13.

[84] Glenn Snyder and Paul Diesing, *Conflict among Nations: Bargaining, Decision Making, and System Structure in International Crises* (Princeton, NJ: Princeton University Press, 1977), p. 30.

[85] Cross, *Conflict in the Shadows*, p. 140.

[86] Quote comes from John F. Kennedy, "Inaugural Address" (Washington, DC, January 20, 1961).

by allowing the Salvadorian military "to continue to ignore political reality" as it carried out war with the insurgents.[87]

Whereas adverse selection results from the lack of information about the agent's true preferences, a moral hazard is created when the principal lacks the ability to directly observe the agent's actions. This inability to observe can manifest in multiple ways. In some instances, it can be a literal lack of information, such as occurred prior to 1962 when President Diem strictly limited the presence of American personnel in the South Vietnamese countryside. In other instances it can stem from uncertainty about the degree to which the client government's actions are leading to observed outcomes. In El Salvador, the conservative defense minister Jose Guillermo Garcia appeared to support the socio-economic reforms urged by the United States – including the need to reduce human rights violations – yet atrocities continued on his watch. American observers were uncertain whether this was because Garcia was well intentioned but unable to control rogue elements within the military or he was merely trying to placate his patrons in order to obtain military aid while giving tacit support for continued abuses.[88] Observation can be impeded by the small number of personnel from the patron nation in the local country – such as the congressionally imposed fifty-five-man limit on U.S. trainers in El Salvador – or the distance between the two nations. As a result, the client's knowledge that the patron has difficulty monitoring its behavior provides an incentive to "shirk" on its commitment to engage in meaningful reforms as part of its counterinsurgency strategy or to redirect the patron's aid for its own purposes, without the patron realizing it. This is not to suggest that the local partners are necessarily lazy, evil, or stupid but rather that they are strategic actors focused on what

---

[87] William LeoGrande, "A Splendid Little War: Drawing the Line in El Salvador," *International Security*, 6, no. 1 (Summer 1981), p. 46.

[88] For evidence of Garcia's support for reforms, see Christopher Dickey, "El Salvador Gives Farmers Land to Show Progress in Reforms," *Washington Post*, June 5, 1982; and Shirley Christian, "Salvadorans Battle Erosion of Land Reform," *Miami Herald*, June 13, 1982. For a contrary view, see Telegram 775, San Salvador to State, February 1, 1982, Ronald W. Reagan Presidential Library (RRL). Regarding the difficulties of controlling local police regardless of what was said or done in San Salvador, see Memorandum of Conversation, Bush, Duarte et al., September 21, 1981, Declassified Documents Reference Service (DDRS); and Telegram 89363, State to San Salvador, April 9, 1981, National Security Archive (NSA), George Washington University.

Oliver Williamson called "self-interest seeking with guile," which leads them to undertake "calculated efforts to mislead, distort, disguise, obfuscate or otherwise confuse" to achieve their own preferences.[89]

In coming to the assistance of a client state beset by internal conflict, the supporting power provides aid in an effort to reduce the local political instability.[90] Assistance can take the form of economic aid, such as loans and grants to the client government; training and equipment for the local security forces and intelligence services; as well as diplomatic support, which can bolster the allied state in international forums and enhance its international legitimacy. The challenge facing supporting powers in such circumstances is that aid, even when well intentioned, can be a double-edged sword.

The very same economic and military assistance that can be used to subsidize reform, stimulate growth, broaden the government's base of support, and protect the local populace from insurgent violence can also be employed to forcibly repress dissent and bribe dissatisfied elites. This diversion of external aid could take the form of the outright misallocation of funds in ways that run counter to the patron's intentions, or it can occur indirectly when foreign aid replaces the funds the government would have otherwise spent, allowing that money to be used to enrich the regime or its supporters. In the short term, providing an ally with needed sources of money, materiel, and military expertise may stabilize its government and allow it to weather a temporary crisis.[91] In the longer term, however, this very same aid may "hollow out" the regime, making it more vulnerable to collapse or overthrow. Protracted foreign assistance can undermine the very stability and self-sufficiency the aid was intended to achieve in the first place.[92] Therefore, as Kaplan argued, "[T]he impact of aid thus depends largely on the extent to which the aid-giver can affect motivations, public policy and private-sector decisions – whether by formal agreement, by persuasion and cajolery, or by the announced fact of aid giving."[93]

---

[89] Oliver Williamson, *The Economic Institutions of Capitalism* (New York: Free Press, 1985), p. 47.

[90] Michael N. Barnett and Jack S. Levy, "Domestic Sources of Alliances and Alignments: The Case of Egypt, 1962–73," *International Organization*, 45, no. 3 (Summer 1991), p. 374.

[91] Carney, "International Patron-Client Relationships," p. 49.

[92] Knorr, "International Economic Leverage," p. 191.

[93] Jacob J. Kaplan, *The Challenge of Foreign Aid* (New York: Praeger, 1967), p. 137.

As an independent actor, the partner nation will respond to the incentives created for it by the supporting power. The ability to obtain abundant economic and military assistance from abroad can divorce a government from its dependence on its broader society, reduce its incentives to govern prudently, alleviate the need to build popular support for its policies, and retard reforms that strengthen the capacity of the state and lay the foundation for long-term economic prosperity.[94] Unsurprisingly, an almost inverse relationship has been posited between external support for a government and its prospects for undertaking meaningful domestic political and economic reform.[95]

When faced with an insurgency, such externally supported regimes frequently centralize power and authority with an increasingly narrow clique of insiders and divert resources to actions with short-term pay-offs, such as funding repression or bribing rivals, which foreign aid renders less costly than measures that could promote longer-term stability such as addressing popular grievances or broadening their political support base.[96] The economy is further weakened because repression deters productive economic activity, while corruption – which is correlated with high levels of foreign aid – encourages citizens to focus on rent-seeking activities.[97] The net result is a fragile regime

---

[94] Dave Dollar and Lant Pritchett, *Assessing Aid. What Works, What Doesn't and Why, World Bank* (New York: Oxford University Press, 1998), p. 1; Karen Remmer, "Does Foreign Aid Promote the Expansion of Government?" *American Journal of Political Science*, 48, no. 1 (2004); Nicolas Van de Walle, *African Economies and the Politics of Permanent Crisis, 1979–1999* (New York: Cambridge University Press, 2001). For a similar phenomenon among countries with abundant natural resources, see Terry Karl, "The Perils of the Petro-State: Reflections on the Paradox of Plenty," *Journal of International Affairs*, 53, no. 1 (Fall 1999), p. 37.

[95] Hilton L. Root, *Alliance Curse: How America Lost the Third World* (Washington, DC: Brookings Institution Press, 2008), p. 22.

[96] Simeon Djankov et al., "The Curse of Aid," *Economics Working Papers 870* (Department of Economics and Business, Universitat Pompeu Fabra, 2005), pp. 4–5; Tim Harford and Michael Klein, "Aid and the Resource Curse," *View Points 291* (Washington, DC: World Bank, 2005), pp. 2–3; Mancur Olson, "Dictatorship, Democracy and Development," *American Political Science Review*, 87 (September 1993), p. 571. For a general critique that external aid simply maintains the status quo in a developing country by entrenching the position of those already in power, see P. T. Bauer, *Equality, the Third World, and Economic Delusion* (Cambridge, MA: Harvard University Press, 1981), pp. 100–10.

[97] Yi Feng, "Political Freedom, Political Instability and Policy Uncertainty: A Study of Political Institutions and Private Investments in Developing

with a narrow base of support that is vulnerable to organized political opposition and insurgency – the exact situation foreign aid was intended to avoid. As a result, Thompson suggests that in counter-insurgency, "the less aid is given and the more the threatened country is compelled to rely on its own resources, the more effective the results will be."[98] A host of cases ranging from Diem's Vietnam to Somoza's Nicaragua to the Shah's Iran suggest that the provision of assistance – well intentioned though it may have been – can actually promote the very instability in the client state it was seeking to prevent. Even if a total collapse is avoided, the patron's position will be undermined if the security of its regional interests depends on an unstable partner government that only survives at the point of a bayonet.

Bound by Obligation?

Before moving to an examination of ways to mitigate the principal-agent problem in counterinsurgency, it is necessary to address two questions raised by the discussion so far:

1. Why would states make such strong commitments to clients if they can be so counterproductive? and
2. Why wouldn't such states simply reduce support for a client discovered to have sharply divergent preferences?

The answer to the first question is a consequence of the fact that talk is cheap in the anarchic international system. In situations ranging from extended deterrence to economic negotiations, states must take costly actions to credibly signal to allies and adversaries alike that they are not merely bluffing when they issue threats or make promises.[99] Supporting counterinsurgency is no different: a patron state not only

Countries," *International Studies Quarterly*, 45, no. 2 (June 2001), pp. 271–9; Jonathan Isham et al., "Civil Liberties, Democracy and the Performance of Government Projects," *World Bank Economic Review*, 11, no. 2 (1997), pp. 234–5; Kevin Murphy et al., "Why Is Rent-Seeking So Costly to Growth," *American Economic Review*, 83, no. 2 (May 1993), pp. 413–14. The links between aid and corruption are discussed in Alberto Alesina and Beatrice Weder, "Do Corrupt Governments Receive Less Foreign Aid?" *American Economic Review*, 92, no. 4 (September 2002), pp. 1126–37.

[98] Thompson, *Defeating Communist Insurgency*, p. 163.

[99] James Fearon, "Domestic Political Audiences and the Escalation of International Disputes," *American Political Science Review*, 88, no. 3 (September 1994).

seeks to reassure its client via public commitments but also to send important signals to the insurgents and those countries perceived to be their patrons. Such signals are not necessarily just symbolic. During the Cold War, several prominent scholars, such as Robert Osgood, Thomas Schelling, and Glenn Snyder, all suggested that strong American commitments to defend smaller nations made a substantive and positive contribution to U.S. national security goals by stabilizing the friendly governments in question, while simultaneously deterring hostile aggression globally.[100] The 2006 U.S. *Counterinsurgency Field Manual* embraced this logic, arguing that

U.S. support can be critical to building public faith in [the host nation] government's viability. The populace must have confidence in the staying power of both the counterinsurgents and the HN [host nation] government. Insurgents and local populations often believe that a few casualties or a few years will cause the United States to abandon a COIN effort. Constant reaffirmations of commitment, backed by deeds, can overcome that perception and bolster faith in the steadfastness of U.S. support.[101]

Strong public statements may also be necessary to generate action in the domestic realm, where it may be easier for policymakers to rally popular and congressional support for unambiguous commitments to clients by overstating their importance to U.S. national security or clearly identifying them as "good" and their opponents as "bad." Scholars of U.S. foreign policy have noted a tendency for political leaders to oversell the rationale for intervention in a particular situation in order to generate both elite consensus and public backing for their desired course of action.[102] "We made our points clearer than the truth" is how Secretary of State Dean Acheson described the overselling of containment to a skeptical American public in the early Cold War.[103] As a result, unambiguous commitments, sweeping rhetoric,

---

[100] For a discussion of "global commitment theory," see Bruce Jentleson, "American Commitments in the Third World: Theory vs. Practice," *International Organization*, 41, no. 4 (Autumn 1987), pp. 670–5.

[101] Field Manual 3–24, *Counterinsurgency Operations*, p. 43.

[102] Theodore Lowi, "Making Democracy Safe for the World: On Fighting the Next War," in John Ikenberry, ed., *American Foreign Policy: Theoretical Essays* (New York: HarperCollins, 1989), p. 273; Ole Holsti, *Public Opinion and American Foreign Policy* (Ann Arbor: University of Michigan Press, 2004), pp. 319–21.

[103] Dean Acheson, *Present at the Creation* (New York: Norton, 1969), pp. 374–5.

and hyperbole can replace limited commitments, precision, and nuance in the domestic debate over U.S. foreign policy. In this vein, John F. Kennedy called South Vietnamese president Ngo Dinh Diem "the cornerstone of the Free World in Southeast Asia, the keystone to the arch, the finger in the dyke," while Lyndon Johnson proclaimed that he was the "Winston Churchill" of Asia.[104] Although such techniques can be effective in generating public support, they can also constrain a government's freedom of action and lead to a deeper commitment than initially anticipated because these messages are sent to multiple audiences at once.

Turning to the second question, why doesn't a patron simply withdraw from a situation when it discovers the client's priorities are so divergent that the local government appears unwilling to take even basic steps to save itself? A great power patron may be aware of the client's shortcomings but decides to assist it anyway because it believes that the alternative – insurgent victory – would be worse. As the CIA suggested with respect to several weak or authoritarian regimes backed by the United States in the 1950s, "[B]y definition, the present governments in these states, whatever their deficiencies, are preferable to Communist governments."[105] From this standpoint, a failure to follow through with assistance to such regimes could court disaster. Indeed, several observers have argued that the principal cause of the collapse of friendly regimes in South Vietnam, Iran, and Nicaragua was the failure of the United States to vigorously uphold its commitments to those clients.[106]

The need to be seen to uphold commitments to clients was a particular worry during the Cold War where the belief that all of America's commitments to its allies and partners worldwide were interrelated created a deep concern that a failure to support a client in one part of the world would call into question the credibility of its

---

[104] John F. Kennedy, "America's Stake in Vietnam," in Wesley Fishel, ed., *Vietnam: Anatomy of a Conflict* (Itasca, IL: F. E. Peacock, 1968), p. 144; Stanley Karnow, *Vietnam: A History* (London: Pimlico, 1994), p. 267.

[105] CIA, "Certain Problems Created by the U.S. Military Assistance Program," January 30, 1959, p. 10, Joseph M. Dodge Papers, Dwight D. Eisenhower Presidential Library (Dodge Papers).

[106] Norman Podhoretz, *Why We Were in Vietnam* (New York: Simon & Schuster, 1984); Michael Ledeen and Michael Lewis, *Debacle: The American Failure in Iran* (New York: Knopf, 1981); and Jeane Kirkpatrick, "Dictatorships and Double Standards," *Commentary*, 68, no. 5 (November 1979), pp. 34–45.

commitments in other areas.[107] Moreover, as suggested by the rancor-
ous debate over "Who lost China?" in 1949 – which tarred the
Democrat Party as weak on national security for over a generation –
a political leader may fear that failing to uphold a commitment could
open the door to domestic political repercussions, such as removal
from office.[108] Despite misgivings over Diem's prospects for success
in Vietnam, for example, President Kennedy is alleged to have told
confidants that he shied away from withdrawing American support
because it "would destroy him and the Democratic Party" and that
there was no way he could "give up a piece of territory like that to the
Communists and then get the American people to re-elect me."[109]
As a result, a commitment and its associated reputational effects
could become more important to policymakers than the strategic
value of the regime to which the commitment was made in the first
place.[110] This was particularly true in the case of Vietnam, where,

---

[107] Robert Jervis, "Deterrence Theory Revisited," *World Politics*, 31, no. 2
       (January 1979), p. 322; Nitza Nachimas, *Transfer of Arms, Leverage and
       Peace in the Middle East* (Westport, CT: Greenwood Press, 1988), pp. 8–9;
       Roland A. Paul, *American Military Commitments Abroad* (New Brunswick,
       NJ: Rutgers University Press, 1973), p. 19; Thomas C. Schelling, *Arms and
       Influence* (New Haven, CT: Yale University Press, 1966), pp. 55–6, 65–6;
       Alexander L. George and Richard Smoke, *Deterrence in American Foreign
       Policy: Theory and Practice* (New York: Columbia University Press, 1974),
       p. 41. Huth and Russett find that credibility plays an important role in
       whether opposing states believe that allies will actually intervene in
       a conflict. Paul Huth and Bruce Russett, "Deterrence Failure and Crisis
       Escalation," *International Studies Quarterly*, 32, no. 1 (1988). Weinstein
       suggests American leaders tend to have a "nonsituational" view of
       commitments, resolutely observing them "even in the face of vastly changed
       conditions." Franklin Weinstein, "The Concept of a Commitment in
       International Relations," *Journal of Conflict Resolution*, 13, no. 1 (March
       1969), pp. 51–2.
[108] Fearon, "Domestic Political Audiences and the Escalation of International
       Disputes," pp. 581–2, 585; Bruce Bueno de Mesquita et al., "An Institutional
       Explanation of the Democratic Peace," *American Political Science Review*, 93,
       no. 4 (December 1999), p. 794; Schelling, *Arms*, p. 55; Alastair Smith,
       "International Crises and Domestic Politics," *American Political Science
       Review*, 92, no. 3 (September 1998); Snyder and Diesing, *Conflict among
       Nations*, p. 216. For a skeptical view of the impact of audience costs, see
       Marc Trachtenberg, "Audience Costs: An Historical Analysis," *Security
       Studies*, 21, no. 1 (March 2012), pp. 3–42.
[109] Quoted in Richard Reeves, *President Kennedy: Profile in Power* (New York:
       Simon & Schuster, 1993), pp. 261, 484.
[110] This is not strictly an American phenomenon. With regard to the Soviet
       intervention in Afghanistan, Foreign Minister Andrei Gromyko argued,

writing on the cusp of full-scale American intervention, Assistant Secretary of Defense John McNaughton explained in a March 1965 memo to the Secretary of Defense that U.S. aims in Vietnam were "70% – to avoid a humiliating U.S. defeat (to our reputation as a guarantor). 20% – to keep SVN (and the adjacent territory) from Chinese hands. 10% – to permit the people of SVN to enjoy a better, freer way of life."[111] Having made a commitment to a local ally, even a superpower may find that it does not have the freedom to easily disengage should it wish to do so.[112] As Alexander George has noted, "[A]n abrupt change or reversal of foreign policy is never easy in a democratic system; it must generally await a severe crisis that drives home unmistakably that the policy has become obsolete . . . Even so, the change in policy may not occur until there is a change of administration."[113]

What are the consequences of this behavior for assisting counter-insurgency? A strong commitment to assist an ally can actually under-cut the leverage over that ally. Samuel Huntington has suggested that the level of influence a patron has over its client varies *inversely* with the perceived level of commitment to that client.[114] Robert Jervis concurs, suggesting that "to restrain yet not alienate its allies, a state may want to prevent them from being confident that it will fulfill its obligation . . . a nation will lose bargaining leverage if their allies are sure they can count on it to live up to the original commitment."[115] Having publicly pledged its support for the client government's counterinsurgency

"[U]nder no circumstances can we lose Afghanistan . . . If we lose Afghanistan now, it will move away from the Soviet Union, that will be a blow to our politics." Quoted in Andrei Doohovskoy, "Soviet Counterinsurgency in the Soviet Afghan War Revisited," master's thesis Harvard University, September 2009, pp. 30–1.

[111] *The Pentagon Papers, Gravel Edition*, vol. 3 (Boston: Beacon Press, 1971), pp. 694–702. This view is supported by Leslie Gelb, "Vietnam: The System Worked," *Foreign Policy*, no. 3 (Summer 1971).

[112] Blaufarb, *Counterinsurgency Era*, p. 307; Hoffman, "Restraints and Choices in American Foreign Policy," p. 678.

[113] Alexander L. George, *Bridging the Gap* (Washington, DC: U.S. Institute of Peace, 1993), p. 34.

[114] Richard M. Pfeffer, ed., *No More Vietnams? The War and the Future of American Foreign Policy* (New York: Harper & Row, 1968), p. 230. See also Snyder and Diesing, *Conflict among Nations*, pp. 223–5, 432.

[115] Robert Jervis, *The Logic of Images in International Relations* (Princeton, NJ: Princeton University Press, 1970), pp. 87–8. Michael Handel also suggests that it is particularly beneficial to strong states to leave their commitments

campaign, the patron can find itself embroiled in what has been called "the Commitment Trap."[116] This is a situation in which the perceived strength of a great power's commitment to a small ally renders it unable to influence the ally's policies or prevent it from acting in a way that is harmful to the great power's long-term interests, yet simultaneously, the great power believes it is unable to withdraw its support from the ally for fear of damaging its credibility. Reviewing American partnerships with Nationalist China, South Korea, South Vietnam, the Shah's Iran, and the Philippines under Marcos, Hilton Root argues that

it was the implicit strength of the U.S. commitment that allowed these client regimes to ignore external requests for accommodation and reform – notions that often enjoyed strong support among client regime populations. Thus, the commitment trap turns a great power into a creature of a smaller power. The tail wags the dog.[117]

In the specific context of counterinsurgency, Douglas Blaufarb describes the situation similarly, with the United States repeatedly "becoming the reluctant prisoner of an unsavory and incompetent regime which we continue to aid despite its obvious failures because it is too difficult to back out."[118]

If the local government believes that its patron cannot withdraw support without suffering harm to its reputation, then the supported regime can attempt to "pass the buck" for its security to its larger ally.[119] It is also free to ignore its patron's requests to change its policies as well as their threats to withhold aid should such actions not be forthcoming.[120] Aware that it is not in the patron's interest to punish them for noncompliance, clients can freely discount such ultimatums in the belief that the patron will still assist them when presented with their

ambiguous so as to not be manipulated by weaker allies. Handel, *Weak States*, p. 122.

[116] Douglas J. Macdonald, *Adventures in Chaos: American Interventions for Reform in the Third World* (Cambridge, MA: Harvard University Press, 1992), pp. 259–262.

[117] Root, *Alliance Curse*, p. 175. See also Shoemaker and Spanier, *Patron-Client*, p. 13.

[118] Blaufarb, *Counterinsurgency Era*, p. 307.

[119] Klaus Knorr, *On the Uses of Military Power in the Nuclear Age* (Princeton, NJ: Princeton University Press, 1966), p. 156.

[120] Hans Morgenthau, *Politics Among Nations: The Struggle for Power and Peace* (New York: Knopf, 1961), pp. 545–6.

fait acompli because of its interest in the client's long-term stability.[121] Benjamin Schwarz described these dynamics in El Salvador, where

[s]ince 1981 [American] policymakers believed that victory in El Salvador could be won by influencing the regime to do what was necessary to win its people's hearts and minds; and the United States believed that the $6 billion in support it provided bought considerable leverage in that effort. But the Salvadorans had America trapped. They realized that the United States was involved in their war for its own national security interests ... How, then, could the Salvadoran armed forces and far right be pressured to reform by threats to cease aid if Washington repeatedly affirmed its determination to "draw a line" against communism in El Salvador? So while the ruling Salvadorans gestured appropriately in response to U.S. conditions, whenever the U.S. imposed reforms threatened to alter fundamentally the status quo – their very object – they were emasculated.[122]

The end result of this process, as Richard Schultz described with respect to Vietnam, is one in which "the United States found itself ... supporting a client with little chance of success and unwilling to reform."[123]

Mitigating Principal-Agent Problems in Counterinsurgency

Agency theory allowed a structured exploration of the problems of adverse selection and moral hazard that can arise when assisting counterinsurgency. The same body of literature can also provide insights into managing these particular challenges. To mitigate the agency losses incurred by delegation, scholars have identified four principal mechanisms for controlling adverse selection and moral hazard: (1) contract design, (2) screening and selection, (3) monitoring and reporting, and (4) institutional checks.[124] Depending on the particular features of the agency relationship, some of these mechanisms will be more feasible than others.[125] Institutional checks, which seek to limit the scope of the agent's behavior by empowering other agents with the power to veto

---

[121] James M. Buchanan, "The Samaritan's Dilemma," in Edmund S. Phelps, ed., *Altruism, Morality and Economic Theory* (New York: SAGE, 1975), pp. 71–86.

[122] Schwarz, *American Counterinsurgency Doctrine*, p. xiii.

[123] Richard Shultz, "Strategy Lessons from an Unconventional War: The U.S. Experience in Vietnam," in Sam Sarkesian, ed., *Nonnuclear Conflicts in the Nuclear Age* (New York: Praeger, 1980), p. 169.

[124] Kiewiet and McCubbins, *The Logic of Delegation*, p. 27.   [125] *Ibid.*, p. 34.

the agent's unilateral actions, are effective in domestic bureaucratic settings in which the principal has free rein to create or alter the characteristics of its agents. When the actors involved are sovereign states, however, this method for aligning the agent's actions with the principal's objectives is of little use because, much as they might like, the patron cannot freely manipulate the structures and organizations of the host nation's government and society in the context of a limited intervention. Nor can they create new government bodies or agencies that can block or constrain the policy choices of an independent government. Similarly, although the preferred means of reducing adverse selection is to carefully screen agents and select only those whose preferences align closely with those of the principal, when assisting counterinsurgency, screening and selecting will be a less feasible tool for controlling adverse selection than it might be in other settings.[126] In theory this could be highly effective at the point where a decision to intervene is taken, however, as previously discussed, a patron assisting a client state in counterinsurgency rarely has the option of selecting an optimal agent beforehand and may – due to perceived geopolitical imperatives, reputational concerns, or domestic political pressures – knowingly decide to back a flawed regime against hostile insurgents, making what George Tanham and Dennis Duncanson term a "choice between evils."[127] Therefore, attention turns to the two remaining tools for mitigating agency losses: monitoring and reporting and contract design.

Of the two principal-agent problems, the moral hazard is more straightforward to deal with in a counterinsurgency setting because the primary solution suggested by agency theory is improved monitoring and reporting of the agent's behavior.[128] Although at first blush requiring the agent to report regularly to the principal on its actions would appear to be an ideal method for dealing with the problems of the agent's hidden actions, it has some limitations. Self-reporting by the agent is unreliable because the agent retains a strong incentive to reveal information in a strategic manner that reflects most favorably on

---

[126] *Ibid.*, p. 48.
[127] George K. Tanham and Dennis J. Duncanson, *Foreign Affairs*, 48, no. 1 (October 1969), p. 113. See also William J. Olson, "U.S. Objectives and Constraints," in Richard Shultz et al., eds., *Guerrilla Warfare and Counterinsurgency* (Lexington, MA: Lexington Books, 1993), p. 35.
[128] Kiewiet and McCubbins, *The Logic of Delegation*, p. 31.

itself.[129] For this reason, the principal often has to resort to monitoring of the agent's behavior to overcome the information asymmetry. Compared to reporting, monitoring is a second-best solution because it is costly for the principal to implement in terms of both time and effort. In the case of indirect intervention in counterinsurgency, monitors may require specialized knowledge – such as language ability – to do their jobs effectively, which can be both time-consuming or expensive for the personnel from the patron government to cultivate. Monitoring can also carry with it political costs for the patron nation. Close monitoring of a client government may require intrusive measures, such as placing monitors in the host nation's government offices, which could be a source of tension in bilateral relations. Moreover, there is a potential tradeoff between depth of monitoring and the perceived level of commitment to the client. More extensive monitoring typically means a larger presence in the client country and the perception of a larger commitment to that client. In Vietnam in mid-1962, after the United States assigned advisory personnel to every South Vietnamese military unit down to the battalion level and the CIA and USAID began to station their personnel in rural areas, the quality and quantity of information Washington received on the various shortcomings of the South Vietnamese military and government increased tremendously. The cost of this monitoring, however, was the deployment of 11,500 American military personnel to Vietnam, which undercut any notion of a limited involvement in the conflict and paved the way for future escalation. Conversely, the notional fifty-five-man limit on U.S. military trainers in El Salvador helped to constrain the visible American presence on the ground in the country but also limited the ability of the United States to monitor the behavior of government forces in the field.

Monitoring can take the form of either direct supervision of the client by the patron government, referred to as a *police-patrol oversight*, or the more passive *fire alarm monitoring*, which relies heavily on responding to the complaints of interested nongovernmental groups such as journalists and human rights organizations.[130] The effectiveness of this mechanism can be hindered by the host nation's purposeful

---

[129] *Ibid.*, pp. 31–2.
[130] Matthew McCubbins and Thomas Schwartz, "Congressional Oversight Overlooked: Police Patrols versus Fire Alarms," *American Journal of Political Science*, 28, no. 1 (February 1984).

attempts to obfuscate or limit monitoring. The refusal of the South Vietnamese government to allow American personnel to be based in the provinces prior to 1962 forced the United States to rely on Saigon's own intelligence agencies, which delivered overly optimistic reports on the progress of the conflict. This illusion was only dispelled when Diem finally allowed American civilian and military advisors to deploy into the countryside, where they discovered numerous deficiencies in the execution of South Vietnam's counterinsurgency strategy.[131] As this example suggests, the solution to the problem of the agent's hidden actions is often to increase the effectiveness of monitoring by improving either its quantity or its quality. Since this can be costly, however, a principal must carefully weigh the costs and benefits of additional information.

Turning to the second principal-agent problem, managing adverse selection is relatively more difficult because it relates to uncertainty over the local partner's true preferences for outcomes and its willingness to engage in risky behavior. As noted previously, would-be clients have a strong incentive to misrepresent their preferences to attract patron support. If it is not possible to control selection of the client, agency theory suggests that the next-best solution is to minimize the effects of adverse selection by shaping the client's behavior. When coming to the client's assistance, the principal must carefully craft its bargain or security guarantee (*contract*) with the agent to establish performance expectations along with a clear set of rewards and punishments for compliance and noncompliance. Although such a bargain may not appear to be a contract in the formal sense, in the principal-agent literature, a contract "may refer to a formal document ... to an implicit contract ... or to some penalty-reward system which may not formally be a contract at all."[132] Outcome-based incentives can be a key means of overcoming the problems of adverse selection by aligning the preferences of the agent with those of the principal – since both parties achieve their "payoff" by having the same action occur.[133]

[131] Memorandum, Heavner to Nolting, April 27, 1962, *Foreign Relations of the United States 1961–1963*, vol. II, Vietnam, 1962 (FRUS 1962), p. 363; Blaufarb, *Counterinsurgency Era*, p. 116.

[132] Rees, "The Theory of Principal and Agent, Part 1," p. 3.

[133] Michael Jensen and William Meckling, "Theory of the Firm: Managerial Behavior, Agency Costs and Ownership Structure," *Journal of Financial Economics*, 3, no. 4 (October, 1976).

The offer of rewards and the threat of sanctions can create incentives for the agent to serve the principal's interests. Full compliance, however, can never be expected. Inevitably, in any principal-agent interaction, the outcome achieved by the principal via delegation falls short of its desired end state. Although the principal saves in terms of the cost of carrying out a task, it must accept a "cost" in the form of suboptimal execution: agency losses are essentially the price of delegation. As Matthew McCubbins, Roger Noll, and Barry Weingast note, "[A] system of rewards and punishments is unlikely to be a completely effective solution to the control problem. This is due to the cost of monitoring, limitations in the range of rewards and punishments, and for the most meaningful forms of rewards and punishments, the cost to the principals of implementing them."[134] The fact that punishing an agent imposes costs on a principal may undercut the credibility of such threats. This is no guarantee, however, that the patron would not punish defection by the client. A host of documented international interactions ranging from economic sanctions to nuclear deterrence involve attempts to coerce another party through the threat of actions that, if implemented, would be harmful to the implementing party.[135] Not only have such threats proven to be credible, in certain instances, they can actually imbue the threatening party with bargaining leverage. In terms of providing assistance to counterinsurgency, this suggests that patrons should establish a clear "contract" with their client state at the outset of an intervention and apply conditions to its aid in an effort to both shape the client's actions and limit the perceived scope of the commitment to that client. The challenges of implementing this approach are explored in Chapter 3.

Conclusion

On its own, counterinsurgency is a challenging undertaking. The difficulties are compounded when a state has to work with or through a local ally. Among the criticisms of American counterinsurgency

---

[134] Matthew McCubbins et al., "Administrative Procedures as Instruments of Political Control," *Journal of Law, Economics and Organization*, 3, no. 2 (Autumn 1987), pp. 251–2.

[135] James Fearon, "Rationalist Explanations for War," *International Organization*, 49, no. 3 (1995); Paul Huth, "Deterrence and International Conflict," *Annual Review of Political Science*, 2 (1999).

support efforts, two recurring themes have emerged: a failure to properly understand the character and preferences of it local partners and a failure to appreciate the potentially deleterious effects that providing support can have on the behavior of those partners. Despite counterinsurgency theorists' advocacy of reform, reorganization, and policy changes in response to political violence, the local government's divergent interests can inhibit its willingness to respond in a manner preferred by its external patron. Moreover, unless aid to an incumbent regime is carefully directed and controlled, it can skew the local government's incentives in a manner that runs counter to the patron's goals. Agency theory identifies two relevant mechanisms by which a principal can attempt to ameliorate these problems: effective monitoring of the agent and the design of the "contract" between the two parties. In Chapter 3, the utility of these two tools are compared to the predictions of power asymmetry, aid dependence, strategic utility, and selectorate theory to explain the ability of the patron to gain influence over its client in order to induce or compel reform and policy change in the host nation's counterinsurgency strategy.

3 | *Influencing Clients*

As Chapter 2 outlined, successfully assisting an ally's counterinsurgency effort may require a patron to be able to compel policy change on the part of its client. Yet, as critics have noted, despite the overwhelming military and economic power of the United States and the apparent dependence of a local ally on external support for its continued survival, American policymakers have often found themselves in the frustrating position of being unable to gain sufficient influence over the military or government of the partner nation.[1]

The insights from agency theory in Chapter 2 suggest that attention should focus on the ability of the patron to (1) undertake sufficient monitoring to mitigate the effects of moral hazard and (2) develop a "contract" with the client to ameliorate the effects of adverse selection. Before investigating these mechanisms further, however, we should first consider whether or not there are any structural factors in the patron-client relationship that could determine the patterns of influence. To accomplish this, the predictions of power asymmetry, aid dependence, strategic utility, and selectorate theory, as well as the monitoring aspects of agency theory, are all compared to the actual influence patterns observed in the detailed case studies of the Philippines, Vietnam, and El Salvador examined in Chapters 4 through 6. Each of these explanations is found wanting, so attention then focuses on the "contract" between the two parties, and two alternate means for using aid to influence a client, *inducement* and *conditionality*, are described and their observable implications specified.

Competing Theories of Influence

Scholars of international relations have advanced a number of theories to explain the relative balance of influence between large and

---

[1] For this phenomenon more generally, see Robert Keohane, "The Big Influence of Small Allies," *Foreign Policy*, no. 2 (Spring 1971).

small states. In this section neither power asymmetry, aid dependence, the strategic utility of the client state, selectorate theory, nor the monitoring aspects of agency theory are found to accurately predict the patterns of influence observed in the three cases studied here.

The discrete influence episodes examined in great detail in Chapters 4 through 6 are summarized in Tables 3.1 through 3.3. As these tables indicate, across the three cases, the United States exercised the greatest level of influence over the Philippine government and the least over the Vietnamese government. The United States achieved a moderate degree of influence over the government of El Salvador, characterized by high levels of influence in some areas and low levels in others.

Table 3.1 *Degree of Compliance with U.S. Policy Prescriptions in the Philippines, 1946–54*

Date	Event	Compliance
1949–50	Restructuring of the Philippine constabulary	High
1950–1	Implementation of the Quirino-Foster Agreement	High
1950	Appointment of Magsaysay as Secretary of Defense	High
1952	Removal of General Castañeda and Brigadier Ramos	High
1952–3	Prevention of backsliding by Liberal Party	High

Table 3.2 *Degree of Compliance with U.S. Policy Prescriptions in Vietnam, 1957–63*

Date	Event	Compliance
1957–9	Durbrow's press for political liberalization	Low
1961	Counterinsurgency plan	Low
1961	Joint action plan	Low
1961	Limited partnership	Low
1963	Final push for reform	Low

Table 3.3 *Degree of Compliance with U.S. Policy Prescriptions in El Salvador, 1979–91*

Date	Event	Compliance
1980	Christian Democrat entry into Junta	High
1980	Prevent military coup	High
1980	Improve human rights in return for helicopters	Low
1980	Restructure Junta and purge human rights abusers	High
1980	Control human rights abuses and death squads	Low
1981	Sustain Junta reforms and reduce human rights abuses	Low
1981–91	Adapt the Salvadoran military for counterinsurgency	Low
1981	Prevent right-wing coup and prosecute churchwomen case	High
1981–4	Congressional certification requirements	Low
1982	Include Christian Democrats in coalition government	High
1982	Defend "land-to-the-tiller" program	High
1983	Vice President Bush's "new contract"	High
1984–5	Implement economic austerity measures	High
1984–6	Prosecution of additional suspects in land reform murders	Low
1990	Promote the military's cooperation with Jesuit investigation	Low
1990–1	Prosecute the Jesuit murders and negotiate with the FMLN	High

Power Asymmetry

From the standpoint of conventional power analysis, the idea that the United States would have difficulty influencing the counterinsurgency efforts of objectively dependent partner is perplexing.[2] Ulf Lindell and Stefan Persson have gone so far as to term the "paradoxical" phenomenon of great powers being unable to get their way with smaller ones or

---

[2] Game theory predicts that a weak client should be strongly susceptible to patron influence. Snyder and Diesing, *Conflict among Nations*, pp. 145–7.

even being influenced by them in return as "a genuine puzzle."[3] In this vein, international negotiation theorists expect that in an unequal bargaining encounter, the stronger party will exploit the weaker party, who will act submissively in return.[4] This view is shared by some liberal international relations theorists such as Richard Rosecrance, who suggests that "influence normally succeeds where there is a hierarchical relation between influencer and influencee."[5] In this vein, some scholars of patron-client relationships assert that the influence of the stronger party, the patron, "almost always exceeds that of his inferior ally."[6] Consequently, "the dominant flow of influence is from patron to the client, rather than the reverse."[7]

Yet there are many situations where great powers have been unable to translate their economic and military strength into influence over smaller states and indeed some instances where it appears that "the tail wags the dog."[8] If national power were as easily translated into influence as the scholars cited above suggest, in the three cases examined here we should see a steady pattern of increasing U.S. influence over the client state as the ratio of U.S. power to client state power increases, with similar levels of influence achieved over states that have a power

---

[3] Ulf Lindell and Stefan Persson, "The Paradox of Weak State Power," in *International Relations: Contemporary Theory and Practice* (Washington, DC: CQ Press, 1989), p. 287.

[4] Jeffrey Rubin and Bert Brown, *The Social Psychology of Bargaining and Negotiation* (New York: Academic Press, 1975), p. 199. For general arguments that the weaker side will concede faster in a negotiation, see F. Robert Dwyer and Orville C. Walker, "Bargaining in an Asymmetric Power Structure," *Journal of Marketing*, 55, no. 1 (Winter 1981), p. 110 and Arthur Lall, *Modern International Negotiation: Principles and Practice* (New York: Columbia University Press, 1966), p. 338.

[5] Richard Rosecrance, "Reward, Punishment and Interdependence," *Journal of Conflict Resolution*, 25, no. 1 (1981), p. 37.

[6] Carl Lande, "The Dyadic Basis of Clientelism," in Steffen W. Schmidt et al., eds., *Friends, Followers, and Factions: A Reader in Political Clientelism* (Berkeley: University of California Press, 1977), p. xxvi.

[7] Joseph Helman, "The Politics of Patron-Client State Relationships: The United States and Israel, 1948–1992," Ph.D. dissertation, George Washington University, 2002, p. 317.

[8] Michael Handel, "Does the Dog Wag the Tail or Vice Versa? Patron-Client Relations," *Jerusalem Journal of International Relations*, 6, no. 2 (1982). See also Richard Betts, "The Tragicomedy of Arms Trade Control," *International Security*, 5, no. 1 (Summer 1980), p. 100; Keohane, "Big Influence"; Klaus Knorr, *The Power of Nations: The Political Economy of International Relations* (New York: Basic Books, 1975), pp. 180–7.

asymmetry with the United States of the same order of magnitude. While some scholars use gross domestic product (GDP) or military expenditure as a proxy for national power, the Composite Index of National Capability (CINC) provides a comprehensive measure of state power by assessing a country's share of the world's economic, military, and demographic strength.[9]

As Table 3.4 indicates, while there was the greatest power differential ("CINC ratio U.S.:client") between the United States and El Salvador, Washington achieved only a relatively moderate level of influence over the host nation's counterinsurgency efforts. Moreover, in the cases that exhibited the greatest (Philippines) and least (South Vietnam) degree of influence, the power ratios, though different, were of the same order of magnitude compared with El Salvador and would not be expected to exhibit such divergent results if the predictions of power asymmetry were correct.

Aid Dependence

A second group of scholars argues that it is not aggregate power differences but the client state's degree of dependence on its patron for security or economic well-being that determines influence patterns.[10] As Robert Keohane argued in his early work, the "more dependent a state is on a great power for trade, aid or protection, the more responsive it is likely to be to pressure."[11] Nitza Nachimas is even more explicit, suggesting that "the client state's dependence on its patron state will result in leverage that could be measured and identified."[12] Such dependence would be

---

[9] J. David Singer, "Reconstructing the Correlates of War Dataset on Material Capabilities of States, 1816–1985," *International Interactions*, 14, no. 2 (April 1987). The CINC is very similar to Waltz's components of state power: population, size of territory, natural resource endowment, economic capacity, military strength, and political competence. Waltz, *Theory of International Politics*, p. 131. Where data in Singer conflict with archival data, the latter are used.

[10] Shoemaker and Spanier, *Patron-Client*, p. 15; Johan Galtung, "A Structural Theory of Imperialism," *Journal of Peace Research* 8, no. 2 (1971), 81–117; Robert Gilpin, *U.S. Power and the Multinational Corporation: The Political Economy of Foreign Direct Investment* (New York: Basic Books, 1975), pp. 25–33; Adrienne Armstrong, "The Political Consequences of Economic Dependence," *Journal of Conflict Resolution*, 25, no. 3 (1981), pp. 422–3.

[11] Robert Keohane, "Political Influence in the General Assembly," *International Conciliation*, no. 557 (1966), p. 18.

[12] Nachimas, *Transfer*, p. 3.

Table 3.4 *Comparative Elements of State Power*

Country	Steel production (1,000s tons)	Energy use (1,000s coal-ton equivalent)	Military size (1,000s)	Military expenditure (1,000s of $)	Urban population (1,000s)	Total population (1,000s)	CINC (% of world)	CINC ratio U.S.: client	Relative level of influence
USA (1947–53)	85,317.3	1,305,245.7	2,363.4	$26,315,715.0	43,781.6	152,283.9	30.06%	93:1	High
Philippines	0.0	118.6	28.7	$85,192.1	1,993.6	20,353.3	0.32%		
USA (1957–63)	90,239.1	1,487,528.3	2,522.1	$47,789,860.6	50,407.7	180,691.1	22.32%	59:1	Low
South Vietnam	0.0	68.3	262.9	$219,904.7	1,327.6	14,120.0	0.38%		
USA (1979–91)	88,146.8	3,244,149.2	2,180.6	$230,792,461.5	60,523.8	238,646.1	13.43%	214:1	Moderate
El Salvador	2.7	3,159.6	39.1	$156,931.5	1,038.4	4,863.0	0.06%		

Note: Figures in the table are average values over the course of the intervention. All dollar figures are historical values.

expected to produce a particularly high degree of leverage during a crisis – like the counterinsurgency episodes studied here – when the client requires sustained access to the patron's largesse.[13] Not surprisingly, throughout the Cold War, American policymakers consistently expected that dependence on U.S. aid would necessarily translate into influence over the policies of the recipient state.[14] Indeed, in El Salvador, some Carter administration officials believed that the behavior of the Salvadoran Armed Forces could be influenced by 'making them dependent on American military aid, an effort that sought to, in the words of an unnamed official, "wean the military off the teat of the oligarchy and on to ours."[15]

Yet other scholars report that the provision of significant amounts of military or economic aid to a client state does not necessarily translate into considerable leverage over the client's behavior.[16] In fact, even highly dependent states have repeatedly demonstrated the ability to resist the demands of their patrons for behavior or policy change and even sometimes exercise reverse leverage over their stronger allies.[17]

[13] Robert Harkavy, *Arms Trade and International Systems* (Cambridge, MA: Ballingar, 1975), p. 101.

[14] Scholars reporting this finding include Barry M. Blechman, et al., "Negotiated Limitations on Arms Transfers: First Steps towards Crisis Prevention?" in Alexander L. George, ed., *Managing U.S.-Soviet Rivalry: Problems of Crisis Prevention* (Boulder, CO: Westview Press, 1983), p. 257; Richard W. Cottam, *Competitive Interference and Twentieth Century Diplomacy* (Pittsburgh: University of Pittsburgh Press, 1967), p. 59; Michael Klare, *American Arms Supermarket* (Austin: University of Texas Press, 1984), p. 30; Keith Krause, "Military Statecraft: Power and Influence in Soviet and American Arms Transfer Relationships," *International Studies Quarterly*, 35, no. 3 (1991), p. 314; Nachimas, *Transfer*, pp. 1–2; T. V. Paul, "Influence through Arms Transfers: Lessons from the U.S.-Pakistani Relationship," *Asian Survey*, 32, No. 12 (December 1992), p. 1078.

[15] Quoted in Christopher Dickey, "Oligarchy Takes Stand against Salvadoran Land Reform," *Washington Post*, April 4, 1980.

[16] Knorr, *Power of Nations*, pp. 181–3; William Mott, *United States Military Assistance: An Empirical Perspective* (Westport, CT: Greenwood Press, 2002), pp. 14–15; Stephen Walt, *The Origins of Alliances* (Ithaca, NY: Cornell University Press, 1987), pp. 43–4.

[17] Jacob Bercovitch, "Superpowers and Client States: Analyzing Relations and Patterns of Influence," in Moshe Efrat and Jacob Bercovitch, eds., *Superpowers and Client States in the Middle East: The Imbalance of Influence* (London: Routledge, 1991), p. 19; James A Blessing, "The Suspension of Foreign Aid: A Macro-Analysis," *Polity*, 13, no. 3 (Spring 1981), p. 533; Gordon Crozier, *Foreign Aid and Political Reform: A Comparative Analysis of Democracy Assistance and Political Conditionality* (New York: Palgrave, 2001), p. 202;

As Table 3.5 suggests, in the three cases examined in this book, there is no clear correlation between the amount of aid received and client state compliance. Although it has been suggested that economic aid disbursements exceeding 10 percent of the recipient state's GDP would provide "substantial leverage" over a recipient, Vietnam breached that threshold yet had the lowest level of compliance with U.S. wishes.[18] There is also no evidence that military assistance in particular leads to compliance: U.S. military aid to South Vietnam was nearly two-thirds the size of Saigon's total military expenditures, yet Washington was unable to translate this largesse into significant leverage. In contrast, both the Philippines and El Salvador received significantly less aid than Vietnam (as a share of GDP and as a share of defense spending), yet the United States achieved greater influence in these two cases. Moreover, while the aid given to these two countries was relatively proportional, both as a percentage of GDP and as a share of military expenditure, the levels of influence achieved by the United States were notably different in the two cases. Thus aid levels alone are unable to adequately explain these influence patterns.

Strategic Value and Reverse Leverage

A third factor posited to affect the balance of influence between a patron and its client is the relative strategic importance of the client state to the patron. When dealing with a client government that is perceived to be strategically important, the patron may find it has less grounds to influence its local partner than it might expect. As Stephen Walt suggests, "[T]he more important the recipient is to the donor, the more aid it is likely to receive but the less leverage such aid will produce."[19]

Annette Baker Fox, "The Power of Small States: Diplomacy in World War II," in Christine Ingebritsen et al., eds., *Small States in International Relations* (Seattle: University of Washington Press, 2006), p. 40; Zeev Moaz, "Power Capabilities and Paradoxical Conflict Outcomes," *World Politics*, 46, no. 2 (January 1989), pp. 241–5.

[18] Stephen Brown, "Donors' Dilemmas in Democratization: Foreign Aid and Political Reform in Africa," Ph.D. dissertation, New York University, 2000, pp. 6–7. Stephen Walt also characterizes a state receiving 10 percent of its GDP in aid as "especially dependent" on its donor. Walt, *Alliances*, pp. 235–6.

[19] Walt, *Alliances*, pp. 43–4. For similar views, see David Baldwin, *Economic Statecraft* (Princeton, NJ: Princeton University Press, 1985); and Shoemaker and Spanier, *Patron-Client*, pp. 20–1.

Table 3.5 *Aid and Influence*

Country	Average annual U.S. aid ($m)	U.S. aid/client GDP	Average U.S. military aid ($m)	U.S. military aid/ client military expenditure	Relative level of influence
Philippines (1947–53)	$168.4	2.5%	$33.9	39.7%	High
South Vietnam (1957–63)	$343.7	12.0%	$148.4	67.5%	Low
El Salvador (1979–91)	$325.0	2.6%	$83.2	37.8%	Medium

Note: All dollar figures are historical values. Figures are drawn from the Bureau for Legislative and Public Affairs, "U.S. Overseas Loans and Grants: Obligations and Loan Authorizations, July 1, 1945–September 30, 2008," U.S. Agency for International Development, Washington, DC, 2008; and Kristian Gleditsch, "Expanded Trade and GDP Data," *Journal of Conflict Resolution*, 46, no. 5 (October 2002).

Therefore, the military and economic aid given to a strategically important client is rarely employed to advance the patron's interests but
instead become "a resource at the disposition of the recipient for domestic or external use regardless of the stated purpose for which given."[20]
Hans Morgenthau has warned that the mere perception of strategic
utility can also render a client blasé or even dismissive of its patron's
concerns.[21] Philippine president Elpidio Quirino, for example, deflected
stern warnings from the Truman administration that his government
needed to undertake significant political, economic, and military reform
in order to gain further U.S. assistance in the battle against the
Hukbalahap insurgents. Instead, he confidently predicted that America
would extend assistance to his government regardless of what he did
because it was in America's interest to see him succeed.[22] Michael Shafer
takes this argument one step further and suggests that a strategically
important client state beset by a major crisis – such as the insurgencies
studied here – will actually have the ability to exercise "reverse leverage"
over its patron.[23] Consequently, despite the local government's objective
dependence on external aid for its continued survival, the patron may
have little ability to shape a strategically important client's behavior.

Although the clients of great powers are often portrayed as pawns or
puppets, in point of fact they have repeatedly demonstrated the ability
to exploit the patron's interests for their own ends. Classic client
strategies for gaining reverse leverage over a patron include the threat
of defection, the invocation of shared sacrifice, and the threat of
collapse. Throughout the Cold War, it is well documented that
a number of strategically located "frontline" anti-Communist states
threatened to realign or accept aid from a hostile power in an effort to
gain significant concessions from the United States while simultaneously resisting American influence over their own policies.[24]

---

[20] Lewis, "Political Influence," p. 196.
[21] Hans Morgenthau, "Alliances in Theory and Practice," in Arnold Wolfers, ed.,
Alliance Policy in the Cold War (Baltimore: Johns Hopkins University Press,
1959), p. 211.
[22] Telegram 752, Manila to State, September 27, 1950, Box 12, Melby Papers.
[23] Shafer, *Deadly Paradigms*, p. 120.
[24] See, e.g., Keohane, "Big Influence," pp. 170–1; Chang Jin Park, "The Influence
of Small States upon the Superpowers: The United States–South Korean
Relations as a Case Study, 1950–1953," *World Politics*, 28 (1975);
Rouhollah Ramazani, *The United States and Iran: The Patterns of Influence*
(New York: Praeger, 1982), p. 38; John H. Spencer, *Ethiopia at Bay: A Personal*

In Vietnam, the Diem government sought to deter the Kennedy administration from pressing for reform by cultivating the impression that it was engaged in secret negotiations with North Vietnam to "neutralize" the country, an action that would have hindered American attempts to contain the spread of Communism in Southeast Asia.[25] Client states have also attempted to gain concessions or deflect pressure by emphasizing the sacrifices they are supposedly making on their patron's behalf. In El Salvador, senior military officers attempted to guilt the Reagan administration into supporting them despite a failure to enact key reforms by emphasizing that their soldiers were the ones fighting and dying to contain communism so that American soldiers would not have to.[26] Raising the specter of military defeat or internal collapse should the great power fail to provide sufficient aid is another classic client strategy for gaining reverse leverage. Thomas Schelling explained the logic: "[W]hen a person or country has lost the power to help himself, or the power to avert mutual damage, the other interested party has no choice but to assume the cost or responsibility."[27] As a result, the client could actually blackmail its patron into supporting it under the assumption that the cost to the patron of "losing" the client state far outweighs the harm caused by the particular policy or behavior that the patron is seeking to change.[28] This strategy was employed by the Salvadoran government to deflect the Carter administration's pressure for reform by bluntly informing Washington it

---

Account of the Selassie Years (Algonac, MI: Reference Publications, 1984), pp. 305–9; Theodore White, ed., *The Stilwell Papers* (New York: W. Sloane Associates, 1948), pp. 125–6.

[25] Memorandum of Conversation, Rusk, Hilsman, Nolting et al., August 30, 1963, *Foreign Relations of the United States 1961–1963*, vol. IV, Vietnam, August–December 1963 (FRUS 1963/2), p. 55; Telegram 391, Saigon to State, August 31, 1963, FRUS 1963/2, p. 68; Memorandum of Conversation, Rusk, Hilsman, Nolting et al., August 31, 1963, FRUS 1963/2, p. 72; CIA Telegram [no. redacted], Saigon to Langley, September 2, 1963, FRUS 1963/2, pp. 89–90; CIA Telegram 0698, Saigon to Langley, September 6, 1963, FRUS 1963/2, pp. 125–6; Research Memo, Hughes to SecState, September 11, 1963, FRUS 1963/2, p. 184.

[26] Central Intelligence Agency Cable, "Military Commanders' Resentment and Opposition to U.S. Government Pressure," January 25, 1984, Central Intelligence Agency FOIA Electronic Reading Room (CIA).

[27] Thomas C. Schelling, *The Strategy of Conflict* (Cambridge, MA: Harvard University Press, 1960), p. 37.

[28] Keohane, "Big Influence," p. 171; Rothstein, *Alliances and Small Powers*, p. 261.

faced a choice: "[E]ither support the present government of El Salvador totally, or see the country fall to Communism."[29]

While the deductive logic of the strategic utility proposition is compelling, it is not substantiated by the cases under examination. The strategic utility of a client state can be assessed along three axes: (1) the inherent power of the client state, (2) the substantial importance of the client state's territory for facilitating the patron's national security strategy, and (3) the symbolic importance of the client state to the patron. As the CINC figures reported in Table 3.4 demonstrate, neither Vietnam nor El Salvador contributed significantly to the global balance of power between the United States and the Soviet Union during the Cold War, yet they took on disproportionate political significance. In both cases U.S. interests were largely symbolic (i.e., to "draw a line in the sand" against Communist expansion) and involved concerns about the reputational effects of not upholding commitments. This was particularly true in the case of South Vietnam, where the U.S. Joint Chiefs of Staff argued in a 1962 memo to Secretary McNamara that the importance of Vietnam, and all of Southeast Asia, "lies in the political value that can accrue to the Free World through a successful stand in that area. Of equal importance is the psychological impact that a firm position by the United States will have on the countries of the world – both free and Communist."[30] Vietnam was not innately important but achieved significance primarily for its symbolism. This view is confirmed by John McNaughton's subsequent memo, referenced in Chapter 2, which indicated that the primary American interest in Vietnam was "to avoid a humiliating U.S. defeat (to our reputation as a guarantor)."[31] Similarly, both the Carter and Regan administrations saw El Salvador's importance to the United States in symbolic rather than substantive terms. Officials in the State Department's Latin America Bureau asserted that "the Carter people tended to assume that what happened in Central America really wasn't all that much business of theirs."[32] Indeed, National Security Advisor Zbigniew Brzezinski admitted that prior to the 1979 revolution in neighboring Nicaragua, the Carter administration had given El Salvador "only

---

[29] Telegram 8421, San Salvador to State, December 3, 1980, U.S. State Department FOIA Virtual Reading Room (STATE).

[30] *The Pentagon Papers*, vol. 2, pp. 662–6. [31] *Ibid.*, vol. 3, pp. 694–702.

[32] Luigi Einaudi, interview, September 10, 1987, *Oral History of the Conflict in El Salvador (OHCES)*, vol. 1, p. 4, MHI.

sporadic attention."[33] This is hardly a declaration of deep and enduring strategic interest. However, it did befit the one Central American
state with which the United States had little historical interaction. Like
McNaughton, President Reagan also focused on American credibility
with respect to El Salvador, arguing that if the United States failed to
draw the line against perceived Communist adventurism there, "our
credibility would collapse, our alliances would crumble and the safety
of our homeland would be in jeopardy."[34] As with Vietnam, El
Salvador was not strategically important per se, but it mattered largely
due to its symbolic value.[35]

In sharp contrast to Vietnam and El Salvador, the Philippines was of
both symbolic and substantive importance to the United States.
In symbolic terms, the Truman administration saw Philippine independence as a "model," the success of which could convince America's
Dutch and French allies to peacefully surrender their colonial possessions in the region. This would head off "the crucial immediate issue in
Southeast Asia of militant nationalism" that Washington feared would
be easily co-opted by Communists.[36] On the other hand, following the
"loss" of China in 1949, a failure to arrest the insurgency in the
Philippines would discredit America, in the words of then Assistant
Secretary of State Dean Rusk "throughout the length and breadth of
Asia."[37] Thus the archipelago was seen as a key battleground in the
emerging Cold War.[38] At the same time, unlike in Vietnam and El
Salvador, the Philippines also was of substantive strategic importance.
Although the CINC figures in Table 3.4 do not indicate that the
Philippines is of major importance to the global balance of power in
and of itself, U.S. naval bases and air fields in the country were crucial
for projecting American power in Southeast Asia and beyond. The U.S.

[33] Quoted in "U.S. Policy to El Salvador and Central America," Minutes of Special
Coordinating Committee Meeting, White House, January 28, 1980, NSA.
[34] U.S. Department of State, *American Foreign Policy: Current Documents, 1983*
(Washington, DC: GPO, 1984), p. 1320.
[35] For a British assessment of El Salvador's "global insignificance," see Letter,
Christopher Crabbie (Washington, DC) to FCO, December 10, 1980, FCO 99/
577, National Archives of the United Kingdom (NAUK).
[36] National Security Council Report, "U.S. Policy Towards Southeast Asia,"
July 1, 1949, p. 16, DDRS.
[37] Memorandum, Rusk to Matthews, "United States Military Assistance
Program in Southeast Asia," January 31, 1951, *Foreign Relations of the United
States 1951*, vol. VI, East Asia and the Pacific (FRUS 1951), p. 24.
[38] Memorandum, Jessup to Acheson, October 10, 1950, 796.00/10–1050, RG 59.

Joint Chiefs of Staff termed the Philippines "an essential part [of] the strategic position of the United States in the Far East," while George Kennan, the architect of containment, described the archipelago, alongside Japan, as "the corner-stones of . . . a Pacific security system" and "a bulwark of U.S. security in that area."[39]

Comprehensively comparing the relative strategic importance of three different countries in three different time periods is a task that goes beyond the scope of this subsection. However, without privileging substantive strategic value over the purely symbolic, if the proposed relationship between strategic utility and leverage were to hold true, it would not be reasonable to assume that a client state that was of both substantive and symbolic value to a patron would be less able to fend off unwanted influence than clients which are only of strategic importance in one of these aspects. Even if one were not to accept this formulation, at a minimum, all three countries were seen to be of strategic importance to the United States at the time of intervention and if the strategic utility argument was valid they should have at least had a roughly equal ability to deflect American pressure. Yet, contrary to either formulation, the United States enjoyed far greater leverage in the Philippines than in either Vietnam or El Salvador.

Selectorate Theory

A fourth potential explanation for the influence patterns observed in these cases is *selectorate theory*, which posits that the size of the domestic political coalition necessary to sustain a leader in power affects the policy choices of that leader. With respect to interstate influence, the key factor is the regime type of the influenced state.[40] Since autocratic governments require a smaller coalition of supporters to remain in office than do democracies, selectorate theory suggests that they have a greater ability to make policy concessions to a patron state in return for foreign aid that can be used to reward their

---

[39] Memorandum, JCS to SecDef, September 6, 1950, *Foreign Relations of the United States 1950*, vol. VI, East Asia and the Pacific (FRUS 1950), p. 1485; Report by the Policy Planning Staff, February 24, 1948, *Foreign Relations of the United States 1948*, Volume I, Part 2, General (FRUS 1948), pp. 510–29.

[40] Bruce Bueno de Mesquita et al., *The Logic of Political Survival* (Cambridge, MA: MIT Press, 2003).

supporters.[41] In contrast, democratic leaders can make relatively fewer concessions to a patron in return for aid because remaining in office requires them to make policy choices that are supported by the majority of the voting population.[42] As a result, Hilton Root notes that a host of great powers has found it easier to "co-opt leaders who rule through the disbursement of private goods to small coalitions," than to work with more democratic regimes.[43] While generally suggesting an inverse relationship between degree of democracy and influence level, in particular, selectorate theory argues that the less competitive the selection of the client state's chief executive is, the less open the recruitment of the chief executive is, and the less freely alternative preferences for policy and leadership can be pursued in the political arena, the greater the degree of influence the patron's aid will have on that client.

As Figure 3.1 indicates, the widely used Polity IV database of political regime characteristics identifies the governments of the Philippines (1947–53) and South Vietnam (1957–63) as "anocracies" – states where power is vested in competing elite groups rather than strong public institutions – which renders them neither fully democratic nor fully autocratic due to the weakness of central authority.[44] Comparatively, the post–World War II Philippine government was coded as being closer to democracy than autocracy, while the South Vietnamese government of Ngo Dinh Diem was relatively more autocratic than democratic. The government of El Salvador was considered to be an autocracy immediately prior to the 1979 coup by a group of reform-minded junior officers that installed a civilian-led Junta. However, due to the post coup chaos and weakness of the Junta, it was an anocracy for the first five years of the insurgency (1979–84), transitioning to democracy in successive steps in 1984 and 1991.

In terms of the competitiveness and openness of the selection of chief executives and domestic political participation, Table 3.6 shows that the Philippines was rated slightly more competitive than the other two

---

[41] Provided, of course, that such concessions do not threaten the regime's support base. Bruce Bueno de Mesquita, *Principles of International Politics* (Washington, DC: CQ Press, 2009), pp. 246–72; Root, *Alliance Curse*, p. 21.

[42] Root, *Alliance Curse*, p. 22. The assumption that patron and majority preferences diverge is endogenous to the analysis of selectorate theory. I thank Nina Silove for pointing this out.

[43] *Ibid.*, p. 23.

[44] "Polity IV Project: Political Regime Characteristics and Transitions, 1800–2008" (Vienna, VA: Center for Systemic Peace, 2008).

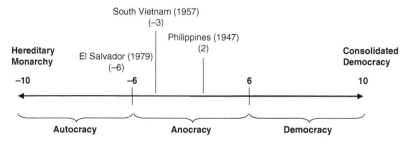

Figure 3.1 Polity IV measures of regime type at the start of the conflict.

countries due to the electoral-based method of choosing the Philippine president, while the governments of both Vietnam and El Salvador were chosen through a process characterized by informal competition within a ruling elite. In terms of political participation, both the Philippines and South Vietnam were characterized by parochial-based political factions that sought to promote the welfare and interests of narrow groups in society, while in El Salvador the regime systematically limited political participation in ways that excluded significant portions of the society. However, for the purposes of selectorate theory's predictions about a government's susceptibility to the influence of patron aid, there is no substantive difference between these three cases in this dimension. These results suggest that we would see a relatively equal level of influence wielded by the United States in its dealings with the governments in San Salvador and Saigon, with less compliance achieved in its relationship with the relatively more democratic government in Manila. In fact, none of these propositions are correct. The United States achieved the greatest influence in its dealings with the government that was relatively the most democratic and open of the three and met with relatively more success in its attempts to shape the counterinsurgency campaign in El Salvador than it did in South Vietnam despite the comparatively similar attributes of the two countries' domestic political arrangements.

Monitoring Agents

As discussed in detail in Chapter 2, one of the counterinsurgency-relevant mechanisms that principals can employ to mitigate the agency costs of delegation is monitoring of their agent's behavior to reduce the problems

Table 3.6 *Characteristics of Key Political Institutions*

	Competitiveness of executive recruitment	Openness of executive recruitment	Competitiveness of participation
Philippines (1947)	Election (3)	Open (4)	Parochial political factions (3)
South Vietnam (1957)	Selection by Elites (1)	Open (4)	Parochial political factions (3)
El Salvador (1979)	Selection by Elites (1)	Open (4)	Participation suppressed (2)

Source: Monty G. Marshall, "Polity IV Project: Dataset Users' Manual," Center for Systemic Peace, Vienna, VA, November 12, 2010.

associated with hidden actions. There are certainly good reasons to believe that this could be effective. For example, in the early years of American involvement in El Salvador, when death squad activity and human rights abuses were at their worst, the U.S. MILGROUP commander complained that as a result of the congressionally mandated limit on the number of American trainers in the country, it was "difficult at first to really pin down who is doing it, in part because we didn't have enough people in country to oversee every unit" or know what was really happening in the Salvadoran countryside.[45] In contrast, later in the conflict when American trainers had been deployed more widely, insurgent leaders actually lamented that "the most damaging thing that occurred during the war was putting American trainers in the [Salvadoran Army] brigades" because it reduced the human rights abuses that were the FMLN's best recruitment tool.[46]

One way to approximate the patron's ability to monitor the client is to look at the ratio of advisors deployed to the client state vis-à-vis the

[45] John D. Waghelstein, interview, January 31, 1985, Senior Officers Oral History Program (SOOHP), MHI; John D. Waghelstein, interview, February 23, 1987, *Oral History of the Conflict in El Salvador*, vol. 6, MHI, p. 34.

[46] Quoted in Kalev Sepp, "The Evolution of United States Military Strategy in Central America, 1979–1991," Ph.D. dissertation, Harvard University, 2002, p. 225.

Table 3.7 *Monitoring of Client Behavior (Advisor Ratio)*

	Philippines		Vietnam		El Salvador	
	1947	1952	1957	1963	1981	1984
No. of advisors	58	64	740	21,000	55	~125
No. of local army	25,000	56,000	150,000	250,000	20,000	40,000
Ratio of advisors to army	1: 431	1:875	1:202	1:12	1:300	1:320
Relative Influence	High		Low		Medium	

size of its armed forces. We would expect that influence would be positively correlated with the advisor–armed force ratio.

A second proxy for the relative ease of monitoring a client government is the distance between the two capitals. Ease of visitation should greatly improve monitoring because elected officials from the patron nation, not just foreign affairs and military specialists, are able to travel to the country in question to assess the situation firsthand. As one U.S. ambassador in San Salvador noted, "El Salvador was close enough that you could get your work done in Washington, get on an airplane, spend the weekend in El Salvador, and then get back to work on Monday … virtually every member of the Congress got to El Salvador."[47] One former embassy official recounts that, in a single twelve-month period alone, 212 members of Congress and their staff visited the country.[48] Given the increasing ease of international travel over the four decades in question, this measure should be temporally biased toward the more recent cases.

Despite the compelling logic, the data presented in Tables 3.7 and 3.8 cast doubt on the notion that monitoring can explain the degree of influence over client state behavior. With respect to the idea of directly monitoring the client via in-country personnel, the experiences of the

[47] Deane Hinton quoted in David Jeffrey Mouritsen, "The United States in El Salvador, 1979–1992: Success through the Eyes of the Diplomats," master's thesis, Brigham Young University, June 2003, p. 72.

[48] Recollection of the public affairs spokesman at the embassy in San Salvador. Donald R. Hamilton, "Strategic Communications in El Salvador 1982–1986: A Personal Perspective," presented at the Research and Education in Defense and Security Studies Seminar, Center for Hemispheric Defense, Santiago, Chile, 2003, p. 9.

Table 3.8 *Monitoring of Client Behavior (Distance)*

	Manila	Saigon	San Salvador
Miles from Washington, DC	8,570	9,006	1,887
Relative influence	High	Low	Medium

Philippines, Vietnam, and El Salvador actually demonstrate an inverse relationship between the advisor–armed forces ratio and the relative level of influence. By 1963, the United States had one solider deployed to South Vietnam for every twelve members of the South Vietnamese Army, yet client state compliance was comparatively low. In contrast, with a ratio of 875 Filipino soldiers per advisor, the American mission in the Philippines was far more successful in shaping the client's behavior. In terms of the "visibility" by policymakers – as measured by the distance from Washington – Manila and Saigon were virtually equidistant, but the level of influence achieved in the two capitals was significantly different. San Salvador was the closest capital by far and the beneficiary of the most contemporary airline technology – both of which should have combined to make it the most susceptible to monitoring of the three cases – yet it only experienced a medium degree of patron influence.

These results do not discount the role of monitoring in toto but question whether direct monitoring of clients is a panacea in these scenarios. The persistence of moral hazards when assisting another country's counterinsurgency campaigns may be less the result of the unobservability of the local governments' actions than a failure of key policymakers in the patron country to appreciate the deleterious effects of their local partner's policies or even a conscious decision to turn a blind eye to them.[49] This latter pressure would have been particularly strong in the context of the Cold War, where a zero-sum mentality meant that one side's loss was often perceived as the other's gain. Despite recognizing the shortcomings of South Vietnamese president Ngo Dinh Diem, for example, at the outset of American support to his government in 1954, the U.S. ambassador forcibly argued that "we

[49] Evan N. Resenick, "Strange Bedfellows: U.S. Bargaining Behavior with Allies of Convenience," *International Security*, 35, no. 3 (Winter 2010–11), pp. 158–9.

would assist a Communist takeover by a withholding of our aid, even if it must necessarily be given to a government which is less than perfect."[50] Thus the challenge of managing moral hazards in a partner nation may be one of political will rather than the mere availability of information.

Patron-Client Influence Strategies

Since the theories examined in the preceding section failed to sufficiently explain the patterns of influence between the United States and its local allies observed in the three cases, we take up the insights of agency theory from Chapter 2 and turn our attention to the "contract" between the two parties. The purpose of the contract is to align the preferences of the principal and agent by properly structuring incentives for the agent's compliance with the principal's desires as well as punishments for noncompliance. This section examines two prototypical patron-client influence strategies to explore the means by which a patron could shape its client's behavior, manage its perceived level of commitment, and enhance the credibility of its threats to withhold assistance should the client not perform.

As Daniel Drezner has noted, the three principal tools available to a state that wishes to alter the behavior of another one are *military compellence, economic inducement,* and *economic coercion.*[51] For obvious reasons, in the context of indirect intervention in counter-insurgency, it is possible to rule out the option of employing military force to influence a friendly state. As a result, the primary approaches available for shaping a client state's behavior are economic: *inducement* (the unilateral provision of incentives and other positive sanctions intended to solicit reciprocal cooperation) and *conditionality* (a type of coercion that ties aid to specific action on the part of the client governments and does not release it until after implementation).[52] While it

---

[50] Memorandum, Heath to Robertson, December 17, 1954, *Foreign Relations of the United States 1952–1954,* vol. XIII, Indochina, part 2 (FRUS 1952–4), p. 2391.

[51] Daniel Drezner, "Are Carrots and Sticks Good for You? The Utility of Economic Statecraft," Ph.D. dissertation, Stanford University, 1996, p. 179.

[52] Abraham Ben-Zvi and Joseph Helman identify a similar bifurcation of strategies of patron-client influence. Abraham Ben-Zvi, *The United States and Israel: The Limits of the Special Relationship* (New York: Columbia University Press, 1994), pp. 13–27; Helman, "Patron-Client State Relationships," p. 316.

may be said that all influence relationships contain elements of both incentives and coercion, inducement and conditionality do represent distinct approaches to shaping the behavior of a client.[53]

Inducement

When it comes to the question of influencing a client, given that both patron and client value their consensual partnership, some scholars argue that a patron will not exploit its superior strength to command obedience from its clients.[54] Instead, they will achieve influence by providing clients with inducements to change their behavior.[55] Inducement influence strategies focus on the use of incentives to encourage specific actions. Such incentives can include both intangible rewards, such as security guarantees and diplomatic backing, and tangible rewards in the form of military hardware and economic aid. As Celia Reynolds and Wilfred Wan describe, "Senders use positive inducements as persuasive measures to cajole the recipient into changing its behavior."[56] Given the cooperative relationship between the two parties, unilateral grants of aid are expected to generate positive reciprocity and cooperative behavior from the recipient.[57] Moreover, because these incentives can mitigate the client's cost of undertaking a desired policy change, these methods are believed to increase the chances that the client will comply. As William Long argued, "[E]conomic incentives can affect a state's definition of its preferences by changing its external payoff environment and its domestic politics and, in some cases, alter its chosen policies."[58] Befitting

---

[53] Richard Ned Lebow, *The Art of Bargaining* (Baltimore: Johns Hopkins University Press, 1996), p. 72.

[54] Bercovitch, "Superpowers and Client States," p. 15; Shoemaker and Spanier, *Patron-Client State Relationships*, p. 20.

[55] Bercovitch, "Superpowers and Client States," p. 16; Helman, "The Politics of Patron-Client State Relationships," p. 316.

[56] Celia L. Reynolds and Wilfred T. Wan, "Empirical Trends in Sanctions and Positive Inducements in Nonproliferation," in Etel Solingen, ed., *Sanctions, Statecraft, and Nuclear Proliferation* (Cambridge: Cambridge University Press, 2012), p. 58.

[57] Tit-for-tat strategies produce optimum outcomes in an iterative prisoners' dilemma game. See Robert Axelrod, *The Evolution of Cooperation* (New York: Basic Books, 1984).

[58] William Long, *Economic Incentives and Bilateral Cooperation* (Ann Arbor: University of Michigan Press, 1996), p. 11.

a strategy that seeks to gain influence via the unilateral provision of aid, inducement strategies favor public and unambiguous commitments to client states to gain their trust and bolster their confidence.

Scholars working in the constructivist tradition have suggested that inducement-type strategies can lead to a cooperative focus on shared interests by building trust between governments.[59] In this respect, proponents of inducement believe that it is superior to more coercive approaches because it maintains friendly relations between patron and client since the patron is "convey[ing] an impression of sympathy and concern."[60] In terms of prestige, as Schelling has argued, it is easier for a target state to accede to an inducement than to acquiesce to a threat.[61] In contrast, proponents of inducement worry that attempts to coerce a policy change by threatening a client with harm for noncompliance can backfire by hardening the target's resolve.[62]

Past scholarship on the use of this approach by the United States finds that inducements were generally met with reciprocity from the other party and that positive sanctions have a favorable track record in influencing a target state's behavior. Scholarly examination of U.S.-Soviet interactions during the Cold War has found that concessions by one party were generally met with reciprocity from the other.[63] Similarly, Miroslav Nincic finds that the use of inducements to influence "renegade regimes" in the post–Cold War era generates superior results to the use of punitive pressures – particularly when the regime in question is experiencing a degree of domestic instability.[64] Turning to

---

[59] Deborah Welch Larson, "Crisis Prevention and the Austrian State Treaty," *International Organization*, 41, no. 1 (Winter 1987); Alexander Wendt, "Anarchy Is What States Make of It: The Social Construction of Power Politics," *International Organization*, 46, no. 2 (Spring 1992), pp. 420–2.

[60] David A. Baldwin, "The Power of Positive Sanctions," *World Politics*, 24, no. 1 (1971), p. 32; Knorr, *Power of Nations*, p. 174; Arnold Wolfers, *Discord and Collaboration: Essays in International Politics* (Baltimore: Johns Hopkins University Press, 1962), pp. 107–8.

[61] Schelling, *Arms*, pp. 70–8.

[62] Roger Fisher, *International Conflict for Beginners* (New York: Harper & Row, 1969), p. 28; Knorr, *Power of Nations*, pp. 166–206.

[63] Lloyd Jensen, "Negotiating Strategic Arms Control, 1969–1979," *Journal of Conflict Resolution*, 28, no. 3 (September 1984).

[64] Miroslav Nincic, "Getting What You Want: Positive Inducements in International Relations," *International Security*, 35, no. 1 (Summer 2010), p. 150; Miroslav Nincic, "The Logic of Positive Engagement: Dealing with Renegade Regimes," *International Studies Perspectives*, 7, no. 4 (November 2006), p. 338.

the influence of more friendly states, Joseph Helman's study of U.S. patron-client relations concluded that incentive-based approaches are associated with "the successful use of influence between patron and client."[65] This body of scholarship suggests, in Martin Patchen's words, that "the usual tendency is for one side in a dispute to recipro-cate the [conciliatory] moves of the other, to match incentives if offered with return incentives," rendering concessions an effective tool for changing a state's behavior.[66]

Turning to the behavior of American policymakers, there is substan-tial evidence to suggest a belief in the power of inducements. Nitza Nachimas reports, for example, that during the 1980s, the United States provided Israel with unilateral grants of aid to induce it to make peace with its neighbors.[67] More recently, the George W. Bush administration provided unconditional grants of over $10 billion in military, economic, and development aid to induce Pakistani president Pervez Musharraf to aggressively crack down on Afghan Taliban sanc-tuaries in his country.[68] In the specific context of assisting counter-insurgency, policymakers within the U.S. government have repeatedly advocated inducement strategies, often emphasizing the need to reas-sure client regimes of U.S. support. During the Eisenhower administra-tion, for example, American counterinsurgency expert Edward Lansdale argued strenuously that the United States had to make uni-lateral concessions to the South Vietnamese government to demon-strate that it was "acting in good faith" *before* pressing Saigon to make desired political and economic reforms.[69] Similar logic was

---

[65] Helman, "Patron-Client State Relationships," p. 316.

[66] Martin Patchen, *Resolving Disputes between Nations: Coercion or Conciliation?* (Durham, NC: Duke University Press, 1988), pp. 262–3.

[67] Nachimas, *Transfer*, p. 6.

[68] Craig Cohen and Derek Chollet, "When $10 Billion Is Not Enough: Rethinking U.S. Strategy Towards Pakistan," *Washington Quarterly*, 30, no. 2 (Spring 2007); C. Christine Fair, "Time for Sober Realism: Renegotiating U.S. Relations with Pakistan," *Washington Quarterly*, 32, no. 2 (April 2009).

[69] Memorandum, Lansdale to O'Donnell, September 20, 1960, *Foreign Relations of the United States 1958–1960*, vol. I, Vietnam (FRUS 1958–60), p. 580. For similar views from the Kennedy administration, see Memorandum, Gilpatric to Kennedy, May 3, 1961, FRUS 1961, pp. 92–115, Telegram 1423, Saigon to State, May 20, 1961, FRUS 1961, pp. 140–3, Telegram 1800, Saigon to State, May 26, 1961, FRUS 1961, pp. 158–9; *United States–Vietnam Relations, 1945–1967: A Study Prepared by the Department of Defense* (Washington, DC: GPO, 1971), pp. 136–7.

expressed by State Department officials in the Carter administration who believed it was necessary to signal the credibility of the American commitment to El Salvador by providing military aid without conditions to gain the influence necessary to subsequently push the Salvadoran military for reform.[70] William Mott reports that faith in the efficacy of inducements has traditionally been bolstered by the twin beliefs that the client state shares the United States' priorities – which eliminates the need for more coercive means of influence – and that the provision of aid will result in "a powerful ability to influence the actions and policies of U.S. recipients."[71]

Aside from the core tenet that unilateral grants of aid will be reciprocated by client state compliance with patron policy preferences, the inducement strategy has two other observable implications:

1. Public commitments to a client will make it more amenable to the patron state's requests; and
2. Inducement will be effective regardless of whether or not it is the initial influence strategy employed.

Conditionality

The alternate approach available to patrons seeking to influence a wayward client is the use of conditioned aid. In contrast to inducement, which relies solely on positive rewards, conditionality blends positive benefits with threats to suspend or withhold assistance in the absence of client compliance. The latter measure is a necessary result of the potentially diminishing utility of foreign aid in generating influence. George Kennan noted the "sad and curious fact of human nature: namely that favors granted habitually or unduly prolonged, cease with time to be regarded by the recipients as favors at all and come to be regarded by them as rights."[72] Even if bilateral relations in a patron-client arrangement are consensual and mutually valued, as utility maximizers clients may not readily reciprocate their patron's aid.

---

[70] Memorandum, Bushell to SecState, March 13, 1980, STATE.
[71] Mott, *U.S. Military Assistance*, pp. 66, 307.
[72] George Kennan, *Realities of American Foreign Policy* (New York: Norton, 1966), p. 55.

Rather, they try to obtain the greatest amount of assistance possible while offering the minimum compliance with their patron's wishes.[73] Despite South Korea's dependence on U.S. security guarantees to protect it, for example, American officials in the mid-1970s found it difficult to press for the liberalization of Park Chung-hee's dictatorship: as one U.S. diplomat in Seoul exclaimed, "You've got to have a threat of some kind or they won't listen … there aren't many levers left to pull around here."[74] Consequently, some scholars of international patron-client relations suggest that within the context of an overall benign relationship between patron and client, shaping a client's behavior requires more coercive tools than just grants of aid.[75]

Conditionality seeks to obtain influence by providing the ally with genuine rewards for taking action while also identifying consequences for a failure to act.[76] As Kennan warned, "I view with skepticism our chances for exerting any useful influence unless we learn how to create a respect for our possible disfavor at least as great as the respect for our possible favor."[77] If the client expects assistance as the status quo, the withholding of such aid can be viewed as a form of punishment.[78]

As a tool of foreign policy, David Baldwin reports that withholding aid is as successful at influencing state's behavior, if not more so, than are other means, including military force.[79] This tool may be particularly suited for dealing with recalcitrant clients, since Daniel Drezner has found that economic coercion is more effective when employed against friendly states rather than adversaries because the former are

---

[73] John D. Ciorciari, "A Chinese Model for Patron-Client Relations? The Sino-Cambodian Partnership," *International Relations of the Asia-Pacific*, 15, no. 2 (May 2015), p. 248.

[74] Quoted in Jerome Slater, *Intervention and Negotiation* (New York: Harper & Row, 1970), p. 7.

[75] Ben-Zvi, *The United States and Israel*, p. 2; and Carney, "International Patron-Client Relationships," p. 44.

[76] Scholars emphasizing the need to mix threats and inducements include Baldwin, "Positive Sanctions," pp. 23, 31; K. J. Holsti, *International Politics: A Framework for Analysis* (Englewood Cliffs, NJ: Prentice-Hall, 1977), pp. 167–8; Jervis, "Deterrence Theory Revisited," pp. 304–5; Shoemaker and Spanier, *Patron-Client*, p. 20; Singer, "Inter-Nation Influence," pp. 426–7; George and Smoke, *Deterrence*, pp. 604–10.

[77] Kennan, *Realities of American Foreign Policy*, p. 58.

[78] Baldwin, "Positive Sanctions," p. 23; Blechman et al., "Negotiated Limitations," p. 225; Thomas C. Schelling, *Strategies of Commitment and Other Essays* (Cambridge, MA: Harvard University Press, 2006), p. 8.

[79] Baldwin, *Economic Statecraft*, pp. 318–19.

less concerned with the effects of relative gains on the bilateral relationship and are less worried that they will be exploited by the stronger partner in the future.[80] As a result, when threatened in this manner, allies make larger concessions than adversaries do. In this vein, David Cortright has argued that the credible threat to withhold American military assistance to the Salvadoran Armed Forces provided the necessary catalyst to begin political reform and ultimately accept negotiated settlement with the FMLN insurgents.[81]

The rewards provided to a partner under a conditions-based influence strategy are similar to those used in inducement. The primary difference is in the delivery. In the latter, rewards are provided ex ante – at the time the client agrees to take a certain action or even as an enticement to make an agreement. In contrast, with conditionality, aid is only delivered ex post – once the client government executes the given action.[82] By attaching conditions to aid, the supporting power makes an implicit threat to withhold this aid should the local government not execute the given task.[83] Due to the need to be able to credibly threaten to withhold aid, conditionality favors looser and more ambiguous commitments to the host nation in an effort to create some uncertainty in the minds of client state policymakers about the lengths to which the patron will go in aiding the client.

The logic of conditionality comes from the field of political economy, where international financial institutions (IFIs), such as the International Monetary Fund (IMF) and the World Bank, have attempted to encourage policy reforms in the economies of developing nations by making loans or grants of aid conditional on the implementation of specific reforms. For reasons that should be familiar from the discussion in Chapter 2, it has sometimes proved necessary to attach conditions to aid in an effort to deter the leaders of recipient states from enriching themselves and their supporters at the public's expense, instead of maximizing the welfare of their citizens. The success rate of World Bank and IMF conditionality to engender economic reform in target states is decidedly mixed. Scholars suggest that this is due, in

---

[80] Daniel Drezner, *The Sanctions Paradox: Economic Statecraft and International Relations* (Cambridge: Cambridge University Press, 1999), pp. 27–35.

[81] David Cortright, *The Price of Peace: Incentives and International Conflict Prevention* (Lanham, MD: Rowman & Littlefield, 1997), p. 291.

[82] The ex-ante variant of conditionality is discussed later.

[83] For the coercive nature of such conditions, see Knorr, *Power of Nations*, p. 174.

part, to the fact that such conditionality is overwhelmingly ex ante – local governments receive loans and aid after promising to reform but *before* implementation.[84] Once the loan or aid is received, the local government may choose not to undertake reform. Despite the recipient government's failure to implement promised measures, humanitarian pressures and organizational preferences can lead the IFIs to continue dispersing loans anyway.[85] As a result, the threats to withhold aid made by organizations such as the IMF and the World Bank largely lack credibility.[86]

In contrast, some scholars suggest that delivering aid following implementation of a policy change can be a means to promote reform. In a model of the effects of loan conditionality on domestic policy reform, Eduardo Fernandez-Arias demonstrated that if aid is provided when a successful reform is implemented, the commitment to provide aid in the future "unambiguously accelerates reform."[87] Similarly, Allan Drazen suggested that it may be possible to influence the rent-seeking behavior of local decision makers by giving aid or loans selectively, "only when the government begins to act cooperatively," and holding back assistance otherwise.[88] These propositions are supported by empirical evidence which suggests that making assistance conditional on specific actions can influence the behavior of the recipient government. Evaluation of this approach in the tranching of aid – paying in installments – to African countries by the World Bank in the late 1990s found that it succeeded in generating positive policy outcomes while also reducing the humanitarian and organizational demands on the bank to provide aid when the conditions had not been

[84] Paul Collier et al., "Redesigning Conditionality," *World Development*, 25, no. 9 (1997); David Dollar and Jakob Svensson, "What Explains the Success or Failure of Structural Adjustment Programmes?" *Economic Journal*, 110, no. 466 (October 2000); Van de Walle, *African Economies*, p. 214.

[85] Van de Walle, *African Economies*, p. 224.

[86] D. F. Gordon, "Conditionality in Policy-Based Lending in Africa: USAID Experience," in Paul Mosley, ed., *Development Finance and Policy Reform* (London: Macmillan, 1992), p. 37; Joan Nelson and Stephanie Eglinton, *Global Goals, Contentious Means* (Washington, DC: Overseas Development Council, 1993), p. 44.

[87] Eduardo Fernandez-Arias, "Crisis, Foreign Aid, and Macroeconomic Reform," paper presented at the Fifteenth Meeting of the Latin American Econometric Society, Santiago, Chile, March 1997.

[88] Allan Drazen, "What Is Gained by Selectively Withholding Foreign Aid?" working paper, University of Maryland and NBER, April 1999, p. 19.

met.[89] Likewise, a recent study of the use of conditions on aid to post-conflict reconstruction concluded that the imposition of conditionality on foreign aid is positively associated with the extent of reform undertaken in the recipient country.[90]

In the context of assisting counterinsurgency, to be able to influence the client government via conditionality, the patron must take steps to enhance the credibility of its threat to withhold aid.[91] In particular, Schelling argued that "it is essential, therefore, for maximum credibility, to leave as little room as possible for judgment or discretion in carrying out the threat."[92] Clearly linking specific aid to specific actions in this manner offers patrons a way to make credible threats to promise or withhold aid from their clients while also reducing pressure to deliver assistance in the face of noncompliance. To facilitate enforcement and enhance the credibility of the patron's threat, an aid package can be broken into smaller tranches, each dependent on a specific action, so that later tranches can be withheld if the conditions are not met.[93] As Schelling wrote, "[I]f [a threat] can be decomposed into a series of consecutive smaller threats, there is an opportunity to demonstrate on the first few transgressions that the threat will be carried out on the rest. Even the first few become more plausible, since there is a more obvious incentive to fulfill them as a 'lesson.'"[94] This approach is particularly relevant in situations where the threatening party has a long-term interest in the well-being of the other side:

In foreign aid programs the overt act of terminating assistance may be so obviously painful to both sides as not to be taken seriously by the recipient, but if each small misuse of funds is to be accompanied by a small reduction in assistance, never so large as to leave the recipient helpless nor provoke a diplomatic breach, the willingness to carry it out will receive more

---

[89] Operations Evaluation Department, *Higher Impact Adjustment Lending: Initial Evaluation* (Washington, DC: World Bank, June 1999).

[90] Desha Girod, "Foreign Aid and Post-Conflict Reconstruction," Ph. D. dissertation, Stanford University, 2008, p. 124.

[91] Rosecrance, "Reward," p. 40; Schelling, *Strategies of Commitment*, p. 3; Singer, "Inter-Nation Influence," p. 427.

[92] Schelling, *Conflict*, p. 40.

[93] Allan Drazen, *Political Economy in Macroeconomics* (Princeton, NJ: Princeton University Press, 2000), p. 608; James Boyce, *Investing in Peace* (Oxford: Oxford University Press, 2002), p. 22.

[94] Schelling, *Conflict*, p. 41.

credulity; or if it does not at first, a few lessons may be persuasive without too much damage.[95]

If the patron grants one type of aid unconditionally, it may undermine the credibility of attempts to attach conditions to aid in other realms. A client that is the recipient of unconditional military assistance, for example, may have reason to question its patron's threats to withhold economic assistance in the face of noncompliance because it recognizes that if it is too important to be denied military assistance, economic aid will eventually be forthcoming as well. Consequently, it would appear that if conditionality is to be effective, it must be applied in all instances. The challenge of creating a credible threat may also make it difficult to move from an inducement strategy to a conditionality one because, having received unconditional aid, the client may doubt the patron's resolve to withhold future assistance. Therefore, logic suggests that conditionality will be most effective when it is attached to the patron's aid from the first instance.

There are several reasons why a supporting nation may be reluctant to put conditions on aid. Policymakers may believe that any threat, no matter how mild, to withhold assistance to a friendly government beset by an insurgency is inappropriate. Assistant Secretary of State Thomas Enders highlighted the perceived paradox of conditionality when he noted that it "requires us to threaten to cut off military assistance to achieve the goals of our policy when we know that an actual cut-off would defeat the goals of those policies."[96]

A second reason that patrons may be unwilling to try to force compliance from its client via conditionality is uncertainty about the extent of the influence they possess. Despite the popular image of a client state as a puppet, scholars have found that great powers actually tolerate significant defection by their lesser allies. Since the degree of leverage one state has over another is difficult to measure, Christian Catrina observed that patrons demonstrate a "notable reluctance" to press clients too hard because they are unsure about the limits of their own influence.[97] Similarly, Glenn Snyder and Paul Diesing have argued

---

[95] *Ibid.*

[96] Quoted in U.S. House of Representatives, *Presidential Certification on El Salvador* (Washington, DC: U.S. Government Printing Office, 1982), p. 19.

[97] Christian Catrina, *Arms Transfers and Dependence* (New York: Taylor & Francis, 1988), p. 356.

that patrons are frequently self-deterred from exerting too much pressure on their clients by the fear of alienating them.[98] Rather than risk a client's defection to the Soviet camp, William Mott reports that during the Cold War Washington was frequently reluctant to exercise its potential leverage over smaller allies to actively influence their policy choices.[99] Instead, American policymakers have been found to rationalize continued support for wayward clients despite repeated noncompliance with Washington's desires.[100]

Policymakers may also avoid imposing conditions on aid for fear of provoking a defiant response from the target state, which may choose to engage in a test of wills rather than acquiesce in the dispute.[101] In El Salvador, for example, the CIA reported that frustration within the Salvadoran military over conditions on American aid simply "reinforced their resolve to go it alone, employing their own standards and practices" to achieve victory through a total extermination of the insurgents and their supporters, as in neighboring Guatemala, rather than adopt more discriminating U.S.-backed counterinsurgency strategies.[102] It is not just the target state that the patron has to worry about reacting negatively to conditions on aid. It has been suggested that the use of conditionality can engender reputational effects whereby even mildly coercive measures used against a partner might dissuade other clients from cooperating with the patron in the future.[103]

Conditioning aid on client performance also faces practical problems because most military and economic assistance programs operate according to medium- and long-term plans that can be substantially harmed by having to withhold aid. These efforts are unlikely to be structured to easily accommodate disruptions, and it may be costly to suspend and resume aid. In El Salvador, for example, one U.S. MILGROUP commander recalled that conditions on aid "really screwed our ability to plan long-range" and rendered the Salvadoran

---

[98]   Snyder and Diesing, *Conflict among Nations*, pp. 29, 442–3, 505.

[99]   Mott, *U.S. Military Assistance*, p. 10.

[100] Elise Forbes, "Our Man in Kinshasa: U.S. Relations with Mobutu 1970–1983," Ph.D. dissertation, Johns Hopkins University, 1987. For a contemporary example of American self-deception about the behavior of a client state, see Jeffrey Goldberg and Marc Ambinder, "The Ally from Hell," *The Atlantic*, December 2011.

[101] Holsti, *International Politics*, p. 178.

[102] CIA, "El Salvador: Military Prospects," January 2, 1981, NSA.

[103] Knorr, "International Economic Leverage," p. 113.

military "reluctant to pursue [the war] to the degree they thought they should because they couldn't count on the next shipment of bullets."[104] Finally, if a client does comply as a result of conditions on aid, the patron will have to make tough decisions as to how much of the inevitable backsliding will merit a further aid suspension.

Beyond the expectation that conditions attached to aid will be associated with the client state's implementation of the patron's desired policies, even if the client had previously resisted taking such actions, the conditionality influence strategy has several observable implications:

1. The stronger the public commitment made to the client, the less influence the patron will have;
2. If the patron state fails to apply this approach consistently, it will subsequently be more difficult to make credible threats to withhold aid from the client; and
3. Dividing up grants of aid into discrete tranches that are associated with a specific policy change or reform will allow more credible threats to withhold assistance than untranched aid. If a specific tranche of aid is delivered before the implementation of its associated action, however, implementation of that action will be less likely.

Conclusion

This chapter examined a range of structural factors that could affect the ability of a great power patron to influence its client's counterinsurgency strategy. These included arguments for the deterministic influence of aggregate power, suggestions that the client's dependence on the patron will result in significant influence over their policy choices, the notion that the perceived strategic utility of a client state will undermine a patron's leverage, the impact that the regime type of the client state has on the patron's ability to influence it, and the utility of direct monitoring for controlling the client's behavior. Finding all of these approaches unable to explain the variance in influence patterns observed in the three case studies, this chapter advanced the argument that the manner in which aid is provided to the client government is a key factor affecting the relative level of influence between patron and

---

[104] Waghelstein, interview, *OHCES*, p. 8.

client. Two archetypical client-management strategies were described: inducement, which employs bribes to buy compliance, and conditionality, which links aid to client behavior. The case studies in the next three chapters provide a body of evidence that is used to analyze the relative utility of these two approaches in an effort to determine which one offers the best guide to influencing clients in counterinsurgency.

4 | *America's Boy? The Philippines, 1947–1953*

PART I CRAFTING A STRATEGY, 1947–1950

The Huk (pronounced "hook") Rebellion was one America's first experiences assisting a partner nation in counterinsurgency during the Cold War. In early 1950, the government of the Philippines appeared to be on the verge of succumbing to a revolutionary insurgent movement just like Chiang Kai-shek's government had in China the previous year. Yet, by 1954, the veteran Huk guerrillas had been attrited to the point where they no longer posed a serious threat.

How did this rapid transformation come about? Some scholars downplay the American role in this episode, suggesting that its importance was secondary to that of indigenous, reform-minded Philippine leadership or even asserting that the American assistance effort was "irrelevant" because it exercised virtually no influence over the Philippine government.[1] In contrast, this chapter suggests that significant credit can be given to the active intervention by the United States. Recognizing the intertwined economic, political, and security challenges posed by the Huk Rebellion, American personnel in Washington and Manila worked to ensure that military and economic aid was strictly conditioned in an effort to persuade, cajole, and coerce the government of the Philippines into substantive reform while creating an environment in which indigenous reformers, who played a critical role, could come to the fore. Despite active opposition by the Philippine government to American reform proposals and the expectation that Washington would provide aid regardless of what it did, a conditionality-based influence strategy resulted in a significant degree of American leverage over the government in Manila. This, in turn, led

---

[1] The centrality of indigenous leadership rather than U.S. aid and advice is discussed in Blaufarb, *Counterinsurgency Era*, p. 38. Arguments for the lack of U.S. leverage over the Philippine government are found in Shafer, *Deadly Paradigms*, pp. 223–6.

to a significant reorientation of the security forces' strategy and tactics, key economic reforms that shored up the government, and political reforms that denied the insurgents a justification for continued violence.

World War II and the Origins of the Hukbalahap

Following the arrival of explorer Ferdinand Magellan in 1521, the Philippines fell under Spanish dominion and soon became a key hub linking Madrid to its Pacific coast possessions in the New World. By the time the country passed into U.S. control in the wake of the Spanish-American War, its political economy was characterized by a quasi-feudal agricultural system in which large landlords were the dominant political force.[2] Although consisting of more than 7,000 individual islands, in 1950 nearly half the Philippines' 20 million people lived on the central island of Luzon. Larger than South Korea, it was home to both the seat of government, Quezon City, and the most fertile farm-land in the archipelago.[3]

Agriculture was the country's most important industry, accounting for an estimated 58 percent of national income and either directly or indirectly employing 72 percent of the working population.[4] Many farmers did not own the land they worked, and in central Luzon, tenancy rates were as high as 70 percent.[5] As the mechanization of farming spread during the first decades of the twentieth century, the relative value of labor declined and traditional patron-client relation-ship between landlords and tenants broke down.[6] Increasingly indif-ferent to their tenants' welfare, landlords demanded more than half of a harvest as compensation for the use of land, seed, and farming implements.[7] With agricultural incomes stagnant, by the early 1940s, the supermajority of tenant-farmers were deeply indebted to their landlords.

---

[2] CIA, "Current Situation in the Philippines," June 27, 1950, p. 3, DDRS.
[3] *Ibid.*, p. 9.
[4] Letter, Abbey to Cowen, November 27, 1951, Box 1, Philippine and Southeast Asian Division (PSEAD), RG 59.
[5] *Ibid.*   [6] Brian Crozier, *The Rebels* (Boston: Beacon Press, 1960), p. 38.
[7] Office of Intelligence Research, Report No. 5209, "The Hukbalahaps," September 27, 1950, p. iii, DDRS.

In 1935, the U.S. government granted the Philippines self-governance as part of a ten-year transition to independence by 1945. This plan was disrupted by Japan's surprise invasion in December 1941, which threw the highly stratified society of the Philippine Commonwealth into chaos. After the official surrender of U.S. and Filipino forces on Corregidor the following May, President Manuel Quezon escaped to lead a government in exile. In the place of the Commonwealth government, a Japanese-sponsored administration was established under former Supreme Court Justice José Laurel that employed a large number of the country's political and economic elite.[8]

Resistance to the Japanese and their collaborationist allies centered around two main groups. The "official" guerrillas of the U.S. Army Forces Far East (USAFFE) consisted of American and Filipino soldiers who had escaped capture by the Japanese, supplemented by civilian volunteers. They primarily collected intelligence on the Japanese for the Supreme Commander Allied Forces Southwest Pacific, General Douglas McArthur, and secondarily waged a campaign of sabotage against the occupying troops. It was the peasants of the Hukbalahap (the Tagalog acronym for the "People's Army against the Japanese"), however, who formed the largest and most aggressive anti-Japanese resistance group. Consisting of urban labor unions and tenant farmers from central Luzon, led by the Philippine Communist Party in a "united front," the Huks possessed a mass base of support in the population and established a shadow government in the areas they controlled. While fighting against the Japanese and their Philippine collaborators, the Huks also seized large estates that had been abandoned by their owners and gave them to landless farmers. Numbering roughly 10,000 full-time guerrillas and another 100,000 part-time militia members, the Huks claimed responsibility for killing over 25,000 of "the enemy" – 80 percent of whom were Filipino collaborators – in more than 1,200 engagements, which denied the Japanese access to much of the valuable rice harvest in Luzon.[9]

---

[8] Although some of those who cooperated with and served in the puppet government did so in hopes of shielding their people from harm, many others collaborated for personal gain.

[9] Memorandum, Peralta to Roxas, "Capability of MPC to Deal with Huk Problem," August 19, 1946, Series IV, Box 18, Manuel A. Roxas Papers, University of the Philippines Diliman (Roxas Papers); Eduardo Lachica, *The Huks: Philippine Agrarian Society in Revolt* (London: Praeger, 1971), p. 115; Alvin Scaff, *The Philippine Answer to Communism* (Palo Alto, CA: Stanford University Press, 1955), p. 23.

Despite their war against a common foe, significant tensions existed between the USAFFE and the Huks that occasionally led to bloody intraguerrilla clashes.

When peace finally came in 1945, war, occupation, and liberation had shattered the country. In terms of physical destruction, Dwight Eisenhower is said to have observed that "of all the wartime capitals, only Warsaw suffered more damage than Manila."[10] The postwar Philippine economy was in shambles, and even basic commodities were scarce. The Truman administration sought to reestablish the prewar status quo as quickly as possible in order to grant the Philippines independence on July 4, 1946. Inflation saw the cost of living quintuple as American money, equipment, medicine, and food flooded into the impoverished nation with little oversight – a situation exploited by Filipino officials who, in the words of one American diplomat, "demonstrated a rather impressive appetite for corruption."[11]

Following liberation, the Philippine government refused to recognize the Huks as legitimate anti-Japanese guerrillas – which would have carried with it compensation and benefits from the U.S. government – and replaced the officials they had appointed to govern the towns and provinces under their control.[12] Suspicious of their apparent Marxist leanings, American officials did not intervene on the Huks' behalf. Former collaborators were inducted into the country's security forces; however, Huks were specifically excluded and ordered to disarm.[13] In Luzon, landlords employed private militias known as *civil guards* – the largest of which were over 1,000 men strong – to forcibly collect back rent from their tenants for the period of Japanese occupation and eject squatters from their plantations.[14] Attempts to reimpose the prewar social order by force were met with active resistance as Huk

[10] Robert Smith, *Philippine Freedom, 1946–1958* (New York: Columbia University Press, 1958), p. 115.
[11] "The Current Situation in the Philippines," *Intelligence Review*, no. 40 (November 14, 1946), p. 17; Letter, Melby to Jessup, August 25, 1949, Box 6, Melby Papers.
[12] Edward. G. Lansdale, *In the Midst of Wars: An American's Mission to Southeast Asia* (New York: Harper & Row, 1972), p. 8.
[13] Benedict Kerkvliet, *The Huk Rebellion* (Los Angeles: University of California Press, 1977), p. 116.
[14] Letter, Locket to Marshall, August 15, 1948, 896.00/8–1548, RG 59; Memorandum, Peralta to Roxas.

fighters – already alienated by the open collaboration of many Filipino officials with the Japanese – regrouped to defy returning landlords.[15]

With large numbers of the country's economic, political, and legal elite, not to mention civil servants, compromised by service to the Japanese, the issue of collaboration dominated the election that occurred in the run-up to Philippine independence.[16] With all 24 senate and 100 house seats up for grabs, in addition to the presidency, the winner of the contest was Liberal Party candidate Manuel Roxas. A minister in the Laurel government, Roxas escaped punishment for collaboration when his old friend General MacArthur exonerated him, despite the widespread belief that he was the "guiltiest of the puppets."[17] American assessments noted that the new government in Manila remained the preserve of the upper classes, who "talked of reestablishing 'law and order,' yet seemed blind to injustice in the administration of the law and the prejudicial imbalance of the order they desired."[18] For the Huks, who fought against an occupation that claimed the lives of tens of thousands of Filipinos, the world seemed to be upside down: the collaborationist landlord class was returned to positions of authority (forty-five members of the pro-Japanese government had been elected to Congress), while those who actually fought the invaders were regarded with hostility.

Nevertheless, the Huks had attempted to press their reform agenda at the ballot box by backing candidates from the Democratic Alliance (DA). They were thwarted, however, when President Roxas charged six DA congressmen with electoral fraud and barred them from office.[19] Evidence supporting the allegations was flimsy, and the political calculations behind the move were clear: the presence of these opposition members would have denied Roxas' Liberal Party a filibuster-proof majority in Congress. After a prominent peasant

[15] Luis Taruc, *Born of the People* (Bombay: People's Publishing House, 1953), pp. 228–31.

[16] CIA Report, ORE 11–48, "Enclosure A: Collaboration in the Philippines," April 28, 1948, p. 4, DDRS.

[17] Hernando Abaya, *Betrayal in the Philippines* (New York: A.A. Wyn, 1946), p. 9; William Owens, *Eye-Deep in Hell: A Memoir of the Liberation of the Philippines* (Dallas: SMU Press, 1989), pp. 194–5.

[18] OIR Report No. 4818, "The Philippine Congress in 1948," July 21, 1949, pp. 8, 11–12, DDRS; Lansdale, *In the Midst of Wars*, p. 28.

[19] Three senators from the opposition Nationalistas were similarly barred. Telegram 138, Manila to State, January 14, 1949, 896.00/1–1449, RG 59.

leader died while in government custody, the Huks traded their political efforts for military action.[20]

The Insurgency Takes Root

The political leadership of the Huk movement was made up of urban intellectuals from the Philippine Communist Party.[21] With a rallying cry of "Land for the Landless," they proclaimed an intention to form a government of "the proletariat, peasants, middle class, intellectuals, and progressive bourgeois" that would redistribute large estates and nationalize industry, as well as eject the American "imperialists" and their military bases.[22] Among the rank-and-file guerrillas, however, the motivations for rebelling were more pragmatic.[23] In a letter to President Roxas, Huk military commander Luis Taruc explained that most of his fighters took up arms because "it has become impossible to live and earn their livelihoods peacefully" in the face of the landlords attempts to perpetuate a feudal economic structure in rural areas and the "atrocities and plunder" of their private armies.[24] Repression by the security forces did not trigger the turn to armed violence, but it left many believing that it was their best choice: as one former guerrilla noted, he fought to stop "the civilian guards and [police] from beating up my family" and see "the DA congressman hold office."[25]

The Huks' initial strategy was to tie down the security forces by launching a host of small raids, which required the government to disperse their limited numbers of men to defend large areas of the countryside.[26] Influenced by the example of the Chinese communists, however, the insurgents eventually sought to establish liberated areas from which they could develop into a regular army that could directly

---

[20] Lachica, *The Huks*, p. 121.
[21] Memorandum, Reinhold to Roberts, "Anti-Government Rebels in the Philippines," May 7, 1953, FO 371/105614, p. 1, NAUK.
[22] Kerkvliet, *The Huk Rebellion*, p. 224.
[23] Analysts at the U.S. Embassy believed the motivations of the Huks were "essentially socio-economic." Memorandum, O'Neal, February 19, 1948, 896.00/2–948, RG 59.
[24] Letter, Del Castillo and Taruc to Roxas, August 17, 1946, Series IV, Box 18, Roxas Papers.
[25] Kerkvliet, *The Huk Rebellion*, pp. 143, 164.
[26] Telegram 311, Manila to State, March 21, 1949, 896.00/3–2149, RG 59.

engage and defeat the government's forces in the field.[27] By 1949, the Huks possessed roughly 12,000 active guerrillas, organized into 100-man squadrons, which operated at will across central Luzon.[28] Coalescing into formations several hundred strong for particular operations, the Huks ambushed civilian guards and police patrols, hijacked commercial trucking, robbed provincial treasuries, and soon after progressed from guerrilla tactics to mobile warfare in certain parts of Luzon.[29] The Philippine government was astounded by the quality of Huk intelligence, which seemed to know the routes, strength, and composition of its troops the second they deployed on an operation. Information passed to the insurgents from both a sympathetic public and agents in the government at every level from the barrio to Malacañang Palace allowed them to remain one step ahead of the security forces.[30] As one contemporaneous scholar judged, "[I]n numbers, organization and small arms the Huk fighting units were comparable to the government forces. In terms of morale and civilian support in the areas of their operations they had a decided advantage."[31]

Retaining their wartime base of support, large swaths of Luzon, including 6,000 square miles of the richest rice-growing region in the country, were soon known as "Huklandia" in recognition of the insurgents' domination. Following independence, the economic gap between the peasantry and the upper classes had actually widened, which induced many to willingly flock to the Huk banner, and a training camp, called "Stalin University," was established in the Sierra Madre mountains to conduct military training and political indoctrination of new recruits.[32] The Philippine government believed

---

[27] Airpouch 1057, Manila to State, January 24, 1951, Melby Papers.

[28] Larry E. Cable, *Conflict of Myths: The Development of American Counterinsurgency Doctrine during the Vietnam War* (New York: New York University Press, 1986), p. 50; Scaff, *The Philippine Answer to Communism*, p. 28.

[29] Kerkvliet, *The Huk Rebellion*, p. 205.

[30] JUSMAG, "Semi-Annual Report, January 1, 1951–June 30, 1951," Records of Interservice Agencies, U.S. National Archive at College Park, Maryland (RG 334). For one such example of government officials cooperating with the Huks, see Memorandum, "Intelligence Project on Arm Smuggling Deal: Lt. Col. Benjamin Santillioin," October 29, 1951, Box "for indexing," Ramon Magsaysay Papers, Ramon Magsaysay Award Foundation, Manila (Magsaysay Papers).

[31] Scaff, *The Philippine Answer to Communism*, p. 28.

[32] For an independent view of the Philippine government's role in generating support for the Huks, see "Unrest in the Philippines," *Times of London*, September 20, 1950.

that 35 percent of the population in Luzon actively supported the Huks; however, independent assessments put the number at closer to 50 percent.[33] Where political sympathy was lacking, threats of violence ensured that the uncommitted provided assistance to the insurgents in the hopes of being left alone.[34] Huk militias established in local villages provided a support base for recruits, intelligence, and supplies. Forming a shadow administration, the insurgents collected taxes from the population, offered competent governance, and publicly executed landlords, unpopular local officials, and government sympathizers.[35]

Roxas' Mailed Fist

With a strength of 37,000, the Philippine security forces – which consisted of the Armed Forces of the Philippines (AFP) and the paramilitary police of the Philippine Constabulary (PC) – were in no position to contend with an organized insurgency.[36] The 13,000 men of the AFP, who were under the Department of National Defense, provided external security for the country, while internal security was the responsibility of the 24,000-man PC. Administratively, the constabulary was under the control of the Minister of the Interior – who the U.S. embassy described as a "reactionary member of the landed gentry" – and largely served to advance the interests of large landlords vis-à-vis agricultural workers.[37] The Constabulary Commander, Brigadier Alberto Ramos, had been a collaborator and was alleged to have personally overseen the execution of American and Filipino guerrillas on behalf of the Japanese.[38] The U.S. embassy judged that Ramos – who was also suspected of involvement in illegal arms trafficking – "does not appear to be well qualified" for his job; however, his personal loyalty

[33] Telegram 458, Manila to State, April 13, 1950, 796.00/4–1350, RG 59; "AFP Brief for Melby Mission," September 19, 1950, Melby Papers.
[34] Telegram 561, Manila to State, June 16, 1949, 896.00/6–1649, RG 59.
[35] Telegram 444, Manila to State, February 10, 1950, 796.00/2–1050, RG 59.
[36] Scaff, *The Philippine Answer to Communism*, p. 27.
[37] Telegram 1862, Manila to State, September 24, 1948, 896.00/9–2848, RG 59.
[38] *Ibid.*; JUSMAG Weekly Summary of Activities, August 3, 1950, p. 1, RG 334; Donald Berlin, "Prelude to Martial Law: An Examination of Pre-1972 Philippine Civil-Military Relations," Ph.D. dissertation, University of Southern Carolina, 1974, p. 55.

to the president secured his role.[39] Under Ramos, the PC was a political tool of the ruling Liberal Party that they used to falsify electoral registers, close hostile newspapers, as well as attack opposition candidates and their supporters.

On March 6, 1948, President Roxas declared that the Hukbalahap and the Philippine Communist Party were illegal organizations seeking to overthrow the government.[40] Although the mere 2:1 ratio between the constabulary and the insurgents led some Philippine officials to conclude that the PC "cannot 'solve' the Huk question" through military means – even with the assistance of the army and civil guards – the Philippine president pledged to forcibly restore order in Luzon within sixty days.[41] Insisting that "the only way to fight force is to meet it with superior force," he dispatched the PC to eradicate the Huks in a "mailed fist" campaign.[42]

Employing the conventional tactics of positional war, the constabulary repeatedly attempted to encircle the highly mobile Huks and bring them to battle, which proved to be as ineffective as it was destructive.[43] Without effective intelligence on the Huks, the PC relied on less-discriminate measures to separate the guerrillas from the population: large-scale cordon-and-search operations, food denials, and collective punishment. The latter included the slaughter of livestock, the destruction of crops, the demolition of dwellings, mass arrests, and the summary execution of suspected sympathizers.[44] It is not without

---

[39] Airgram A-160, Manila to State, March 31, 1949, 896.00/3–3149; Letter, Chapin to Gullion, April 20, 1950, Box 2, Office of Philippine Affairs, both in RG 59.

[40] Dispatch 366, Manila to State, April 9, 1948, 896.00/4–949, RG 59.

[41] *Ibid.*; Memorandum, Peralta to Roxas.

[42] Quoted in "Roxas to Force Huk Showdown," *Manila Chronicle*, January 23, 1948; Scaff, *The Philippine Answer to Communism*, p. 28. Roxas did take some measures to ameliorate rural discontent, most notably signing into law legislation that allowed tenant farmers to keep 70 percent of their harvest. These mild reforms proved to have little practical impact, however, as landlords ignored the legislation – using their militias to forcibly collect half their tenants' harvest.

[43] Telegram 492, Manila to State, May 17, 1949, 896.00/5–1749; Telegram 1011, Manila to State, April 8, 1950, 796.00/4–850, both in RG 59.

[44] Walter C. Ladwig III, "When the Police Are the Problem: The Philippine Constabulary and the Hukbalahap Rebellion," in C. Christine Fair and Sumit Ganguly, eds., *Policing Insurgencies: Cops as Counterinsurgents* (Oxford: Oxford University Press, 2014), p. 32.

justification that some scholars judged that the constabulary conducted itself "like an army of occupation" in central Luzon.[45]

The effect of the security forces' heavy-handed tactics was magnified by their indiscipline. The U.S. embassy reported that the poorly paid and poorly trained enlisted members of the PC would "seize foodstuffs without paying for them, become drunk and disorderly, extract information by inhumane methods, abuse women, shoot up country towns and generally mistreat the populace."[46] Frequently, delayed pay meant that the PC had to loot supplies from the local peasantry, while checkpoints on roads – notionally established to hinder the insurgent's freedom of movement – became opportunities to collect "tolls" to supplement their earnings.[47] Constabulary officers were accused of enriching themselves by levying illegal taxes on plantations and forcing farmers to thresh their rice in PC-run mills.[48] Not only did these practices foster widespread corruption, they also further harmed the government's relations with the local population.

When not pursing offensive operations, the PC was scattered in penny packets across Luzon, which left them vulnerable to a concentrated assault by the insurgents. Moreover, they lacked the mobility to pursue the guerrillas should they actually foil an ambush or surprise attack.[49] Instead of protecting major population centers, constabulary units were frequently redeployed to guard the estates of influential landlords, which left towns and villages vulnerable to infiltration by the insurgents. Stocked with political loyalists at the highest levels, the PC's professionalism was further eroded by its politicization: instead of accurately reporting the situation in the field, senior officers repeatedly assured authorities in Manila that the Huks were being defeated and that "ultimate victory was in sight."[50]

Unleashing the constabulary drove civilians in Luzon into the insurgents' arms. As guerrilla leaders readily admitted, "the great majority

[45] Lawrence Greenberg, *The Hukbalahap Insurrection* (Washington, DC: U.S. Army Center of Military History, 1987), p. 70; Lachica, *The Huks*, p. 121.
[46] Telegram 432, Manila to State, April 7, 1950, FRUS 1950, p. 1436; Telegram 1152, Manila to State, April 21, 1950, 896.00/4–2150, RG 59.
[47] Napoleon D. Valeriano and Charles T. R. Bohannan, *Counter-Guerrilla Operations: The Philippine Experience* (Westport, CT: Praeger, 2006), p. 79.
[48] "Embassy Briefing," Melby Mission, September 19, 1950, Melby Papers.
[49] U.S. Department of the Army, G-2, "The Philippine Constabulary," Intelligence Research Project No. 7557, December 15, 1952, p. 1, DDRS.
[50] Smith, *Philippine Freedom, 1946–1958*, pp. 145–6.

of Huks joined because of repression by the Philippine Government . . .
and civilian guards. Many felt it was either join or be killed without at
least putting up a fight."[51] The U.S. embassy concurred that it was
"reasonable to assume that some of the Huks are merely trying to
avenge mistreatment at the hands of the PC."[52] From the American
perspective, the Philippine government was unlikely to gain the upper
hand unless these abuses were curtailed.

Quirino Dithers and the Americans Worry

Little more than a month after launching his campaign against the
Huks, President Roxas suddenly died of a heart attack. He was suc-
ceeded by his vice president, Elpidio Quirino, who was described by
American analysts as a "weak, vacillating, and bewildered" figure
lacking diplomatic tact, "control of his Party," or "the loyalty of his
Cabinet."[53] Declaring an amnesty, Quirino unsuccessfully attempted
to negotiate with the insurgents, promising reforms if they disarmed.[54]
The Huks had no incentive to entertain the deal, however, because they
were winning on the battlefield and gaining popular support.[55]
As fighting spread to the neighboring provinces of Bataan, Laguna,
Rizal, Nueva Ecija, Quezon, and Zambales and thousands of peasants
fled central Luzon, Quirino declared a state of rebellion.[56]

---

[51] Huk political leader Jesus Lava quoted in Kerkvliet, *The Huk Rebellion*, p. 227.
     For a similar view from the Huks' military commander, see Luis Taruc, *He Who
     Rides the Tiger: The Story of an Asian Guerrilla Leader* (New York: Praeger,
     1967), p. 38.
[52] Telegram 1152, Manila to State, April 21, 1950, 896.00/4–2150, RG 59;
     Telegram 432, FRUS 1950, p. 1436.
[53] CIA, "Current Situation," p. 6. The British ambassador in Manila concurred
     with this assessment, noting that Quirino had "no great political following,"
     and described his cabinet as "nonentities." Dispatch 53, Clinton-Thomas to
     Eden, March 31, 1952, FO 371/99648, NAUK. For an example of Quirino
     having to chastise his own Secretary of the Interior for the repeated "impropriety
     of hurling attacks against the leaders of this administration," see Letter, Quirino
     to Zulueta, May 29, 1948, Box 14, Elpidio R. Quirino Papers, Filipinas Heritage
     Library, Manila (Quirino Papers). On his lack of diplomatic tact, see Letter,
     Edelstein to Roxas, May 22, 1947, Series I, Box 3, Roxas Papers.
[54] "Situation in the Philippines: Failure of Amnesty for Hukbalahap Dissidents,"
     October 27, 1948, FO 371/99648, NAUK.
[55] Greenberg, *The Hukbalahap Insurrection*, p. 61.
[56] Telegram 1752, Manila to State, September 13, 1948, 896.00/9–1348, RG 59.

Despite clear evidence to the contrary, by January 1949, the officer overseeing anti-Huk operations declared, "Central Luzon is virtually free of outlaw depredations."[57] The government's failure to contain the insurgency was shockingly illustrated four months later when several squadrons of Huks ambushed and killed the widow of Manual Quezon – the country's beloved wartime president-in-exile – along with her daughter, son-in-law, the head of Philippine Army intelligence, and the mayor of Quezon City while they were on the way to open a hospital in the former president's hometown.[58]

Seemingly oblivious to the role of government corruption, tenant-landlord relations, or collaboration in fueling discontent, Quirino was pilloried by the press for possessing "neither the necessary force to wipe out" the insurgents "nor the willingness to institute genuine reforms which would revitalize" the government.[59] In the lead-up to the 1949 presidential election, Quirino attempted to shore up his political position by providing patronage to local provincial officials, running up significant budget deficits in the process.[60] The opposition Nationalista Party nominated José Laurel, head of the Japanese puppet government, as its candidate for president. Despite his collaboration with the Japanese – 132 counts of treason against him had been wiped away by a general amnesty – Laurel's fiery nationalism made him a popular figure, and the U.S. embassy believed that he could triumph in an honest election.[61] To ensure victory, Quirino appointed loyalists to the senior leadership of the PC, while his brother Antonio organized a group of Liberal Party "enforcers" to suppress opposition turnout.[62] The U.S. embassy received widespread reports of fraud and violence: electoral registers were falsified, valid ballots were destroyed, local newspapers were shut down, and in rural areas opposition candidates

---

[57] Airgram A-3, Manila to State, January 5, 1949, 896.00/1–549, RG 59. For a contrasting view, see Telegram 2043, Manila to State, October 18, 1948, 896.00/10–1848 and Telegram 2100, October 26, 1948, 896.00/10–2648, both RG 59.
[58] Telegram 1126, Manila to State, April 28, 1949, 896.00/4–2849, RG 59.
[59] Teodoro Locsin, "Year of Disgrace," *Philippine Free Press*, January 1, 1949. Quirino's assessment of the situation in the countryside can be found in Elpidio Quirino, "Initial Views on the Huk Problem," in *The New Philippine Ideology* (Manila: Bureau of Printing, 1949), pp. 16–17.
[60] Telegram 2317, Manila to State, October 4, 1949, 896.00/10–449, RG 59.
[61] Telegram 2528, Manila to State, November 4, 1949, 896.00/11–449, RG 59.
[62] Lansdale, *In the Midst of Wars*, p. 25.

and their supporters were attacked at polling stations by Antonio's thugs working in conjunction with the constabulary.[63] In the final tally, twenty-four people were killed in election-day violence and another eighteen were wounded.

With official records estimating that more than 20 percent of ballots were counterfeit, the fraud was so extensive in some regions that people openly joked that "the birds, the trees and the dead had voted."[64] Quirino triumphed over Laurel by 485,000 votes – the majority of which came from the two provinces where allegations of intimidation and fraud were most widespread – and his party maintained control of the House and Senate.[65] The CIA reported that "coercion, fraudulent voting, and miscounting were so blatant as to cause frustration and disgust among the majority of Filipino voters," which "continue to contribute to the common people's distrust of their government."[66] The American counsel general in Cebu was even blunter, proclaiming that the contest marked "the death of democracy in the new republic."[67]

The primary beneficiaries of Quirino's fraud were the Huks, who now possessed an estimated 15,000 to 20,000 guerrillas under arms at any one time (drawn from a pool of 30,000 to 50,000 part-time fighters), backed by 100,000 members of their clandestine political organization and nearly 2 million active sympathizers.[68] Emboldened by the growing discontent, the Huks increased the frequency of attacks

[63] Telegram 2485, Manila to State, October 28, 1949, 896.00/10–2849 and Telegram 2528, Manila to State, November 4, 1949, 896.00/11–449, both RG 59.

[64] José Veloso Abueva, *Ramon Magsaysay* (Manila: Solidaridad Publishing House, 1971), p. 141–2.

[65] *Ibid.*; Stephen Shalom, "Counter-Insurgency in the Philippines," *Journal of Contemporary Asia*, 7, no. 2 (1977), p. 154.

[66] CIA, "Current Situation," p. 5

[67] Letter, Henderson to Hester, November 14, 1949, 896.00/11–4949, RG 59.

[68] For views that the electoral fraud directly benefited the insurgents from both Huk leaders and Philippine government officials, see Taruc, *He Who Rides the Tiger*, p. 60; Carlos Romulo, *Crusade in Asia* (New York: John Day, 1955), p. 88. Estimates of Huk strength in this period vary. Joes puts their strength at 20,000 in Joes, *America and Guerrilla Warfare*, p. 193. This figure is backed by Philippine Army intelligence reports, HQ National Defense Forces G-2, "Estimate of Situation," August 12, 1948, Box 126, Quirino Papers. However, most other sources cite the lower 15,000 number. Telegram 458; Charles Bohannan, "Antiguerrilla Operations," *Annals of the American Academy of Political and Social Sciences*, 341 (May 1962), p. 21; Kerkvliet, *The Huk Rebellion*, p. 211; Shalom, "Counter-Insurgency in the Philippines," p. 155.

tenfold and spread their operations into outlying districts of Manila.[69] By April 1950, an estimated 500,000 Filipinos had been displaced by the fighting.[70] Worryingly, Philippine military intelligence also began to report that dissident Nationalista supporters were taking up arms and making common cause with the Huks.[71]

The security situation soon became so precarious that armored cars were deployed on the streets of the capital, and President Quirino took to sleeping on his yacht lest he need to make a quick escape.[72] Those local government officials who had not been co-opted by the Huks refused to remain in central Luzon after dark – returning nightly to the relative safety of Manila – thus further weakening the link between the government and the governed. As the head of the American military mission laconically advised Quirino, "[T]he capacity of the government to assure internal security in the Philippines is lower today than it has been at any time since liberation."[73]

The deteriorating situation in the Philippines caught the attention of U.S. State Department personnel, who worried that they had "another China" on their hands.[74] This theme was taken up by the *Washington Post*, which commented on the "ominous parallel" with the situation in

Chiang Kai-shek's China just before it fell to the Communists. The parallel elements are unmistakable: maladministration and epidemic corruption; a threat of financial breakdown; widespread loss of confidence not only in the government, but in the whole order of things; growing lawlessness and political thuggery; finally an armed rebellion in the peasant hinterland under Communist leadership.[75]

---

[69] Greenberg, *The Hukbalahap Insurrection*, p. 65; "Pomeroy's Own Story," Unpublished Manuscript, p. 7, Box 1, Alvin Scaff Papers, Hoover Institution Archives, Stanford University (Scaff Papers).
[70] Memo, Perez to Quirino, April 14, 1950, Box 7, Quirino Papers.
[71] Telegram 2829, Manila to State, November 19, 1949, 896.00/11–1949; Telegram 2646, Manila to State, November 22, 1949, 896.00/11–2249; Telegram 2659, Manila to State, November 23, 1949, 896.00/11–2349, all RG 59.
[72] Edward Lansdale, "Oral History Interview," April 25, 1971, p. 27, HRA; Telegram 2694, November 11, 1949, 896.00/11–1149, RG 59.
[73] Letter, Anderson to Quirino, January 3, 1950, Box 23, Quirino Papers. See also Memo, Doty to Anderson, "Brief Summary of Law and Order," March 31, 1950, Box 23, Quirino Papers.
[74] Memo, Ely to Butterworth, October 15, 1949, 896.00/10–1549, RG 59.
[75] Harold R. Isaacs, "Philippines Reported Near Political, Economic Collapse," *Washington Post*, June 12, 1950.

The alienation of moderate, non-Communist political opposition had doomed Chiang's Nationalist Party (Kuomintang) in China. In the Philippines, the disqualification of the Democratic Alliance congressmen radicalized and alienated many in central Luzon. In the absence of a non-Communist organization championing substantive social change, the disaffected increasingly turned to the Huks and armed violence.[76] The similarities were not lost on Huk leaders, who explicitly prophesized that Quirino would suffer "the inevitable fate of Chiang Kai-shek."[77]

The situation was extremely concerning for Washington because the Philippines possessed both symbolic and substantive importance to the United States. Demonstrating that an independent Philippines could be a "showcase of democracy" was central to the Truman administration's efforts to persuade America's European allies to peaceably relinquish their colonies in Southeast Asia.[78] U.S. officials were particularly concerned that, without imminent decolonization, indigenous nationalists could be co-opted by Communism – a worry heightened by the outbreak of a host of Communist-linked insurgencies from Greece to Indochina. Following the victory of Mao Tse-tung's Communist Party in China, loss of the Philippines would, Assistant Secretary of State Dean Rusk argued, "more than any other single factor discredit the United States throughout the length and breadth of Asia ... If we fail there, the rest of Asia will certainly consider [that] we have nothing to offer elsewhere."[79] Conversely, other officials believed that the Philippines was a venue where the United States could take a stand and successfully offset Communist gains in the region.[80]

On a substantive level, U.S. military facilities at Clark Field and Subic Bay were key facilitators of American air and naval power projection in Asia. The Joint Chiefs of Staff argued that "the Philippines are an essential part of the Asian offshore island chain of bases on which the strategic position of the United States in the Far East depends."[81] Their loss could risk "rapid disintegration of the entire structure of

[76] Frances Starner, *Magsaysay and the Philippine Peasantry* (Los Angeles: University of California Press, 1961), p. 193.
[77] Airgram A-3, Manila to State, January 10, 1949, 896.00/1–1049, RG 59.
[78] Meeting Notes, Webb and Connally, May 10, 1950, 796.00/5–1050, RG 59; National Security Council Report, "U.S. Policy towards Southeast Asia," July 1, 1949, p. 16, DDRS.
[79] Memorandum, Rusk to Matthews, FRUS 1951, p. 24.
[80] Memo, Jessup to Acheson, October 10, 1950, 796.00/10–1050, RG 59.
[81] Memo, JCS to SecDef, FRUS 1950, p. 1485.

anti-Communist defenses in Southeast Asia ... including Japan."[82]
Secretary of Defense Louis Johnson concurred with the military's
assessment, noting that "the strategic importance of the Philippines is
not open to question."[83] Aside from the risk that the Huks might grow
in strength to seriously threaten the government, the CIA warned that
a continuation of the status quo under Quirino could lead "a non-
Communist junta or a strong man" to size power which would "be
inclined to reduce and eventually eliminate U.S. influence in the
Philippines and probably would gradually accommodate to
Communism."[84] This concern for the Philippines would only be ampli-
fied after June 25, 1950, when, on a rainy Sunday morning, North
Korean armored divisions smashed through the defenses on the 38th
parallel and began moving down the western side of the Korean
Peninsula toward Seoul.

President Truman was "anxious" that the United States "do everything possible to keep the Philippines not only friendly to the U.S., but
close to the U.S." while avoiding a repeat of the "recent catastrophe in
China."[85] The widespread corruption that marked postwar reconstruction made American officials wary of unconditional grants of aid
to Quirino's government, while the main lesson learned from the
unsuccessful effort to assist Chiang Kai-shek in China was that simply
providing aid to a country beset by insurgency was not enough to
persuade the government to address its shortcomings or encourage it
to save itself.[86] An interagency group including the Departments of
State, Defense, and Treasury debated the feasibility of imposing conditions on aid to the Philippines in an effort to foster internal reform.
They recognized that in the process of providing assistance,
Washington must avoid backing Manila too strongly lest Quirino
believe the United States was so committed to his survival that he
could ignore his domestic troubles.[87] Indeed, when President Quirino
attempted to elicit a high-profile sign of American support during

[82] *Ibid.*
[83] Memo, Johnson to Acheson, September 16, 1949, Box 81, Records of the U.S.
      Secretary of Defense, U.S. National Archive at College Park, Maryland
      (RG 330).
[84] CIA, "Current Situation," p. 2.
[85] Memorandum of Conversation with the President, "Philippine Policy,"
      April 25, 1949, 896.00/4–2549, RG 59.
[86] Memo, Reed to Butterworth, March 25, 1949, Box 5, PSEAD, RG 59.
[87] Memo, Webb to Steelman, May 19, 1949, 896.00/5–1949, RG 59.

a state visit ahead of the 1949 election, the Truman administration specifically downplayed the significance of his trip, emphasizing that it did not convey "any material commitments on the part of the United States" to his government. For his part, the Philippine president was reportedly quite piqued by the lack of pomp and circumstance he received in Washington.[88]

Quirino Seeks Assistance, but Conditions Are Attached

To respond to the growing instability in his country, Quirino appealed for $35 million in American military aid.[89] The ambassador to the Philippines, Myron Cowen, warned Washington that unconditioned military aid would further incline Quirino to seek a military solution to his problems.[90] Since the repressive actions of the security forces were a key factor driving support for the insurgency, augmenting their capacity without altering their behavior could be extremely counter-productive. Cowen believed it was necessary for the government to win back the support of the population rather than simply attempt to crush dissent.[91] This view was shared by the U.S. Joint Chiefs of Staff, who saw the problems in the Philippines as "primarily political and economic" and warned that "military action should not be an alternative for a stable and efficient government based on sound economic and social foundations."[92]

On the ground in Manila, the fifty-eight officers and men of the Joint U.S. Military Assistance Group (JUSMAG) were charged with over-seeing training of the Philippine Armed Forces, providing them with logistical support, and advising the Philippine government on military matters.[93] The JUSMAG commander had been lobbying Quirino since mid-1948 to reorganize the security forces by shifting responsibility for the counterinsurgency campaign to the AFP and consolidating the

---

[88]   Memorandum of Conversation, Elizalde, Acheson, Cowen, and Butterworth, July 19, 1949, Box 65, Dean G. Acheson Papers, Harry S. Truman Presidential Library (Acheson Papers); Memo, Melby to Butterworth, January 7, 1949, Box 6, Melby Papers; Letter, Melby to Cowen, February 3, 1950, Box 6, Melby Papers.
[89]   Letter, Quirino to Jones, March 3, 1949, Box 23, Quirino Papers.
[90]   Memo, Ely to Allison, February 2, 1949, 896.20/2–249, RG 59.
[91]   Airpouch 307, Manila to State, March 15, 1950, 796.00/3–1550, RG 59.
[92]   Memo, JCS to SecDef, September 6, 1950, FRUS 1950, pp. 1488–9.
[93]   Telegram 1194, Manila to State, February 15, 1951, FRUS 1951, p. 1510; OIR, Report No. 5209, "The Hukbalahaps," p. 49.

constabulary under the command of the Secretary of National Defense.[94] The present organizational structure, the American advisor argued, "results in financial waste, as well as lack of cohesion and quality and a decided loss of potential strength," which produces a force that is "completely inadequate to cope with the current situation."[95] In contrast, bringing all the security forces under a single command would enhance the coordination of counterinsurgency operations and allow U.S. military aid – which could not legally be provided to police forces – to benefit the PC.

Both the Philippine Secretary of the Interior and the Secretary of National Defense objected to the American proposal, arguing that it "would be dangerous" to blur the lines between policing and war fighting.[96] JUSMAG observers believed, however, that they opposed integration of the PC into the military chain of command because it would put the constabulary beyond the influence of Liberal Party politicians who frequently used the force for their own ends.[97] This was, of course, precisely what the JUSMAG intended.[98]

The United States was willing to provide the military aid Quirino sought, but it came with conditions: the constabulary must be integrated into the army, and the JUSMAG must share decision making with Philippine authorities in both military planning and the use of American-provided funds.[99] Quirino assented to the joint planning but resisted reorganizing the security forces. Instead, he attempted to secure military aid by promising to integrate half the PC into the army, in the hopes that a mere promise would be sufficient to appease the Americans. The Philippine president made no effort, however, to actually follow through on the measure.[100] In the face of Quirino's attempted deception, the embassy and JUSMAG withheld military aid

---

[94] Letter, Jones to Quirino, May 15, 1948, Box 23, Quirino Papers.
[95] Anderson to Quirino, January 3, 1950; Anderson to Quirino, April 1, 1950, Box 23, Quirino Papers.
[96] Memorandum, Baluyut to Quirino, March 9, 1949, Box 14, Quirino Papers; *Manila Times*, March 8, 1949.
[97] JUSMAG, "Weekly Summary of Activities," November 4, 1949; JUSMAG, "Weekly Summary of Activities," December 8, 1949, both RG 334.
[98] Anderson to Quirino, January 3, 1950; Anderson to Quirino, April 20, 1950, Box 23, Quirino Papers. For the JUSMAG reorganization plans, see Memorandum, Bertsch to Chief Advisor JUSMAG PHIL, "Staff Study," June 10, 1950, Box 23, Quirino Papers.
[99] Abueva, *Ramon Magsaysay*, p. 146.
[100] JUSMAG Weekly Summary of Activities, December 22, 1949, RG 334.

until movement was seen on the constabulary's status. To send a clear signal of American displeasure with Quirino's foot dragging, the JUSMAG commander had his staff curtail their work with the armed forces, which was reported in the Philippine press as a clear threat that military aid would be suspended.[101]

Quirino's government attempted to turn the tables on the United States by openly criticizing the Truman administration's failure to concretely assist the Philippines. Philippine Secretary of National Defense Ruperto Kangleon and head of the AFP General Mariano Castañeda publicly condemned the conditions on American military aid, claiming that the United States had "welched" on its responsibility to defend the country.[102] With Quirino's tacit support, the pair tried to placate the Americans with a superficial change: the PC was organizationally made a part of the army; however, day-to-day authority remained vested with the hard-line Department of the Interior.[103] The Americans were not duped by the maneuver. Even if the reorganization of the constabulary had been implemented, however, it would have only partially improved the situation because command of the Philippine military remained in the hands of General Castañeda, a corrupt yet affable figure who led a factionalized officer corps that had developed a conservative and unhurried approach to military operations under his watch.[104] The stalemate over reorganization of the security forces would drag on for the next six months.

Economic Problems

The Huks were hardly the only problem facing Manila. By the end of 1949, the Philippine government appeared to be on the verge of a full-blown economic crisis. Quirino's deficit spending ahead of the election

---

[101] JUSMAG Semi-Annual Appraisal, March 25, 1950, RG 334. For Philippine press coverage, see Philippine Press Analysis 147, March 20, 1949 896.00/3–3049, RG 59.

[102] Telegram 674, Manila to State, March 6, 1950, FRUS 1950, p. 1418; Abueva, *Ramon Magsaysay*, pp. 146–7.

[103] JUSMAG, "Weekly Summary of Activities," April 8, 1950, RG 334; Telegram 1011, Manila to State, April 8, 1950, 796.00/4–850, RG 59.

[104] Telegram 1880, January 5, 1951, FRUS 1951, p. 1492; Lansdale, *In the Midst of Wars*, p. 37. Reportedly, President Roxas also did not believe that he was "sufficiently competent" for command of the military. Despatch 591, Manila to State, February 27, 1947, 896.20/2–2747, RG 59.

had exhausted the treasury's coffers: public works projects ground to a halt, and the government would soon be unable pay the army, the constabulary, and other government employees.[105] Although the country's economy was rapidly expanding, key sectors – including large landlords and businesses linked to the Liberal Party – paid almost no tax.[106] U.S. officials believed that Quirino's reliance on American aid, rather than domestic taxation, prevented his government from developing sufficient administrative capacity to govern effectively.[107]

The State Department also reported that corruption and growing economic inequality were "being exploited by the Communist-led Hukbalahap movement to incite lawlessness and disorder."[108] As the *Washington Post* argued in a scathing editorial, "The ugly truth is that the Quirino regime is bankrupt both morally and financially. Graft and corruption have reached staggering proportions and the leading culprits appear to be so close to the President that he is unable or unwilling to oust them."[109] Nevertheless, Quirino insisted to his American patrons that everything would be fine "without the application of any painful measures" (i.e., significant reforms).[110]

In fact, the Truman administration was growing frustrated with Quirino's failure to demonstrate the capacity to address his country's economic problems, let alone restore internal security. As Secretary Acheson briefed the president in early 1950, "efforts by American representatives to induce the Philippine Government to take the necessary measures have thus far proven unavailing."[111] Acheson believed that American aid must be conditioned on Philippine reforms if the

[105] Radiogram 1135, Romulo to Quirino, September 25, 1950, Box 66, Quirino Papers; A. V. H Hartendorp, *History of Industry and Trade of the Philippines* (Manila: ACCP, 1958), pp. 293–5.

[106] Memorandum, Acheson to Truman, August 31, 1950, Box 162, President's Secretary's Files, Harry S. Truman Presidential Library (HST).

[107] Memorandum, Acheson to Truman, February 2, 1950, FRUS 1950, pp. 1407–8.

[108] State Department Report, "The Philippines," October 10, 1950, DDRS.

[109] "Suppressed Report," *Washington Post*, October 24, 1950.

[110] Memorandum of Conversation, Quirino, Acheson et al., August 9, 1949, 896.00/8–949, RG 59. For the failures of the "wealthy propertied class" to see the need for reform, see National Security Council, "The Position of the United States with Respect to the Philippines," November 9, 1950, FRUS 1950, p. 1518.

[111] Memorandum for the President, "Recent Developments in the Philippine Situation," March 14, 1950, 796.00/3–1450, RG 59.

country's deteriorating fiscal situation was to be reversed. Wary of "the classic Philippine maneuver of playing one part of the American government against another part," he warned Truman that unconditional assistance would undercut the leverage Ambassador Cowen had to push for reform. American aid would only be helpful if it supported "drastic reforms undertaken by the Philippines itself." Importantly, the Philippine government needed to be disabused of the notion that it could "always count on the United States to bail it out."[112] As things stood, State Department analysts reported that "President Quirino ... is supremely confident that no matter what he does, the United States will always provide whatever funds are needed to solve his problems."[113]

Since aid would signal a tacit endorsement of Quirino, Ambassador Cowen advised Washington to wait until it was clear "whether the growing discontent will lead to the necessary reforms or chaos."[114] This left two basic options for dealing with the Philippine government: the United States could either provide aid to strengthen the government but essentially take a "hands off" approach to Quirino's policies or it could "tie tight the strings to any aid" in an attempt "to force him into less suicidal paths." The second choice would require the United States to "clearly and publicly specify" the conditions attached to future aid and perhaps "lay down the law" to Quirino.[115] Acheson signaled the new U.S. approach in a speech at the National Press Club in Washington, where he called on the Philippine government to be more self-reliant and indicated that the United States would expect stricter accountability for future aid: "It is the Philippine Government which is responsible. It is the Philippine Government which must make its own mistakes. What we can do is advise and urge and if help continues to be misused to stop giving help."[116]

The belief that forceful intervention was needed to redirect the Philippine government's economic policies was hardly confined to U.S. government circles. Andres Soriano, a Quirino supporter,

---

[112] Memorandum, Acheson to Truman, FRUS 1950, p. 1404.
[113] State Department Report, "The Philippines," October 10, 1950, DDRS.
[114] Minutes, Interdepartmental Meeting on the Far East, April 13, 1950, 796.00/4–1350, RG 59.
[115] Telegram 1063, Manila to State, April 13, 1950, 796.00/4–1350, RG 59.
[116] U.S. Department of State Bulletin, 22, no. 552 (January 23, 1950), p. 117.

a former Finance Minister and then president of Philippine Airlines, implored American interlocutors that "[s]omeone in the top level of the American government" needed to sit Quirino down "and tell him the hard facts of life."[117] Quirino's own vice president, Fernando López, concurred that it was necessary to "force Quirino to take steps necessary for his own survival – steps which he would not take merely on the basis of good advice tendered privately."[118]

The political and economic situation in the Philippines was deteriorating at such a rapid rate that by mid-April the Secretary of State cautioned Truman that a "rapid decline into chaos" would occur if the United States was not able to bring about a change in the policies and behavior of Quirino's government.[119] In Washington, an attempt was made to forge a unified approach to the growing problems in the Philippines. While the United States had to act to protect its long-term interests in the region, an interagency task force concurred that unconditional American aid would only reinforce the Philippine government's present course of action and signal an endorsement of Quirino's ineffectual policies.[120] Strict conditions on aid were seen as a means of compelling the Quirino government to act while guaranteeing that assistance was productively employed.[121] Importantly, both the U.S. military and the State Department concurred that "military measures . . . can only be a temporary expedient. Remedial political and economic measures must be adopted by the Philippine Government in order to eliminate the basic causes of discontent among the Philippine people."[122] Yet, as the embassy reported, "in the grass-roots, politico-military campaign for the mind and loyalties of Filipinos, the Huks are forging ahead while the Government too largely marks time."[123]

An economic assessment mission led by former Under-Secretary of the Treasury Daniel Bell spent two months in the Philippines surveying

---

[117] Memorandum of Conversation, Soriano, Ely, and Melby, December 28, 1949, Box 17, PSEAD, RG 59.

[118] Telegram 1197, Manila to State, April 26, 1950, 796.00/4–2650, RG 59.

[119] Memo, Rusk to Acheson, May 17, 1950, 796.00/5–1750, RG 59.

[120] Interdepartmental Meeting on the Far East.

[121] Telegram 1063, Manila to State, April 13, 1950, 796.00/4–1350; Memo, Merchant to Rusk, April 19, 1950, 796.00/4–1950; Memo, Rusk to Acheson, May 8, 1950, 796.00/5–850, all in RG 59.

[122] Memo, JCS to SecDef, FRUS 1950, p. 1487. See also State Department Report, "The Philippines," October 10, 1950, DDRS.

[123] Telegram 145, Manila to State, July 28, 1950; 796.00/7–2850, RG 59.

the country's fiscal needs and confirmed that the government was facing financial collapse in a period of high national income. In his report to President Truman, Bell recommended that the United States grant the Filipino government $250 million in aid over the next five years. In light of the need for both "competent and vigorous military action" as well as social reform to deal with the Huk situation, this aid was to be conditioned on the implementation of specific socioeconomic measures by the Philippine government, including increasing industrial production and agricultural output, expanding public health and education programs, and a sweeping revision of the government's tax policy that would enhance revenue in an equitable fashion.[124] To avoid the problems of corruption that plagued the immediate postwar reconstruction aid, Bell suggested that the money be supervised and administered by American personnel.[125] Reportedly "horrified" by the state of affairs, Truman indicated that he wished to see "the most vigorous possible effort made to act ... as soon as possible."[126]

Bell's recommended approach fit well with the interagency consensus that had developed in support of conditionality. Washington approached Manila about a wide-ranging series of reforms, including "political, financial, economic and agricultural reforms in order to improve the stability of the country," reorganization of the armed forces, removal of several incompetent government officials, and a reduction in governmental corruption.[127] Acheson counseled Truman that "it is apparent ... that the Philippine Government will not take adequate action on its own initiative," which meant that "financial assistance for economic and social development ... must be firmly conditioned on satisfactory performance by the Philippine Government and must be effectively utilized as a lever to obtain such performance."[128] Therefore, although the United States offered to provide $250 million in aid over five years, as Bell had recommended,

---

[124] Memorandum of Conversation, Truman, Bell, and Marshall, September 11, 1950, Acheson Papers; OIR, "The Hukbalahaps," pp. 41, 50; Economic Survey Mission to the Philippines, *Report to the President of the United States*, Department of State Publication 4010, Far Eastern Series 38 (Washington, DC: Department of State, 1950), pp. 3–5.

[125] MemCon, Truman, Bell, and Marshall, pp. 105–6.   [126] *Ibid*.

[127] NSC 84/2, "The Philippines," November 9, 1950, FRUS 1950, pp. 1514–20; Letter, Cowen to Dewey, February 18, 1952, Cowen Papers.

[128] Acheson to Truman; State Department Report, "The Philippines," October 10, 1950, DDRS.

this assistance was to be made "contingent upon the institution of these reforms by the Philippine Government."[129]

Though arguably necessary, the measures the United States had proposed would likely weaken Quirino's already fragile grip on power by alienating government loyalists and risking a nationalist backlash over the apparent surrender of sovereignty over economic policy to the United States. However, support for an allied country was not the same as support for a specific government: Acheson counseled Truman that, as the experience with Chiang Kai-shek demonstrated, "[I]f we are confronted with an inadequate vehicle it should be discarded or immobilized in favor of a more propitious one."[130]

Quirino Resists American Oversight

While happy to accept $250 million in American aid, Quirino was less enthused about the restrictions and oversight that came with it.[131] To preempt Washington's efforts to impose conditions on the assistance, the Filipino president publicly announced that he would "not consider any American aid if extended with American government supervision" – a position that was supported by the leader of the opposition Nationalistas.[132] In private, Quirino expressed confidence that the United States would aid the Philippines because it was in their interest to do so.[133] The Philippine establishment's expectation that America would provide help was summed up in an editorial in the *Manila Chronicle* that pointed out Washington's "moral and political obligation to stabilize the Philippine economy."[134] In Washington, the Philippine Foreign Minister warned Acheson about the negative effect conditions on American aid would have on his government's

[129] NSC 84/2, FRUS 1950, pp. 1514–19.
[130] Draft Memorandum, Acheson to Truman, April 20, 1950, FRUS 1950, p. 1442.
[131] Elpidio Quirino, "Summary of Philippine Stand on the Bell Report," November 6, 1950, Box 21, Quirino Papers. See also Letter, Romulo to Quirino, November 2, 1950, Box 66, Quirino Papers.
[132] "Quirino to Reject U.S.-Supervised Bell Aid," *Manila Chronicle*, October 18, 1950. For the political opposition's hostility to conditions on U.S. aid, see "Supervision of Bell Aid by PI Urged," *Manila Times*, October 16, 1950.
[133] Telegram 752, Manila to State, September 27, 1950, Melby File.
[134] "What Does Supervision Mean?" *Manila Chronicle*, October 18, 1950.

nationalist credentials, noting that it "played directly into unfriendly hands."[135]

Quirino's attempts to counteract American pressure largely fell flat as few Filipinos responded to his attempts to stoke nationalist sentiment against American interference in Philippine domestic affairs. In fact, a survey of attitudes across twenty-four provinces by a major daily newspaper found that a majority of Filipinos, regardless of party affiliation, supported American supervision over its assistance package – largely due to the perception that the Philippine government was corrupt and incompetent.[136] Opposition political groups took this view less out of principle than out of the recognition that tightly controlled aid was less likely to be diverted by Quirino as patronage to solidify his political position.

The Quirino-Foster Agreement

The U.S. assistance strategy was formally defined in a November 1950 agreement reached between Quirino and William Foster, head of the Economic Cooperation Administration, which committed the U.S. and Philippine governments to addressing the country's problems in accordance with the recommendations of the Bell Report. In his assessment, Bell had judged that "the economic situation will deteriorate further and political disorder will inevitably result" if Quirino's government did not obtain an immediate injection of $20 million to $30 million.[137] To sweeten the deal and overcome Quirino's resistance, the U.S. Treasury agreed to provide a $35 million emergency loan to the government of the Philippines to tide it over while the reforms called for in the Quirino-Foster agreement took effect. Requiring matching funds from the Filipino government, $250 million in grants and loans from the United States would be provided over seven years once the Philippine government had

---

[135] Memorandum of Conversation, Romulo, Acheson et al., December 27, 1950, Box 65, Acheson Papers.

[136] Survey reported in the *Manila Bulletin*, November 1, 1950. See also "What Does Supervision Mean?" *Manila Chronicle*, October 18, 1950 and Teodoro Locsin, "It Must Not Happen Again," *Philippine Free Press*, November 11, 1950.

[137] Economic Survey Mission to the Philippines, *Report*, p. 1.

1. Implemented an equitable tax program that had the goal of raising 565 million pesos in tax by January 1, 1951, to provide revenues to balance the budget and counteract inflation;
2. Enacted a minimum-wage law for all farm workers; and
3. Expressed, via a congressional resolution, a "determination ... to bring about social and economic well-being in the Philippines ... through total economic mobilization and the bold implementation of measures that will bring about a high degree of social justice."[138]

In addition to providing monetary aid, the United States also committed itself to providing the Philippine government with policy advisors and governmental specialists.

American officials were explicit about the conditionality, referring to the Quirino-Foster agreement as a "bribe" that attempted to compel the Philippine government to "live up to the 'quid pro quo' required of it."[139] In conversations with Quirino, Foster emphasized that "the United States congress [would] not appropriate a cent of the amount recommended by the Bell Mission until steps were taken by the Philippine government to implement the Bell recommendations substantially."[140] Nevertheless, Filipino officials were not necessarily convinced by the Truman administration's "tough guy" act, and within weeks of the Quirino-Foster agreement, they were pressing U.S. officials for the release of the first $15 million in aid, which they thought was likely to be given in light of the deteriorating situation in Korea.[141]

PART II IMPLEMENTING MILITARY AND ECONOMIC REFORM, 1950–1951

Reforming the Philippine Armed Forces

Throughout the first half of 1950, Quirino continued to oppose the incorporation of the constabulary within the army and attempted to placate the JUSMAG with window-dressing reforms. Undeterred, the

---

[138] "Philippine Aid Plan Forecasts New Era," *New York Times*, November 18, 1950.
[139] Memorandum, Shohan to Lacy, January 12, 1951, FRUS 1951, p. 1498.
[140] Memorandum of Conversation, Quirino and Foster, November 7, 1950, Box 21, Quirino Papers.
[141] Salvador Bigay, "Initial U.S. Loans Urged by Council," *Manila Chronicle*, November 30, 1950.

American mission maintained its pressure for real organizational change within the security forces. Meanwhile, in late March 1950, the Huks launched a series of large-scale coordinated attacks across Luzon that threw the security forces on the defensive.[142] As the insurgents overran military outposts and captured villages in the vicinity of Manila, the U.S. embassy considered evacuating its nonessential personnel.[143] Within metropolitan Manila, Huk units rendered working-class neighborhoods "no-go" zones and nearly succeeded in assassinating the army's chief of staff.[144] American personnel began to receive reports that some PC units were purposefully patrolling areas known to have no insurgent presence to avoid combat, while government officials in Huk-dominated areas appeared to be paying off the insurgents to avoid assassination.[145]

Employing the same influence strategy as the Quirino-Foster agreement, military assistance to the Philippine Armed Forces was made conditional on the reorganization of the PC into the army and the implementation of concrete reforms to reduce the security force's abusive treatment of the civilian population. To increase the credibility of its threat to withhold aid, the United States split its military assistance package into a series of smaller tranches that were linked to particular actions by the Philippine government. Thus, in late July 1950, when Quirino finally transferred 5,000 men from the PC to the army and placed the agency under the operational control of the Department of National Defense, the JUSMAG released thirty-seven tons of small arms and equipment conditioned on reorganization of the security forces.[146]

Reorganization of the PC was merely the first step in the process of enhancing the military aspects of the Philippine government's counterinsurgency effort. Having played a role in facilitating Quiernio's victory in the fraudulent election of 1949, the constabulary was widely seen as a tool of the landed elite. Moreover, their habit of quickly vacating a given area if they made contact with Huks did little to incline

---

[142] Lachica, *The Huks*, pp. 128–30.
[143] Telegram 941, Telegram 942, and Telegram 946, all Manila to State, March 31, 1950, 796.00/3–3150, RG 59.
[144] William Pomeroy, "The Philippine Peasantry and the Huk Revolt," *Journal of Peasant Studies*, 5, no. 4 (1978), p. 511.
[145] Airpouch 814, Manila to State, June 28, 1950, 796.00/6–2850, RG 59.
[146] Telegram 211, Manila to State, July 26, 1950, 796.00/7–2650 and Telegram 220, July 27, 1950, 796.00/7–2750, both RG 59; JUSMAG, "Weekly Summary of Activities," July 29, 1950, RG 334. See also, Macdonald, *Adventures in Chaos*, p. 142.

civilians to risk informing on the insurgents: U.S. analysts noted that "many people have come to believe that cooperation with the Constabulary would be a dangerous undertaking even if other obstacles to such cooperation were removed."[147]

The JUSMAG proposed that the combined AFP-PC force be organized into 1,200-man battalion combat teams (BCTs) – a reinforced infantry battalion complete with reconnaissance assets.[148] To increase mobility and reduce collateral damage, the battalion's artillery and heavy mortars were replaced with additional rifle companies: heavy weapons were only deployed for specific purposes on an as-needed basis.[149] As a combined arms force, it was envisioned that a BCT would be capable of independent operations in the rough terrain of Luzon while having more mobility and flexibility than the PC formations it replaced. In practice, the effectiveness of the BCTs was hampered by the army's preference for conventional encirclement tactics – which repeatedly failed to catch the highly mobile guerrillas – and standoff artillery strikes on insurgent positions that the U.S. embassy reported would "break up ... Huk concentrations and keep them on the move but ... inflict few casualties."[150]

In order to be able to take offensive actions against the insurgents, the JUSMAG Commander, General Leland Hobbs, believed that the security forces required energetic leadership. He also emphasized the need to engage the insurgents in close-quarters battle instead of relying on long-range artillery strikes, which could inflict significant collateral damage. The American officer counseled aggressive patrolling and night operations to separate the Huks from the population, while a revamped intelligence system and strengthened police could attack the Huks' support infrastructure to ensure that the guerrillas did not simply return when the army moved on.[151] Although the JUSMAG personnel spent much of their time in the field inspecting Filipino units,

[147] OIR, "The Hukbalahaps," p. 47
[148] JUSMAG, "Weekly Summary of Activities," December 8, 1949, RG 334.
[149] Napoleon D. Valeriano and Charles T. R. Bohannan, *Counter-Guerrilla Operations: The Philippine Experience* (London: Pall Mall Press, 1962), p. 133.
[150] Telegram 376, Manila to State, February 3, 1950, 869.00/2–350 and Telegram 1011, Manila to State, April 8, 1950, 869.00/4–850, both RG 59; Lansdale, *In the Midst of Wars*, p. 21.
[151] JUSMAG, "Semi-Annual Appraisal," March 25, 1950, p. 5 and JUSMAG, "Semi-Annual Appraisal," January 18, 1951, pp. 29–30, both RG 334.

American advisors were never assigned to them on a permanent basis, nor were they allowed to join army units on combat operations.[152] In an effort to bolster the leadership of the AFP, both State Department and Philippine government officials wanted to assign dozens of Americans to army units as tactical combat advisors and even suggested that American officers could command Filipino units in the field.[153] General Hobbs successfully rebuffed such proposals, however, as antithetical to efforts to "get the Philippine military to stand on its own feet."[154] Instead, the emergence of new leadership in the Department of National Defense would help to move the AFP toward Hobbs' ideal.

Ramon Magsaysay and the Revitalization of the Armed Forces of the Philippines

As members of the U.S. mission pushed the AFP for reform, they cultivated an ally in Liberal Party Congressman Ramon Magsaysay. During the Japanese occupation, Magsaysay had been a member of a USAFEE guerrilla unit and now served as chairman of the House National Defense Committee. The congressman had a keen interest in military matters and shared the JUSMAG's views about the need for reorganization of the AFP.[155] In his role as chairman, Magsaysay came to rely heavily on American military advisors for advice.[156]

By the third quarter of 1950, the Huks were operating across the breadth of Luzon and had spread to the adjacent islands of Panay and

---

[152] JCS Memo, November 1947, Box 46, Geographic Files 1948–50, Records of the U.S. Joint Chiefs of Staff, U.S. National Archive at College Park, Maryland (RG 218).

[153] For the desire of civilian embassy staff, including Ambassador Cowen, to deploy tactical combat advisors, see State Department Report, "The Philippines," October 10, 1950, DDRS; Letter, Melby to Cowen, February 13, 1951, Box 8, Melby Papers; Letter, Cowen to Melby, March 29, 1951, Box 8, Melby Papers; Letter, Melby to Cowen, April 10, 1951, Box 8, Melby Papers; Telegram 432, FRUS 1950, pp. 1436–7. For a similar view from the Philippine Secretary of National Defense, see Letter, Cowen to Melby, March 29, 1951. American command of Philippine units is discussed in Memo, Hobbs to Bradley, July 31, 1950, Box 48, JCS Geographic Files, 1948–50, RG 218.

[154] JUSMAG opposition to these proposals are found in Letter, Cowen to Melby, March 29, 1951, Box 8, Melby Papers; Telegram 1802, Manila to State, June 15, 1951, FRUS 1951, p. 1549; Hobbs to Bradley.

[155] Abueva, *Ramon Magsaysay*, pp. 147–8.   [156] *Ibid.*, p. 143.

Mindanao.[157] Frustration boiled over in the Philippine government
after an insurgent offensive attacked a dozen towns across Luzon,
captured two provincial capitals, and overran a PC base – massacring
the nurses, patients, and doctors in the facility's hospital before burning
it to the ground. In response, Secretary of National Defense Kangleon
resigned. Openly blaming Quirino for the setback, he asserting that the
president had refused to retire several dozen senior officers, including
General Castañeda – the "deadwood of the army" – who were bungling
the anti-Huk campaign. Kangleon also alleged that army officers were
being promoted based on their relationships with prominent political
figures rather than battlefield competence.[158] American observers
concurred that a large portion of the problem lay with General
Castañeda's attempt to counter "guerrilla tactics with poorly disciplined troops and with generally incompetent officers who employ
positional tactics against elusive dissident commandos."[159]

As Quirino considered replacing Kangleon with a staunch political
loyalist that had served the Japanese puppet government or even
assuming the defense portfolio himself, General Hobbs and
Ambassador Cowen pushed for Ramon Magsaysay to fill the role to
ensure strong leadership at the top of the AFP. Although Magsaysay
had the support of important Filipino politicians, such as Speaker of the
House Eugino Pérez, American pressure played a key role in his
selection.[160] The message that future military aid was conditional on
Magsaysay's appointment was delivered by John Melby, the State
Department's Director of the Office of Philippine Affairs, who told
Quirino directly that he had to name Magsaysay as the new Secretary of

[157] Telegram 680, Manila to State, November 20, 1950, 796.00/9–2050, RG 59.
[158] Abueva, *Ramon Magsaysay*, pp. 155–6; José Lava, "Twenty Years of Struggle
      of the CPP," Unpublished Manuscript, p. 23, Box 1, Scaff Papers.
[159] OIR, "The Hukbalahaps," p. 39.
[160] Telegram 53, Manila to State, July 7, 1950, 796.00/7–750, RG 59; Letter,
      Melby to Lacy, September 30, 1950, Box 12, Melby Papers; Lansdale, *In the
      Midst of Wars*, p. 43; Romulo, *Crusade in Asia*, p. 123; Starner, *Magsaysay and
      the Philippine Peasantry*, p. 32. Following Magsaysay's appointment, the
      Americans attempted to downplay their role. Not only was Quirino extremely
      sensitive to discussions of American pressure forcing Magsaysay on him, but
      there was also fear that such rumors would undercut Magsaysay's credibility.
      See the discussions in Letter, Cowen to Dewey, February 18, 1952, Box 6,
      Cowen Papers. The leaders of the opposition Nationalistas believed that
      Magsaysay's presence in Qurinio's cabinet was due to the U.S. Telegram 1840,
      Manila to State, November 20, 1951, 796.00/11–2051, RG 59.

National Defense. When the Philippine president shrugged and replied, "You know, you're asking me to commit political suicide," Melby responded, "Yes, I know that, but unless you do it there's no more American military aid forthcoming."[161] In the face of this threat, Quirino acquiesced.

Once in office, Magsaysay approved a comprehensive list of recommendations put forth by the JUSMAG. He also sought to reenergize the military, raising morale while simultaneously building public confidence in the security forces. Having come to rely on American military advisors, the JUSMAG chief and his staff officers became functionally part of Magsaysay's leadership team.[162] One American advisor of particular note was U.S. Air Force intelligence officer Edward Lansdale, who served as Magsaysay's chief of staff, advisor, and confidant – accompanying him everywhere he went.[163]

Magsaysay's counterinsurgency strategy sought to reduce support for the Huks by curtailing AFP mistreatment of the civilian population. He also empowered vigorous field commanders to target the insurgent's "liberated zones," denying them access to food and supplies. He provided a means for rank-and-file guerrillas to rally to the government's side while offering lucrative rewards for the capture of their leaders. He attempted to depoliticize the military by dismissing corrupt officers while increasing training for regular soldiers to enhance their professionalism. Increased pay and logistical support for units in the field eliminated the need to prey on the civilian population. American military and economic aid facilitated Magsaysay's efforts, providing the funding to raise the salaries of AFP personnel and undertake civic action projects in rural areas. The limits placed on American aid and personnel, however, forced the AFP to develop its own solutions to the challenge posed by the Huks.

Reform and Reorganization

Acting on JUSMAG recommendations, Magsaysay streamlined the military's command structure, which reduced duplication of staff

---

[161] John F. Melby, "Oral History Interview," November 21, 1986, p. 239, HST.

[162] Abueva, *Ramon Magsaysay*, p. 172.

[163] Charles Bohannan, "Oral History Interview," March 10, 1981, Ramon Magsaysay Award Foundation, Manila (RMAF).

functions and established an uninterrupted chain of command.[164] Embracing the JUSMAG's battalion combat team concept, Magsaysay accelerated their creation, raising the number of combat-ready infantry battalions from two to ten by the end of 1950, with another five on the drawing board – a move that pleased General Hobbs, who believed that the AFP needed every available unit in the field operating against the Huks.[165] As the constabulary was integrated into the AFP, army officers were assigned to command former PC units, which received modern weapons and advanced unit training.

To disrupt the Huks' "safe zones," central Luzon was blanketed with battalion combat teams that focused on a half or a third of a province.[166] The majority of BCTs initially assumed static defensive positions as the army focused on protecting the civilian population from Huk raids and developing local intelligence networks. Roadblocks and curfews established in major villages allowed BCTs to disrupt the link between the guerrillas and their supporters.

JUSMAG advisors had been counseling the leadership of the Philippine military on the shortcomings of their small-units tactics for some time; however, they found a receptive audience in the new Secretary of Defense.[167] To reorient the army's tactical approach, American advisors designed a twelve-week training program that emphasized reconnaissance, small-unit patrolling, close-quarter battle drills, and night operations.[168] The conspicuous large-sweep operations favored by General Castañeda were to be replaced with small, highly mobile units that pursued insurgents deep into their base areas.[169] Not only was it relatively easy for the lightly armed insurgents to avoid large-scale operations, abuse of the civilian population occurred most frequently during these sweeps, as the security forces vented their frustration at failing to find the guerrillas on local civilians. Whereas the security forces had previously only conducted desultory patrols along major roads adjacent to their cantonments, under

---

[164] JUSMAG, "Semi-Annual Appraisal," January 18, 1951, p. 7 and JUSMAG, "Semi-Annual Appraisal," July 18, 1951, both in RG 334.
[165] Letter, Hobbs to MacArthur, September 25, 1950, RG 10, MacArthur Memorial Library and Archives, Norfolk, Virginia (DAM).
[166] Kerkvliet, *The Huk Rebellion*, p. 208.
[167] JUSMAG, "Weekly Summary of Activities," June 24, 1950, RG 334.
[168] Erskine Mission Briefing Minutes, August 1950, Box 6, RG 334.
[169] Kerkvliet, *The Huk Rebellion*, p. 241.

Magsaysay, off-road and night patrolling by squadron- or platoon-sized units became a major focus.

At General Hobbs urging, Quirino gave Magsaysay a free hand to promote deserving officers and, more importantly, to court martial incompetents.[170] This latter power was employed liberally: Thirteen unfit senior officers were dismissed during his first month in office and over 400 by the middle of 1953.[171] Magsaysay personally appointed energetic, young officers – many of whom were in their early thirties – to command the BCTs and empowered them to remove unqualified enlisted personnel.[172] Since the Philippine counterinsurgency operations were increasingly decentralized – providing a high degree of tactical flexibility to local commanders to respond to the particular situation in their area of responsibility – vigorous leadership was especially important.

For several years, JUSMAG had advised that the "niggardly attitude" toward the "pay, clothing and substance allowance" of enlisted men was hindering the AFP's professionalization.[173] Magsaysay prioritized the procurement of sufficient rations to ensure that army units could sustain themselves in the field without stealing from the population, which appreciably improved relations with the local peasantry.[174] In 1950, the average Filipino solider did not earn enough to pay for his daily meals. Magsaysay used American aid to triple the wages of enlisted men, which raised morale and further reduced their incentives to rob or extort civilians.[175]

The landlords' civil guards were responsible for a significant portion of the abuse that was alienating the rural population. Although the JUSMAG urged these private militias be abolished, the Philippine security forces lacked the capacity to secure Luzon without them.[176]

---

[170] Lansdale, *In the Midst of Wars*, p. 43.
[171] Donn Hart, "Magsaysay: Philippine Candidate," *Far Eastern Survey*, 22, no. 6 (May 1953), p. 67.
[172] Jacinto Gavino, "Oral History Interview," October 29, 1981, RMAF.
[173] Letter, Jones to Quirino, May 5, 1948, Box 23, Quirino Papers.
[174] Osmundo Mondeñedo, "Oral History Interview," January 16, 1982, RMAF; William Thorpe, "Huk Hunting in the Philippines, 1946–1953," *The Airpower Historian* (April 1962), p. 98; Valeriano and Bohannan, *Counter-Guerrilla Operations*, p. 208.
[175] Greenberg, *The Hukbalahap Insurrection*, p. 85.
[176] Letter, Anderson to Quirino, April 13, 1950, and Letter, Anderson to Quirino, April 20, 1950, both Box 23, Quirino Papers.

Instead, Magsaysay brought the civilian guards under government control by assigning them noncommissioned officers from the army to act as instructors and commanders. Although initially a liability – Huks frequently disarmed them without a fight – these units eventually proved their worth by guarding farms, roads, bridges, and other important locations, which freed the army for offensive operations against the insurgents.[177]

To ensure that his orders were being carried out, Magsaysay functioned as his own inspector general. Accompanied by Lansdale, he conducted surprise inspections of units in the field to reward and punish officers as appropriate. Soldiers who killed insurgents were typically promoted and given a personal letter of commendation in an effort to instill an aggressive spirit among the military.[178] The JUSMAG supplemented Magsaysay by visiting up to three BCTs in the field a week to correct deficiencies and advise field commanders on how to maintain continuous pressure on the guerrillas.[179] The combination of "inspections and Magsaysay's rapid corrective actions," the JUSMAG assessed, "had a considerable impact on the armed forces," contributing to "improvements in their operational results."[180]

Civic Action

Recognizing that abuses by the security forces and the difficult economic circumstances faced by tenant farmers in central Luzon were driving support for the Huks, JUSMAG advisors emphasized the nonmilitary aspects of the conflict, especially the need to "improve the attitude and behavior of troops towards civilians."[181] Accepting this analysis, Magsaysay decreed that the first task for the army was to convince the local people that it was on their side. While previously the security forces entered every village in Huklandia poised for combat, Magsaysay insisted that unless there was a clear danger, soldiers should

[177] Valeriano and Bohannan, *Counter-Guerrilla Operations*, p. 165; JUSMAG, "Semi-Annual Report, 1 July–31 December 1952," February 1, 1953, p. 15, RG 334.

[178] Carlos Romulo and Marvin Gray, *The Magsaysay Story* (New York: Pocket Books, 1957), pp. 133–4.

[179] JUSMAG, "Semi-Annual Appraisal," January 18, 1951, p. 2.

[180] JUSMAG, "Semi-Annual Appraisal," July 18, 1951, p 49; Lansdale, *In the Midst of Wars*, p. 43.

[181] Lansdale, *In the Midst of Wars*, p. 70.

"conduct themselves as though they were coming among friends."[182] Officers ignoring these instructions were immediately relieved of duty.[183] To facilitate the reporting of abuse, Magsaysay established a nickel telegram service that would allow any Filipino to report a problem directly to him.

To demonstrate that the military could be a force for good, the army undertook what Lansdale coined "civic action," digging wells in remote areas, repairing roads, building schools, and providing basic medical treatment to the population. With American aid, 300 miles of new roads were laid, and over 2,000 wells were dug across Luzon over the subsequent four years.[184] Magsaysay also ordered army lawyers to provide pro bono representation to tenant farmers and others pursuing legal action against landlords or abusive military personnel.[185]

As important as these measures were for their substantive impact, their effect on popular opinion was far greater. Peasants in Luzon heaped praise on Magsaysay, claiming he "cleaned up the PC and Philippine army" and "got rid of the civilian guards."[186] After the alienation wrought by rehabilitation of the collaborationists, government corruption, and the fraudulent election of 1949, this change in perception was critical. One provincial Huk commander noted that "all the reforms that were promised and partially implemented [by Magsaysay], even though small and show-case in nature, were encouraging for people. Many people believed in the government; they believed in Magsaysay."[187]

Intelligence

The Philippine government's counterinsurgency intelligence effort was hindered by the fact that it could rarely detain suspected insurgents very long. The country's legal system was designed to protect citizens from capricious and unfair treatment at the hands of the authorities, which posed difficulties when the government attempted to respond to

---

[182] Valeriano and Bohannan, *Counter-Guerrilla Operations*, p. 165.
[183] Robert Smith, *The Hukbalahap Insurgency: Economic, Political and Military Factors* (Washington, DC: Office of the Chief of Military History, 1963), p. 103.
[184] Greenberg, *The Hukbalahap Insurrection*, p. 139.
[185] Lansdale, *In the Midst of Wars*, p. 48.
[186] Quoted in Kerkvliet, *The Huk Rebellion*, p. 208.   [187] *Ibid.*, p. 238.

a large-scale insurgency. Because captured insurgents were entitled to the same due-process protections as any other citizen, if a guerrilla was not presented before a judge within six hours of his arrest and a prima facie case presented against him within twenty-four hours, he was automatically released by the court. As U.S. observers noted, the PC "found it almost impossible to hold a dissident captive, since the time-space element from the field to the court offices . . . is frequently greater than six hours."[188] Moreover, if the charge filed against the insurgent was anything short of murder, he had a right to demand to be released on bail. Consequently, one JUSMAG officer noted, "[I]t was literally true that a Huk captured in a fire fight could be free and back with his unit within seventy-two hours or less."[189] General Hobbs urged Quirino to take temporary legal measures to increase the government's ability to prosecute subversives.[190] However, politicians from the ruling Liberal Party were unwilling to propose suspending the writ of habeas corpus, aware that such a move would be deeply unpopular after the brutality of the Japanese occupation and could devastate their party's future electoral chances.

These legal obstacles were only one barrier to effective intelligence collection. According to JUSMAG assessments, the Philippine government's intelligence capability was "extremely poor."[191] Until the end of 1951, responsibility for gathering intelligence on the insurgents was fragmented across sixteen different agencies, including the Philippine Constabulary, the Military Intelligence Service (MIS), the National Bureau of Investigation, the Manila Police Department, and a host of others.[192] With "phenomenal" redundancy of effort and "rampant" bureaucratic jealousy, one JUSMAG veteran claimed the situation "would have frightened any organization-minded intelligence officer."[193] Moreover, the government did not have a systematic program for the interrogation of captured insurgents: prisoners were simply locked away and occasionally beaten for information.

---

[188] JUSMAG, "Semi-Annual Appraisal, January 18, 1951."
[189] Valeriano and Bohannan, *Counter-Guerrilla Operations*, p. 54.
[190] Letter, Hobbs to Quirino, August 10, 1950, attached to Letter Hobbs to McArthur, August 11, 1950, Box 3, RG 5, DAM.
[191] JUSMAG Brief for Melby Mission, September 18, 1950, Box 12, Melby Papers.
[192] Bohannan, "Oral History Interview"; Valeriano and Bohannan, *Counter-Guerrilla Operations*, p. 138.
[193] *Ibid.*, pp. 138–9.

To assist the AFP in cultivating information from civilians and captured guerrillas, General Hobbs added six combat intelligence officers with prior knowledge of the Philippines to the JUSMAG staff.[194] A January 1951 intelligence reorganization designed by the JUSMAG made the MIS the lead agency for counterinsurgency intelligence. Intelligence teams were assigned to all the BCTs, which decentralized intelligence collection and dissemination: local commanders, rather than a separate intelligence agency, were now responsible for cultivating intelligence in their areas of operation.[195] To provide the necessary personnel, Lansdale created an intelligence school that trained 240 officers and 570 enlisted men in its first eighteen months of operation.[196] Magsaysay ended the maltreatment of prisoners, making them more likely to cooperate with interrogators and their comrades in the field more likely to surrender. With American guidance, the AFP built a network of informants and began to interrogate the families and friends of known Huks.[197]

To generate information about the insurgents while simultaneously delegitimizing them, Magsaysay offered large cash bounties for information leading to the capture of Huk leaders. The basic reward began at a rate of 5,000 pesos – ten times the average annual agricultural wage – and went as high as 100,000 pesos for senior commanders. This created divisions among the rank-and-file insurgents and their leaders, who worried that such large rewards created temptation for betrayal.[198] To reduce the Huks' heroic image, they were always portrayed as criminals wanted for a specific act of robbery, arson, or murder. The combination of better treatment of the civilian population and rewards for cooperation began to pay off in the form of reliable information about the insurgents and their organization, which previously had been notably lacking.[199]

Even before it had a practical effect on counterinsurgency operations, Magsaysay's new approach paid dividends when the Huk commander for greater Manila rallied to the government's side,

---

[194] Memorandum, Hobbs to Joint Chiefs of Staff, June 30, 1950, Box 48, JCS Geographic Files, 1948–50, RG 218.
[195] JUSMAG, "Semi-Annual Report, January 1, 1951–June 30, 1951."
[196] JUSMAG, "Semi-Annual Report," August 1, 1952, RG 334.
[197] JUSMAG, "Semi-Annual Report, January 1, 1951–June 30, 1951."
[198] Shalom, "Counter-Insurgency in the Philippines," p. 160.
[199] Telegram 38, British Legation Manila to Foreign Office, March 1, 1952, FO 371/99648, NAUK.

providing the location of the insurgents' safe houses in the capital. The simultaneous raid on twenty-two locations across the city resulted in the arrest of over one hundred people, including a large number of the organization's politburo as well as two truckloads of documents.[200] Although the arrest of so many senior leaders was a blow for the Huks, the captured documents revealed that the insurgents were much stronger and better organized than many realized.[201] More worryingly, there was evidence that, "having seen the handwriting on the wall," elements of the government, including half a dozen field-grade Army officers, a senator, President Quirino's police advisor, and an unnamed "ranking government official" – believed to be Speaker of the House Eugenio Pérez – had all reached out to the Huks to arrange a modus vivendi should the insurgents succeed in overthrowing the government.[202] The public revelation of the size and scope of the Huk organization provided Quirino with political cover for temporarily suspending the writ of habeas corpus in conflict zones, which was hindering the investigation and prosecution of insurgents. That, in turn, enhanced the ability of the government to collect intelligence on the Huks.[203]

In the months following the raids, the Huks maintained daily attacks while expanding their operations into new areas – leading Lansdale to conclude that "they were not weakened by the capture of the Manila members of their Politburo."[204] Indeed, the Huks themselves judged that the capture of the politburo only resulted in a "slight lowering of the morale of the ordinary rank-and-file member of the party," while their remaining leadership actually debated whether their forces had become strong enough to transition from guerrilla warfare to conventional operations against the Philippine military.[205]

---

[200] Abueva, *Ramon Magsaysay*, p. 167; Air Pouch 1057, Manila to State, January 24, 1951, Box 7, Melby Papers.

[201] Lansdale, *In the Midst of Wars*, pp. 63–4.

[202] Airpouch 1057, Manila to State, January 24, 1951, Box 7, Melby Papers; Airpouch 716, Manila to State, November 20, 1950, 796.00/11–2050, RG 59.

[203] *The Constabulary Story* (Quezon City: Public Information Office, 1982), p. 302.

[204] Lansdale, *In the Midst of Wars*, pp. 85–6.

[205] "Top Secret Report on Communist Military Committee Conference," November 8, 1950, Box 17, Quirino Papers.

Amnesty and EDCOR

Having fought as a guerrilla against the Japanese, Magsaysay knew how hard the life of an insurgent could be. To provide rank-and-file Huks with a way to give up their struggle, he established an amnesty that allowed those who were not guilty of a major crime to reintegrate into society. Surrendered guerrillas were given the tantalizing option of joining the Economic Development Corps (EDCOR), which used American aid to create reintegration settlements on other, less-populated islands.[206] EDCOR offered a surrendered Huk the opportunity to establish a twenty-acre homestead on Mindanao, with government help to clear land, build a home, and purchase supplies. Retired soldiers and their families lived alongside selected ex-insurgents and kept watch over their formerly wayward fellow citizens. If the Huk worked his plot of land for several years, he was granted the title in perpetuity.

Only 950 families were ever resettled by EDCOR – less than a quarter of whom were Huks; – however, the effort directly responded to the insurgents' mantra of "Land for the Landless." [207] News that the government was providing farms to surrendered insurgents triggered a wave of defections: why fight for land and a future when the government was giving it away? Recognizing the threat that EDCOR posed, the insurgents tried to paint the settlements as forced labor camps, however, these charges did not match the images and films coming out of the settlements. The Philippine government estimated that 1,500 active guerrillas surrendered to try to join the program, which would have otherwise tied up thousands of additional government troops had they remained in the field.[208]

By early 1951, Ambassador Cowen was reporting that Magsaysay's leadership was "injecting new enthusiasm in the armed forces, which may be the dominant factor in improving effectiveness."[209] This view was corroborated by Huk leader Jesus Lava, who admitted that "when Magsaysay started making reforms in the Philippine army and in the

---

[206] Romulo and Gray, *The Magsaysay Story*, pp. 167, 221. Since at least 1949, State Department personnel had been recommending that the island of Mindanao "was unpopulated and fertile and would provide a good spot for a large-scale resettlement program." Memorandum, Melby to Jessup, August 25, 1949, Box 6, Philippine General File, HST.
[207] Kerkvliet, *The Huk Rebellion*, p. 239.
[208] Cited in Greenberg, *The Hukbalahap Insurrection*, p. 92.
[209] Telegram 2157, Manila to State, January 26, 1951, 796.00/1–2651, RG 59.

government generally it had an impact not only on the movement's mass support but on the [guerrillas] as well."[210] Nevertheless, transformation of a military, even one as relatively small as the AFP, does not occur overnight. The JUSMAG continued to argue that the armed forces lacked proper training, were overly disbursed in the field, and failed to give proper attention to rooting out the Huks' support base in the civilian population.[211] Similarly, Ambassador Cowen continued to report that the AFP surrendered the initiative to the insurgents through their "disinclination to come into close combat with the Huks."[212] The conflict had clearly turned a corner as a result of the reform and reorganization of the AFP, however, although the Huks were no longer in the ascendancy, their defeat was still several years away.

Managing Conditionality

To capitalize on the momentum the army was generating, Magsaysay requested that the JUSMAG release additional military aid so that he could expand the number of BCTs at a faster rate.[213] Magsaysay's drive and energy created a problem for the United States, however, as progress in the military sphere quickly outpaced political and economic reform. There was a consensus among the Departments of Defense and State and Economic Cooperation Administration (ECA) personnel, both in Manila and Washington, that the military, economic, and political problems plaguing the Philippines were interrelated, which meant that progress was required on all fronts. If the United States provided the military aid Magsaysay's reforms had "earned" while the Filipino Congress delayed action on key economic reforms, there were concerns that it would validate those Filipino leaders who thought American aid would flow no matter what they did. Moreover, unconditioned military aid could lead Quirino to seek a solely military solution to the Huk problem. At the same time, the promise of American aid was a key lever that Magsaysay had used to push through his reforms. If the United States was seen to be changing the terms of the deal, his influence could be undercut.

[210] Quoted in Kerkvliet, *The Huk Rebellion*, p. 238.
[211] JUSMAG, "Semi-Annual Appraisal," January 18, 1951; Telegram 1533, Manila to State, April 25, 1951, 796.00/4–2551, RG 59.
[212] Telegram 1194, FRUS 1951, p. 1510.
[213] Letter, Harrington to Melby, September 6, 1951, Box 7, Melby Papers.

The problem began to undermine the interagency consensus that had formed the previous year. The JUSMAG commander was reluctant to turn down Magsaysay's request, and some embassy personnel, using inducement logic, suggested that the release of military aid could actively engender cooperation from the Philippine government in the political and economic realms. This suggestion was strongly opposed by the local representative of the ECA who took a tough stance on conditionality, arguing that no aid of any kind should be released until nonmilitary reforms had been implemented. A compromise allowed $10 million in aid to fund the creation of six new BCTs – raising the AFP's strength to 60,000 – despite the recognition that this action "may slow down Philippine determination ... to put in some reforms." The JUSMAG chief made it clear, however, that this was a one-time "stopgap" measure until the reforms required by the Quirino-Foster agreement were put in place.[214]

Implementation of the Quirino-Foster Agreement

After some initial dithering, Quirino called a special session of the Philippine Congress in December 1950 to implement the measures called for in his agreement with Foster.[215] In order to balance the budget via "equitable" taxation, American experts assisted in the drafting of legislation to raise sales, income, excise, and corporate taxes.[216] Quirino had relatively little influence over the country's Congress, however, including members of his own Liberal Party, who feared that raising taxes would hurt their chances in the upcoming 1951 midterm election. Moreover, a number of Filipino congressmen publicly expressed doubt that the United States would follow through on conditionality, with one asserting that "the U.S. would give us help when we need it because her prestige is at stake here," while another claimed that "whether the American people like it or not, American aid is coming because of the worsening world condition."[217] Incredulity

---

214 Entire paragraph from the two letters Cowen to Melby, March 6, 1951 and Letter, Melby to Cowen, March 20, 1951, all in Box 8, Melby Papers. See also Telegram 2190, Neri to Romulo, September 22, 1951, VVM, Box 1, Magsaysay Papers, RMAF.

215 "Congress Called to Special Meet," *Manila Chronicle*, November 24, 1950.

216 "Finance Experts Press Adoption of Tax Measures," *Manila Chronicle*, December 3, 1950.

217 Congress of the Philippines, *Congressional Record*, December 21, 1950, p. 843.

was also expressed that the United States would spend billions of dollars to rehabilitate its wartime enemy, Japan, but would force an ally to comply with burdensome conditions before it received much-needed assistance.[218]

Nevertheless, the United States stuck to its position. In Washington, the ECA announced that it was waiting for Philippine compliance with tax and minimum-wage measures before funding the first $15 million in aid grants, while in Manila, embassy officials delivered the same message to the Philippine Central Bank and the Philippine Congress.[219] In response, Quirino resumed his offensive against conditionality, bolstered by the growing hostility among Filipino elites over the delay of American aid.[220] The president publicly insisted that the United States should be providing economic assistance and military equipment to the Philippines, while in private he attempted to placate Ambassador Cowen with promises of reform in an effort to convince him to deliver aid despite congressional inaction.[221] The United States responded to these entreaties with an ultimatum: if the necessary legislation was not passed by the end of June 1951, not only would Quirino's government lose the initial tranche of aid associated with those reforms, but the entire aid program would be canceled.[222] From Washington, the Departments of Defense and State and the ECA impressed on their representatives in Manila the need to maintain a "united front" to bring the "utmost pressure" on the Philippine government to implement the agreement.[223]

Only days before his agreement with Foster, Quirino had been on the record opposing tax increases.[224] In light of the American ultimatum, however, he personally appealed to Congress to support the tax

[218] Ernesto Del Rosario, "Off the Beat," *Manila Chronicle*, January, 20, 1951.
[219] Morris Harris, "PI to Implement Accord – Romulo," *Manila Chronicle*, January, 21, 1951; "Address to Bear Cowen's Views," *Manila Chronicle*, January, 21, 1951.
[220] Letter, Cowen to Melby, January 21, 1951, Box 8, Melby Papers.
[221] "EQ Deplores ECA Impositions," *Manila Chronicle*, February 23, 1951; "Cowen, Checchi May Ask U.S. to Relax Terms," *Manila Chronicle*, February 27, 1951.
[222] "The President's Week," *Philippine Free Press*, March 24, 1951.
[223] Economic Cable 151, ECA to Manila, February 22, 1951, FRUS 1951, p. 1512.
[224] Celso Cabrera, "EQ Opposes Supervision," *Manila Chronicle*, October 31, 1950.

increases because they were essential steps to gaining U.S. financial assistance.[225] Although he publicly protested that American conditions were "too hard," Quirino also pressed Congress to pass minimum-wage legislation for agricultural and unskilled laborers – over the staunch opposition of the country's influential sugar cane producers – as the final requirement to gain the assistance promised under the Quirino-Foster agreement.[226] Quirino eked out a victory, and in late March, he signed the minimum-wage regulations and the new taxes into law.[227] Soon after the measures were passed, Washington announced the release of the first $15 million in grants.[228]

Debates in the Philippine Congress over the legislation made it clear that conditions on U.S. aid were a key impetus to the approval of both reforms.[229] Filipino politicians privately referred to the U.S. assistance mission and its conditioned aid as a "magical organization" that had "balanced the Philippine budget and passed the minimum wage law . . . without spending any money here."[230] As a contemporaneous scholar of Philippine politics observed,

Few would have dared predict six months earlier that the Philippine Congress could pass in short order two laws, such as the minimum wage and the increased corporate income tax . . . In sum, the leverage of proffered foreign aid had produced the legislative authorization for social change probably not possible otherwise.[231]

With the tax increases in place, government revenues doubled in the space of just two years. This allowed an increase in defense spending while simultaneously funding social programs and other necessary expenditures.[232] At the same time, the minimum-wage law saw real

---

225 "Address to Bear Cowen's Views."
226 Telegram 2608, Manila to State, March 2, 1951, 796.00(w)/3–251, RG 59; Elpidio Quirino, "Statement on Congressional Approval of the Minimum Wage Bill," n.d., Box 22, Quirino Papers.
227 Leon Ty, "Inside Congress," *Philippine Free Press*, March 24, 1951.
228 Letter, Foster to Quirino, April 17, 1951, Box 22, Quirino Papers.
229 Congress of the Philippines, *Congressional Record*, March 16, 1951, p. 791.
230 Quoted in, Letter, Cowen to Melby, April 2, 1951, Box 8, Melby Papers.
231 David Wurfel, "Foreign Aid and Social Reform in Political Development: A Philippine Case Study," *American Political Science Review*, 53, no. 2 (June 1959), p. 466.
232 Frank Golay, *The Philippines: Public Policy and National Economic Development* (Ithaca, NY: Cornell University Press, 1961), p. 85.

wages of unskilled and agricultural workers increase by approximately 22 percent between 1950 and 1953.[233]

Things Look Up

By the third quarter of 1951, the military assistance program was under way, and the Philippine government had implemented key provisions of the Quirino-Foster agreement to stabilize the economy and address some of the economic issues underpinning support for the insurgents. However, the United States still desired to see a shakeup in the military's high command. In particular, the United States sought the removal of the Army Chief of Staff, General Castañeda, and the Constabulary Commander, Brigadier Ramos, the architects of the Philippine government's abusive and ineffective response to the Huk insurgency – as a way to substantially boost the morale of the AFP.[234] The embassy and JUSMAG reported that Castañeda refused to cooperate with Magsaysay's reform efforts, while adding that "beyond protecting perpetrators of abuses," Ramos has "done nothing but draw his breath and his salary."[235] With U.S. Secretary of Defense George Marshall convinced that giving American aid to a politicized military would not enhance its capacity, it was imperative to cultivate a "strong, competent and nonpolitical military leadership" in the AFP.[236] Moreover, Ambassador Cowen believed that the removal of Castañeda and Ramos was essential to prevent the military from becoming a tool of the ruling Liberal Party.[237] Since both men had substantially aided Quirino in winning the 1949 election, attempts to press the president on this front were "met with an explosion" of "violent protestations."[238] After several recent coup attempts in the

[233] Central Bank of the Philippines, "Statistical Bulletin," December 1956, p. 237.
[234] Airgram A-160, Manila to State, March 31, 1949, 896.00/3–3149 and Letter, Chapin to Gullion, April 20, 1950, Box 2, Office of Philippine Affairs, both RG 59; Letter, Melby to Cowen, January 22, 1951, Box 6, and Letter, Cowen to Melby, March 6, 1951, box 8, both Melby Papers.
[235] Telegram 1880, FRUS 1951, p. 1492.
[236] Telegram 1880, FRUS 1951, p. 1491; Memorandum of Conversation, Cowen and Magsaysay, January 22, 1951, FRUS 1951, p. 1504.
[237] Letter, Cowen to Melby, April 6, 1951, Box 6, Melby Papers.
[238] Melby Survey Mission, Embassy Brief, September 18, 1950, Box 12, Melby Papers; Letter, Cowen to Melby, April 6, 1951, Box 8, Melby Papers; Letter, Cowen to Dewey, February 18, 1952, Box 6, Cowen Papers.

region, Quirino was particularly fearful about the loyalty of his armed forces and favored reliability over capability.

Defense Secretary Kangleon's criticisms of Castañeda and Ramos had led to his break with Quirino, and Magsaysay – who judged that the men knew nothing about guerrilla warfare – threatened to resign unless they were fired. Magsaysay's bargaining position was bolstered by the conditioning of America's 1952 military aid budget on the retirement of the pair "from all government service immediately."[239] In an effort to bypass Ambassador Cowen and the State Department, Quirino dispatched his Foreign Minister to Washington to lobby the White House directly for the expedited delivery of military aid without changes to the military high command. However, the Truman administration was adamant "not a centavo of the ten million dollar military budget aid will be forthcoming unless and until Castañeda is retired."[240] Under duress, Quirino complied.

The new leadership of the military and the reforms instituted by Magsaysay began to have an impact. The additional BCTs increasingly blunted the Huks' progress and began to push the insurgents onto the defensive, forcing them to abandon Luzon's fertile agricultural plains for the sanctuary of mountains and swamps. With morale on the rise, the AFP were displaying increasing levels of competence and finally demonstrated a willingness to engage the insurgents in close combat.[241] With the army killing Huks at the rate of forty to fifty a week, Philippine defense officials claimed that 2,000 insurgents had been killed in 1951 and an equal number captured.[242] By the spring of 1952, the army had twenty-six BCTs in the field, which allowed the military to maintain a constant presence in central Luzon and reassert government authority.[243] Despite the heavy wear and tear on the AFP, JUSMAG observers were pleased to note that the AFP were making "steady progress" and that the peace and order situation in the country had improved markedly.[244] An ever-tightening army cordon herded

---

[239] Telegram 2760, Manila to State, March 14, 1951, 796.00/3–1451, RG 59.
[240] Letter, Cowen to Melby, April 23, 1951, Box 8, Melby Papers; Romulo, *The Magsaysay Story*, p. 105.
[241] Dispatch 324, Manila to State, August 30, 1951, 796.00/8–3051, RG 59.
[242] Lachica, *The Huks*, p. 131.
[243] JUSMAG, "Semi-Annual Report," February 14, 1952, RG 334.
[244] Memo, "Military Situation in the Philippines," appended to letter, Pierson to Renne, August 8, 1952, Box 1, JUSMAGPHIL Central Admin Files, 1949–53, RG 334.

the remaining Huks into the tiny area of Mount Arayat, while locally raised pro-government militias prevented the insurgents' political organizations from reestablishing themselves in cleared zones. Increasingly cut off from the population and lacking both supplies and solid intelligence, the Huks were soon spending more time and energy merely evading government forces than planning offensives.[245] The estimate of the number of guerrillas in the field had fallen from 15,000 to 8,000, and the embassy was reporting that the "dissident problem [had been] reduced from military threat . . . to nuisance raids."[246] Although it was "still not . . . entirely safe [to] travel anywhere outside Manila after dark," by early 1953, the insurgency was believed to be in a state of "continued deterioration," having been "winnowed down to diehards."[247] Roughly 1,500 full-time guerrillas and 33,000 active sympathizers remained in the field, a fraction of the 15,000 to 20,000 fighters and 2 million active supporters they possessed in 1950.[248]

On the economic front, the Philippine budget had been balanced, tax intake increased 70 percent, and 90 percent of workers had seen their wages rise.[249] As a result of these socioeconomic reforms and Magsaysay's vigorous leadership, the embassy reported a marked increase in the "willingness of the residents of small towns and villages to cooperate with the armed forces in the struggle against the Hukbalahap."[250] In contrast to the precarious situation in late 1949, the security forces were gaining initiative against the insurgents, abuses of the population were down, and the government's fiscal situation had stabilized. In reflecting on these successes, Ambassador Cowen judged that "without exception [these steps] were made possible only by continuously applied pressure" on the Philippine government, however, it remained to be seen "whether or not this reinforced structure will hold together when pressure is removed." [251]

---

[245] Telegram 1214, Manila to State, October 24, 1952, 796.00/10–2452, RG 59
[246] Telegram 2318, Manila to State, January 4, 1952, 796.00/1–452, RG 59.
[247] Telegram 1794, Manila to State, December 19, 1952, 796.00/12–1952, and Telegram 2200, Manila to State, January 23, 1953, 796.00/1–2353, both RG 59.
[248] Tomas Tirona, "The Philippine Anti-Communist Campaign," *Air University Quarterly Review* (Summer 1954), p. 52.
[249] Letter, Checchi to Cowen, October 11, 1951, Box 8, Melby Papers.
[250] Dispatch 324.
[251] Telegram 729, Manila to State, August 21, 1951, 796.00/8–2151, RG 59.

PART III THE POLITICAL EFFORT, 1951–1953

The Election of 1951

With the counterinsurgency campaign gaining steam, the U.S. embassy worried that the forthcoming congressional election in November – where the Liberal Party faced a choice between "honesty and defeat on the one hand and fraud and victory on the other" – could undo all the progress the U.S. assistance effort had registered.[252] Toward that end, American officials warned all Filipino political parties that electoral malfeasance would jeopardize continued American aid.[253]

Beyond making threats to withhold assistance, the United States took active steps to check electoral fraud. The embassy encouraged both Philippine and American journalists to monitor the polls to report any malfeasance.[254] Behind the scenes, the CIA dispatched an election-law expert to lead the nascent National Movement for Free Elections (NAMFREL). This nongovernmental organization brought together civil society groups, such as Rotary, the Junior Chamber of Commerce, and the YMCA, which consisted of active, politically aware young professionals who wanted to raise public awareness about the value of free and fair elections.[255] To support its operations, the JUSMAG covertly channeled American aid to NAMFREL.[256]

Equally important, the embassy convinced the Philippine Electoral Commission to request Magsaysay's assistance in ensuring an honest election.[257] In rural areas that were traditionally subject to fraud, the army protected voters from both the insurgents and armed political partisans. They also secured ballot boxes, immediately reporting the

---

[252] Telegram 1640, Manila to State, May 14, 1951, 796.00/5–1451, RG 59.
[253] Telegram 70, Manila to State, July 5, 1951, 796.00/7–551; Dispatch 67, State to Manila, July 28, 1951, 796.00/7–2851, RG 59; Telegram 1194, Manila to State, February 15, 1951, FRUS 1951, pp. 1506–7; Telegram 186, State to Manila, April 25, 1951, FRUS 1951, pp. 1536–7.
[254] Memo, Bell to Wanamaker, October 16, 1951, 796.00/10–1651, RG 59.
[255] Letter, Cowen to Melby, August 13, 1951, Melby Papers; Melby, "Oral History Interview," pp. 184, 203, HST; Joseph Smith, *Portrait of a Cold Warrior* (New York: Putnam, 1976), pp. 107–8. NAMFREL's CIA origins are examined in Nakano Satoshi, "Gabriel L. Kaplan and U.S. Involvement in Philippine Electoral Democracy: A Tale of Two Democracies," *Philippine Studies*, 52, no. 2 (2004).
[256] Cecil Currey, *Edward Lansdale, the Unquiet American* (Washington, DC: Brassey's, 1998), p. 109.
[257] *Ibid.*, p. 108.

local vote tallies by radio to Manila so that they could not be tampered with.[258] The Chief of Staff of the AFP issued several stern warnings to all officers of severe punishment should they act in a politically partisan manner.[259]

With these measures in place, the balloting was exceptionally clean by local standards, resulting in a landslide for the opposition Nationalistas.[260] Although Quirino himself was not up for election, corruption in his administration was the primary issue in the campaign.[261] In a reverse of 1949, the relatively fair contest in 1951 sapped much of the Huks' justification for armed violence and triggered a groundswell of popular support for the government.[262] Although the British ambassador in Manila suggested that the result came about "thanks to no little prodding from the United States ambassador and the actions of NAMFREL," ordinary Filipinos credited Magsaysay with the "honest and peaceful election" as well as with restoring "the confidence of the majority in the present administration."[263] The prestige of the army was also enhanced for its role in ensuring the integrity of the vote.[264]

The Liberals Retrench

Early 1952 saw a change at the U.S. embassy as World War II hero Admiral Raymond Spruance succeeded Myron Cowen as ambassador. Cowen exhorted his successor to maintain pressure on the Quirino administration via conditions on aid in order to push forward with the kind of reforms necessary to help the Philippines become a "stable outpost of American democracy in the Far East" rather than "buying temporary stability through the continued handing out of United States

---

[258] Telegram 306, Manila to State, July 20, 1951, 796.00/7–2051, RG 59.

[259] Memorandum from Gozun to all officers, June 25, 1951; Memorandum from Duque to all officers, August 4, 1951, both Box 8, Melby Papers.

[260] Telegram 194, British Legation Manila to London, December 27, 1951, FO 371/99648, NAUK.

[261] Telegram 971, Manila to State, January 21, 1951, 796.00/1–2151, RG 59.

[262] Telegram 1784, Manila to State, November 15, 1951, 796.00/11–1551, RG 59.

[263] The British views are contained in Telegram 194, British Legation Manila to London. For the credit given to Magsaysay, see Letter, Residents of Urdaneta to Quirino, December 29, 1951, Box 17, Quirino Papers; Telegram 52, Cebu to State, January 4, 1952, 796.00/1–452, RG 59.

[264] JUSMAG, "Semi-Annual Report," February 14, 1952.

government largesse."[265] Meanwhile, in the wake of their electoral defeat, several prominent Liberal Party leaders attempted to undo the reforms that had weakened their hold on power. The Speaker of the House, Eugenio Pérez, called for the constabulary to be separated from the army and pressed Quirino to remove Magsaysay and replace him with General Castañeda.[266] To prevent Magsaysay from policing the 1953 presidential election, Perez also attempted to weaken the Secretary of National Defense's authority, claiming that concentrating too much power in his hands of risked provoking a coup.[267] The embassy expressed strong concern that these partisan political machinations were threatening the centralization of command that had been so important for achieving unity of effort in the counterinsurgency campaign.[268]

In the face of this attempted backsliding, the JUSMAG let it be known that an independent PC would be cut off from American aid, while officials from President Truman down quietly let Quirino know the importance they attached to Magsaysay's continued work.[269] To raise Magsaysay's stature further and make it difficult for Quirino to replace him, the State Department invited the Secretary of National Defense to the United States, where he was feted by the press and had closed-door meetings with President Truman and Secretary of State Acheson, as well as senior Pentagon officials.[270] As the Undersecretary of State recounted to President Truman, "[T]he United States government has successfully expended some money and much time to situate Magsaysay both politically and militarily in a decisive position."[271]

---

[265] Letter, Cowen to Spruance, April 29, 1952, Cowen Papers.
[266] Telegram 2000, Manila to State, December 4, 1951, 796.00/12–451, and Airpouch 339, April 15, 1952, 796.00/4–1552, both RG 59.
[267] Telegram 2012, Manila to State, December 5, 1951, 796.00/12–551, RG 59; Abueva, *Ramon Magsaysay*, p. 204.
[268] Telegram 3598, Manila to State, April 16, 1952, 796.00/4–1652, RG 59; *ibid.*, p. 207.
[269] Memorandum, Allison to Webb, November 18, 1951; 796.00/11–1851, Telegram 2033, Manila to State, December 7, 1951; 796.00/12–751, and Letter, Truman to Quirino, December 8, 1951, 796.00/12–851, all RG 59; Memorandum, Cowen to Melby, December 3, 1951, Box 8, Melby Papers.
[270] Abueva, *Ramon Magsaysay*, p. 213.
[271] Letter, Webb to Truman, December 6, 1951, Box 1573, Official File, HST.

Magsaysay for President

Magsaysay's growing popularity was resented by Quirino and his role in preserving the 1951 election caused tension with the Liberal Party establishment. In early March 1953, after Quirino publicly denigrated Magsaysay's part in combating the insurgency by saying he was "only good for killing Huks," the Defense Secretary resigned to head an alliance of the Nationalistas and several other opposition parties in an effort to unseat Quirino.[272] In his letter of resignation, Magsaysay asserted

[W]e cannot solve the problem of dissidence simply by military measures. It would be futile to go on killing Huks while the administration continues to build dissidence by neglecting the problems of our masses ... [the] solution lies in the correction of social evils and injustice, and in giving the people a decent government, free from dishonesty and graft.[273]

Crisscrossing the country in a populist campaign, Magsaysay forged a coalition of rural farmers, reform-minded professionals, business-men, and former guerrillas that stood in sharp contrast to the Liberal Party's tried-and-true methods of winning adherents by dispensing patronage from the public coffers.[274] Working on behalf of the CIA, Edward Lansdale bolstered Magsaysay's reputation with the American press.

Seeing Washington's hand behind Magsaysay's candidacy and resentful of the "heavy hand" with which Ambassador Cowen had been pushing reform, Quirino adopted an increasingly nationalist and anti-American line.[275] He claimed that Magsaysay "has always been known to be servile to Americans," while in contrast, on several

---

[272] Telegram 2288, Manila to State, January 23, 1953, 796.00/1–2353, RG 59; Smith, *Portrait of a Cold Warrior*, pp. 109–11; Starner, *Magsaysay and the Philippine Peasantry*, p. 28. Rumors of Magsaysay's impeding candidacy had been circulating for over a year. Letter, Cowen to Melby, February 26, 1952, Box 8, Melby Papers.

[273] Letter, Magsaysay to Quirino, February 28, 1953, Series 9, Box 13, Magsaysay Papers, RMAF. See also Smith, *Philippine Freedom, 1946–1958*, p. 165.

[274] Airpouch 1277, Manila to State, May 12, 1953, 796.00/5–1253, RG 59.

[275] Quirino quoted in Memorandum, Lacy to Allison, October 31, 1952, 796.00/10–3152, Telegram 2017, Manila to State, January 8, 1953, 796.00/1–853, Airpouch 77, Cebu to State, January 27, 1953, 796.00/1–2753, Telegram 2959, Manila to State, March 30, 1953, 796.00/3–3053, and Telegram 2967, Manila to State, March 31, 1953, 796.00/3–3153, all RG 59.

occasions, he had "foiled" American attempts to "force their will" on the Philippines.[276]

Believing that Quirino "cannot win if the elections are honest," U.S. officials suggested that it would require a major effort to prevent electoral fraud, "possibly even going so far as to threaten to cut off both economic and military assistance."[277] The threat of an aid cutoff was made explicit by Ambassador Spruance, who warned Philippine officials that the U.S. Congress would cease economic and military aid to any government that achieved office through deceit.[278] This had a temporary ameliorating effect, with embassy personnel reporting that for the next several months "Quirino has slowed down perceptibly in his efforts to prepare for rigged elections."[279]

Before long, however, the Liberal Party's standard bearer was again harassing opposition leaders, who were denounced as Communists and arrested on trumped-up civil charges.[280] The U.S. embassy believed that NAMFREL remained the "best hope for arousing wide popular demand for honest elections."[281] Unsurprisingly, it came under attack from the Quirino administration as a partisan organization.[282] With financial support for NAMFREL coming from American-linked sources such as the local Coca-Cola distributor, the Catherwood Foundation, the Free Asia Foundation, and the JUSMAG, Liberal Party leaders denounced it and fellow pro-democracy civic groups as "insincere political organizations financed by aliens and supporting one candidate."[283] Reports soon circulated that the military had been ordered to close them down.

[276] Telegram 2967; Telegram 1151, Manila to State, November 19, 1953, 796.00/11–1953, RG 59. See also Tillman Durdin, "Quirino Makes U.S. Chief Vote Target," *New York Times*, October 9, 1953.

[277] Letter, Tannenwald to Paul, November 10, 1952, Box 8, Tannenwald Papers.

[278] Telegram 1592, Manila to State, December 3, 1952, 796.00/12–352, RG 59. See also Telegram 1716, Manila to State, December 15, 1952, 796.00/12–1552, RG 59.

[279] Letter, Lacy to Allison, February 17, 1953, 796.00/2–1753, RG 59.

[280] Telegram 3336, Manila to State, May 7, 1953, 796.00/5–753, Telegram 3348, Manila to State, May 8, 1953, 796.00/5–853, both RG 59; Memo, Lacy to Allison, October 31, 1952; Abueva, *Ramon Magsaysay*, p. 244.

[281] Telegram 971, Manila to State, January 21, 1953, 796.00/1–2153, and Telegram 1417, Manila to State, November 14, 1953, 796.00/11–1453, both RG 59.

[282] Letter, Lacy to Bonsal, May 4, 1953, 769.00/5–453, RG 59.

[283] Telegram 1680, Manila to State, December 10, 1952, 796.00/12–1052, and Telegram 377, Manila to State, August 17, 1953, 796.00/8–1753, both RG 59; Document, "Where NAMFREL and Other Allied Organizations Are Getting

Meanwhile, Quirino also attempted to pressure the United States to cease its meddling in the coming election. The president's brother, Antonio – appointed as a lieutenant colonel in the military intelligence agency – directed his agents to intimidate Americans perceived to be close to Magsaysay. Embassy personnel suspected that Antonio had spies in the chancery who were trying to determine the extent of American contact with the opposition parties.[284] To disarm Magsaysay of one of his key advisors, Quirino and his Foreign Minister publicly alleged that Lansdale was a CIA agent, which created embarrassment for the U.S. mission and required him to leave the country for a period.[285] These pressure tactics had some impact on the new Eisenhower administration, which had succeeded Truman in January 1953. Secretary of State John Foster Dulles instructed the U.S. embassy to remain "absolutely impartial" in the election campaign.[286]

After the ameliorating effects of the 1951 election, the coming presidential contest appeared to run the risk of undoing much of what had been accomplished. As the U.S. Chargé d'Affairs warned Secretary Dulles, "[I]f the election is clearly fraudulent and Quirino should win, the embassy fears organized armed resistance will be inevitable."[287] American personnel received reports that the central government was arming Liberal Party "goon squads" in rural areas, provincial officials and PC commanders were being replaced by party loyalists, and "large shipments of arms," excess election ballots, and cases of ink eradicator were being delivered "to unknown consignees."[288] Mindful of the important role the army had played in policing the polls in 1951,

Funds," December 24, 1952, Box 128, Quirino Papers. The Catherwood Foundation would later be revealed to be one of several conduits through which the CIA surreptitiously provided grants to educational, religious, labor, and other civil society groups in the U.S. and abroad. "Foundations, Private Organizations Linked to CIA," *Congressional Quarterly Almanac* February 24, 1967, p. 1.

[284] Memo, Lacy to Allison, October 31, 1952; U.S. Embassy Manila, "Changes in the Philippine National Defense Establishment following the Resignation of Defense Secretary Magsaysay," March 16, 1953, 796.00/3–1652, RG 59; Letter, Lansdale to Cowen, June 11, 1953, Box 6, Cowen Papers.

[285] Letter, Lansdale to Cowen, June 11, 1953, Box 6, Cowen Papers; Memorandum, Day to Drumright, November 6, 1953, 796.00/11–653, RG 59.

[286] Telegram 2840, State to Manila, March 6, 1953, 796.00/3–653, and Telegram 2854, State to Manila, March 14, 1953, 796.00/3–1453, both RG 59.

[287] Airpouch 415, Manila to State, October 14, 1953, 796.00/10–1453, RG 59.

[288] Memorandum, Lansdale to Spruance, October 3, 1953, 796.00/10–353, RG 59; Airpouch 415, Manila to State, October 14, 1953, 796.00/10–1453,

Liberal Party congressmen introduced legislation outlawing its involvement.[289] Once again, the Speaker of the House attempted to appoint General Castañeda as the Secretary of National Defense and separate the constabulary from the army. Again, the JUSMAG and the embassy informed the Philippine government that military aid was conditioned on the PC remaining under the authority of the armed forces and Castañeda playing no role in government.[290] The threat largely prevented the Philippine government from following through, although the PC was given independent jurisdiction in a few provinces outside Luzon, where American observers reported opposition candidates had their rallies broken up by "hired bands of thugs" and PC troops.[291]

Throughout the year, Quirino attempted to reassert control over the AFP by replacing officers suspected of pro-Magsaysay sentiments with party loyalists, while rumors continued to circulate that General Castañeda would be named as the Secretary of National Defense.[292] The Philippine ambassador to the United States warned the State Department that the manipulation of the security forces was far more extensive than the Americans realized and urged the United States not to recognize an electoral result brought about by fraud and intimidation.[293] In response, Dulles authorized Ambassador Spruance to threaten to cut American military aid, and as before, Quirino backed down from his attempts to politicize the AFP.[294]

As the election day approached, the JUSMAG chief – directly contravening instructions from the State Department – deployed his officers to supervise the PC and army personnel who were working as poll watchers. In the embassy's estimate, this action had a significant effect

RG 59; Telegram 415, Manila to State, October 14, 1953, 796.00/10–1553, RG 59; and Lansdale, *In the Midst of Wars*, pp. 118–20.

[289] Telegram 1339, Manila to State, April 15, 1952, 796.00/4–1552, and Telegram 1953, Manila to State, January 5, 1953, 796.00/1–553, both RG 59.

[290] Telegram 1953.

[291] Telegram 3890, Manila to State, June 29, 1953, 796.00/6–2953, and Telegram 1021, Manila to State, November 13, 1953, 796.00/11–1353, both RG 59; Lansdale, *In the Midst of Wars*, p. 116.

[292] *Manila Bulletin*, September 9, 1953; Lansdale to Spruance, October 3, 1953; Telegram 498, Manila to State, September 2, 1953, 796.00/9–253, RG 59.

[293] Telegram 1051, Manila to State, November 6, 1953, 796.00/11–653, RG 59.

[294] Telegram 876, Manila to State, October 10, 1953, 796.00/10–1053, and Telegram 503, Manila to State, September 2, 1953, 796.00/9–253; Dispatch 617, State to Manila, September 3, 1953, 796.00/9–353, all RG 59.

in "encouraging local provincial officials to maintain rectitude."[295]
Thanks to a concerted American effort that billed the Philippines as
a democratic showpiece in Asia, the country was teeming with foreign
journalists on election day who provided an additional check against
blatant fraud.[296]

Dénouement

In one of the most peaceful and lawful electoral contests in Philippine
history, Magsaysay received twice as many votes as Quirino, winning
forty-eight of the country's fifty-two provinces – including 70 percent
of the votes from the provinces of central Luzon.[297] It would, of course,
be both unfair and inaccurate to give sole credit for the success of the
1953 elections to the Americans.[298] Whatever its origins, NAMFREL
rallied a large cross section of Filipino civic society to work for
a legitimate electoral process. In addition, local institutions, ranging
from the Catholic Church – which claimed that it was a mortal sin not
to vote "when there is danger of evil men obtaining control of the
government" – to the Supreme Court – which blocked Quirino's
attempts to invoke emergency powers to rule by decree – all played
important roles in sustaining the democratic process.[299] The effect that
the combination of enhanced civic engagement and nonpartisan policing of the polls had on the Philippine political system should not be

---

[295] Dispatch 1043, State to Manila, October 16, 1953, 796.00/10–2353; Memo,
Bonsal to Halla, October 23, 1953, 796.00/10–2353; Telegram 996, Manila to
State, October 29, 1953, 796.00/10–2353; Telegram 1079, Manila to State,
November 11, 1953, 796.00/11–1153, all RG 59. Despite complaints from
Quirino, local observers report that "virtually the entire rank and file of the
Philippine armed forces welcomed this U.S. military presence." Telegram 1151,
Manila to State, November 19, 1953, 796.00/11–1953; Dispatch 740, State to
Manila, September 18, 1953, 796.00/9–1853; Telegram 1168, Manila to State,
November 24, 1953, 796.00/11–2453, RG 59; Lansdale, *In the Midst of Wars*,
p. 121.

[296] Telegram 176, Manila to State, August 18, 1953, 796.00/8–1853, and
Memorandum of Conversation, Peabody, Bonsal et al., August 24, 1953,
796.00/8–2453, both RG 59.

[297] *Current Intelligence Weekly*, November 20, 1953, p. 8, DDRS.

[298] For other American efforts, see Letter, Lacy to Bell, December 2, 1953,
796.00/2–1253, RG 59.

[299] Airpouch 115, Manila to State, July 27, 1953, 796.00/7–2753, RG 59; Joint
Pastoral Letter on Elections, Catholic Welfare Organization, September 16,
1953.

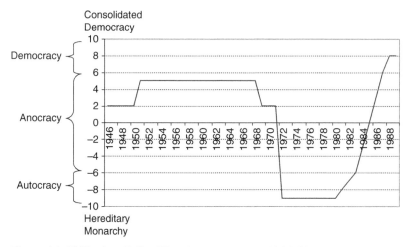

Figure 4.1 Philippines Polity IV regime type score, 1946–89.

understated. Scholars who study democratization record the elections of 1951 and 1953 as a major transition (see Figure 4.1) that left the political system just shy of democratic status – a high-water mark of political liberalization that would not be eclipsed until the fall of the Marcos dictatorship in 1986.[300]

Following Magsaysay's election, the remaining insurgents attempted to negotiate a truce that would allow them to reconstitute themselves as a legitimate Communist Party. As Huk leaders admitted, the peasants of Luzon now saw "elections as alternatives to rebellion."[301] When those negotiations failed, the insurgent's military commander and most popular leader, Luis Taruc, surrendered to the government in May 1954 – receiving a twelve-year prison sentence.[302] A few diehards refused to follow his lead; however, their numbers continued to decline. By the end of 1956, there were fewer than 700 full-time guerrillas and 30,000 supporters remaining, with approximately a tenth of that number still active in 1965.[303]

---

[300] "Polity IV Project: Political Regime Characteristics and Transitions, 1800–2008," Center for Systemic Peace, Vienna, VA, 2008.
[301] Kerkvliet, *The Huk Rebellion*, p. 238.
[302] Scaff, *The Philippine Answer to Communism*, pp. 130–1.
[303] Lachica, *The Huks*, p. 14.

Magsaysay attempted to continue his reformist ways once in office, but his efforts were stymied by vested interests in the Philippine Congress. The conditions placed on American aid – which had been so effective at forcing reform in the past – were no longer wielded on his behalf.[304] Although both Ambassador Spruance and Vice President Nixon had recommended that the United States "do everything possible to make Magsaysay's administration a success," without the threat of the Huk insurgency, American concerns about inequality, corruption, and other barriers to establishing a stable democracy waned.[305] In March 1957, while he was campaigning for reelection in Cebu, Magsaysay's plane crashed into Mount Manunggal. More than 2 million Filipinos attended his funeral.[306]

Assessment

The Philippine government's initial response to the outbreak of the Huk Rebellion was to deploy its poorly trained and led security forces in an unsophisticated search-and-destroy campaign against the insurgents and their supporters. This indiscriminate violence alienated much of the rural population and ceded initiative to the Huks, who used the government's repression, corruption, and other failings to expand the ranks of their active and passive sympathizers. Consequently, the multipronged American support effort sought to compel the Philippine government to ameliorate the most glaring sources of discontent by reducing the abusive practices of the security forces, enhancing rural standards of living, and bolstering the legitimacy of the Philippine political process as a viable alternative to armed violence. The combination of these efforts was a counterinsurgency strategy that not only proved to be militarily effective but also convinced the population that

[304] NSC Progress Report; Memorandum, Howe to Lourie, "Prospects for the Magsaysay Administration," February 24, 1954, 796.00/2–2454, RG 59; Wurfel, "Foreign Aid and Social Reform," p. 473. This was foreseen by some American analysts. See, e.g., Memorandum, Bell to Day, "Philippine Elections," November 16, 1953, 796.00/11–1653, RG 59.

[305] Telegram 1181, Manila to State, November 24, 1953, 796.00/11–2453, RG 59; National Security Council, "Notes on Planning Board Discussion of February 3, 1954," DDRS.

[306] For an assessment of Magsaysay's tenure, see David Wurfel, "Philippine Agrarian Reform under Magsaysay, Part I," *Far Eastern Survey*, 27, no. 1 (January 1958), pp. 24–5.

the government was worthy of support, undercut most of the justification for violent rebellion, and provided real incentives to the insurgents to give up the fight.[307] This latter point can be seen in the fact that the number of insurgents who surrendered to the government between 1947 and 1953 (15,866) was larger than the numbers captured (4,269) and killed (9,695) combined.

How did the United States compel the Quirino administration to adopt these measures which – in some instances – had been bitterly resisted? The dominant influence approach was the use of conditioned aid and constant pressure on the Philippine government, which is perfectly in line with the expectations of conditionality discussed in Chapter 3. Of particular importance is the fact that the United States applied conditions to both military and economic aid because, as State Department personnel recognized, tying military aid to the progress of political and economic reform provided "a far stronger lever than an economic aid program alone would have ever given us."[308] The case also suggests the utility of tranching aid, where specific blocks of assistance are attached to specific reforms. In line with the predictions of the conditionality approach, U.S. threats to withhold specific aid until a particular reform was implemented were believed to be credible by Filipino officials across the government and helped to overcome their prior expectations that American assistance would be forthcoming regardless of what they did.

With respect to the role that commitments to the client played in generating influence, this case supports the prediction that ambiguous or limited commitments are associated with greater leverage. In approaching the Philippines, the Truman administration deflected several attempts by Quirino to secure a strong endorsement from Washington for himself and his party. Moreover, the U.S. government never conflated Quirino or the Liberals, on the one hand, with the Philippine government or the country, on the other. They kept lines of communication open with opposition leaders, and when circumstances dictated it, they empowered indigenous leaders such as Ramon

---

[307] Admittedly some of these measures proved to be more symbolic than substantive; however, as Greenberg has noted, in counterinsurgency, "image building was as important as nation building." Greenberg, *The Hukbalahap Insurrection*, p. 149.

[308] Memorandum, Wanamaker to Melby, March 28, 1951, Box 1, Office of Philippine Affairs, RG 59.

Magsaysay – who shared U.S. prescriptions for strengthening the country – even at the expense of the incumbent government. In so doing, it may be argued that the United States subverted a friendly regime, but the focus of American policy was on securing its own interests – and the perceived interests of the Philippines as a whole – not those of a particular local leader.

Unlike in the subsequent case of Vietnam, where bureaucratic disagreements over the optimal approach to the client were exploited by the South Vietnamese government, the unified interagency approach adopted by American officials both on the ground in Manila and in Washington repulsed Quirino's attempts to subvert pressure for reform from one part of the U.S. government by appealing to another.[309] Quirino's attempt to circumvent Ambassador Cowen's policy of conditioning military aid on the removal of Ramos and Castañeda, for example, by appealing directly to the White House for military assistance was firmly rebuffed. Of particular note in this regard is the fact that in an effort to ensure that the JUSMAG's military efforts complemented the political and economic assistance being rendered by the State Department and other agencies in country, the JUSMAG chief directly liaised with the U.S. ambassador. From 1951, at the JUSMAG commander's request, the unit was brought under the ambassador's direct control rather than that of the regional military authority, the Commander-in-Chief, Pacific, in Hawaii.[310] This would not prove to be the case in Vietnam.

Before concluding this chapter, it is necessary to address the question of whether this episode has particular features that render it an outlier. It could argued that the unique historical relationship that the United States had with the Philippines provided it with more leverage than is normal for an American patron-client relationship. In fact, historical ties hardly inclined Filipino leaders to heed American advice. If anything, these links between the United States and the Philippines left the latter with a strong sense of entitlement. As demonstrated throughout this chapter, the dominant belief among Filipino elites was that irrespective of their compliance with American policy proposals, the United States *owed* assistance to the Philippines, both for the

---

[309] Memorandum, Merchant to Acheson, January 26, 1950, Box 1, Office of Philippine Affairs, RG 59.
[310] Memorandum, Nash to SecDef, June 16, 1952, Box 74, RG 330.

destruction wreaked on their country during World War II and for the imperatives of Cold War geostrategy. Indeed, this perception was shared by some American officials: John Melby, the State Department's director of the Office of Philippine Affairs, wrote of the Philippines, "[T]oward no other country in the world does the United States have quite the kind of commitment and moral obligation that it does here."[311] As a result, despite the unique historical relationship with this country, it still required constant pressure and the use of tough conditions on aid to generate the influence required to alter the Philippine government's counterinsurgency policies.

---

[311] John Melby, "Report of the Joint State-Defense MDAP Survey Mission for Southeast Asia," September 29, 1950, Box 12, Melby Papers. For evidence that President Truman shared this view, see Telegram 2321, Elizalde to Roxas, February 10, 1948, Series I, Box 6, Roxas Papers.

5 | The Puppet That Pulled Its Own Strings? Vietnam, 1957–1963

In sharp contrast to the preceding case study, where the U.S. assistance effort relied almost exclusively on conditionality to shape the client's behavior, in Vietnam the United States primarily employed inducement to influence the South Vietnamese government (GVN), with far less success. Throughout both the Eisenhower and Kennedy administrations, aid programs were notionally cast as exchanges of aid for reform. However, significant pressure was rarely brought to bear to push President Ngo Dinh Diem to adopt measures that Washington believed would ensure the long-term stability of his government, nor was he ever held to account for his failure to deliver on his promises. Despite the Saigon government's apparent dependence on U.S. assistance for its survival, leaders in Washington were unable to achieve the influence that they expected such dependence would engender. The fact that the United States struggled to shape the behavior of the Diem government has been well documented. What has not been previously explored in great detail, however, is the alternate influence strategies used by the United States in this case and the different outcomes they appeared to achieve. On two occasions the United States employed conditionality instead of inducement to influence the Diem government: first in negotiating the 1961 limited partnership and second in the period leading up to the 1963 coup. In both cases the United States appeared to gain greater influence over South Vietnam's policies; however, neither effort was sustained enough to have a meaningful impact.

The Republic of Vietnam

American intervention in Vietnam's wars occurred as early as May 1950, when President Truman approved an emergency grant of $10 million to support French Union forces fighting the Communist

Vietminh guerrillas. U.S. involvement began in earnest, however, following the 1954 Geneva Accords, which ended France's seven-year war against the Vietminh and temporarily divided Vietnam in two: the government of Ho Chi Minh in Hanoi administered the 15 million Vietnamese living north of the 17th parallel, while the government in Saigon oversaw the 16 million people in the south, roughly two-thirds of whom resided in the vicinity of Saigon or the Mekong Delta. The leader of the fledgling Republic of South Vietnam was its bachelor president Ngo Dinh Diem.[1] A former mandarin in the Imperial Court, as well as a devout Catholic and an ardent nationalist, Diem saw Communism as a "moral evil," as embodied by the Vietminh agents who murdered his older brother and nephew when they refused to join Ho Chi Minh's cause.[2] Embracing French philosopher Emmanuel Mounier's concept of *personalism*, he hoped to build a modern communitarian state in Vietnam that eschewed the excesses of both liberal individualism and Marxist collectivism, elevating the common good of the community above other considerations. Untainted by collaboration with either the Japanese or the French, his honesty, integrity, and incorruptibility won him much praise; however, even close family members recognized that his stubborn commitment to principle could render him rigid and inflexible when dealing with those who did not share his vision.[3] As one British official remarked, "Diem has a genius for making enemies where he need not do so."[4]

Given the widespread economic devastation in South Vietnam inflicted by the war for independence, the lack of experienced administrators following the end of French colonial rule, and the fact that the government's authority barely extended beyond Saigon, few observers

[1] Ngo is the family name of South Vietnam's first president; however, it is extremely common in both Vietnamese custom and the historiography of the conflict to refer to Vietnamese personages by their first name rather than their family name.

[2] Letter, Fredrick Nolting to Marguerite Higgins, July 7, 1965, Box 12, Fredrick Nolting Papers, Alderman Library, University of Virginia (Nolting Papers); Karnow, *Vietnam*, pp. 232–3.

[3] Telegram 19, Saigon to Foreign Office, April 15, 1957, FO 371/129704. The comments of his brother Luyen are found in Foreign Office Minutes, November 11, 1960, FO 371/152743, both in NAUK.

[4] Comment by McGhie on coversheet for Letter, Murray to Williams, 22 May 1963, FO 371/170142, NAUK.

expected Diem's tenure would be a lengthy one.[5] The South Vietnamese leader astounded his critics, however, by employing a sophisticated divide-and-conquer strategy to outmaneuver political rivals, rally a rebellious army to his side, and suppress the independent warlords who had flourished under French rule. At the same time he resettled 800,000 Catholic refugees (6.6 percent of South Vietnam's population) who had fled the Communist-dominated north and oversaw increases in agricultural production that contributed to South Vietnam's apparent rising standard of living. This astonishing series of successes in a brief period of time won the South Vietnamese president accolades in the United States, where one contemporaneous scholar proclaimed, "[H]istory may yet judge Diem as one of the great figures of twentieth century Asia."[6] In Washington, President Eisenhower called Diem the "miracle man" of Asia, while the junior senator from Massachusetts, John F. Kennedy, praised him as "the cornerstone of the Free World in Southeast Asia, the keystone to the arch, the finger in the dyke."[7] The Eisenhower administration pledged to provide South Vietnam with aid and support to assist in "developing and maintaining a strong, viable state, capable of resisting attempted subversion or aggression through military means." In return, Eisenhower informed Diem, "the Government of the United States expects that this aid will be met by performance on the part of the Government of Vietnam in undertaking needed reforms ... that will contribute effectively toward an independent Vietnam endowed with a strong government ... [that is] responsive to the nationalist aspirations of its people."[8] On this score, the Americans would be sadly disappointed.

Despite the superficial veneer of prosperity in South Vietnam, the main beneficiaries of economic growth were the country's urban middle class. In rural areas, where nearly 90 percent of the population resided, the standard of living stagnated. Both the government and economy were highly dependent on American aid: in 1958, more

---

[5] Edward Miller, *Misalliance: Ngo Dinh Diem, the United States, and the Fate of South Vietnam* (Cambridge, MA: Harvard University Press, 2013), pp. 87–95.

[6] William Henderson, "South Viet Nam Finds Itself," *Foreign Affairs*, 35, no. 2 (January 1957), p. 285.

[7] Karnow, *Vietnam*, p. 245; Kennedy, "America's Stake in Vietnam," p. 144. See also Spector, *Advice and Support*, p. 304.

[8] Letter, Eisenhower to Diem, in Marilyn Young et al., eds., *The Vietnam War: A History in Documents* (Oxford: Oxford University Press, 2003), p. 49.

than 80 percent of Saigon's military expenditures and 40 percent of its nonmilitary outlays were paid for by the United States, down from 90 percent of military expenditures the year before.[9] Although the United States provided considerable economic assistance to South Vietnam, the supermajority of this aid was diverted to security purposes by the Vietnamese government, which hindered economic development and social welfare projects.[10]

Diem's Government

Lacking experienced administrators to govern South Vietnam, Diem relied heavily on his family, who had shepherded his political fortunes during years of self-imposed exile under French rule.[11] His brother Nhu – a Sorbonne graduate – held no official position but served as Diem's chief political strategist and de facto head of the intelligence services. Another brother, Thuc, was archbishop of the former Imperial Capital of Hue, and a third, Can, was the political boss for all of central Vietnam, while various other relatives and family loyalists held positions throughout the government.[12] The state's administrative machinery was dominated by Western-educated urban elites, many of whom had served the French colonial administration.

The extensive power of the president – who directly controlled economic policy, internal security, foreign affairs, and administration – was bolstered by the "rubber stamp" national assembly, where nearly 75 percent of parliamentarians were considered staunch supporters of the government.[13] In the countryside, Diem abolished the traditional elected councils that governed the country's semi-autonomous villages for fear that they would be subverted by Communists.[14] These were replaced by government-appointed administrators – chosen for their

[9] Spector, *Advice and Support*, p. 306.
[10] Douglas C. Dacy, *Foreign Aid, War and Economic Development: South Vietnam, 1955–1975* (Cambridge: Cambridge University Press, 1986), pp. 25–9, 34–7, 206–9; Spector, *Advice and Support*, p. 307.
[11] Miller, *Misalliance*, p. 42.
[12] Samuel Myers, "Oral History Interview," February 8, 1980, U.S. Army Center for Military History, Fort McNair, Washington, DC (CMH).
[13] Bernard Fall, *The Two Viet-Nams: A Political and Military Analysis* (London: Praeger, 1963), p. 270.
[14] Rufus Phillips, "Oral History Interview I," March 4, 1982, p. 25, Lyndon B. Johnson Presidential Library (LBJ).

political loyalty rather than their ability – which severed the link between the local population and their government. When sufficient civil servants were unavailable to fill administrative posts, the army stepped in, which rapidly militarized the governance of rural areas.[15]

The Ngo family's political vehicle was the semi-secret Can Lao Party (Personalist Labor Revolutionary Party), which ironically mirrored the "state within a state" role of the Communist Party in the USSR. Can Lao membership facilitated advancement in the military and the civil service and was also a means by which the Ngos dispensed political favors and lucrative government contracts to supporters. With cells of informers at all levels of civil society, the party's more pernicious role was to stifle political dissent throughout South Vietnam. This simultaneously undercut the effectiveness of the South Vietnamese government and provoked discontent. Can Lao cadres in the civil service deferred decisions on matters of consequence to superiors because their advancement depended on political patronage. At the same time, this patronage system alienated non-Communist nationalists outside the party and deepened elite discontent with the government, which, in turn, prompted further attempts by Diem to control South Vietnam's politics, military, and economics.

Building the Army of the Republic of Vietnam

The task of assisting the development of South Vietnam's armed forces fell to the 740-man U.S. Military Assistance Advisory Group (MAAG) under the command of General Samuel "Hanging Sam" Williams, a veteran of World War II and Korea. The decision to train and develop the Army of the Republic of Vietnam (ARVN) was pushed by Secretary of State John Foster Dulles over the objections of the U.S. Joint Chiefs of Staff (JCS), who believed that the undertaking would fail without a "reasonably strong, stable, civil government in control."[16] With agencies ranging from the JCS to the CIA agreeing that subversion was the major threat facing South Vietnam, Dulles believed that Vietnam only required a 50,000-man force focused on internal security.[17] Instead, with Diem's blessing, Williams and the MAAG treated the threat of

---

[15]   Eric Bergerud, *Dynamics of Defeat: The Vietnam War in Hau Nghia Province* (Boulder, CO: Westview Press, 1993), p. 55.
[16]   Quoted in *The Pentagon Papers*, vol. 1, p. 215.
[17]   Spector, *Advice and Support*, p. 272.

a "Korean-style" cross-border invasion by North Vietnam as the primary danger to the country.[18] This necessitated a conventional army several times the size of Dulles's envisioned force. The threat posed by insurgents was discounted by the MAAG's leadership, who assumed that forces capable of maintaining external security automatically had the ability to provide for internal security.[19]

Under the MAAG's direction, the old French Colonial Army was organized into a 150,000-man force consisting of seven infantry divisions supplemented by an airborne brigade, four armor battalions, a small green-water navy, and an air force.[20] On the American model, ARVN training focused on operations by large tactical formations that employed overwhelming firepower to minimize friendly casualties.[21] Although some ARVN officers – particularly those who had experience fighting with the Vietminh against the French – found the structure and training "too constraining, too conventional and ill-suited to the war conditions in Vietnam," they acquiesced to their patron's plans in order to gain access to American largesse.[22]

Each Vietnamese division had an American colonel assigned to it as a senior advisor, with a major assigned to advise each subordinate infantry regiment. Focusing on staff work and training, MAAG advisors were not allowed to accompany their units into combat.[23] Although advisors became well acquainted with their unit's deficiencies, they were implicitly discouraged from reporting these shortcomings back to MAAG headquarters in Saigon for fear of provoking General Williams' ire.[24]

Since French nationals had previously provided both officers and technicians for the Colonial Army, Vietnamese units lacked experienced leadership and neither officers nor men exhibited significant national spirit.[25] "The Vietnamese officer," one American general

---

[18] Samuel T. Williams, "Oral History Interview I," March 2, 1981, p. 30, LBJ.
[19] *The Pentagon Papers*, vol. 2, p. 433.   [20] *Ibid.*, p. 408.
[21] Tran Ngoc Chau, "From Ho Chi Minh to Ngo Dinh Diem," in Harvey C. Neese and John O'Donnell, eds., *Prelude to Tragedy: Vietnam, 1960–1965* (Annapolis, MD: Naval Institute Press, 2001), p. 193.
[22] Cao Van Vien, *The U.S. Advisor* (Washington, DC: U.S. Army Center of Military History, 1980), p. 73; Letter, Stewart to Warner, June 11, 1960, FO 371/152778, NAUK.
[23] Spector, *Advice and Support*, pp. 286, 291.   [24] *Ibid.*, pp. 294–5.
[25] *Ibid.*, p. 281. Many senior ARVN officers had been captains or majors under the French. Williams, "Oral History I," p. 23.

assigned to the MAAG noted, "is inclined to be passive, cautious, lacking in initiative and unwilling to risk casualties to achieve results."[26] At the ARVN's highest levels, the appointment of senior officers based on their loyalty to the Ngo family brought uninspired leaders into positions of responsibility.[27] In a number of instances, American advisors offered scathing appraisals of their counterparts. One senior advisor questioned the competence, dedication, and mental health of the corps commander he worked with, while another caustically remarked that the Vietnamese Chief of Army Staff would have made "a real good sergeant."[28]

In an effort to prevent any single general from acquiring too much influence, individual officers were frequently rotated from one position to another and military commanders were given overlapping areas of responsibility which created conflicting chains of command. The commanders of the country's four corps' tactical zones should have had sole authority over units conducting operations in their areas of responsibility. However, the regional commander of a given unit's garrison, the local province chief, or even service branch superiors would issue orders to units without informing the corps commanders. At times, Diem would simply bypass the entire convoluted command structure to issue orders directly to units in the field, while politically connected subordinate commanders would bypass their superiors and contact the president directly to request instructions or support during operations.[29]

The MAAG's top-down training efforts focused on the regiment level and above, leaving the rank-and-file forces – who would be in actual contact with the enemy – largely bereft of individual and small-unit training. Consequently, the British military attaché in Saigon noted that the MAAG proudly worked to establish a Vietnamese West Point – complete with "a four year course designed to produce not merely young officers but fully educated university undergraduates" – while in the field, the ARVN

---

[26] Edward Rowny, Senior Officer Debriefing Report, September 6, 1963, p. 2, MHI.

[27] Memo, Wilson to McGarr, October 15, 1961, Box 3, Wilbur Wilson Papers, Military History Institute, Carlisle, Pennsylvania (Wilson Papers); Eugene Stein, "Oral History Interview," June 18, 1980, p. 2, CMH.

[28] III Corps commander General Dinh was the officer referred to in Memo, Wilson to Commander MACV, October 17, 1963, Box 3, Wilson Papers; John Ruggles, "Oral History Interview," February 24, 1977, p. 18, CMH.

[29] Ruggles, "Oral History," pp. 17–8, 28–9.

consisted of "a number of generally immature officers, put in charge of a number of semi-trained and none-too-well disciplined soldiers."[30]

Internal Security Forces

With the MAAG preparing the ARVN for conventional warfare, the job of providing security to the population fell to the Self-Defense Corps (SDC) and the Civil Guard (CG). The SDC were a part-time militia – approximately 50,000 strong – that defended Vietnam's 6,000 villages and hamlets.[31] Operating in their home villages, the militia's primary asset was their detailed knowledge of the local physical and political geography. The Civil Guard was a uniformed paramilitary police force responsible for maintaining order and collecting intelligence in rural areas. Mobile and better armed than the SDC, the CG was envisioned as a quick-response force in the countryside that would deal with threats beyond the capacity of the self-defense corps.

Despite their importance for internal security, the South Vietnamese government neglected the CG and SDC in favor of the army. "Poorly trained and equipped, miserably led, and incapable of coping with insurgents," these local security forces, according to American observers, could "scarcely defend themselves, much less secure the farmers."[32] Rather than protecting the population, the paramilitary forces frequently preyed on them – alienating villagers with their poor discipline.[33]

Lacking Intelligence

The MAAG did not have intelligence personnel attached to it, and it had no way of cultivating reliable information on the internal security

[30] Memorandum, Military Attaché Saigon to War Office, "Annual Appreciation on the Army of South Vietnam," January 3, 1958, FO 371/13151, NAUK; Letter, Stewart to Petersen, May 29, 1961, FO 371/160111, NAUK.
[31] Memo for the Record, January 27, 1956, *Foreign Relations of the United States 1955–1957*, vol. I, Vietnam (FRUS 1955–7), p. 611.
[32] *The Pentagon Papers*, vol. 1, p. 256. General Williams concurred, noting that they "hadn't as much training as a good Boy Scout in the United States." Samuel T. Williams, "Oral History Interview II," March 16, 1981, p. 15, LBJ.
[33] Joseph Zasloff, *Origins of the Insurgency in South Vietnam, 1954–1960* (Santa Monica, CA: RAND Corporation, 1968), p. 27.

situation in Vietnam.[34] Instructing advisors that it was their "military obligation to support the incumbent government," the American mission further compromised its political awareness by ordering personnel not to discuss politics with their Vietnamese counterparts, lest the Vietnamese confuse individual opinion for U.S. policy.[35] Without an independent intelligence network, the United States was heavily reliant on South Vietnam's fractious, poorly trained, and politicized intelligences services.[36] The country had no less than ten intelligence agencies, each operating independently and reporting directly to Diem or Nhu. The result, the Commander of U.S. Army Special Forces in Vietnam described, was "a duplication of effort, incompetence, gross security le akage, and exaggerated and false reporting for prestige purposes."[37] Rather than focusing attention on Communist insurgents, these agencies primarily monitored each other and non-Communist political dissidents.[38] As late as 1962, South Vietnam's vice president would candidly inform foreign interlocutors that "the intelligence agencies of [South Vietnam] scarcely know the enemy at all."[39] In Diem's government, an American observer noted, "[C]oordination among agencies to achieve unity of effort and effect for the common good is almost unknown: more than this, it is zealously avoided as an undesirable encroachment on individual agency prerogatives."[40]

The Rise of the Vietcong

To eliminate the Communist cadres that stayed behind in South Vietnam after the Geneva Accords, legislation was adopted in 1955 to make being a Communist or assisting one a capital offense.[41] In the

[34] Williams, "Oral History I," p. 80; and William E. Colby, "Oral History Interview I," June 2, 1981, p. 2, both LBJ.
[35] MAAG Memo, Lessons Learned 28, April 18, 1963, Center for Army Lessons Learned, Fort Leavenworth, KS (CALL).
[36] Graham Cosmas, *MACV: The Joint Command in the Years of Escalation, 1962–1967* (Washington, DC: Center for Military History, 2005), p. 52.
[37] U.S. Army Special Forces Vietnam, Debriefing of George Morton, November 6, 1963, p. 23, MHI.
[38] Letter, Stewart to Warner, April 22, 1960, FO 371/152748, NAUK.
[39] Memorandum of Conversation, Mendenhall and Tho, June 26, 1962, FRUS 1962, p. 477.
[40] Letter, Lasche to Williams, July 27, 1960, Samuel T. Williams Papers, Hoover Institution Archive, Stanford University (Williams Papers).
[41] Fall, *The Two Viet-Nams*, pp. 271–2.

field, the police and paramilitary forces proactively detained suspected Communists, while the ARVN swept through former Vietminh base areas. The effort devastated South Vietnam's Communist cadres – who lost up to 90 percent of their members by 1958 – and the internal security situation in South Vietnam improved markedly.[42] Allegations surfaced, however, that members of opposition parties and non-Communist nationalists were also caught up in the heavy-handed anti-Communist purge that saw as many as 40,000 political prisoners arrested and more than 12,000 put to death in the space of three years.[43] Moreover, American analysts noted that the government "has tended to treat the population with suspicion or coerce it and has been rewarded with an attitude of apathy or resentment."[44] This disaffection would prove to be fertile recruiting ground as the government's policy began to provoke scattered resistance in the countryside.

The Vietcong (VC) drew their strength from veterans of the war against the French as well as those alienated by the Saigon government. Local resistance was supplemented by infiltrators from the north who had been specially trained in the military and political aspects of revolutionary war.[45] Although the infiltrators were important in providing leadership and technical skills to the insurgency, intelligence estimates indicated that 80 to 90 percent of the insurgents were locally recruited.[46] The Vietcong received vital logistical assistance from North Vietnam, but their primary base of support was South Vietnam's rural villages and hamlets, particularly in the Mekong Delta region – some sections of which had never been brought under Saigon's control.

[42] Memo, Williams to Durbrow, October 9, 1957, FRUS 1955–7, p. 846; William Duiker, *The Communist Road to Power in Vietnam* (Boulder, CO: Westview Press, 1981), p. 183; Merle L. Pribbenow, *Victory in Vietnam: The Official History of the People's Army of Vietnam, 1954–1975* (Lawrence, KS: University Press of Kansas, 2002), pp. 15–16; Carlyle Thayer, "Southern Vietnamese Revolutionary Organizations," in Joseph Zasloff and MacAlister Brown, eds., *Communism in Indochina* (Lexington, MA: Lexington Books, 1975), p. 42.

[43] Gabriel Kolko, *Vietnam: Anatomy of a War, 1940–75* (New York: HarperCollins, 1986), pp. 88–9.

[44] *The Pentagon Papers*, vol. 1, p. 258.

[45] Spector, *Advice and Support*, pp. 313–15, 330.

[46] Special National Intelligence Estimate 53-2-61, "Bloc Support of the Communist Effort against the Government of Vietnam," October 5, 1961, p. 4, The Virtual Vietnam Archive, Texas Tech University (VVA).

To extend their influence throughout the countryside, the Vietcong employed a mix of persuasion and force. Political organizers would build support at the village level by vowing to address local grievances – mainly those against landlords and the local government. These political approaches were paired with the selective use of violence against government officials. On occasion, armed propaganda teams would execute corrupt or abusive officials after trying them for "crimes against the people." More frequently, however, it was particularly effective hamlet chiefs, teachers, or civil guard commanders who would be targeted for assassination because they were the strongest bastions of government authority in rural areas.[47] As the security forces proved unable to protect local administrators, these officials withdrew from direct contact with their charges in the hamlets to more secure areas, breaking the link between the peasantry and Saigon. This political vacuum was quickly filled by the Vietcong, who established shadow governments in underadministered areas.

The Vietcong's military element had a three-tiered structure. At the lowest level, lightly armed and largely untrained hamlet militia provided local defense as well as logistical support to the full-time fighters. One step up from the militias were the combat guerrillas, who operated at the squad or platoon level and undertook small-scale attacks beyond the immediate confines of their home village.[48] At the highest level were the VC's mobile main forces, which were eventually organized into units as large as regiments and carried modern weapons and equipment. Unlike the combat guerrillas, who primarily remained within their home province, the main forces eventually operated across the breadth of the country and would prove capable of directly engaging ARVN units.[49] By 1960, the Vietcong was estimated to have between 10,000 and 15,000 fighters in its ranks.[50]

---

[47] Jeffrey Race, *War Comes to Long An* (Berkeley: University of California Press, 1972), p. 83.

[48] George Tanham, *Communist Revolutionary Warfare: From the Vietminh to the Viet Cong* (New York: Praeger, 1967), pp. 138–9.

[49] *Ibid.*, pp. 140–1.

[50] "Basic Counterinsurgency Plan for Viet-Nam," January 4, 1961, FRUS 1961, p. 7; National Security Action Memorandum 12, February 6, 1961, FRUS 1961, p. 29.

The American Approach to Vietnam: Hands Off in Washington, Confusion in Saigon

Believing that Diem's early successes had left his government in a strong position, the Eisenhower administration let Vietnam drift from its attention during the second half of the 1950s, distracted by a host of international events ranging from the Hungarian Uprising to the Cuban Revolution. Washington's persistent disengagement meant that the country team played a critical role in managing the U.S. support effort. In addition to the State Department and the MAAG, the U.S. mission in Vietnam included elements of the CIA, the U.S. Information Agency, and the International Cooperation Administration (ICA).

Although the ambassador notionally directed the actions of all U.S. agencies in the country, in practice, individual agencies carried out their own programs with little coordination or central guidance. This was particularly true in the case of the MAAG, where General Williams reported directly to the Commander-in-Chief, Pacific, in Hawaii rather than to the ambassador.[51] Having won Diem's trust, Williams would regularly meet with him to discuss defense- or security-related matters without anyone from the State Department present.

In May 1957, Elbridge Durbrow – a career Foreign Service officer and ardent anti-Communist – was appointed ambassador to Vietnam. Arriving in Saigon, he quickly came to believe that Washington's rosy view of events was far from accurate. In a report that harshly critiqued Diem's government, Durbrow cataloged a laundry list of weaknesses, including a failure to delegate authority, a focus on security to the exclusion of economic development, and the infiltration of the Can Lao Party into all aspects of the country's political and social life.[52] Moreover, it was noted that Diem had a marked preference for responding to subversion by attempting to eradicate dissent – despite the clearly "diminishing or even negative returns" of repression – rather than attempting to eliminate the underlying causes of dissatisfaction.[53]

---

[51] Colby, "Oral History Interview I," pp. 10–11.

[52] Spector, *Advice and Support*, p. 305. For similar concerns expressed by the CIA, both in Saigon and in Washington, see Thomas L. Ahern, Jr., *CIA and the House of NGO: Covert Action in South Vietnam, 1954–1963* (Washington, DC: Center for the Study of Intelligence, 2000), p. 115. These worries were also echoed by the French. Letter, Paris to Foreign Office, January 11, 1958, FO 371/136116, NAUK.

[53] Telegram 18, Hue to State, March 19, 1958, 751G.00/3–1958, RG 59.

Notwithstanding strong urging by the embassy, Diem had failed to undertake reforms to ameliorate discontent that were easily within his grasp, leading Durbrow to argue that it was necessary to impose conditions on American aid to refocus Diem's attention away from a military-only response to the ongoing Communist subversion.[54] The ambassador also pushed for a reorientation of the ARVN toward counterinsurgency operations and questioned whether or not the force was too heavily equipped and road bound to be of use in fighting guerrillas.[55]

In a pattern that would play out frequently over the course of the U.S. involvement in Vietnam, the CIA station chief and the local head of the ICA concurred with Durbrow's assessment, while General Williams strongly disagreed with both Durbrow's report and his views on using aid to leverage policy changes. Rather than focus on the government's failings – which, he believed, would play into the hands of the Communists – the general argued that America should seek to build Diem's confidence.[56] Contrary to Durbrow, Williams believed that the ARVN was giving too much time to counterinsurgency operations to the detriment of "fundamental, sound, advanced individual and basic unit training."[57] The lack of consensus between the civilian and military elements of the country team as to the best way to respond to the insurgency would have an acute impact on the efficacy of U.S. assistance to South Vietnam. Moreover, the increasingly hostile relationship that developed between Durbrow and Williams soon spread to other U.S. civilian and military personnel in the country.

In Washington, Eisenhower administration officials acknowledged the ambassador's arguments but generally shared Williams' view that restoring internal security was a necessary precursor to undertaking political or economic reform.[58] Instead of criticizing his approach, the

[54] Telegram 191, Saigon to State, December 5, 1957, FRUS 1955–7, pp. 869–84.
[55] Letter, Durbrow to Parsons, April 19, 1960, FRUS 1958–60, pp. 396–400. For a similar view from British military sources, see Despatch 37, Saigon to Foreign Office, April 28, 1958, FO 371/136117.
[56] Letter, Williams to Lansdale, August 30, 1961, Box 42 Edward Lansdale Papers, Hoover Institution Archive, Stanford University (Lansdale Papers).
[57] Letter, Williams to Stump, November 16, 1957, FRUS 1955–7, pp. 862–3; Memorandum, Williams to Durbrow, June 1, 1960, FRUS 1958–60, pp. 475–9.
[58] Assistant Secretary of State for Far Eastern Affairs Walter Robertson asserted that "no lasting economic development is possible without security against aggression," in Memorandum of Conversation, Vu Van Mau, Tran Van Chuong et al., November 17–18, 1958, FRUS 1958–60, p. 101.

message that was delivered to Diem from the various congressmen, senators, and senior military officers who visited Vietnam was one of unconditional support. In Williams' words, the South Vietnamese leader was repeatedly told: "Mr. President, you're doing exactly right. We're behind you 100 per cent. You keep on pitching, and we're going to back you up to the hilt."[59] Despite the lack of encouragement from his superiors, Durbrow continued to express concern about Diem's single-minded focus on security to the detriment of establishing a solid political base of support, which required broad-based economic growth and tangible improvements in the rural quality of life.[60] As the insurgency gained momentum, Durbrow pressed the South Vietnamese government to reach out to non-Communist opposition groups and enhance the country's economic self-sufficiency. The vast quantities of aid that the United States bestowed on Diem, however, did little to incline him to heed that advice.[61] Moreover, the perception that defending South Vietnam was the West's top priority encouraged Vietnamese officials to ignore their patron's concerns.[62]

Durbrow Pushes to Condition U.S. Aid and Is Rebuffed

While American policy drifted, the situation in Vietnam deteriorated. By 1959, Diem had declared that the entire Mekong Delta was in a state of siege.[63] Insurgent attacks were averaging more than 100 per month, and the CIA was reporting that they had achieved "virtual control over whole villages and districts" in certain provinces.[64]

Ambassador Durbrow believed that the ability of the Vietcong to operate largely unhindered demonstrated the South Vietnamese

[59] Williams, "Oral History II," p. 61.

[60] Telegram 4, Saigon to State, July 1, 1957, FRUS 1955–7, p. 825; Letter, Williams to Riley, April 14, 1959, FRUS 1958–60, p. 182; Dispatch 115, Saigon to State, October 8, 1957, 751G.00/10–857 and Dispatch 452, Saigon to State, June 13, 1958, 751G.00/6–1358, both RG 59.

[61] Telegram 263, Saigon to State, August 13, 1958, FRUS 1958–60 pp. 74–5.

[62] For British judgments to this effect, see Telegram 56, Saigon to Foreign Office, June 23, 1958, FO 371/136125, NAUK.

[63] USARPAC Intel Bulletin, October–November 1959, quoted in Spector, *Advice and Support*, p. 332.

[64] CIA Currently Weekly Intel Summary, April 9, 1959 quoted in *Ibid.*, p. 332.

population's "growing disillusionment" with the government. At the same time, the concentration of decision making in Diem's inner circle was paralyzing the government's ability to respond to the insurgency.[65] British sources reported that even Diem's closest advisors were growing "restive and embittered" at his refusal to delegate authority, while loyal Diem supporters were increasingly critical of the Can Lao and the role of the extended Ngo family in government.[66] To counteract these developments, Durbrow urged Diem to rally popular support by curtailing the Can Lao's operations, sending his intensely unpopular brother Nhu abroad, devolving authority to the national assembly, and controlling the actions of rural officials whose arbitrary manner was antagonizing their charges.[67] Diem acknowledged the failings of some of his administrators but declined to act against Nhu or the Can Lao, arguing that allegations of malfeasance were part of an "organized campaign of calumny" by opposition groups and Communists.[68] Moreover, the South Vietnamese leader continued to insist that the increasing insurgent violence was a sign of desperation rather than strength, the last gasp of a rebellion being defeated by the government's countersubversion efforts.[69]

When Diem requested supplemental military aid to respond to the increased Vietcong threat, Durbrow cabled Washington for permission to put "teeth" into his persuasion by attaching conditions in order to spur the South Vietnamese government into action. These requirements included both reforms essential to ameliorate popular grievances, as well as measures that would enhance counterinsurgency prowess such as establishing an effective central intelligence agency and rationalizing

[65]   Telegram 267, Saigon to State, March 2, 1960, FRUS 1958–60, pp. 294–9; Telegram 278, Saigon to State, March 7, 1960, FRUS 1958–60, pp. 301–2.

[66]   Telegram 22E, Saigon to Foreign Office, February 18, 1958, FO 371/136137, and Dispatch 27, Saigon to Foreign Office, June 24, 1960, FO 371/152740, both NAUK.

[67]   Elbridge Durbrow, "Undiplomatic History: The Stealthful Soviet Saga," Box 40, Elbridge Durbrow Papers, Hoover Institution Archive, Stanford University (Durbrow Papers), p. 176; Telegram 279, Saigon to State, March 2, 1959, FRUS 1958–60, pp. 144–70; Telegram 2622, Saigon to State, March 10, 1960, FRUS 1958–60, p. 326.

[68]   "Special Report on the Internal Security Situation in Vietnam," March 7, 1960, FRUS 1958–60, p. 316; Telegram 2622, FRUS 1958–60, pp. 325–8; Telegram 2884, Saigon to State, April 7, 1960, FRUS 1958–60, pp. 375–9.

[69]   Telegram 251, Saigon to State, February 16, 1960, FRUS 1958–60, p. 285; Ahern, *CIA and the House of NGO*, p. 133.

the military chain of command.[70] The last of these items was identified by the MAAG as the "most essential single provision" to increase the effectiveness of the military portion of the counterinsurgency campaign.[71] Conditioning military aid in particular was necessary, Durbrow judged, because "Diem could not care less if we cut off some economic development aid." Although admittedly a drastic step in light of the deteriorating security situation, unless the United States was "prepared to stick by our guns and refuse to give extra help at this time," the American ambassador counseled, "Diem will not come to his senses."[72] Given the president's "unrealistically optimistic and stubborn" beliefs that his government was winning against the insurgents, several senior South Vietnamese officials – including the country's vice president – concurred that American pressure was necessary to convince Diem to ameliorate some of the discontent in Vietnam rather than focusing exclusively on military measures to combat the insurgency.[73]

Durbrow's desire to pressure Diem into addressing political and economic grievances aggravated the institutional split within the American mission over how to deal with the South Vietnamese government.[74] General Williams argued that South Vietnam's problems were caused largely by a "hard core of Viet Cong agents left in the south ... augmented ... by new blood shipped in from the north" rather than social or economic conditions in Vietnamese society.[75] The Vietcong, he insisted, had little popular appeal and were gaining the assistance of the rural peasantry through violence and intimidation.[76] Instead of political-economic action, the MAAG chief argued that the key to success was enhancing the efficiency of the security forces through "centralized direction, coordination and motivation."[77] Williams'

---

[70] Telegram 3095, Saigon to State, May 3, 1960, FRUS 1958–60, pp. 434–6.

[71] Lionel McGarr, "First Twelve Month Report of Chief MAAG, Vietnam," September 1, 1961, Box 49, Lansdale Papers, p. 10.

[72] Telegram 3095.

[73] Memorandum of Conversation, Ladejinsky and Durbrow, April 24, 1959, FRUS 1958–60, pp. 188–90; Telegram 3152, Saigon to State, May 9, 1960, FRUS 1958–60, pp. 450–1; Letter, Durbrow to Anderson, July 18, 1960, FRUS 1958–60, pp. 514–15.

[74] In contrast, Durbrow had little trouble coordinating his approach to Diem with his British and French colleagues. Telegram 129, Saigon to Foreign Office, May 7, 1960, FO 371/152739, NAUK.

[75] Spector, *Advice and Support*, p. 335.

[76] Williams, "Oral History II," pp. 13–14.

[77] Spector, *Advice and Support*, p. 335.

superiors in Pacific Command, the Joint Chiefs of Staff, and the Office of the Secretary of Defense – where Edward Lansdale was monitoring events in Vietnam – opposed using military aid to pressure a friendly government fighting for its survival.[78] Instead of "demanding compliance" with Durbrow's "ill-conceived political innovations" by threatening to with-hold aid, defense officials such as Lansdale argued that more could be accomplished through friendly persuasion.[79] Securing a stronger base of support for Diem's government might be a worthwhile objective, but not at the risk of upsetting relations with Saigon or harming the war effort.

The deadlock over how to deal with Saigon had reached such an impasse that in early May 1960 Vietnam was discussed at the National Security Council for the first time in years. The deputy director of the CIA expressed apprehension about Diem's growing political isolation from the Vietnamese people, as well as the increasing criticism "at all levels of government" that his rule "had fostered corruption, condoned maladministration, and permitted dictatorial practices," which were driving support for the insurgents.[80] The security situation in the coun-tryside, he contended, appeared "similar to that which characterized the last days of the French regime." Although President Eisenhower acknowledged that Diem appeared "blind to the situation," Durbrow's proposal to condition military aid on political reform was rejected and replaced by watered-down threats to suspend some relatively inconse-quential economic aid as a signal of American concern.[81] Without the ability to link aid – particularly military assistance – to specific reforms, American leverage on these critical matters would prove to be limited.[82]

The Situation Worsens

Throughout the summer of 1960, the Vietcong intensified their activ-ity. Operating in units of up to several hundred fighters, they disrupted

[78] Memorandum, Lansdale to Douglas, February 12, 1960, FRUS 1958–60, pp. 280; Memorandum, May 4, 1960, FRUS 1958–60, pp. 439–41.
[79] Memorandum, Lansdale to Douglas, FRUS 1958–60, p. 280.
[80] Memorandum of Discussion at the 444th Meeting of the National Security Council, May 9, 1960, FRUS 1958–60, p. 446.
[81] *Ibid.*; Telegram 2037, State to Saigon, May 9, 1960, FRUS 1958–60, pp. 448–9.
[82] Letter, Durbrow to Anderson, July 18, 1960, FRUS 1958–60, p. 515. Retrospectively, British officials would identify the lack of pressure to ensure follow-through here as a key failing in the American intervention. Letter, Stewart to Warner, July 3, 1961, FO 371/160113, NAUK.

economic activity, attacked defended villages, and inflicted twice as many casualties on government forces in just six months than they had in the previous two years.[83] Nearly 2,100 government officials were assassinated in 1960, a threefold increase from 1958.[84] A CIA assessment released in August reported "indications of increasing dissatisfaction with the Diem government" in rural areas, while urban elites were growing alienated by "Ngo family rule ... and the growing evidence of corruption in high places." Unless these trends were reversed, the CIA predicted that "they will almost certainly in time cause the collapse of Diem's regime."[85] The following month, the government of North Vietnam gave formal approval to an intensified effort to "liberate" South Vietnam.[86]

Deeply concerned by these developments, Durbrow urged Diem to include several senior members of the non-Communist opposition in his government, as well as devolve authority to his cabinet and allow election of village officials. [87] He also advised that Nhu be sent abroad on a diplomatic assignment. As Durbrow forcibly contended to his superiors in Washington, "[O]ur main problem is not to pamper Diem by giving him more security forces with which to beat people into line but to ... bring all other pressures on him to take essential steps which will win over the population by other methods than sheer force."[88]

Durbrow's attempts to pressure Diem were undercut by General Williams, who assured the South Vietnamese president that the U.S. government would assist him regardless of his commitment to economic and political reform.[89] In Washington, Lansdale advised

---

[83] Telegram 495, Saigon to State, August 30, 1960, FRUS 1958–60, pp. 544–7; Spector, *Advice and Support*, pp. 305, 337–48.

[84] George C. Herring, *America's Longest War: The United States and Vietnam, 1950–1975* (Philadelphia: Temple University Press, 1986), p. 68.

[85] Special National Intelligence Estimate, "Short-Term Trends in South Vietnam," August 23, 1960, FRUS 1958–60, pp. 536–41.

[86] George McTurnan Kahin, *Intervention: How America Became Involved in Vietnam* (New York: Knopf, 1986), pp. 114–15.

[87] Telegram 624, Saigon to State, September 16, 1960, FRUS 1958–60, pp. 578–9; Editorial Note, FRUS 1958–60, pp. 585–6; Telegram 157, Saigon to State, October 15, 1960, FRUS 1958–60, pp. 598–602; Durbrow, "Undiplomatic History," p. 176. The Australian, British, and French ambassadors in Saigon were also raising these issues. Letter, Hohler to MacDermott, October 8, 1960, FO 371/152739, NAUK.

[88] Letter, Durbrow to Parsons, September 6, 1960, FRUS 1958–60, p. 566.

[89] Kathryn Statler, *Replacing France: The Origins of American Intervention in Vietnam* (Lexington: University Press of Kentucky, 2007), p. 256.

senior defense officials to oppose Durbrow's approach, arguing that the ambassador needed to convince Diem that he was "acting in good faith" by delivering "something which Diem has long desired" *before* pressing the South Vietnamese leader for policy changes.[90]

Apropos of this recommendation, Diem was informed that the United States would extend military assistance to the paramilitary CG, a move Diem had long requested and Durbrow had long opposed. This increased commitment was made, as defense officials pushing the inducement approach urged, without linkage to the political and social reforms Durbrow was attempting to encourage.[91] Eisenhower paired the expanded assistance program with a public reiteration of support when he sent the South Vietnamese president a letter on the country's fifth anniversary praising his "courage and daring" in resisting Communist imperialism and promising "for so long as our strength can be useful, the United States will continue to assist Vietnam in the difficult yet hopeful struggle ahead."[92]

The increased American aid and the public pledge of support had the counterproductive effect of reducing American leverage over Saigon. As General Williams would later admit, "I'm afraid that [Diem] got an idea that 'I can go as far as I want to because the United States is going to back me up.'"[93] South Vietnam's perceived importance to arresting Communist expansion in Southeast Asia led its government to believe it could simply ignore American demands for reform.[94]

In response to Durbrow's pressure, Diem announced several initiatives, including a partial cabinet reshuffle and a partial devolution of authority over economic policy and counterinsurgency operations.[95] In time, these measures proved to be merely cosmetic changes intended to placate the American observers and disgruntled Vietnamese. The embassy reported that Diem was increasingly aware of his deteriorating political position, but he still refused to broaden his government by including opposition members, curb the Can Lao, or

[90]   Letter, Durbrow to Parsons, July 27, 1960, FRUS 1958–60, p. 525; Memorandum, Lansdale to O'Donnell, FRUS 1958–60, p. 580.
[91]   Telegram 802, Saigon to State, October 15, 1960, FRUS 1958–60, pp. 595–6; Telegram 805, Saigon to State, October 15, 1960, FRUS 1958–60, p. 597.
[92]   Memorandum, Herter to Eisenhower, October 20, 1960, FRUS 1958–60, pp. 609–11.
[93]   Williams, "Oral History II," p. 61.   [94]   Karnow, *Vietnam*, p. 251.
[95]   Telegram 866, Saigon to State, October 20, 1960, FRUS 1958–60, pp. 606–7; Airgram G-196, Saigon to State, November 3, 1960, FRUS 1958–60, p. 623.

reduce Nhu's stature—casting doubt on the notion that building Diem's confidence and giving him what he wanted were the best way to bring about a change in the government of Vietnam's policies.[96]

The Paratrooper Revolt

The depth of discontent within the military was exposed on the morning of November 11, 1960, when three battalions of the army's elite paratroopers mutinied against Diem. Surrounding Independence Palace in Saigon, the rebels made it clear that their goal was to reform the government so that it could more effectively combat the Communist insurgency. This necessitated the removal of Diem, they claimed, "because he is so unpopular that no effective leadership against the Viet Cong is possible while he is in office."[97] Pretending to negotiate with the rebels, and even accede to their demands, the South Vietnamese president stalled for time while loyalist units rallied to his side.[98]

Although quickly suppressed, the U.S Secretary of State believed that the revolt demonstrated "a serious lack of support" within the military and other sectors of Vietnamese society for many aspects of Diem's policies.[99] Indeed, many of the issues brought up by the mutineers, such as ending corruption and embracing non-Communist nationalists, were similar to those that the U.S. embassy and civilian critics had been raising.[100] Durbrow advised Eisenhower not to send the South Vietnamese president a letter congratulating him for having survived the uprising as it "might detract from the stern attitude we may soon have to take towards Diem."[101] The Commander of the MAAG drew the opposite conclusion, reporting to the Pentagon that "Diem has emerged from this severe test in a position of greater strength with

---

[96] Telegram 802, FRUS 1958–60, p. 596; Airgram G-196, Saigon to State, November 3, 1960, 751K.11/11–360, RG 59.

[97] Telegram 1035, Saigon to State, November 12, 1960, FRUS 1958–60, pp. 642–3; Telegram MAGTN-PO 1434, MAAG to CINPAC, November 12,1960, FRUS 1958–60, p. 648.

[98] Miller, *Misalliance*, pp. 203–4.

[99] Telegram 782, State to Saigon, November 12, 1960, FRUS 1958–60, pp. 654–5.

[100] Telegram MAGTN-PO 1434, FRUS 1958–60, p. 647; Dispatch 59, Saigon to Foreign Office, November 19, 1960, FO 371/152744, NAUK.

[101] Telegram 1103, State to Saigon, November 18, 1960, FRUS 1958–60, pp. 682–3.

visible proof of sincere support behind him in both the armed forces and the civilian population."[102] As a result, officials in the U.S. Department of Defense argued it was now more important than ever that Diem be "convinced of the sincerity of the U.S. government and that he has its full support."[103] Agreeing with Durbrow, the State Department withheld a public affirmation to avoid furthering Diem's belief that U.S. support was "absolute," which would "weaken our own pressures for government reform and liberalization."[104]

Unduly suspicious of an American hand behind the uprising and recognizing the less than absolute commitment the Eisenhower administration had signaled in its aftermath, the Ngos attempted to gain reverse leverage over their patron to resist pressure for liberalization measures that they believed only invited more trouble.[105] Viewing the French as a possible counterweight to pressure from the United States, Nhu urged his brother "to work more closely with the French since he could not trust the Americans."[106] At the same time, government-linked organizations attempted to stoke popular resentment against the United States by accusing American "colonialists and imperialists" of inspiring the paratroopers' revolt.[107] The embassy surmised that this was part of Nhu's effort to "prevent us from bringing further pressures on Diem to make drastic political changes."[108]

Rather than interpreting the paratrooper revolt as a sign that a change of course was required, Diem and Nhu saw the outcome as a validation of the divide-and-rule tactics they had used to consolidate power in the early years of the republic.[109] The government arrested a number of prominent opposition politicians and Diem became more resistant than ever to proposals that would enhance the effectiveness of

[102] Telegram SGN 236, MAAG to Lansdale, November 13, 1960, FRUS 1958–60, p. 660.
[103] Memorandum, French to Erskine December 6, 1960, FRUS 1958–60, p. 717. See also Memorandum, Lansdale to Gates, November 12, 1960, FRUS 1958–60, pp. 653–4.
[104] Memo, Wood to Anderson, December 2, 1960, FRUS 1958–60, pp. 705–7.
[105] Elbridge Durbrow, "Oral History Interview I," June 3, 1981, pp. 43–4, LBJ.
[106] Nhu quoted in Statler, *Replacing France*, p. 244.
[107] Telegram 1093, Saigon to State, November 17, 1960, 751K.00/11–1760, RG 59.
[108] Telegram 1096, Saigon to State, November 17, 1960, FRUS 1958–60, p. 672; Memorandum of Conversation, Parsons, Chuong et al., November 18, 1960, FRUS 1958–60, pp. 679–81.
[109] Miller, *Misalliance*, p. 211.

the military at the cost of lessening his direct control over the armed forces, such as promoting officers based on merit rather than political reliability.[110] Embassy officials were soon inundated with disaffected South Vietnamese military officers, opposition politicians, and other urban elites who warned that, absent a concerted effort to liberalize, the government would likely fall to the Communists or an internal coup. Given the perceived gravity of the situation, many of the informants expressed surprise that the United States was not leveraging its massive aid program to compel Diem to act.[111] As the British ambassador noted, "[T]he Americans are criticized not for intervening too much, but too little."[112]

In the waning days of the Eisenhower administration, Durbrow proposed a final attempt to press for liberalization. Saigon had requested enhanced military aid to expand the ARVN by 20,000 men, a move Diem was "desperate" to undertake.[113] To facilitate approval of the request, Vietnamese officials assured the embassy that pending action on press freedom, devolution of power to the National Assembly, and a rural civic action program would be forthcoming.[114] However, Durbrow's proposal to use the additional military aid as a "bargaining counter" to ensure that the South Vietnamese government followed through on these pledges was overruled by the Secretary of State, who was concerned by the continuing crisis in South Vietnam.[115] Without conditionality linking aid to reform, Durbrow quickly found Diem "dragging his feet" on the promised reforms and once again stressing a military response to the

---

[110] Dennis Duncanson, *Government and Revolution in Vietnam* (London: Oxford University Press, 1968), p. 268; Spector, *Advice and Support*, pp. 370–1.

[111] Telegram 1151, Saigon to State, December 4, 1960, 751K.00/12–460; Dispatch 261, Saigon to State, December 23, 1960, 751K.00/12–2360, RG 59; Annex A, "The Situation in Vietnam," attached to Memorandum, French to Erskine, December 6, 1960, FRUS 1958–60, pp. 715–6.

[112] Dispatch 64, Saigon to Foreign Office, December 12, 1960, FO 371/152744, NAUK.

[113] Letter, Lansdale to Secretary of Defense, January 14, 1961, Box 49, Lansdale Papers.

[114] Telegram 1119, Saigon to State, November 23, 1960, FRUS 1958–60, pp. 686–91.

[115] Telegram 862, Saigon to State, December 9, 1960, FRUS 1958–60, pp. 720–1. The Commander-in-Chief Pacific also saw the force increase as potential "bargaining material" with Diem. Naval Message 6555, CINPAC to CHMAAG Vietnam, October 29, 1960, Box 49, Lansdale Papers.

insurgency.[116] The American ambassador continued to advise that pressuring Saigon for social, economic, and political reforms was the best way to react to the Vietcong, but time had run out. Believing that "future exhortation [would] likely be counterproductive," the Secretary of State instructed Durbrow to back off.[117] Vietnam would be a problem left to the Kennedy administration.

PART II THE ORIGINS OF THE KENNEDY COMMITMENT, 1961

In the weeks before Kennedy took office, Edward Lansdale traveled to Vietnam to provide an assessment of the situation for the Department of Defense.[118] Finding relations between Durbrow and Diem strained by the former's continued push for reform and confidence in the MAAG shaken by their apparent preparation of the ARVN for the wrong war, Lansdale's report criticized the U.S. mission in Saigon for failing to visibly support the South Vietnamese president. He judged that the precariousness of the situation made it impossible for Diem to undertake the types of reforms that Durbrow proposed and argued that if there was any hope of making South Vietnam an anti-Communist bulwark, it was necessary to regain the Ngos' trust. Rather than imposing conditions on military and economic assistance, Lansdale advised that America should unconditionally "aid and abet" South Vietnam as China and the USSR were doing for North Vietnam.[119] As a symbol of that approach, Lansdale suggested that President Kennedy should issue a strong public statement of support for Diem.[120] Such an undertaking would be welcomed in

[116] Telegram 1176, Saigon to State, December 15, 1960, 751K.00/12–1560, RG 59.

[117] Telegram 961, State to Saigon, December 31, 1960, FRUS 1958–60, pp. 751–2.

[118] Navy Message, Felt to Lansdale, December 10, 1960, Box 49, Lansdale Papers. For a discussion of Lansdale's role in the early days of the Kennedy administration, see Lawrence Freedman, *Kennedy's Wars: Berlin, Cuba, Laos, and Vietnam* (Oxford: Oxford University Press, 2000), pp. 287–8.

[119] Memorandum, Lansdale to Secretary of Defense, January 17, 1961, 751K.00/1–1961, RG 59; Meeting Notes, Rusk and Parsons, January 28, 1961, FRUS 1961, pp. 19–20. On the state of U.S.-Vietnamese relations, see Letter, Hohler to Warner, June 24, 1960, FO 371/152753 and Letter, Stewart to Peck, December 23, 1960, FO 371/152777, both NAUK.

[120] Navy Message, Lansdale to Durbrow, January 17, 1961, Box 49, Lansdale Papers.

Saigon, where the Diem government hoped to reset relations with the United States and its young president.[121]

In sharp contrast to Lansdale's recommendations, Durbrow continued to argue that a strong pledge of support for Diem personally "might further convince him that we have no alternative but to support him no matter what he does." [122] This, in turn, would reduce the South Vietnamese leader's incentives to adopt the reforms his regime required. Conditions on aid, the ambassador insisted, were the only way to engender a meaningful policy change.

These two viewpoints collided in the "Basic Counterinsurgency Plan for Vietnam." By the South Vietnamese government's own estimates, more than half the population was outside its effective control.[123] Believing that "the principal task facing the GVN is restoration of individual security," the MAAG had drafted a plan of action for Saigon, including a series of organizational and administrative reforms that would increase the effectiveness of the South Vietnamese government's counterinsurgency operations. In response for implementing these measures, the United States would provide South Vietnam with an additional $41.1 million in military aid to fund the 20,000-man expansion of the army that Diem had requested, as well as the training of the Civil Guard.[124] Although this would increase annual American defense payments to $267 million – firmly establishing Saigon as the second-largest recipient of U.S. aid in the world – in adopting the plan as the foundation for his administration's approach to South Vietnam, Kennedy's primary query for his staff was "Why so little?"[125]

Per Durbrow's advice, the aid from the Counterinsurgency Plan would not be released until the Vietnamese government implemented a number of specific administrative measures to reduce Diem's arbitrary interference in counterinsurgency operations, such as streamlining

---

[121] Miller, *Misalliance*, p. 213.
[122] Telegram 1329, Saigon to State, February 1, 1961, FRUS 1961.
[123] Miller, *Misalliance*, p. 222.
[124] "Basic Counterinsurgency Plan for Vietnam," FRUS 1961, pp. 1–12;
       Memorandum, Kennedy to Rusk and McNamara, January 30, 1961, Box 193,
       NSF:VN, JFK; Letter, Elbridge Durbrow to Fredrick Nolting, February 21,
       1961, Box 12, Nolting Papers; William Gibbons, *The U.S. Government and the
       Vietnam War*, vol. 2 (Princeton, NJ: Princeton University Press, 1986),
       pp. 13–14.
[125] Memorandum, Rostow to Bundy, January 30, 1961, FRUS 1961, p. 16;
       Durbrow, "Oral History I," p. 30.

national security planning and centralizing intelligence collection.[126] The plan also identified specific actions to rally popular support, such as reducing Can Lao corruption, engaging opposition leaders, decreasing Nhu's influence, devolving power to the National Assembly, and expanding civil liberties.[127] While the Kennedy administration viewed the plan as a new initiative to defeat the insurgency, in reality, Durbrow had been trying unsuccessfully for years to get Saigon to adopt many of the recommended measures.

Secretary of State Dean Rusk was sympathetic to Durbrow's "unpalatable task" of pressing Diem to reform while simultaneously assuring him of American support.[128] Although the Counterinsurgency Plan primarily responded to the proximate military concerns, it was recognized that ultimate success required Diem to gain active support from the citizens of South Vietnam.[129] Rusk instructed the ambassador to inform the South Vietnamese government that the increased military aid was only being offered for 1961, with future support influenced by developments in both the political and the security situation. Durbrow was also directed to provide Washington with a strategy for achieving Diem's cooperation should he be recalcitrant, including the suspension of future U.S. aid.[130]

The American proposal was met with the announcement of a series of reforms: the government would be restructured to promote transparency and efficiency; new departments would be created to improve rural administration; and provincial and village councils would be established to decentralize some authority and increase participation in government at the local level.[131] In practice, however, the reorganization was largely administrative, barely implemented, and fell short of the bold measures that Durbrow believed were necessary to seize the

---

[126] "Basic Counterinsurgency Plan," FRUS 1961, pp. 3, 13; Mark Moyar, *Triumph Forsaken: The Vietnam War, 1954–1965* (New York: Cambridge University Press, 2006), pp. 440, n. 410.

[127] "Basic Counterinsurgency Plan," FRUS 1961, p. 8; details on the political proposals are contained in FRUS 1958–60, pp. 575–9, 707–11, 739–41.

[128] Meeting Record, Kennedy, Johnson, Rusk et al., January 28, 1961, FRUS 1961, p. 15.

[129] Privately, Durbrow believed "it will take a lot of doing and a long time to really put the Commies on the full defensive." Letter, Durbrow to Nolting.

[130] Telegram 1054, State to Saigon, February 3, 1961, 751K.00/2–361, RG 59.

[131] Airpouch G-309, Saigon to State, January 30, 1961, 751K.00/1–3061, RG 59.

initiative from the insurgents.[132] Instead of devolving authority, "the main effect," as one historian has noted, was "to concentrate power further in the hands of the regime's shrinking inner circle."[133]

Throughout the spring, Diem resisted pressure to agree to all of the provisions of the Counterinsurgency Plan – particularly those involving political reform. Durbrow informed Washington that "there are strong indications that [the] GVN will continue to delay necessary actions unless highly pressured to act promptly and decisively."[134] Although Diem willingly implemented the minor organizational changes that would improve the efficiency of his government, he opposed the measures that would require him to actually decentralize decision making. No new powers were given to the National Assembly, opposition politicians were not brought into the cabinet, the provincial councils were not created, the Can Lao Party was not reformed, and military commanders in the field were not given operational control over counterinsurgency missions.[135]

The Kennedy administration was increasingly concerned by the lack of progress in Saigon, while the intelligence community warned that failure to address the issues that had provoked the paratrooper revolt made another coup attempt likely.[136] On the battlefield, the ARVN conducted large-scale sweeps on the basis of deficient intelligence with little result, while the SDC and CG focused more on protecting themselves than defending their villages or confronting the Vietcong. Kennedy believed that Vietnam required "rapid and energetic action," but he decided to wait until after Diem had contested the April 1961 presidential election to attempt to induce him to act.[137]

A New Ambassador and a New Approach

With the machinery of government at his disposal and no organized political opposition to speak of, Diem easily defeated what the CIA

---

[132] Telegram 1351, Saigon to State, February 8, 1961, FRUS 1961, pp. 29–30.
[133] Miller, *Misalliance*, p. 223.
[134] Telegram 1444, Saigon to State, March 5, 1961, 751K.5-MSP/3–561, RG 59.
[135] Memorandum, Bundy to Battle, March 14, 1961, Box 193, NSF:VN, JFK; Telegram 1606, Saigon to State, April 15, 1961, 751K.5-MSP/4–1561, RG 59.
[136] National Intelligence Estimate, "Outlook in Mainland Southeast Asia," March 28, 1961, FRUS 1961, p. 59.
[137] Memorandum, Rostow to Kennedy, March 29, 1961, Box 193, NSF:VN, JFK; Memorandum, Bundy to Battle, March 14, 1961.

described as "two little known and poorly qualified candidates" in early April to win a second five-year term.[138] American analysts judged that although the "outcome was never in doubt," Diem had won 89 percent of the vote "without resorting to any blatant manipulation or corruption."[139] With voter turnout reaching 90 percent, the *New York Times* suggested the election was a "resounding defeat" for Communist elements that had called for a boycott of the polls.[140]

Although Diem had previously claimed that liberalization would have to wait until after the election, in his second term the South Vietnamese president continued to rebuff the political and social reforms called for by the Counterinsurgency Plan.[141] Instead, he responded to U.S. pressure by publicly charging that the growth of the Vietcong was a direct result of America's failure to provide South Vietnam with sufficient aid.[142] This critique touched a sore spot because Democrats in general were sensitive to the charge of being soft on Communism, and Kennedy in particular had campaigned against the Eisenhower administration's perceived passivity in the face of Soviet advances.[143]

Despite Diem's public criticism, Durbrow implored Washington to hold back supplemental military aid until Saigon implemented the Counterinsurgency Plan's political, economic, and social reforms to ensure that the government of Vietnam did not have to simultaneously contend with an alienated political opposition while fighting the Vietcong.[144] With senior Vietnamese officials suggesting to American interlocutors that Diem might never implement the Counterinsurgency Plan's political and economic measures, a number of Kennedy's advisors began to echo Durbrow's concern that providing military

---

[138] CIA, "Conduct of the South Vietnamese Election of 9 April 1961," November 14, 1961, DDRS. Durbrow later denounced the election as a "sham" and "mock democratic polling." Elbridge Durbrow, "Undiplomatic History: The Stealthful Soviet Saga," Box 40, Durbrow Papers, pp. 177, 183, HIA.

[139] CIA, "Conduct of the South Vietnamese Election of 9 April 1961."

[140] Robert Trumbull, "Ngo Sweeps Vote in SVN," *New York Times*, April 10, 1961.

[141] Meeting Record, Kennedy, Johnson, Rusk et al., FRUS 1961, p. 15; Memorandum, Komer to Rostow, April 28, 1961, Box 193, NSF:VN, JFK.

[142] Telegram 1599, Saigon to State, April 12, 1961, 951K.62/4–1261, RG 59.

[143] Walt Rostow, *The Diffusion of Power: An Essay in Recent History* (New York: Macmillan, 1972), p. 270.

[144] Telegram 1599.

assistance without insisting on reform would undermine America's ability to press Diem to fulfill his commitments.[145]

Conditionality continued to be opposed by both the uniformed military and the Department of Defense. In Saigon, General Williams' departure in September 1960 did not result in a policy change because the new MAAG Commander, General Lionel McGarr, continued his predecessor's firm opposition to linking military aid to reform.[146] In Washington, senior Department of Defense (DoD) officials were also "leery" of conditioning counterinsurgency assistance on social and political reforms.[147] As the Chairman of the Joint Chiefs of Staff saw things, the question was clear:

Does the U.S. intend to take the necessary military action now to defeat the Viet Cong threat or do we intend to quibble for weeks and months over details of general policy, finances, Vietnamese Gov't organization, etc., while Vietnam slowly but surely goes down the drain of Communism as North Vietnam and a large portion of Laos have gone to date?[148]

From the Pentagon, Lansdale pushed for Durbrow's removal, arguing that the ambassador had permanently lost Diem's trust by failing to support him unconditionally.[149]

Arguments for conditionality fell on deaf ears as the Kennedy administration's Vietnam Task Force, led by the Deputy Secretary of Defense, specifically advocated delinking U.S. aid from the progress of political and economic reform.[150] Diem's confidence in the United States had been undermined by Durbrow's "vigorous efforts to get him to mend his ways politically," the task force concluded, which made restoring the South Vietnamese leader's faith and trust in the United States a top priority.[151] Seeing Communist aggression in Southeast Asia as primarily a security matter, Secretary of State Rusk deferred to the DoD on Vietnam policy. Although not doubting the accuracy of Durbrow's assessments, Rusk concurred that a change was needed in Saigon.[152]

---

[145] Memorandum, Sorensen to Kennedy, April 28, 1961, FRUS 1961, pp. 84–5; Memorandum, Komer to Rostow, April 28, 1961, FRUS 1961, pp. 85–6; Telegram 1656, Saigon to State, May 3, 1961, 751K.5-MSP/5–361, RG 59.
[146] Letter, McGarr to Palmer, March 3, 1961, FRUS 1961, p. 43.
[147] Memo, Nolting to Rusk, April 29, 1961, FRUS 1961, pp. 87–8.
[148] Telegram UK 70272, Lemnitzer to JCS, May 8, 1961, FRUS 1961, p. 127.
[149] Memorandum, Lansdale to Secretary of Defense.
[150] Memorandum from Gilpatric to Kennedy, FRUS 1961, p. 97.   [151] *Ibid.*
[152] Meeting Notes, Rusk and Parsons, FRUS 1961, pp. 19–20.

With pressure from the Vietcong increasing and fears of another "Who lost China?" debate emerging over Vietnam, the administration took a new approach to influencing the South Vietnamese government.[153]

President Kennedy set the tone for an inducement influence strategy by sending a letter to Diem congratulating him on his reelection and reaffirming America's support for Vietnam.[154] This message was reiterated a few months later by Vice President Lyndon Johnson, who traveled to Saigon to publicly signal a renewed U.S. commitment to Diem, whom the bombastic Texan famously described as the "Winston Churchill" of Asia.[155] Although many Vietnamese opposition figures hoped that Johnson would press Diem for reforms, instead he promised enhanced military aid and economic assistance.[156] The message received by the Ngo family was that "the sky was the limit."[157]

This new approach was to be executed by the new ambassador to Vietnam, Fredrick "Fritz" Nolting, who was tasked with making certain that American aid enhanced the government's counterinsurgency capabilities and generated popular support for Diem.[158] Rather than pressure Diem, Nolting was specifically instructed to use friendly persuasion, winning the South Vietnamese president's trust and confidence by assuring him of complete U.S. support.[159] Echoing the view of successive MAAG Commanders and the DoD, Nolting alleged that America's ability to encourage Diem to reform was "in proportion to the confidence he has in us."[160]

The administration put the inducement strategy into action in mid-May 1961, when President Kennedy approved National Security Action Memorandum (NSAM) 52, which committed the United States to "military, political, economic, psychological and covert" action to "prevent Communist domination of South Vietnam." NSAM-52

---

[153]   McGarr to Lemnitzer, p. 4; Rostow, *The Diffusion of Power*, p. 270.
[154]   Letter, Kennedy to Diem, April 26, 1961, FRUS 1961, p. 81.
[155]   Karnow, *Vietnam*, p. 267.
[156]   Telegram 1740, Saigon to State, May 13, 1961, FRUS 1961, pp. 136–8. On the hopes of opposition figures, see "Report on Vietnam," May 19, 1961, FO 371/160112, NAUK.
[157]   Diem's brother, Ambassador Ngo Dinh Luyen, quoted in Letter, Hohler to Warner, July 14, 1961, FO 371/160114, NAUK.
[158]   Several other senior embassy personnel were also changed to ensure a fresh start in Saigon. William Trueheart, "Oral History Interview," March 2, 1982, pp. 2–3, LBJ.
[159]   Fredrick Nolting, "Oral History Interview," November 11, 1982, p. 1, LBJ.
[160]   Telegram 70, Saigon to State, July 14, 1961, FRUS 1961, p. 218

sanctioned an expansion of the ARVN by 20,000 and assigned the MAAG to train both the Civil Guard and the Self Defense Corps.[161] Diem's stalling tactics had won him the U.S. support called for by the Counterinsurgency Plan without having to implement any of the reform measures he disliked.[162]

Saigon welcomed the grant of aid without conditions, which was interpreted as a sign that Washington sought to move past the tension that had characterized U.S.-Vietnamese relations in recent years.[163] The impact of giving Diem what he wanted appeared to register results almost immediately: in late May, Ambassador Nolting was informed that the government reorganization agreed to in February would finally take place.[164] Initially, it appeared that the willingness to devolve political authority, empower the National Assembly, and reshuffle the cabinet indicated that inducement was working. Once again, however, the actual implementation of these measures fell well short of expectations. Rather than truly broadening the government or devolving authority, the changes were primarily organizational. Diem retained authority in key areas, such as defense and internal security.[165] The blatant attempt to placate Washington was not lost on local observers: The day after the reforms were announced, six prominent South Vietnamese diplomats simultaneously resigned in protest at the clear demonstration that Diem intended "no real change in his method of governing."[166] In the wake of the Kennedy administration's decision to unilaterally expand its support of the South Vietnamese security forces and Vice President Johnson's public expression of the American commitment to Diem, Saigon appeared noticeably less willing to engage with the United States on the reform measures called for by the Counterinsurgency Plan.

The Joint Action Plan

Having won support for a 20,000-man expansion of the ARVN, Diem sent Kennedy a direct appeal for yet more military aid. This new

[161] Bundy to Secretary of State, "National Security Action Memorandum Number 52," May 11, 1961, JFK.
[162] For a similar assessment, see Macdonald, *Adventures in Chaos*, p. 197.
[163] Miller, *Misalliance*, p. 226.
[164] Telegram 1805, Saigon to State, May 29, 1961, 751K.00/5–2961, RG 59.
[165] Telegram 1817, Saigon to State, May 30, 1961, 751K.13/5–3061, RG 59.
[166] Telegram 1838, Saigon to State, June 2, 1961, 751K.00/6–261, RG 59.

allotment was intended to expand the army by an additional 100,000 men over the next two years to cope with the increased infiltration of Communist cadres from North Vietnam. Diem promised that once this security situation was stabilized, the political and social programs called for under the Counterinsurgency Plan could finally be implemented. This "security first" argument was not well received by some administration officials, who argued that recent experience demonstrated that Diem would not reciprocate American concessions with reform.[167] Kennedy delayed a decision on the matter pending the outcome of a joint U.S.-Vietnamese review of South Vietnam's ability to finance domestic economic development as well as its growing security forces.[168]

The Special Financial Group's "Joint Action Plan," delivered to Kennedy in July 1961, called for the United States to provide an additional $85.5 million to expand the ARVN by 30,000 men, train civil administrators in rural areas, and develop programs to enhance the well-being of the rural population as well as strengthen the country's industrial base.[169] In return, the South Vietnamese government would undertake both immediate and longer-term social and economic restructuring. The new economic aid plan reopened the interagency dispute over influence strategies. Officials from the State Department and the Budget Office made the case for conditionality, arguing that Washington should "insist upon much more in the way of political action by Diem as a condition for additional aid" and that Vietnamese follow-through on outstanding political and economic liberalization "is much more likely to be forthcoming if our aid is specifically conditioned upon Vietnamese performance with respect to particular [*sic*] needed reforms." In contrast, defense officials continued to insist that creating a "general atmosphere of cooperation and confidence" was the best way to bring about the desired policy changes.[170]

President Kennedy split the difference by casting the Joint Action Plan as a grand bargain but stopped short of applying strict conditions

---

[167] Memorandum, Johnson to Rostow, June 15, 1961, Box 193, NSF:VN, JFK.
[168] "Editorial Note," FRUS 1961, p. 179.
[169] Staley Mission, "Summary of Joint Action Program," n.d., Folder 7/22/ 61–7/26/61, Box 193, NSF:VN, JFK; Letter, Kennedy to Diem, August 5, 1961, FRUS 1961, p. 265.
[170] Memorandum, Johnson to Rostow, July 27, 1961, Box 193, NSF:VN, JFK; Memorandum, Rostow to Kennedy, August 4, 1961, Box 194, NSF:VN, JFK.

on American aid. He promised Diem "substantial resources to assist you in carrying out the military and economic and social components of the special action program" and urged his counterpart to delegate "maximum authority" to the Vietnamese officials who would execute the plan.[171] Diem was reminded that Kennedy's support for his government had recently been criticized by Congress and the press. Implementation of the liberalization measures, however, would guarantee that South Vietnam was one of the administration's highest priorities.

Diem did not react enthusiastically to Kennedy's offer. He objected to the idea of devolving authority for execution of the Joint Action Plan and avoided committing himself to anything specific in return for additional American aid.[172] Accepting Ambassador Nolting's argument that the immediate provision of unconditional aid was necessary to maintain the "momentum and confidence" of the U.S.-South Vietnamese relationship, Washington revised the bargain: the United States would provide the military and economic assistance called for by the Joint Action Plan, but the associated political and social reforms would be dealt with through other channels, and Diem would not be pressed to devolve authority for execution of the plan.[173] Once again, Diem managed to obtain additional support from the Kennedy administration without committing to address the sociopolitical issues consistently identified as a major cause of South Vietnam's deteriorating internal security situation.

For policymakers who believed that winning Diem's trust through unconditional support was the key to gaining influence over Saigon, government-to-government relations at long last appeared to be on track. By late August, Nolting was optimistically predicting that it would finally be possible to "mount a 'break-through' program" against the Vietcong.[174] For those who believed that hard bargaining and conditioned aid were the only way to elicit real change from Saigon, the picture was far less rosy.

---

[171] Letter, Kennedy to Diem, FRUS 1961, pp. 263–6.
[172] Telegram 192, Saigon to State, August 8, 1961, FRUS 1961, p. 272. For Diem's continued resistance to delegating authority, see Telegram 392, State to Saigon, October 6, 1961, 751K.5-MSP/10–661, RG 59.
[173] Telegram 66, Saigon to State, July 14, 1961, FRUS 1961, p. 214; Telegram 226, State to Saigon, August 23, 1961, Box 194, NSF:VN, JFK.
[174] Telegram 304, Saigon to State, August 31, 1961, FRUS 1961, p. 289.

The Security Situation Deteriorates and More Unilateral Aid Is Provided

Events on the ground soon proved Nolting wrong: reports of increased infiltration coincided with large-scale attacks by battalion-sized units of guerrillas, which demonstrated to MAAG analysts a "significant increase" in Vietcong capabilities.[175] After a VC force of 1,500 fighters besieged the provincial capital of Phouc Vinh – less than forty miles north of Saigon – the situation appeared to deteriorate at such a rapid pace that, by late September, officials in Washington were convinced that the South Vietnamese government required an immediate infusion of military aid simply to "retain the capacity to defend itself."[176] Rural security was identified as a particular failing. Despite bearing the brunt of the fighting, the SDC had the lowest priority for training and was equipped with "antique weapons" and "ammunition that was so old that it often did not fire."[177] Meanwhile, the ARVN – which was primarily tied down in static protection duty – appeared to do more harm than good as it failed to carry out any civic action projects and, as a senior State Department official noted, "generally treated the population in a very callous fashion."[178] Shocked by the insurgents' gains, Diem declared a national state of emergency that curtailed civil liberties and allowed him to rule by executive decree.[179]

This fresh crisis prompted a renewed debate among Americans about the best way to respond. Advisors in the field suggested that Saigon misunderstood the nature of the conflict. "Most of us are sure," one American officer assigned to the Mekong Delta wrote, "that this problem is only fifteen per cent military and eighty-five per cent political. It's not just a matter of killing Viet Cong but of coupling security with welfare."[180]

---

[175] Message 1473, MAAG to CINCPAC, September 21, 1961, FRUS 1961, pp. 296–8; Memorandum, Johnson to Rostow, September 15, 1961, Box 194, NSF:VN, JFK; Message 1543, MAAG to CINCPAC, September 21, 1961, Box 194, NSF:VN, JFK.

[176] Draft Telegram, State-Defense to Saigon, September 20, 1961, Box 194, NSF: VN, JFK.

[177] Memorandum, Johnson to Rostow, October 6, 1961, Box 194, NSF:VN, JFK.

[178] *Ibid*; Dispatch 56, Saigon to Foreign Office, October 8, 1961, FO 371/160116, NAUK.

[179] Telegram 508, Saigon to State, October 18, 1961, FRUS 1961, p. 830; Telegram 504, Saigon to State, October 18, 1961, 751K.00/10–1861, RG 59.

[180] Denis Warner, "Fighting the Viet Cong," *Army*, 12, no. 2 (September 1961), p. 20.

Officials in the State Department and the National Security Council placed the blame on Diem's failures to improve the quality of rural administration, streamline his government, or devolve authority, let alone engage the political opposition in a meaningful way.[181] These views were echoed by senior officials within the South Vietnamese government and the military, who suggested to American interlocutors that it might be necessary to "force" reform on the South Vietnamese leader.[182] Unless Diem took vigorous action on the various counter-insurgency proposals the United States had drawn up in the past year – to both provide local security and ameliorate the sources of discontent that were alienating the rural population – these Vietnamese officials believed that "no amount of U.S. military or economic aid could save the country."[183]

Although financial inducements and public pledges of support had not led to reform in the past, Nolting and McGarr pushed increased military assistance as the best response to the worsening political-military situation. While acknowledging the value of administrative and political reform over the long term, they believed that the short-comings of the South Vietnamese security forces could be addressed by additional U.S. advisors and a more vigorous effort by the MAAG. The deployment of American combat troops to the border regions was also proposed as a means to help stem the tide of Communist infiltration.[184] Despite awareness of Diem's failings, Nolting argued that "our present policy of all-out support to the present government here is ... our only feasible alternative."[185]

Short-term military necessity carried the day as Kennedy authorized an expansion of the MAAG to nearly 2,000 personnel and allowed American advisors to accompany Vietnamese units into combat. He

[181]   Telegram 392; Memorandum, Cottrell to Wood, October 13, 1961, 751K.00/10–1361, RG 59.
[182]   Telegram 545, Saigon to State, October 25, 1961, 751K.00/10–2561, RG 59; Telegram 556, Saigon to State, October 27, 1961, 751K.00/10–2761, RG 59.
[183]   Telegram 392; CIA Information Report, TDCS 3/490.230, October 18, 1961, Box 194, NSF:VN, JFK.
[184]   Telegram 337, Saigon to State, September 22, 1961, FRUS 1961, pp. 307–8; Telegram 448, Saigon to State, October 7, 1961, 751K.00/10–761, and Telegram 457, Saigon to State, October 9, 1961, 751K.00/10–961, both RG 59; Memorandum for the Record, Worth H. Bagley, October 12, 1961, Box 194, NSF:VN, JFK.
[185]   Telegram 445, Saigon to State, October 6, 1961, 751K.00/10–661, RG 59.

also approved the deployment of a squadron of American "air commandos" that flew secret combat missions under the guise of training the South Vietnamese Air Force.[186] Despite the critical situation engendered by South Vietnam's continued political and administrative shortcomings, Diem was not asked to do anything in return for this expanded American support.

The Taylor Mission, Limited Partnership, and the Threat of Conditioned Aid

The year 1961 had not been a kind one for the Kennedy administration, nor perceptions of the U.S. position in the world. The failure of U.S.-trained Cuban exiles at the Bay of Pigs was followed by the construction of the Berlin Wall and a resumption of Soviet nuclear testing. While Soviet premier Nikita Khrushchev bellicosely sanctioned "wars of national liberation," the United States appeared to be on the back foot. Within Southeast Asia, a string of defeats for the American-backed Royal Laotian Army by North Vietnamese troops supporting the Communist Pathet Lao led the Kennedy administration to accept negotiations to "neutralize" Laos. As regional allies expressed concern about America's commitment to arresting Communist expansion, Kennedy believed the time had come to take a stand: "[W]e have a problem in making our power credible and Vietnam looks like the place" to do it.[187]

In mid-October 1961, the president dispatched his military advisor, General Maxwell Taylor, to Vietnam to evaluate the U.S. assistance effort. In particular, he was to focus on the question of deploying American combat troops and the advisability of conditioning future aid on meaningful political and administrative reforms by the South Vietnamese government and military.[188] Taylor found that the ARVN's anti-guerrilla operations were hampered by a lack of intelligence, insufficient mobility, and political interference in the chain of

---

[186] NSAM 104, October 13, 1961, Meetings and Memos, NSF, JFK Presidential Papers, JFK; Darrel Whitcomb, "Farm Gate," *Air Force Magazine*, 88, No. 12 (December 2005).

[187] Quoted in John Hellmann, *American Myth and the Legacy of Vietnam* (New York: Columbia University Press, 1986), pp. 50–1. For further discussion of these various episodes, see Freedman, *Kennedy's Wars*.

[188] Rostow, *The Diffusion of Power*, pp. 270–9; Maxwell Taylor, *Swords and Plowshares* (New York: W.W. Norton, 1972), pp. 227–45.

command. Moreover, he noted that Diem's attempts "to maintain all the strings of power in his own hands" were hindering the ability of the government to take effective action against the insurgency. His report to Kennedy recommended a mix of political and military measures to respond to the emergency in South Vietnam, including efforts to ameliorate the discontent of the rural population and opposition elites – who had been alienated by the government's heavy-handed rule – as well as a significant expansion of U.S. aid and a "a radical increase" in American advisors "at every level." With senior South Vietnamese officials insisting the "situation was so serious that nothing but American military intervention would restore the morale of the population," Taylor also recommended that the United States significantly increase the visibility of its commitment to South Vietnam by deploying 8,000 troops to demonstrate the "seriousness of U.S. intent to resist a Communist take-over."[189]

Reaction to the Taylor report highlighted the divergence between the proponents of inducement and those of conditionality. While the MAAG chief and the ambassador welcomed the increased American commitment to Vietnam, Secretary Rusk cautioned that such a significant expansion – particularly the deployment of troops – would eliminate any leverage the United States had to push Diem for action on the social-political-economic front and that the United States could not continue to provide unconditional support to a "losing horse."[190]

Rusk's arguments carried the day, and the troop proposal was-shelved. In late November 1961, the United States switched influence strategies, making a fresh attempt to condition an enlarged commitment to Vietnam on internal reform. Washington offered to provide theaid called for in the Taylor Report, including airlift assets, expedited training for the Civil Guard and the Self Defense Corps, experienced advisors for the South Vietnamese government, intelligence support, and economic assistance for civic action projects. In return, the United States expected Diem to take "prompt and appropriate" action to rally against the insurgent threat, including a "decentralization

---

[189]   Letter, Taylor to Kennedy, November 3, 1961, FRUS 1961, pp. 477–532.
Nguyen Dinh Thuan, Secretary of State for the Presidency, quoted in Telegram 710, Saigon to Foreign Office, November 6, 1961, FO 371/160118, NAUK.
[190]   *The Pentagon Papers*, vol. 2, p. 105; Telegram SECTO 6, Hakone to State, November 1, 1961, FRUS 1961, p. 464.

and broadening of the government so as to realize the full potential of all non-Communist elements in the country," delegation of "adequate authority" to government agencies directing counterinsurgency operations and a restructuring of "the military establishment and command structure" to enhance military effectiveness.[191]

The expansion of U.S. assistance was clearly linked to action by the South Vietnamese government. As Rusk instructed Nolting, "If we are to give substantial support, we must be able to point to real administrative, political, and social reforms and a real effort to widen its base."[192] Recalling Diem's previous attempts to placate the United States with superficial reform, the Secretary of State noted that he must make "changes that will be recognized as having real substance and meaning."[193] Apropos of that, a scathing editorial in the *New York Times* declared "the inadequacies of the government of President Ngo Dinh Diem are the weakest component in South Vietnam's struggle against Communism," with "the basic requisite for success" being "government reform in Saigon."[194]

When Nolting outlined the U.S. proposal to Diem, the South Vietnamese leader was disquieted. Decrying conditionality as an infringement on the country's sovereignty, he argued that the appearance of South Vietnam as an American "protectorate" would give "a monopoly on nationalism" to the Vietcong.[195] He rebuffed the urgency the United States attached to internal reforms with the familiar claims that it was impossible to undertake major changes until order was restored and that the lack of "trained and able" government officials outside his immediate family made further delegation of authority impractical.[196] Instead, he accused the United States of repeating the mistakes of China, where insistence on reform and liberalization in Chang Kaishek's Nationalist government had been blamed for bringing about its defeat at the hands of the Communists.[197]

---

[191] NSAM 111, November 22, 1961, Meetings and Memos, NSF, JFK Presidential Papers, JFK
[192] Telegram 619, State to Saigon, November 14, 1961, 751K.00/11–1561.
[193] Telegram 678, Saigon to State, November 18, 1961, FRUS 1961, p. 643.
[194] "Ngo Dinh Diem's Responsibility" *New York Times*, November 26, 1961.
[195] Telegram 678, FRUS 1961, p. 643; Telegram 708, Saigon to State, November 25, 1961, FRUS 1961, p. 667.
[196] *Ibid.*
[197] CIA Information Report, "Views of President Ngo Dinh Diem," November 29, 1961, FRUS 1961, pp. 692–3.

Diem attempted to strengthen his bargaining position by reducing his dependence on the United States. He made contact with Chang Kai-shek's government to see if military advisors from Taiwan could replace the American trainers being held up by the negotiations.[198] At Nhu's behest several of the government-influenced daily newspapers stoked anti-American sentiment with a series of front-page stories denouncing Washington's interference in Vietnam's internal affairs. The articles specifically condemned the conditioning of U.S. aid – although such proposals were secret – and suggested that American policy was on a course toward failure in Vietnam, as it had in China and Cuba, where local allies were insufficiently supported in the face of a Communist insurgency.[199] The dispute between the two sides was openly discussed, with the *New York Times* commenting on the painfully obvious fact that "ruling circles in South Vietnam appear to have hardened their resistance to the government reforms reported to have been demanded by the United States as part of a joint effort to defeat communism there."[200]

Holding the line in the face of these pressure tactics, the United States purposefully delayed the delivery of the military equipment and advisors offered under the deal, some of which were already in transit to Vietnam. Despite the South Vietnamese government's urgent need for assistance, it was recognized that if such items arrived before a comprehensive agreement had been reached, the U.S. bargaining position would be "weakened significantly."[201] In light of Diem's recalcitrance, the Americans made their bargain more attractive by offering additional economic aid, but they held the line on the issue of conditionality. At the same time, they increased the pressure on Saigon by letting it be known that Ambassador Nolting would be recalled to Washington for consultations if progress was not forthcoming.[202]

---

[198] Telegram, CINCPAC to JCS, November 28, 1961, Box 195, NSF:VN, JFK.
[199] Telegram 702, Saigon to State, November 24, 1961, 611K.51/11–2461, RG 59; Telegram 715, Saigon to State, November 29, 1961, 751K.5/11–2761, RG 59; Telegram 707, Saigon to State, November 28, 1961, Box 195, NSF: VN, JFK.
[200] Robert Trumbull, "Saigon Resisting U.S. Reform Plan," *New York Times*, November 27, 1961.
[201] Telegram 683, State to Saigon, November 25, 1961, Box 195, NSF: VN, JFK; Telegram 4145, MAAG to State, November 26, 1961, NSF:VN, JFK.
[202] Max Frankel, "U.S. May Recall Its Envoy if Saigon Refuses Reform," *New York Times*, November 30, 1961.

After a "marathon" negotiation, Nolting reached an agreement with Diem on December 1. As part of the bargain, the United States would increase its aid to Vietnam and allow its advisors to deploy on operations with the ARVN. The conditions placed on American assistance were explicitly articulated in a joint U.S.-Vietnamese memorandum: "Before taking such far-reaching steps, the U.S. has sought, and the GVN has given, assurances that the GVN will take measures to increase its efficiency and to increase its public support in Viet-Nam and abroad."[203] In particular, the effectiveness of the Vietnamese security forces was to be improved by a rationalization of the ARVN's command structure; the collection and dissemination of intelligence would be facilitated by the centralization of the country's multiple intelligence agencies; and close consultation with American advisors would be undertaken in "planning the conduct of the security effort." Overall direction of the counterinsurgency campaign would be devolved to an interagency Internal Security Council. Diem agreed to allow joint U.S.-Vietnamese surveys of the provinces to assess the progress of both military and sociopolitical aspects of the effort against the Vietcong.[204] The agreement also contained measures designed to induce Communist guerrillas to give up their armed struggle as well as to increase the level of support for Diem's government. As part of the latter effort, the government pledged to "take all possible and feasible steps" to achieve further democratization by finally creating the province councils and other advisory bodies that had been promised earlier in the year.

An editorial in the *New York Times* summarized the situation: "The extensive new American commitment in South Vietnam has been made on the basis of parallel commitments by President Ngo Dinh Diem to improve his regime. The effectiveness of what the United States is doing will largely depend on how he proceeds in this respect."[205] In Washington, Kennedy was pleased at Diem's cooperation, while Rusk expressed some concern that the South Vietnamese leader had not "gone as far as we liked," particularly in bringing opposition figures into the government. Nevertheless, the Secretary of

---

[203] Letter, Nolting to Diem, December 5, 1961, FRUS 1961, p. 714.
[204] *Ibid.*, pp. 714–5.
[205] "New Stakes in Vietnam," *New York Times*, December 22, 1961.

State believed that the agreement provided a "sufficient basis on which to move ahead."[206]

The partnership quickly appeared to bear fruit when the South Vietnamese government announced a series of reforms at the end of the year. In addition to implementing the economic policies recommended by the Special Financial Group, the government enhanced the pay of the long-neglected SDC in an effort to boost its morale and outlined a number of policies designed to rally support in rural areas.[207] These measures were also accompanied by signs that the government was finally taking real steps to devolve authority by expanding the role of the National Assembly and creating advisory bodies to guide economic policy.[208] This optimism would soon fade, however, as the United States undercut its leverage by flooding Vietnam with aid without insisting on prior implementation of the government's promised actions.

PART III THE ILLUSION OF PROGRESS AND THE END OF DIEM, 1962–1963

Despite the hard-won battle to convince Diem to accept conditions on American aid, the Department of Defense began to undermine the U.S. position almost immediately by rushing aid into South Vietnam rather than waiting for the agreed-upon reforms to take place. As Secretary of Defense Robert McNamara instructed McGarr, "[T]he political uncertainty of Diem's position and doubts as to his willingness to take steps to make his government more effective must not prevent us from going ahead full blast ... on all possible actions short of the large scale introduction of U.S. combat forces."[209]

As shiploads of military hardware and advisors began to flow into South Vietnam, the Military Assistance Command, Vietnam (MACV) was established in February 1962 to coordinate the expanded military support effort. Under the command of General Paul Harkins, MACV

---

[206] Telegram 725, State to Saigon, December 4, 1961, FRUS 1961, p. 712; Telegram 727, State to Saigon, December 5, 1961, FRUS 1961, p. 716

[207] Telegram 884, Saigon to State, January 3, 1962, 751K.00/1–362, RG 59; Final Report of the Vietnam Task Force, July 1, 1962, FRUS 1962, pp. 484–97.

[208] Telegram 892, Saigon to State, January 5, 1962, FRUS 1962, p. 12.

[209] Def 906345, SecDef to CINPAC and MAAG, November 28, 1961, FRUS 1961, pp. 679–80.

subsumed the mission and personnel of the MAAG.[210] The creation of MACV also institutionalized the de facto fragmentation of the country team: despite warnings that such a move would only facilitate Diem's penchant for playing U.S. agencies off of each other, the MACV commander was made the "co-equal" of the ambassador and autonomous in the military sphere.[211]

In the first half of 1962, "Operation Beef Up" saw a major increase in U.S. advisors as well as the introduction of several hundred American fighter bombers, helicopters, and intelligence-gathering aircraft.[212] The depth and breadth of the American presence was fundamentally altered: by year's end, there would be 11,500 U.S. military personnel in Vietnam, a number that would climb to nearly 16,300 by the end 1963.[213] Each ARVN battalion was assigned a two-man team to provide tactical advice as well as coordinate both close air support and transport by U.S. helicopters.[214] Reorganization of the ARVN's command structure had been one of the conditions attached to military aid, yet as MACV directed a furious military buildup, the ARVN's convoluted chain of command remained untouched.[215]

Conditionality was similarly abandoned in the political and economic spheres. The December agreement called for the deployment of American personnel into rural areas to monitor local administrators, but Diem began to back away from that promise almost immediately.[216] Requiring U.S. agencies to work though the Saigon-based government bureaucracy was a means of maintaining control over both the Americans and provincial officials, whereas disbursement of foreign assistance directly at the province level would amount to a de facto decentralization of authority. With aid flowing into the country, the Vietnamese government delayed undertaking any devolution of

---

[210] Letter, Taylor to Kennedy, FRUS 1962, p. 527; Cosmas, *MACV*, pp. 44–62.
[211] Telegram 801, Saigon to State, December 13, 1961, FRUS 1961, pp. 731–2; Telegram 819, Saigon to State, December 19, 1961, FRUS 1962, pp. 747–9.
[212] Status Report: Project "Beef-Up," Joint Chiefs of Staff (J-3), February 21, 1963, Box 128a, POF:VN, JFK.
[213] James L. Collins, *The Development and Training of the South Vietnamese Army, 1950–1972* (Washington, DC: Center of Military History, 1975), pp. 17–26; Moyar, *Triumph Forsaken*, p. 155.
[214] Martin Dockery, *Lost in Translation: A Combat Advisor's Story* (New York: Ballantine, 2003), pp. 36–40.
[215] Cosmas, *MACV*, p. 86.
[216] Memorandum, Forrestal to Bundy, May 29, 1962, FRUS 1962, p. 430.

authority or even limited liberalization.[217] In Washington, even some DoD officials began to express concern that having "executed in full measure its commitments to Diem," he "continues to resist basic improvements recommended by the U.S.," in particular better administration and political liberalization, which were a "vital part of the U.S.–GVN contract."[218] Nevertheless, the head of the United States Agency for International Development (USAID) personally assured the South Vietnamese president that there would be "no limit" to American help and that Vietnam would be given "whatever aid is necessary" to ensure its freedom.[219]

The growing discontent with Diem's government appeared to manifest itself in late February when two dissident air force pilots bombed the Independence Palace, unsuccessfully attempting to assassinate the president and his brother Nhu. Although the effort did not have widespread support in the ARVN, like the paratrooper revolt, the attack was carried out by self-proclaimed anti-Communist nationalists in reaction to Diem's autocratic rule and his government's failure to prosecute the war against the Vietcong with sufficient vigor.[220] Also like the paratrooper revolt, evidence of violent discontent led Diem to rely even more heavily on his brother Nhu, who clamped down on dissent. Unlike in 1960, however, in the wake of the attack, the Kennedy administration hurried to reassure Diem of its strong support.[221]

The Tide Turns?

In mid-1962, American concerns about the progress of economic and political reform were swept aside as the South Vietnamese government

[217] Memorandum, Cottrell to Harriman, April 3, 1962, FRUS 1962, p. 289; Final Report of the Vietnam Task Force, July 1, 1962, FRUS 1962, p. 495; Fall, *The Two Viet-Nams*, pp. 381–2.

[218] Memorandum, Bagley to Taylor, April 18, 1962, FRUS 1962, pp. 333–4.

[219] Quoted in Bernard Fall (writing under the pseudonym Z), "The War in Vietnam: We Have Not Been Told the Whole Truth," *New Republic*, March 13, 1962. This message was reportedly reinforced by several other high-level American officials. Dispatch 30, Saigon to Foreign Office, June 5, 1962, FO 371/166704, NAUK.

[220] Karnow, *Vietnam*, p. 281; Telegram 58, Phnom Penh to Foreign Office, February 27, 1962, FO 371/166700, NAUK.

[221] Telegram 178A, Saigon to Foreign Office, February 27, 1962, FO 371/166700, NAUK.

appeared to seize the initiative from the insurgents. On the battlefield, aggressive ARVN operations threw the Vietcong on the defensive, while the fortified villages of the Strategic Hamlet Program cut them off from the population.[222] Across South Vietnam, the guerrillas' casualties were increasing, their activity was down, and their recruitment fell dramatically.[223] As Saigon extended its reach across large portions of the country, the country's its rice harvest improved significantly and the government's tax yield doubled.[224] In this environment, optimism abounded: General Harkins proclaimed that the military defeat of the Vietcong was "at hand," while a "euphoric" Diem asserted that "everywhere we are taking the initiative ... sowing insecurity in the Communist strongholds, smashing their units, one after another."[225] This appearance of progress led to a reduction in American pressure for liberalization. Advocates of unqualified support for South Vietnam contended that pressuring the regime would undercut the success of the war effort: Vietnam required the strong leadership Diem was providing, not outreach to disgruntled opposition elements, which would signal to the South Vietnamese the "weakness, if not impending collapse," of the government.[226]

As time went on, the government gains proved to be far less substantial than they first appeared. The deployment of American weapons and equipment significantly improved the ARVN's mobility and firepower, while increased numbers of U.S. advisors enhanced the sophistication of the ARVN's operations. Unprepared to face airmobile assaults or armored personnel carriers, the Vietcong were temporarily thrown on the defensive as the government attacked their remote strongholds along the Cambodian border, in the Central Highlands, and in the Annamite Cordillera to the north of the country. After the initial setback, however, the insurgents adapted their tactics, shifting to

---

[222] Memorandum, Forrestal to Kennedy, September 18, 1962, FRUS 1962, p. 650.

[223] Philip Catton, *Diem's Final Failure: Prelude to America's War in Vietnam* (Lawrence: University Press of Kansas, 2003), p. 151.

[224] Memorandum, Forrestal to Kennedy, FRUS 1962, p. 650; Duncanson, *Government*, p. 326.

[225] Fall, *The Two Viet-Nams*, p. 287; William Rosson, "Four Periods of American Involvement in Vietnam," Ph.D. dissertation, University of Oxford, 1978, p. 123; Dispatch 14, Saigon to Foreign Office, February 28, 1962, FO 371/ 1666701, NAUK.

[226] Memorandum Cottrell to Harriman, FRUS 1962, pp. 146–7; Memorandum, Heavner to Wood, August 3, 1962, FRUS 1962, pp. 574–5.

nighttime operations when South Vietnamese aircraft were less effective. By late 1962, the VC were mounting several attacks on government outposts per day, and their ranks continued to swell despite mounting casualties.[227]

Having been trained for conventional warfare, the ARVN sought to encircle guerrilla units and destroy them rather than focus on denying the insurgents access to the people and the villages from which they drew their support. Featuring sweeps by multiple battalions through areas outside the government's control – which had been "softened up" by artillery or airstrikes beforehand – these operations were described by one State Department official as "more appropriate to the European fronts of World War II than ... guerrilla warfare."[228] Employing intelligence that was "often days, if not weeks old," the ARVN rarely managed to trap the insurgents in the manner envisioned.[229]

Judging such efforts to be "large-scale farces," U.S. advisors in the field quickly concluded that "battalion and larger sized 'sweep' operations are generally unproductive and wasteful in terms of manpower, effort and materials expended."[230] Of the nearly dozen large-scale sweeps undertaken by the ARVN in 1962, only two reported substantial contact with the VC.[231] Moreover, since ARVN units frequently departed the area immediately after an operation concluded, the territory was not denied to the Vietcong, who were free to return once government forces had left.[232] When the ARVN did encounter insurgents, Diem's intolerance for losses engendered great reluctance to

[227] Herring, *America's Longest War*, p. 88; Office of the Military Attache, "Summary for June 1962," July 31, 1962, FO 371/1666749, NAUK.

[228] Andrew Birtle, *U.S. Army Counterinsurgency and Contingency Operations Doctrine, 1942–1976* (Washington, DC: Center of Military History, 2007), p. 323; Fall, *The Two Viet-Nams*, p. 379; Roger Hilsman, *To Move a Nation: The Politics of Foreign Policy in the Administration of John F. Kennedy* (Garden City, NJ: Doubleday, 1967), p. 437.

[229] Rufus Phillips, "Before We Lost in Vietnam," in Harvey C. Neese and John O'Donnell, eds., *Prelude to Tragedy: Vietnam, 1960–1965* (Annapolis, MD: Naval Institute Press, 2001), p. 39; MAAG Memo, Lessons Learned 12, May 10, 1962, CALL; MAAG Memo, Lessons Learned 13, May 16, 1962, CALL.

[230] Denno, "Debriefing," p. 5; MAAG Memo, Lessons Learned 5, April 11, 1962, CALL; MAAG Memo, Lessons Learned 16, June 19, 1962, CALL.

[231] See the various "Lessons Learned" documents for 1962 at CALL.

[232] MAAG Memo, Lessons Learned 14, May 1962, CALL; Andrew F. Krepinevich, *The Army and Vietnam* (Baltimore: Johns Hopkins University Press, 1986), p. 81.

engage the VC in close-quarters battle for fear that sustaining casualties would harm a commanding officer's chances of advancement.[233] Some American advisors reported that their units would not conduct operations after dark – thus conceding the night to the insurgents – while others believed that their units knowingly focused on areas without a Vietcong presence to give the impression of fighting without actually doing so.[234]

All too often the ARVN's use of firepower resulted in civilian casualties and collateral damage, which MAAG analysts noted "only serve to strengthen VC influence over the population, with the final result that the fundamental task of separating the guerrillas from the people will be more difficult."[235] Indeed, the Vietcong would often open fire from populated villages specifically to provoke return fire, which would inevitably kill civilians and create new recruits with a grudge against the government.[236] Not all harm to rural civilians was incidental. To deny the VC access to the population, the ARVN also employed coercive measures, such as burning villages suspected of aiding the insurgents or targeting sections of the country outside of government control with indiscriminate artillery and airstrikes to drive civilians into government-controlled zones.[237] As one American rural development advisor noted, the South Vietnamese government seemed to believe that

[t]hose who do not support the government, or who are not in government-controlled areas, must suffer for this (after all, war is hell), and after suffering enough they will either blame the VC for their suffering, or will come over to government-controlled areas to escape the bombs, shells, etc., which are their lot when the VC are around.[238]

As a result of these operational shortcomings, the influx of American helicopters, armored personnel carriers, and equipment delivered

---

[233] MAAG Memo, Lessons Learned 3, April 11, 1962; MAAG Memo, Lessons Learned 10, May 1, 1962; MAAG Memo, Lessons Learned 16, June 19, 1962, all CALL. For a discussion of the career-minded loss aversion generated by Diem's policy, see Memorandum of Conversation, Wheeler and Harriman, February 9, 1963, POL VIET, RG 59.

[234] This latter practice was derisively referred to as taking "walks in the sun." Birtle, *U.S. Army Counterinsurgency and Contingency Operations Doctrine, 1942–1976*, p. 322; Krepinevich, *The Army and Vietnam*, pp. 82–4.

[235] MAAG Memo, Lessons Learned 20, August 27, 1962, CALL.

[236] Phillips, "Before We Lost in Vietnam," p. 39.   [237] *Ibid.*   [238] *Ibid.*, p. 40.

under "Operation Beef Up" merely allowed the ARVN to conduct its ineffective conventionally oriented operations against the insurgents more energetically. In contrast to the optimism expressed by General Harkins and President Diem from Saigon, an American general sent to observe the operations of U.S. Special Forces in Vietnam found that in the field there was "almost universal skepticism on the part of both U.S. and South Vietnamese personnel that the VC could be defeated expeditiously."[239]

Similarly illusive gains were registered by the Strategic Hamlet Program that sought to reassert the government's control over the countryside, while simultaneously responding to American pressure for a counterinsurgency program that blended social and economic measures with security. In theory, the effort achieved three goals by (1) separating the guerrillas from the population they relied on for food, support, information, and recruits, (2) reestablishing direct contact between the central government and the rural population, and (3) raising rural living standards.[240] Villages in underadministered rural areas were heavily fortified with barbed wire and watchtowers; kept under tight supervision through the use of identity cards, curfews, and checkpoints; and provided with enhanced government services such as schools and medical clinics. An elected hamlet council would prioritize local self-help economic development projects that were funded by Saigon. Men from the hamlet provided security by serving in the local SDC, and radio links were established to the nearest CG or ARVN post, which would respond in case of an attack. In some districts, the insurgents were so effectively cut off from the population by the strategic hamlets that they had to consider abandoning their armed struggle.[241] As a result, the Vietcong undertook a systematic campaign to subvert or destroy the strategic hamlets, a process greatly facilitated by the program's poor administration.

Under Nhu's direction, the effort expanded at a rapid pace, trading quantity for quality. In the space of just six months, the government announced that more than 4 million peasants had been secured, with the total rising to 8 million by May 1963.[242] In reality, only a third of

[239] Rosson, "Four Periods of American Involvement in Vietnam," p. 123.
[240] Duncanson, *Government*, p. 320.
[241] *Ibid.*, p. 326; Pribbenow, *Victory in Vietnam*, p. 110.
[242] Letter, Nolting to Thuan, May 10, 1963, *Foreign Relations of the United States 1961–1963*, vol. III, Vietnam, January–August 1963 (FRUS 1963/1), pp. 298–9; Blaufarb, *Counterinsurgency Era*, p. 120.

the hamlets actually provided the required mix of security and social services.[243] Instead of focusing on areas that had already been cleared of insurgents by military and police action, the strategic hamlets were simultaneously built across the country, many in areas containing active Vietcong cadres that made them subject to infiltration from the start.[244] The rapid proliferation of the strategic hamlets quickly outstripped the ability of the CG to assist hamlets under attack from the insurgents, and in some areas, provincial officials were reluctant to arm local militiamen without verifying their loyalty to the central government.[245] Therefore, as a former CIA station chief recounted, the hamlet's guardians "had to make do with ancient weapons, without shoes and without communications to even advise when they were attacked." Instead of confronting the Vietcong, "their nightly maneuver was limited to closing the barbed wire around their pathetic fort and waiting for morning in hopes that Communist guerrillas would ignore them."[246]

These security failings were compounded by administrative shortcomings that alienated the peasants who lived in the strategic hamlets. Diem's philosophical belief that shared sacrifice and mutual responsibility were the cornerstones of a communitarian, democratic, Vietnam were lost on the peasants, who were required to provide unpaid manual labor to build the hamlet's fortifications and other communal buildings.[247] Moreover, Nhu's insistence that the hamlets be self-sufficient – abetted by a combination of corruption and inefficiency in the administration of the program – meant that Saigon often failed to supply the necessary materials for the construction of fortifications or sufficient funds to finance development projects or pay the SDC cadres, who resorted to petty theft for subsistence – "a chicken here, a pig there" – which estranged the population from their defenders.[248]

None of these failings were readily apparent at the time, however, and together with the ARVN's apparent battlefield success, by the third quarter of 1962 it seemed that the government was making real

---

[243] Memorandum of Conversation, May 1, 1963, Box 40, Lansdale Papers.
[244] Duncanson, *Government*, p. 319.
[245] Memo, Wilson to Dinh, July 7, 1963, Box 6, Wilson Papers.
[246] William Colby, *Lost Victory: A Firsthand Account of America's Sixteen-Year Involvement in Vietnam* (Chicago: Contemporary Books, 1989), p. 61.
[247] Blaufarb, *Counterinsurgency Era*, p. 111.
[248] Memorandum, Heavner to Nolting, April 27, 1962, FRUS 1962, pp. 356–8; Herring, *America's Longest War*, p. 89; Miller, *Misalliance*, pp. 244–5.

progress against the insurgents.[249] Americans involved in the Strategic Hamlet Program bluntly declared that "we are winning the war in Vietnam," a sentiment echoed by senior American officials like Robert McNamara.[250] In Saigon, both Ngo Dinh Diem and his brother Nhu firmly believed that the tide had turned in their favor, and even the Vietcong themselves had concluded that a rapid victory over Diem's government was no longer possible.[251]

Confusion Reigns and Policy Drifts

In the latter half of 1962, Diem's uneven progress in executing the political and economic measures he had agreed to the previous December began to arouse concern in Washington. The South Vietnamese leader had always argued that such actions had to wait for an improvement in the security situation. In light of the government's apparent gains against the insurgents, however, he increasingly lacked a justification for further delaying the promised political liberalization and civic action. Complaints began to circulate among the National Security Council staff that the United States was being too cautious in its dealings with Diem when it was necessary to increase the pressure on him to uphold his side of the bargain.[252] These concerns resonated at the highest levels, with both President Kennedy and

---

[249] For optimistic accounts, see Memorandum, Forrestal to Kennedy, September 18, 1962, FRUS 1962, p. 650; State Department, "Developments in Viet-Nam between General Taylor's Visits – October 1961–October 1962," n.d., FRUS 1962, pp. 679–87. Slightly more nuanced views appear in Telegram 1503, Saigon to State, May 23, 1962, FRUS 1962, pp. 418–26; Southeast Asia Task Force, "Status Report on Southeast Asia," June 27, 1962, FRUS 1962, pp. 478–9.

[250] Rufus Philipps, "Financing and the Future of the Counter-Insurgency Effort in Vietnam," April 30, 1963, Box 40, Lansdale Papers; Neil Sheehan, *A Bright Shining Lie: John Paul Vann and America in Vietnam* (New York: Random House, 1988), pp. 289–90.

[251] Miller, *Misalliance*, pp. 248–9; Gareth Porter, *Perils of Dominance: Imbalance of Power and the Road to War in Vietnam* (Los Angeles: University of California Press, 2005), p. 120.

[252] Memorandum, Forrestal to Kaysen, August 6, 1962, Box 196, NSF:VN, JFK; Memorandum, Forrestal to Bundy, August 8, 1962, FRUS 1962, pp. 583–4. For examples of others urging the need "to make a firm approach to Diem," see Memorandum, Bagley to Taylor, May 9, 1962, FRUS 1962, pp. 377–8.

Secretary McNamara reportedly "very anxious to push on with the civilian side of the counterinsurgency program as fast as possible."[253]

In September, Diem finally agreed to allow the American oversight of rural development programs he had agreed to nine months before. As MACV, the CIA, USAID, and other agencies began to station their personnel in rural areas, the number of Americans in the Vietnamese countryside increased significantly.[254] Reports soon began coming from the field that highlighted deficiencies in ARVN operations and the Strategic Hamlet Program, which contrasted sharply with the more optimistic assessments originating from the embassy and MACV.[255]

A series of fact-finding missions undertaken in late 1962 and early 1963 sought to make sense of the contradictory views flowing back to Washington. At Kennedy's request, Senate Majority Leader Mike Mansfield (D-Montana) – an enthusiastic supporter of Diem in the 1950s – led a bipartisan group of senators to South Vietnam. The result was not encouraging. After eight years of American aid, Mansfield judged that little had appreciably changed in the country. If anything, South Vietnam was more reliant on American assistance than it had been five years before. Mansfield believed that the counterinsurgency effort was unlikely to succeed unless Diem could harness the "initiative and self-sacrifice from a substantial body of Vietnamese," which would require "a diffusion of political power, essentially in a democratic pattern."[256]

Mansfield's gloomy assessment was echoed by the CIA, which reported that after the injection of millions of dollars and thousands of American advisors, South Vietnam was barely "holding its own" in "a slowly escalating stalemate." Although U.S. assistance had increased the ARVN's effectiveness to a degree, the continued appointment of senior officers based on political considerations was retarding the military's battlefield initiative. Despite Saigon's claim to have inflicted 30,000 casualties on the insurgents in 1962, the CIA estimated that the Vietcong had actually expanded by 4,000 to 6,000 fighters over the previous six months, a discrepancy Vice President Tho

---

[253] Memorandum, Forrestal to Kaysen and Bundy, August 18, 1962, Box 196, NSF:VN, JFK.
[254] Blaufarb, *Counterinsurgency Era*, p. 116.
[255] Memorandum, Heavner to Nolting, FRUS 1962, p. 363. For similar views from British sources, see Letter, Hohler to Jones, July 13, 1962, FO 371/166749.
[256] Report, Mansfield to Kennedy, December 18, 1962, FRUS 1962, pp. 781–2.

attributed to the fact that "many of the casualties were not VC at all, but members of the population killed by GVN forces."[257]

A third report by Michael Forrestal of the National Security Council and Roger Hilsman of the State Department leveled criticism at the South Vietnamese government, MACV, and the American embassy in Saigon. The duo asserted that Diem's government lacked any semblance of a long-term plan for achieving victory. Disparaging the ARVN's large-scale "hit and withdraw" operations – which failed to permanently clear the highly mobile Communist guerrillas from a given area – they noted that the few occasions when MACV's protégés attempted to "clear and hold territory," their efforts were marred by poor coordination between the government's civil and military components. Finally, Ambassador Nolting was criticized for his failure to press Diem harder for the "gradual liberalization" called for under the joint agreement. Under Nolting's leadership, the duo alleged, the embassy had failed to cultivate significant relationships with South Vietnam's anti-Communist opposition or "maintain a U.S. position independent of Diem."[258]

Taken together, the three reports suggested that the heavily militarized counterinsurgency campaign was unlikely to bring the conflict under control in the absence of meaningful political and social reforms. As former Undersecretary of State Chester Bowles bluntly stated in a memo to Kennedy, we "appear to be striving, in defiance of powerful indigenous political and military forces, to ensure the survival of an unpopular Vietnamese regime with inadequate roots among the people." The United States had to pressure Diem for political and economic reform, Bowles argued, by making it clear that "our continued assistance to his regime is dependent on his acceptance" of these measures.[259]

In contrast to these negative assessments, American senior advisors attached to the ARVN's I and II Corps in northern and central Vietnam reported that the government had been "clearly, steadily, and as far as I can see, inexorably" winning the fight against the insurgents since

---

[257] CIA, "Current Status of the War in South Vietnam," January 11, 1963, FRUS 1963/1, pp. 19–22; MemCon Mendenhall and Tho, FRUS 1962, p. 477.
[258] Memorandum, Hilsman and Forrestal to Kennedy, January 25, 1963, FRUS 1963/1, pp. 49–62.
[259] Memorandum, Bowles to Kennedy, March 7, 1963, FRUS 1963/1, pp. 136–40.

mid-1962.[260] Similarly, the Joint Chiefs of Staff reported that South Vietnamese military operations were "moving in the right direction," Vietcong morale was "deteriorating," and victory was a "hopeful prospect." Citing the role played by the Strategic Hamlet Program, the JCS noted that an additional half million people had been brought under the control of the government in 1962.[261] This optimistic view was echoed by General Harkins, who believed that the United States and the Vietnamese had "taken the military, psychological, economic and political initiative from the enemy."[262] In contrast to Hilsman and Forrestal, Harkins argued that the ARVN's military strategy – which attacked Vietcong base areas and sought out their regular units – was fundamentally sound and that the South Vietnamese government's civil and military efforts were achieving the necessary level of coordination. Ambassador Nolting reiterated Harkins' positive view and argued that public criticisms of Diem, such as that by Senator Mansfield, make "the government here tighten up rather than liberalize, and have encouraged the enemy."[263]

Indeed, public criticism of the South Vietnamese government by American officials and advisors had created a considerable amount of tension in the relationship between Washington and Saigon.[264] Although they were pleased to have seemingly gained the upper hand against the insurgents, Diem and Nhu remained staunch nationalists who were unhappy with the significant increase in American civilian and military presence necessary to achieve that result.[265] The pair was reported to be upset over "infringements" on Vietnamese sovereignty by American advisors and desired to see their numbers reduced by up to a third.[266] Moreover, the large number of Americans working directly

---

[260] Hal McCowen, Senior Officer Debriefing Reports, October 18, 1963, p. 7, MHI; Denno, "Debriefing," p. 11. For a less optimistic yet still positive assessment from III Corps in the vicinity of Saigon, see Memo, Wilson to Dinh, April 15, 1963, Box 6, Wilson Papers.

[261] JCS Team Report on South Vietnam, January 1963, FRUS 1963/1, pp. 73–94; Minutes of a Meeting of the Special Group for Counterinsurgency, February 7, 1963, FRUS 1963/1, pp, 103–5.

[262] Letter, Harkins to Diem, February 23, 1963, FRUS 1963/1, p. 118; Naval Message, CINCPAC to JCS, March 9, 1963, Box 197, NSF:VN, JFK.

[263] Telegram 824, Saigon to State, March 20, 1963, FRUS 1963/1, p. 162.

[264] *Ibid.*, pp. 246–7.   [265] Colby, "Oral History Interview I," p. 9.

[266] Telegram 1084, State to Saigon, May 13, 1963, FRUS 1963/1, pp. 294–6; CIA Information Report [redacted], "Views of Ngo Dinh Nhu ...," March 6, 1963 and CIA Information Report [redacted], "Views of Ngo Dinh Nhu ...,"

with South Vietnamese military and government officials created the impression that the country was an American colony. Diem felt that this not only undermined his authority but also led the population to ignore local officials because they believed "that the Americans are now the government."[267] In a public critique of their patron's effort, Nhu told a reporter from the *Washington Post* that up to half the U.S. advisors in the country "were not absolutely necessary."[268] American requests to monitor the South Vietnamese government's performance also appeared to be a point of contention. In conversations with Nolting, Diem hinted that while U.S. aid was welcome, the advice and accountability measures that came with it were not.[269] As Nolting pointed out, this was close to a repudiation of the "expanded and deepened advisory effort" that was a cornerstone of the December 1961 agreement.[270] Behind the scenes, Nhu was instructing senior Vietnamese officials "to prepare for a complete withdrawal of American aid," which he asserted Washington was using "as a means of pressuring the GVN and impinging on GVN sovereignty."[271]

The situation on the ground in Vietnam was unclear, there were growing strains in the relationship with Saigon, and the White House was distracted by other domestic and foreign policy issues. As a result, throughout the spring of 1963, American policy drifted: Was the GVN winning or losing? Should Diem be pressed to undertake reforms or should the United States reaffirm its support to shore up his confidence?

The Buddhist Crisis

Diem's "personalist revolution," which was attempting to forge a modern, communitarian society, was not the only nation-building project in South Vietnam. Believing that medieval Vietnam began

April 2, 1963, both Box 197, NSF:VN, JFKL. Discussions of these various reports can be found in Editorial Note, FRUS 1963/1, p. 124; Telegram 852, Saigon to State, March 28, 1963, FRUS 1963/1, pp. 183–4, and Telegram 871, State/AID to Saigon, March 15, 1963, AID(US) S VIET, RG 59.

267 Telegram 882, Saigon to State, April 5, 1963, FRUS 1963/1, pp. 208, 211.

268 Warren Unna, "Viet-Nam Wants 50 Percent of GIs Out," *Washington Post*, May 12, 1963.

269 Telegram 882, pp. 207–13.   270 *Ibid.*, p. 213.

271 CIA Information Report [redacted], "Ngo Dinh Nhu's Statements on Withdrawal of American Aid," April 20, 1963, Box 197, NSF:VN, JFK.

a long decline when its leaders and people turned away from Buddhism, the General Buddhist Association of Vietnam tried to link that faith with Vietnamese nationalism in an effort to bring about a religious and national revival. Ngo Dinh Diem's project thus posed a direct threat to the aims of ardent Buddhist nationalists.[272]

In the summer of 1963, the debate in Washington over how to deal with Saigon was overtaken by events as growing tensions between Buddhist activists and Diem's government sparked a national crisis.[273] In early May, in the old imperial capital of Hue, the violent dispersal of an unauthorized Buddhist rally became a focal point for opposition to Diem's government and triggered demonstrations across the country.[274] In an effort to restore order, martial law was declared in Hue, while in Saigon, Nhu's secret police used teargas to disrupt antigovernment protests.[275] The British embassy judged the deepening crisis to be the most serious challenge to Diem's authority since the 1960 paratrooper revolt.[276]

Despite growing unrest, there appeared to be good prospects for a negotiated resolution when Diem fired several officials responsible for the Hue incident and his government agreed in principle to consider the protestors' complaints about perceived religious discrimination against Buddhists. The attempts at reconciliation were undermined, however, by Nhu and his wife, who issued a series of provocative public statements denouncing the leaders of the protests as liars and traitors using the guise of religion to undermine the government.[277] Behind closed doors, Nhu railed against his brother's conciliatory

---

[272] Miller, *Misalliance*, pp. 262–3.

[273] The exact size of South Vietnam's Buddhist population is the subject of some debate. Most histories describe South Vietnam has having a clear Buddhist majority. However, out of a population of 15 million people, Moyar suggests that between 3 and 4 million were Buddhist, only half of whom actually practiced the faith. Moyar, *Triumph Forsaken*, p. 215. State Department officials at the time cite an even lower total in Letter, Dutton to Wilson, December 5, 1963, POL 27 VIETS, RG 59, and Ambassador Durbrow puts the number of practicing Buddhists at just 10 percent of the population in Durbrow, "Oral History Interview I," pp. 53–4.

[274] Telegram 1155, Saigon to State, June 11, 1963, FRUS 1963/1, pp. 378–381. The protestors wanted to fly flags celebrating the Buddha's birthday, but in the interests of national unity, such sectarian displays wereforbidden in South Vietnam

[275] Telegram 1101, Saigon to State, June 4, 1963, FRUS 1963/1, pp. 346–7; Karnow, *Vietnam*, pp. 295–6.

[276] Dispatch 32, Saigon to FCO, June 12, 1963, FO 371/170143, NAUK.

[277] Miller, *Misalliance*, pp. 269–70.

attitude, suggesting that if Diem was unwilling or unable to enforce order, the government deserved to fall.[278]

Hopes of a quick end to the crisis were dashed on the morning of June 11 when, in a carefully stage-managed propaganda event, a seventy-three-year-old Buddhist monk set himself on fire in front of a crowd of reporters to both protest Diem's government and rally the country's Buddhists.[279] The images of the self-immolation provoked outrage around the world and made Vietnam front-page news.[280] In the United States, approval of Kennedy's Vietnam policy plunged to 28 percent, while in Congress, Senator Frank Church (D-Idaho) introduced a resolution calling for a suspension of U.S. aid to Saigon.[281] Administration officials began to worry that the high-profile problems in Vietnam could jeopardize congressional support for their entire range of foreign aid programs.[282]

The United States pressured Diem to reach an accommodation with the protestors lest the crisis undermine the government's counterinsurgency campaign.[283] However, with a United Nations (UN) fact-finding mission concluding that allegations of widespread religious persecution in South Vietnam were "hearsay," Diem began to backtrack on his earlier policy of conciliation.[284] The South Vietnamese president saw the ongoing protests as a political attack on his government by a group,

---

[278] Ahern, *CIA and the House of NGO*, pp. 167–8.
[279] Telegram 824, Saigon to State, March 20, 1963, FRUS 1963/1, p. 163; Miller, *Misalliance*, p. 272.
[280] Research Memo RFE-57, Denney to Rusk, June 28, 1963, SOC 14–1 SVIET, RG 59.
[281] Telegram 341, State to Saigon, September 9, 1963, POL 1 SVIET-US, RG 59; Gibbons, *The U.S. Government and the Vietnam War*, p. 168; Louis Harris, *The Anguish of Change* (New York: W.W. Norton, 1973), p. 54.
[282] Telegram 1247, State to Saigon, June 19, 1963, FRUS 1961/1, pp. 402–4.
[283] Telegram 1083, Saigon to State, May 31, 1963, FRUS 1963/1, pp. 337–9. The CIA assessed that "the issue could have serious repercussions on government stability" if not resolved quickly. Telegram 1093, Saigon to State, June 3, 1963, FRUS 1963/1, pp. 344–6.
[284] Ambassador Fernando Volio Jiminez quoted in Ross A. Fisher, "The Kennedy Administration and the Overthrow of Ngo Dinh Diem," in Ross A. Fisher, John Norton Moore, and Robert F. Turner, eds., *To Oppose Any Foe: The Legacy of U.S. Intervention in Vietnam* (Durham, NC: Carolina Academic Press, 2006), p. 24. See also Telegram 1083, FRUS 1963/1, pp. 337–9; Guenter Lewy, *America in Vietnam* (New York: Oxford University Press, 1978), p. 26. Despite allegations of favoritism, at times the Diem government also had strained relations with the country's Catholic community. Telegram 25, Saigon to Foreign Office, May 2, 1957, FO 371/129751, NAUK.

seeking to advance its sectarian interests at the expense of the nation, rather than a legitimate religious dispute. Consequently, he was wary of conceding too much lest the loss of "face" undermine his authority and encourage other groups to pursue a similar course of action.[285] Embassy officials candidly informed Diem that if an agreement could not be reached with the demonstrators, the United States "would have to dissociate itself from [the government's] actions," which Secretary Rusk suggested would compel the administration to "reexamine our entire relationship with his regime."[286] Under this intense pressure, Diem agreed to repeal the policies that the militant Buddhists viewed as discriminatory.[287] This was considered a key test of both Diem's intentions and America's remaining influence over its client: if Diem did not follow through on this issue, he was unlikely to keep his word on any agreement that the United States compelled him to make.[288]

Unfortunately, the agreement brought little resolution. The government delayed implementation of the accord while Buddhist activists escalated their antigovernment demonstrations.[289] In the countryside, with the government paralyzed by the growing crisis, the defenses of the

---

[285] Telegram 1155, FRUS 1963/1, pp. 378–381. The Chargé D'affaires at the U.S. embassy shared Diem's view that the "Buddhist crisis" was a political rather than a religious dispute. Trueheart, "Oral History Interview," p. 33. Buddhist leaders stated that they would "seek help from any source [to topple Diem] including the VC." Telegram 1084, Saigon to State, June 1, 1963, FRUS 1963/1, pp. 340–1. Diem's beliefs about the sectarian interests of the demonstrators were not unfounded. As the militant Buddhists grew in influence, they would increasingly demand the suppression of other faiths in Vietnam. See, e.g., Memorandum of Conversation, Lodge, Harkins, Westmoreland, et al., May 12, 1964, *Foreign Relations of the United States 1964–1968*, vol. I, Vietnam, 1964 (FRUS 1964), p. 314 and CIA, "An Analysis of Thich Tri Quang's Possible Communist Affiliations, Personality and Goals," August 28, 1964, DDRS.

[286] Telegram 1136, Saigon to State, June 9, 1963, FRUS 1963/1, p. 367; Telegram 1207, State to Saigon, June 11, 1963, FRUS 1963/1, p. 383; Telegram 1199, State to Saigon, June 10, 1963, SOC 14–1 SVIET, RG 59.

[287] Telegram 1194, Saigon to State, June 16, 1963, SOC 14–1 SVIET, RG 59. The British also credit U.S. pressure with bringing about this change of policy. Dispatch 35, Saigon to FCO, June 26, 1963, FO 371/170143, NAUK.

[288] Research Memorandum, "Implications of the Buddhist Crisis in Vietnam," June 21, 1963, FRUS 1963/1, pp. 405–9.

[289] Telegram 1224, Saigon to State, June 22, 1963, FRUS 1963/1, pp. 409–10; Telegram 5, Saigon to State, July 1, 1963, POL SVIET-US, RG 59; Telegram 173, Saigon to State, August 3, 1963, POL 6 S VIET, RG 59; Telegram 190, Saigon to State, August 8, 1963, SOC 14–1 S RG 59.

strategic hamlets were allowed to deteriorate at the critical moment when they were being actively subverted by the Vietcong.[290] As the situation dragged on through the summer, insurgent activity steadily increased and a host of American assessments warned of the harm being done to South Vietnam's domestic stability. It was judged that an escalated confrontation with the protestors could pose a more serious threat to the government than the insurgents and that a non-Communist coup attempt was likely if there was no resolution to the crisis.[291]

In August, Kennedy appointed former senator Henry Cabot Lodge, Jr., to succeed Nolting as ambassador. The choice of a Republican and a potential opponent in the 1964 presidential election was certainly unconventional; however, as a White House advisor recalls, "[T]he thought of implicating a leading Republican in the Vietnam mess appealed to his instinct for politics."[292] For its part, the Vietnamese government interpreted the replacement of a known friend in Nolting with an ambassador of Lodge's stature as a sign that the United States intended to get tough with Saigon.[293] As Madame Nhu remarked on the new envoy's arrival in Saigon, "[T]hey have sent us a proconsul."[294]

Over the years, bold action and political maneuvering had allowed the regime to triumph in its various confrontations with rebellious army officers, semiautonomous warlords, and nascent political opponents.[295] With America's commitment to Diem in question, coup rumors circulating in Saigon, and militant Buddhists explicitly seeking to bring down the government, Nhu moved to neutralize the threat posed by the mounting protests while presenting the incoming U.S. ambassador with a fait accompli.[296] Fearing that the morale of

[290] Memo, Wilson to Dinh, October 7, 1963, Box 2, Wilson Papers; Colby, "Oral History Interview I," pp. 21–2; Rufus Phillips, "Oral History Interview II," May 27, 1982, p. 25, LBJ.

[291] "Implications of the Buddhist Crisis ...," FRUS 1963/1, pp. 405–9; CIA, "Appraisal of the Ngo Diem Regime as of 26 June 1963," June 28, 1963, FRUS 1963/1, pp. 423–5; Special National Intelligence Estimate, "The Situation in South Vietnam," July 10, 1963, FRUS 1963/1, pp. 483–5.

[292] Arthur M. Schlesinger, *A Thousand Days* (London: Deutsch, 1965), p. 989.

[293] Telegram 1236, Saigon to State, June 25, 1963, FRUS 1963/1, pp. 413–4.

[294] Quoted in Howard Jones, *Death of a Generation* (Oxford: Oxford University Press, 2003), p. 304.

[295] Miller, *Misalliance*, pp. 277–8.

[296] CIA, "Situation Appraisal of the Political Situation as of 1200 hours on 6 July," July 8, 1963, FRUS 1963/1, pp. 473–8; Memo of Conversation, "South Vietnam Situation," September 6, 1963, SOC 14–1 SVIET, RG 59.

their troops was deteriorating, senior ARVN generals had convinced Diem to declare martial law to bring the crisis under control.[297] On August 21, Nhu took advantage of martial law to dispatch elements of the American-trained Vietnamese Special Forces under his direct control to join police raids on the main Buddhist temples in Saigon and Hue. Nearly 1,500 monks and nuns were arrested, including the leaders of the antigovernment protests.[298] By specifically involving military units in the action, Nhu sought to force the Kennedy administration to either accept his coup de main or cut off support for ARVN – a step that Washington had been unwilling to take in any of its previous "confrontations" with Saigon.

Rather than smothering dissent, the raids triggered a new wave of street protests. The government responded forcefully, arresting protestors and proactively detaining opposition leaders.[299] Vietnamese citizens were increasingly critical of the United States for its apparent acquiescence to the crackdown – believing that Washington could force the South Vietnamese government to change its policies if it wished to do so.[300]

Nhu's influence expanded significantly as a result of martial law and Vietnamese government personnel at all levels alleged that he had secretly seized the reins of power from his brother.[301] Diem appeared isolated and ill-informed about events in the country and was reportedly unwilling to accept advice from anyone outside his immediate

---

[297] Telegram 299, Saigon to State, August 21, 1963, FRUS 1963/1, pp. 595–7; Memorandum, CJCS to SecState, August 23, 1963, FRUS 1963/1, pp. 606–10; CIA Telegram 0265, Saigon to Langley, August 24, 1963, FRUS 1963/1, pp. 614–20.

[298] CIA Telegram 0265, FRUS 1963/1, pp. 614–20; Message 16598, CINPAC to State, August 21, 1963, DDRS; Telegram 267, Saigon to State, August 21, 1963, Box 198a, NSF:VN, JFK; Telegram 329, Saigon to State, August 24, 1963, POL 2–4 SVIET, RG 59; Ellen Hammer, *A Death in November: America in Viet Nam 1963* (New York: Dutton, 1987), p. 167; Jones, *Death of a Generation*, p. 306.

[299] CIA Information Report, TDCS 3/557 818, August 28, 1963, Box 198, NSF: VN, JFK.

[300] Message 16048, DIA to White House, August 23, 1963, NSF:VN, JFK; Telegram [no. redacted], Saigon to State, August 26, 1963, POL 25 SVIET, RG 59.

[301] Telegram 470, Saigon to State, September 11, 1963, POL 15 VIET, RG 59; Memorandum, Hughes to SecState, "The Problem of Nhu," September 15, 1963, POL 27 VIET, RG 59; Information Report, "[Redacted] Claims that Nhu is Running the Government," September 20, 1963, CIA.

family.[302] Senior government officials – including Ngo family loyalists – warned of "chaos" if the United States could not remove Nhu from the government, suggesting that Washington should withdraw support if Nhu remained in a position of authority.[303] In the face of the popular backlash against the pagoda raids, high-ranking ARVN officers began to plot against Nhu, surreptitiously approaching the embassy to gauge the potential American reaction to forcibly removing him from power.[304]

Having recently arrived in Vietnam, Ambassador Lodge requested guidance from Washington on how to respond to the nascent coup plot. State Department analysts had identified Nhu as "the primary factor exacerbating the Buddhist controversy" and "the major obstacle" to its resolution.[305] Lodge was advised that the "U.S. Government cannot tolerate a situation in which power lies in Nhu's hands." While Diem should be given an opportunity to remove Nhu from the government, if he refuses to do so, "[W]e must face the possibility that Diem himself cannot be preserved."[306] The ambassador was instructed to pass this information to the coup plotters, but the anti-Nhu movement quickly fizzled as the dissidents failed to amass enough support to carry out their plan.[307]

As the prospect of a putsch faded, Washington focused on persuading the South Vietnamese government to adopt a series of liberalizing measures. President Kennedy himself signaled a determination to see changes in an interview with Walter Cronkite on the *CBS Evening News*, where he opined that South Vietnam would lose its fight with the Communists unless there were "changes in policy and perhaps with

[302] Memorandum, Rufus Phillips to William Trueheart, "Recommendation for Immediate U.S. Action," July 5, 1963, Box 49, Lansdale Papers.

[303] Telegram 324, Saigon to State, August 24, 1963, FRUS 1963/1, pp. 611–2; Telegram 316, Saigon to State, August 24, 1963, POL 25 SVIET, RG 59.

[304] Telegram 274, Saigon to State, August 24, 1963, FRUS 1963/1, pp. 613–4; CIA Telegram 0291, Saigon to Langley, August 25, 1963, FRUS 1963/1, pp. 633–4; Telegram 334, Saigon to State, August 26, 1963, SOC 14–1 SVIET, RG 59.

[305] Hughes, "The Problem of Nhu."

[306] Telegram 243, State to Saigon, August 24, 1963, FRUS 1963/1, p. 628. For a recent assessment of the controversial "Cable 243," see John Prados, ed., *Diem Coup after 50 Years*, National Security Archives Electronic Briefing Book No 444, November 1, 2013.

[307] Telegram 272, State to Saigon, August 29, 1963, FRUS 1963/2, p. 32; MAC 1583, MAAG to JCS, August 31, 1963, FRUS 1963/2, pp. 64–6; Telegram 391, Saigon to State, August 31, 1963, FRUS 1963/2, pp. 66–8.

personnel" in Saigon.[308] This was matched with a delay in the delivery of nonmilitary aid to South Vietnam which was intended to underscore Washington's unhappiness. In Saigon, Ambassador Lodge refused to meet with Diem and granted asylum at the embassy to several leaders of the militant Buddhist movement. The United States was sending a clear signal that its commitment to Diem was in question.[309]

At first, the hard line taken by the administration appeared to compel the Vietnamese government into action. Nhu sought out Lodge to inform him that he would leave the government, that opposition politicians would be brought in, and that reconciliation would be sought with the Buddhists. Soon after, Nhu arranged for several polarizing figures, including his wife, his brother the archbishop, and the head of the intelligence services, to leave the country for an extended period of time.[310] Buoyed by these developments, yet wary of the delaying tactics the Ngo family had employed in the past, the administration pressed for concrete action, including an end to martial law, the release of student protestors, and the recommencement of talks with the leadership of the militant Buddhist movement. As in the past, promises of reform and reconciliation were followed by a renewed crackdown: embassy dispatches soon described the cities of Saigon, Hue, and Da Nang as existing in a miasma of "fear," "anger," and "hate" directed primarily toward Nhu.[311]

To reduce American pressure, Nhu cultivated the impression that he was clandestinely negotiating with Hanoi on a French proposal to neutralize and reunify Vietnam.[312] Given North Vietnam's economic

---

[308] Interview with President Kennedy, September 2, 1963, FRUS 1963/2, pp. 93–5.
[309] Telegram 383, Saigon to State, August 30, 1963, POL 22–9 SVIET, RG 59;
       Telegram 313, State to Saigon, September 3, 1963, AID(US) SVIET, RG 59.
[310] Miller, *Misalliance*, pp. 297–8.
[311] Telegram 403, Saigon to State, September 2, 1963, FRUS 1963/2, pp. 84–5;
       Memorandum, "State of Mind of the Nhus," September 6, 1963, FRUS
       1963/2, pp. 144–5; Message 4688, State to White House, September 7, 1963,
       Box 199, NSF:VN, JFK; Telegram 7, Hue to State, August 31, 1963, POL 26
       SVIET, RG 59.
[312] Memorandum of Conversation, Rusk, Hilsman, et al., August 30, 1963, FRUS
       1963/2, p. 55; Telegram 391, Saigon to State, August 31, 1963, FRUS 1963/2,
       p. 68; Memorandum of Conversation, Rusk, Hilsman, et al., August 31, 1963,
       FRUS 1963/2, p. 72; CIA Telegram 0698, Saigon to Langley, September 6,
       1963, FRUS 1963/2, pp. 125–6, Research Memorandum, "Hanoi, Paris,
       Saigon, and South Vietnam's Future," September 11, 1963, FRUS 1963/2,
       p. 184.

weakness and the appearance that the Vietcong was being defeated in the field, a number of observers found the possibility of such negotiations credible.[313] Believing that the threat of a settlement that did not take into account U.S. interests in Asia would convince the Kennedy administration to back the government "without any strings attached," Nhu confidently predicted to a group of ARVN generals that he could "manage" Ambassador Lodge and that Washington would shortly acquiesce to the government's crackdown.[314] Nhu also reached out to the French, who pressed the United States to cease its attacks on Diem's government.[315] This effort was complemented by a direct assault on the United States in the government-controlled media, which alleged that the CIA had encouraged ARVN officers to mount a coup against Diem.[316] Rumors also circulated that members of the Ngo family had drawn up a "hit list" of U.S. officials who spoke out against the regime, while local Vietnamese employed by the U.S. government reported that they were "under close surveillance" by Nhu's agents.[317]

The Last Push for Conditionality

With dissident ARVN officers no longer planning a coup and the aid slowdown having proved to be insufficient pressure to generate action on the part of the South Vietnamese government, the Kennedy administration attempted to regain influence in its relationship with Saigon. As Secretary Rusk belatedly recognized, the perception that the United States was "inescapably committed to an anti-Communist Vietnam" had undercut its leverage over the regime.[318]

In the face of an uncertain situation on the ground and division among key advisors, Kennedy dispatched a pair of fact-finding missions to make sense of the political and military impact of the Buddhist crisis. The reports varied widely; however, the dominant

---

[313] Miller, *Misalliance*, p. 307; Ahern, *CIA and the House of Ngo*, p. 189.
[314] CIA Telegram [no. redacted], Saigon to Langley, September 2, 1963, FRUS 1963/2, pp. 89–92.
[315] Statler, *Replacing France*, p. 247
[316] Memorandum, "State of Mind of the Nhus," FRUS 1963/2, pp. 122–3; Telegram 355, State to Saigon, September 7, 1963, SOC 14–1 SVIET, RG 59.
[317] Memorandum, "State of Mind of the Nhus," FRUS 1963/2, pp. 122–3; Telegram 7; Phillips, "Before We Lost in Vietnam," p. 55.
[318] Telegram 279, State to Saigon, August 29, 1963, FRUS 1963/2, p. 34.

view was that the military campaign was making progress but the political opposition generated by the Ngo family's repression had the potential to erode this success. The administration considered three options: (1) reconcile with Diem's government, (2) actively promote a coup, or (3) apply "selective short-term pressures" in the form of nonmilitary aid reductions to clarify that America's existing commitments were to Vietnam, not to the Ngo family.[319]

In selecting the third policy, it was acknowledged that while "it is not clear that pressure exerted by the U.S. will move Diem and Nhu to moderation," nevertheless, "unless such pressures are exerted they are almost certain to continue past patterns of behavior."[320] Pressure came in the form of conditions on USAID loans for several major infrastructure projects as well as on the Commercial Import Program, which subsidized 40 percent of South Vietnam's imports. The release of aid was tied to specific military and political actions that would allow South Vietnam to better prosecute the war against the Vietcong. In the military sphere, the United States wanted the government to refocus its efforts away from the sparsely populated Central Highlands toward the security situation in the Mekong Delta, employ "clear and hold" operations to root out Vietcong infrastructure, and provide better training and arms for the hamlet militias. In the political realm, the United States pushed for the release of student protestors, an end to arbitrary arrests, a new land reform program, the appointment of respected public figures to posts in the government, and a visible reduction in Nhu's influence. The latter measure would serve as a "dramatic symbolic move which convinces Vietnamese that the reforms are real."[321] Finally, all future aid to the Vietnamese Special Forces, whom Nhu continued to use to attack dissidents, would be conditioned on their reassignment to the command of the Joint General Staff and employment against the insurgents rather than domestic opponents.[322] In signaling a reduced commitment to Diem, the Kennedy administration hoped to regain the leverage it had lost through its prior unilateral commitments by creating "significant uncertainty in that government and in key Vietnamese groups as to

[319] Memorandum, JCS and SecDef to Kennedy, October 2, 1963, FRUS 1963/2, pp. 336–46.
[320] *Ibid.*
[321] Telegram 534, State to Saigon, October 5, 1963, FRUS 1963/2, pp. 371–9.
[322] *Ibid.*

the future intentions of the United States."[323] They hoped that this would generate momentum within the Vietnamese government to undertake the kind of liberalization that would foster the popular support necessary to overcome the insurgency.

In order to create an opening for Diem to initiate these policy changes without a public loss of face, no public references to conditionality were made. Rusk specifically instructed Lodge to make "every possible effort to limit public knowledge" of the plan because it would undermine its efforts if there was a popular perception that the United States was imposing a list of demands on the South Vietnamese government.[324] American hopes of keeping the matter hidden were quickly dashed when the Vietnamese press denounced the "relentless pressure" being applied to the GVN to compel it to "accept U.S. political advice and guidance" that would harm the war effort.[325]

Believing that the war was still going in their favor and that they would soon be in a position of strength vis-à-vis North Vietnam, the Ngos responded to American pressure by attempting to reinforce their bargaining position.[326] In an address to the National Assembly, Diem sought to arouse nationalist sentiment by blaming many of the country's problems on "traitors and foreign adventurers," the latter an oft-used code for American personnel.[327] Taking things one step further, Nhu told local journalists that the CIA was actively encouraging the militant Buddhists to overthrow the government.[328] To international media, Nhu downplayed the importance of American aid, claiming that "if the Americans were to interrupt their help, it may not be a bad thing after all" because U.S. interference was hindering the Ngos' "revolutionary transformation of society." Instead, Nhu argued that the United States should treat Vietnam like Yugoslavia, "giving them money, but not seeking to influence their

---

[323] Annex to the Draft Report Prepared for the Executive Committee of the National Security Council, October 4, 1963, FRUS 1963/2, p. 360.

[324] Telegram 534, FRUS 1963/2, p. 371

[325] Telegram 647, Saigon to State, October 7, 1963, AID(US) SVIET, RG 59; CIA Memorandum, "Events and Developments in South Vietnam, 5–18 October," October 19, 1963, DDRS.

[326] On the Ngos' views, see CIA Telegram 0698.

[327] Telegram 652, Saigon to State, October 7, 1963, POL 15-1 SVIET, RG 59.

[328] Memorandum, Forrestal to Bundy, "Nhu's Interview in Times of Vietnam," October 21, 1963, FRUS 1963/2, pp. 415–18.

system of government."[329] In an attempt to mitigate the effects of an aid suspension, the South Vietnamese government instituted a belt-tightening campaign that cut the salaries of civil servants and attempted to foster economic self-sufficiency while once again reaching out to Taiwan as an alternate source of military expertise for the ARVN.[330] These measures were accompanied by more sinister attempts to intimidate American personnel. The CIA reported that American officials were being closely monitored by the Vietnamese police, and persistent rumors suggested that Nhu planned to stage a "spontaneous" anti-American demonstration that would result in an attack on the U.S. embassy or the assassination of Ambassador Lodge.[331]

As the South Vietnamese government appeared to dig in for what the CIA termed "a protracted war of attrition with the U.S." to resist pressure for reform, the evidence of a clear split between the United States and Diem spurred dissident ARVN officers to resuming plotting against the regime.[332] Disregarding Kennedy's instructions that no covert encouragement should be given to a coup, local CIA officers, acting on Lodge's orders, repeatedly assured the plotters that the United States would not stand in the way if they decided to move against Diem.[333] While the White House would become increasingly concerned at the mounting evidence that Lodge was independently driving a coup forward, Kennedy did little to rein in his potential political rival.[334]

Through October, American conditionality appeared to be generating movement within the South Vietnamese government. Attempting to gauge American resolve, Diem dispatched his Secretary of State

[329] *Ibid.*
[330] Telegram 632, Saigon to State, October 4, 1963, POL 2 SVIET, RG 59.
[331] Telegram 676, Saigon to State, October 10, 1963, FRUS 1963/2, pp. 394–5; CIA Information Report, "Situation Appraisal as of 12 October 1963," October 14, 1963, FRUS 1963/2, pp. 398–401.
[332] CIA Information Report, FRUS 1963/2, p. 398.
[333] CAP 63560, Bundy to Lodge, October 5, 1963, FRUS 1963/2, p. 379. For Lodge's continual agitation for a coup, from the perspective of a plotter, see Tran Van Don, *Our Endless War* (San Rafael, CA: Presidio Press, 1978), pp. 97–9.
[334] CIA Report, "Contacts with Vietnamese Generals, 23 August through 23 October 1963," October 25, 1963, DDRS; Meeting Recording, October 25, 1963, Tape No. 117/A53, Presidential Recordings, JFK; Telegram [no number], Bundy to Lodge, October 30, 1963, FRUS 1963/2, pp. 501–2. On Kennedy's inability to control Lodge, see Colby, *Lost Victory*, p. 135.

Nguyen Dinh Thuan – the most powerful member of the government after Diem and Nhu – to find out if the United States was planning on delivering the conditioned aid. Thuan, who had previously emphasized to American interlocutors the need for reform within the government and the removal of Nhu, hinted to Lodge that American pressure was having a positive effect and that a resolution to the diplomatic standoff was imminent.[335] Three days later, the ARVN's Joint General Staff assumed control over the Vietnamese Special Forces and began redeploying them from Saigon to take part in counterinsurgency operations in the countryside, which had been a condition for their future receipt of American assistance.[336] Although Nhu publicly claimed that South Vietnam could operate for twenty years without foreign aid, as the country faced shortages of imported foodstuffs and rising prices for commodities, the government's own internal studies confirmed that it could not go on without U.S. assistance.[337]

Following Diem's entreaties to meet with Lodge, Washington cautiously instructed the ambassador to assess whether, as a result of American pressure, Diem might be "moving [in] the direction we desire."[338] By November 1, Diem had asked Lodge to deliver a message to the White House: "Please tell President Kennedy that I am a good and frank ally ... that I take all his suggestions very seriously and wish to carry them out, but it is a question of timing."[339] Holding the government's feet to the fire appeared to be working. The American ambassador reported to Washington that "[i]f we want to make a package deal, I would think we were in a position to do it ... in effect [Diem] said: Tell us what you want and we'll do it."[340] The ultimate effectiveness of this use of conditionality is unknown,

---

[335] Telegram 745, Saigon to State, October 19, 1963, FRUS 1963/2, p. 414
[336] Telegram 770, Saigon to State, October 23, 9163, FRUS 1963/2, p. 424; Message 8250, MACV to CINPAC, October 19, 1963, Box 201, NSF:VN, JFK.
[337] Telegram 804, Saigon to State, October 28, 1961, FRUS 1963/2, p. 441; CIA Report, "Ngo Dinh Nhu's Statements on Withdrawal of American Aid." On Nhu's claims, see CIA, "Views of Ngo Dinh Nhu on Possible Reduction in Foreign Aid," September 12, 1963, CIA.
[338] Telegram 647, State to Saigon, October 25, 1963, FRUS 1963/2, p. 438.
[339] Telegram 841, Saigon to State, November 1, 1963, SOC 14–1 SVIET/UN, RG 59.
[340] *Ibid.*

however, because later that day Diem was overthrown and killed by a group of dissident ARVN generals.

Dénouement

In the immediate aftermath of the coup, the mood in South Vietnam was reported to be "jubilant" and "exuberant."[341] General Harkins' prediction that the dissidents lacked the necessary ability to lead the nation came true, however, as Saigon saw a succession of unstable governments that were wracked by political infighting.[342] Given the opportunity to reset its relationship with its client state, the Kennedy administration remained oblivious to the lessons of its recent history. Rather than clarify its obligations to Vietnam and use its assistance programs as leverage to ensure that the new military government took the kinds of sociopolitical actions to combat the insurgency that Diem had resisted for nearly a decade, Secretary Rusk instructed Ambassador Lodge to inform the Junta that the administration would not "use a delay in resuming aid as summary leverage on the generals."[343]

With the national government paralyzed, the Vietcong had no trouble stepping into the void. Seizing the political and military momentum from the government, the insurgents doubled the rate of their attacks and began operating in even larger military formations.[344] Meanwhile, it quickly became clear that the security situation in the countryside during the previous year was worse than even the pessimists in the U.S. government had thought.

In the eighteen months following Diem's overthrow, the character of the conflict in Vietnam would change dramatically. In 1964, the North Vietnamese Army began sending division-sized units into South Vietnam, marking the start of what became known as "the big unit war." In such circumstances, President Lyndon Johnson – who assumed office following Kennedy's assassination – became convinced that the South Vietnamese could not win on their own and ordered the first U.S. combat troops into Vietnam on March 8, 1965. The need for

---

[341] MAC J-3 8573, MAAG to JCS, November 2, 1963, FRUS 1963/2, p. 543, MAC J-3 8587, MAAG to JCS, November 4, 1963, FRUS 1963/2, p. 552; Jones, *Death of a Generation*, pp. 423–4.
[342] Telegram 822, Saigon to State, October 30, 1963, FRUS 1963/2, p. 482.
[343] Telegram 704, State to Saigon, November 3, 1963, FRUS 1963/2, p. 551.
[344] Memo, Wilson to Commander MACV, November 13, 1963, Wilson Papers.

this move underscored the failure of the counterinsurgency assistance efforts undertaken by the previous two administrations and marked a crucial step in the "Americanization" of the Vietnam War.

Assessment

The government of Ngo Dinh Diem was undoubtedly a flawed instrument for creating a stable, anti-Communist state south of the 17th parallel. The esoteric philosophy guiding the creation of a modern South Vietnam failed to resonate with much of the populace. In his aggressive efforts to stamp out all opposition, Diem angered and radicalized critical segments of the population, which left them vulnerable to co-option by the Vietcong. This was particularly true in the Mekong Delta, where non-Communist political opponents, as well as former Vietminh, quickly joined the armed struggle against his government. Diem's combativeness toward rival political figures and his unwillingness to share power with anyone he did not absolutely trust resulted in a diminished base of able administrators on which the government could rely. As a result, lackeys and sycophants were frequently appointed to high posts in lieu of more capable personnel. This problem was particularly acute in the armed forces, where, in an effort to "coup-proof" the regime, convoluted command structures with overlapping jurisdictions were created to prevent any single general from amassing too much authority.

Although these flaws were recognized, the United States failed to bring about sufficient change in its client to ameliorate them. Indeed, the American experience in Vietnam during the Diem years is a quintessential example of how not to assist an ally in counterinsurgency. The dominant influence strategy toward the South Vietnamese government in both the Eisenhower and Kennedy administrations was *inducement*. For eight years, aid and pledges of support were showered on Diem's government. Yet, despite providing Saigon with the present-day equivalent of nearly $2 billion a year in military and economic assistance (44 percent of South Vietnam's GDP) between 1955 and 1963, the United States was unable to convince Diem to broaden and liberalize his government, rationalize the ARVN's command structure, or undertake any other kind of meaningful reform. Instead, U.S. requests for reform or policy change were met with delay and

obfuscation. This certainly casts doubt on the expectations of inducement discussed in Chapter 3 that the unilateral provision of aid will
lead to a reciprocal concession by the recipient.

Similarly, the belief that clear public commitments to a client will
lead to greater influence is not borne out by this case. In assisting Ngo
Dinh Diem to lead South Vietnam, the United States put its support
behind an individual, rather than a government or a political system,
which may have led the South Vietnamese president to conclude that he
was indispensable. Throughout his tenure, lavish state visits, letters of
support from American presidents, and grandiloquent praise citing him
as a "miracle man" or the "Winston Churchill" of Southeast Asia did
nothing to dispel these notions. Yet every time the United States reiterated its commitment to Diem, his willingness to acquiesce to U.S. policy
proposals declined. As a consequence of this firm American commitment, the South Vietnamese leader had little incentive to compromise
with his domestic opponents, and unlike in the Philippines or El
Salvador, no meaningful political liberalization occurred during the
course of the American intervention (see Figure 5.1). Responding to
political rivals with force and political machinations rather than
accommodation had served Diem well during his consolidation of
power in 1955 and almost succeeded in annihilating Communism in

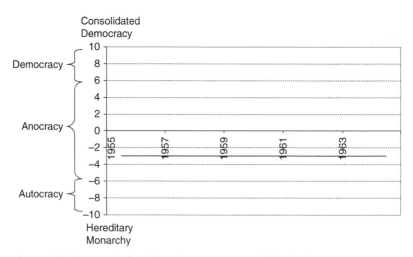

Figure 5.1 Vietnam Polity IV regime type score, 1955–1964.

South Vietnam in the period from 1955 to 1958. However, these tactics sowed the seeds of disaster in the long run.

Inducement was not the only strategy available for influencing Diem. Ambassador Durbrow argued that conditions on U.S. assistance, particularly military aid, would be necessary to pressure the government of Vietnam to undertake the kind of social, economic, and political reforms necessary to overcome the insurgents. While *conditionality* was applied too intermittently in this case to give it a full evaluation, we cannot reject its efficacy, as we can with *inducement*. Indeed, the isolated episodes when conditions were applied to military aid, as with the South Vietnam Special Forces, compliance with U.S. policy preferences was very high. Undoubtedly, attempts to employ conditionality were harmed by the bureaucratic cleavages besetting U.S. policy. With Washington largely taking a hands-off approach during the Eisenhower years, there were serious disagreements between the MAAG commander and his DoD patrons – who both emphasized unilateral grants of aid and confidence-building measures as the key to influencing the regime – and the ambassador, other civilian agencies on the ground, and even some South Vietnamese government officials – who believed that the United States should condition its aid to gain the necessary influence over Diem. These interagency disagreements continued into the Kennedy administration, where, as of late 1962, the embassy in Saigon was said to have no overall plan for coordinating the efforts of "a multitude of independent U.S. agencies and people" in the country.[345]

The Kennedy administration's unconditional support, strong public commitments, and substantial aid granted to Diem under both the Counterinsurgency Plan and the Special Financial Group failed to persuade him to implement the nonmilitary reforms and policy changes being pushed by the United States. In contrast, the administration's singular bargaining success came with the December 1961 agreement on a "joint partnership," which managed to get the South Vietnamese government to accept the idea that U.S. military and economic assistance would be conditioned on specific political actions. The impact of this success was quickly undermined, however, when the DoD rushed aid into Vietnam without waiting for Diem to carry out his part of the bargain. The threat of conditionality elicited promises for action, but

---

[345] Memo, Hilsman and Forrestal to Kennedy, FRUS 1963/1, pp. 49–62.

U.S. failure to hold the line prevented these promises from coming to fruition. Similarly, on the few occasions when American actions created some uncertainty about its future willingness to support the regime, the South Vietnamese government appeared to be more amenable to U.S. requests than it did when it was assured of America's commitment.

In general, the Kennedy administration's few attempts to use conditionality to shape Vietnam's policy decisions were hamstrung by its unwillingness to condition military aid. Ambassador Durbrow had made it clear that Diem privileged military assistance over economic aid.[346] Yet, with the notable exception of the December 1961 "joint partnership" and assistance to the Vietnamese Special Forces in the wake of the "Pagoda Raids," attempts to pressure Diem via aid largely focused on economic assistance. These efforts failed to generate results because they did not target the aid the South Vietnamese government valued the most. Moreover, by providing military aid without conditions, the administration undermined the credibility of the threat to withhold economic aid and failed to properly signal American seriousness about the need for significant political, economic, and social action as part of the counterinsurgency effort. In line with the expectations of conditionality discussed in Chapter 3, because the United States indicated that the military struggle was too important to risk harming by imposing conditions on military assistance, Saigon had every reason to believe that the withheld economic aid would eventually be provided for the same reason. In such circumstances, American leverage over its client was minimal.

---

[346] Telegram 3095, FRUS 1958–60, p. 436.

6 | *The Lesser of Two Evils? El Salvador, 1979–1992*

PART I THE CARTER YEARS, 1979–1980

America's twelve-year involvement in the Salvadoran Civil War gave lie to the notion that the United States was done with counterinsurgency when it left Vietnam in 1973.[1] As with Vietnam and the Philippines before it, the Salvadoran government was plagued with a host of maladies, including corruption, widespread human rights abuses by state security forces, and a lack of democratic legitimacy. These flaws hindered its counterinsurgency efforts and strengthened its armed opposition. However, a decade of American aid and advice allowed San Salvador – which had been on the brink of collapse in late 1979 – to fight the insurgents of the Farabundo Martí National Liberation Front to a standstill and eventually conclude an externally brokered peace agreement.

The amount of influence the United States achieved over the Salvadoran government varied over time and from issue to issue. Washington achieved notable success in shaping the counterinsurgency strategy and behavior of the Salvadorans in some areas but had very little impact in others. Prior scholars have suggested that the combination of the Salvadoran government's dedication to preserving the status quo and the perceived strength of the American commitment to defend the country rendered the client "remarkably immune" to U.S. influence.[2] Although partially true, this argument overlooks the fact that the United States employed different influence strategies at various points in time. This chapter contends that the observed variation in compliance can be explained by the alternate use of inducement and conditionality by three different administrations. Important reforms and policy changes

---

[1] Some of the text in this chapter previously appeared in Walter C. Ladwig III, "Influencing Clients in Counterinsurgency: U.S. Involvement in El Salvador's Civil War, 1979–92," *International Security*, 41, no. 1 (Summer 2016).

[2] See, e.g., Schwarz, *American Counterinsurgency Doctrine*, p. xiii.

occurred when strict conditions were attached to aid and not when inducements were given.[3]

The Salvadoran Government and Armed Forces

Although San Salvador is closer to San Diego than America's Finest City is to New York, the United States did not have a significant history of involvement in El Salvador. A population just under 4 million in 1980 and a land area the size of Massachusetts gave the smallest state in Latin America the region's highest population density, while its extensive mountains, jungles, and swampy coastal areas were particularly conducive to guerrilla warfare. The Salvadoran economy was built around the export of labor-intensive crops such as coffee, cotton, and sugar. These operations were dominated by a landed oligarchy – colloquially known as the "Fourteen Families" – that was among the most economically efficient and modern producers on the continent. Although overall income distribution in El Salvador was no more skewed than in the United States, only Guatemala and Haiti had worse living standards for the bottom tier of society.[4] The limited amount of arable land meant that the country's growing rural population simply could not obtain sufficient income and employment from agriculture.[5] A deep-seated culture of violence routinely saw El Salvador ranked among the most murderous countries in the world.[6] Following the brutal suppression of a Communist-led peasant revolt in 1932 – in which the army killed tens of thousands of suspected rebels – the staunchly anti-Communist upper and upper-middle classes willingly allowed a series of military-led governments to dominate the country's political affairs.[7]

The country's most important institution was its military – the Armed Forces of El Salvador (ESAF) – which consisted of the army

---

[3] In contrast, Benjamin Schwarz dismisses conditions on U.S. aid as empty threats and a weak tool of influence. Schwarz, *American Counterinsurgency Doctrine*, p. vii.

[4] Joes, *America and Guerrilla Warfare*, p. 260.

[5] Telegram 2632, San Salvador to State, May 18, 1979, STATE.

[6] Todd Greentree, *Crossroads of Intervention: Insurgency and Counterinsurgency Lessons from Central America* (Westport, CT: Praeger, 2008), p. 75.

[7] Wickham-Crowley, *Guerrillas and Revolution*, p. 287. This is the major theme of William Stanley, *The Protection Racket State: Elite Politics, Military Extortion, and Civil War in El Salvador* (Philadelphia, PA: Temple University Press, 1996).

and the Public Security Corps (PSC).[8] The 8,000-man army, which focused on external security, possessed four small infantry brigades, an artillery battalion, and a light armor battalion. The paramilitary police forces of the PSC included the National Police (2,500), which provided security in the cities; the National Guard (4,000), which kept order in the countryside; and the Treasury Police (2,000), which functioned throughout the country as a hybrid internal security force and intelligence agency. Control of the ESAF was hindered by the lack of a functioning chain of command.[9] In theory, decision making was highly centralized in the office of the Defense Minister, who sat at the center of a "spider web" of divided and overlapping authority intended to prevent any one commander from amassing sufficient power to mount a coup.[10] In practice, however, the Defense Minister's authority depended on the concurrence of the heads of the three security corps and the quasi-autonomous military commanders of El Salvador's fourteen departments (provinces) who were colloquially known as "the warlords."

A single 500-man officer corps rotated across both the army and the PSC. After enduring four years of "forced marches, beatings, and all-night calisthenics," the approximately twenty or so cadets who graduated annually from the Capitán General Gerardo Barrios Military Academy in San Salvador forged extremely close bonds with their graduating class, their *tanda*.[11] All members of a particular *tanda* were promoted together en masse according to a fixed timetable at every step of their careers – regardless of merit – which meant that corrupt, brutal, or incompetent officers were rarely dismissed from service before reaching retirement age. As a result, outside observers judged that few ESAF officers were suited for anything more taxing than garrison duty, let alone actual combat.[12]

---

[8] In Spanish, this abbreviation is rendered FAES for the "Fuerza Armada de El Salvador."

[9] Fred Woerner, "Report of the El Salvador Military Strategy Assessment Team," November 16, 1981, p. 47, NSA.

[10] Waghelstein, interview, January 31, 1985, *SOOHP*, p. 37, MHI.

[11] William Meara, *Contra Cross: Insurgency and Tyranny in Central America, 1979–1989* (Annapolis, MD: Naval Institute Press, 2006), pp. 47–51, 60–3, 69–70; Joel Millman, "El Salvador's Army: A Force unto Itself," *New York Times Magazine*, December 10, 1989.

[12] Thomas Pickering, interview, August, 28, 1987, *Oral History of the Conflict in El Salvador*, vol. 1, p. 4, MHI.

The Salvadoran Army did not possess a professional noncommissioned officer corps, and the majority of the rank and file was made up
of short-service conscripts. The skill levels of the average soldier were
quite low – even if they had been issued sufficient ammunition for
proper marksmanship training – and the quality of their uniforms
and equipment was so poor that many units in the field tied specific
colored ribbons on their shoulders to avoid being confused with the
guerrillas.[13] Consequently, Americans dealing with the army were
"appalled at the inadequacies of human, organizational and other
resources."[14] In contrast, the enlisted ranks of the PSC were made up
of long-service professionals. They had a negative reputation, however,
for their corruption, wanton brutality, and partiality to the country's
landed elite.[15] In remote rural areas, the National Guard was virtually
a law unto itself, abusing the population with impunity and maintaining domestic order through physical intimidation and the aggressive
use of the Salvadoran National Security Agency's (ANSESAL) grass-
roots network of informants to identify and eliminate potential
subversives.[16]

Origins of the Insurgency and the 1979 Coup

In the 1950s and 1960s, *liberation theology* – which taught that Jesus
was not primarily a peace maker but a staunch opponent of political
and economic injustice – gained traction in the Catholic Church in
Latin America.[17] The appalling living standards of El Salvador's rural
population mobilized Catholic activists, particularly Jesuits, who
organized religiously focused peasant cooperatives. These *base
communities* created a previously unknown level of organization and
politicization of the country's rural populace, which would provide
a fertile recruiting ground for elements inclined to challenge the status
quo through armed violence.

In the 1972 presidential election, widespread fraud denied victory to
a broad-based reformist coalition led by the former mayor of San
Salvador, Christian Democrat José Napoleon Duarte, in favor of yet

---

[13] Telegram 4440, San Salvador to State, June 27, 1980, STATE.
[14] Telegram 7283, San Salvador to State, December 19, 1979, STATE.
[15] Telegram 2632.
[16] Memorandum of Conversation, Bush, Duarte et al, September 21, 1981, DDRS.
[17] "I come not to bring peace, but to bring a sword." Matthew 10:34.

another military officer representing the traditional party of the army-oligarchy alliance, the Party of National Conciliation (PCN).[18] With Duarte tortured and exiled to Venezuela by the ESAF, in the wake of the sham election pressure for change began to resonate with the country's middle classes, leading many in the Catholic Church – a powerful social force in El Salvador – into an implicit alliance with the extreme left. The country's universities and high schools soon preached revolution as the means to achieve social change. The scholars of the Jesuit-run University of Central America – which served as a de facto think tank for the far left – offered a philosophical justification for a revolt, while the University of El Salvador provided a command center, a fertile recruiting ground, and a training base for various radical groups.[19] The government's response to growing unrest was to suspend due process and eliminate dissidents.

A worldwide plunge in the price of coffee in 1978 triggered an economic shockwave that further destabilized large portions of the countryside. In the wake of the July 1979 revolution in neighboring Nicaragua, demands for change in El Salvador among labor unions, peasant groups, students, and segments of the Catholic Church grew stronger and more radical. This dynamic political environment saw the emergence of no fewer than five revolutionary groups across the country, each with its own guerrilla faction as well an overt political wing capable of marshaling tens of thousands of demonstrators.[20]

---

[18] The illegitimate son of a San Salvadoran tailor, Duarte was educated in the United States at an obscure college in rural Indiana known primarily for the irrational expectations of its football fans.

[19] As the U.S. embassy reported, the UCA "has been the above-board fount of pro-FDR/FMLN intellectual theorizing in El Salvador, and virtually nothing of significance has appeared in FDR/FMLN positions or platforms that was not previously or simultaneously published by the UCA press." Telegram 6383, San Salvador to State, May 22, 1985, NSA. See also Memorandum, Office of African and Latin American Analysis to Associate Deputy Director for Intelligence, "Explosions at the Central American University," July 24, 1989, LOC. In a raid on the University of El Salvador, police discovered numerous tunnels connecting to nearby slums where arms were stored and "a well equipped interrogation/torture chamber plus two heavily sound-proofed cells without windows" in addition to "enormous quantities of propaganda material." Telegram 4631, San Salvador to State, July 7, 1980, STATE.

[20] These groups were the Central American Workers' Revolutionary Party, the People's Revolutionary Army, the Farabundo Martí Popular Liberation Forces, the Armed Forces of National Resistance, and the Communist Party of El Salvador's Armed Forces of Liberation.

In a purposeful imitation of the Sandinistas' successful strategy of mass insurrection in Nicaragua, large-scale demonstrations, organized strikes, occupation of foreign embassies, bank robberies, kidnapping for ransom, and bomb attacks became weekly occurrences.

On October 15, 1979, the government of General Carlos Humberto Romero was overthrown, not by Marxist insurgents, but by a movement of reform-minded junior officers, the *Juventud Militar*, who established a civilian-led Junta that included members of centrist and left-wing opposition parties. The *Junta Revolucionaria de Gobierno* promised to bring about "an equitable distribution of national wealth," rein in the PSC, and ensure "a propitious climate for the holding of genuinely free elections" in 1982 for a Constituent Assembly that would write a new constitution for the country.[21] To improve the human rights environment, the Junta disbanded the domestic intelligence agency ANSESAL and purged eighty officers (16 percent of the officer corps) accused of abuses – including the Defense Minister and heads of the National Police and the National Guard – as well as 1,400 enlisted men (10 percent of the ESAF).[22] In taking these actions, the Junta hoped to wrest the reform mantle from the far left while also attracting support from the United States.

Although the coup had been virtually unopposed, only 20 percent of the officer corps was strong proponents of reform. Approximately 10 percent supported the far right, while the vast majority only begrudgingly accepted the bare minimum of reforms necessary to prevent social revolution, but opposed the presence of left-wing politicians in the Junta.[23] Despite the growing threat from the left, the main priority for the bulk of the ESAF's officers was protecting and sustaining their institutional prerogatives.[24] As a result, the idealistic young officers of the *Juventud Militar* were quickly outmaneuvered in the struggle for control of the ESAF, which saw the staunchly conservative Colonel José Guillermo Garcia emerge as defense minister. Although not

---

[21] "Proclamation of the Armed Forces of the Republic of El Salvador," October 15, 1979, reprinted in Stanley, *The Protection Racket State*, pp. 267–9.

[22] Telegram 7163, San Salvador to State, October 16, 1980 and Letter, Office of Central American Affairs to Harrison, November 14, 1980, both STATE.

[23] Brian Bosch, *The Salvadoran Officer Corps and the Final Offensive* (London: McFarland, 1999), p. 43; CIA, "El Salvador: The Right Wing," April 17, 1981, LOC.

[24] Greentree, *Crossroads of Intervention*, p. 82.

associated with the extreme right, Garcia steadily replaced prominent reformers in positions of command with members of his own *tanda*.

Instead of bringing both sides together, fundamental differences between the civilian and military members of the Junta – not to mention among the civilians themselves – produced what one observer termed "a government of national disunity."[25] As state-linked political killings spiked, by January 1980, all the civilian members of the Junta had resigned, blaming Garcia for ongoing repression by the PSC and the slow pace of reforms. This charge was echoed by 186 members of the officer corps who signed an open letter demanding Garcia's immediate removal for obstructing the Junta's reform agenda.[26]

Having paid scant attention to Central America before the Nicaraguan Revolution, the Carter administration inadvertently assisted a consolidation of power by conservative elements in the Salvadoran military. Carter's policy of using human rights as the basis for foreign relations led to strained ties with countries such as Brazil, Argentina, Chile, Uruguay, Guatemala, and El Salvador.[27] Rather than consent to annual American human rights assessments, these countries abrogated mutual defense treaties and forswore military aid, which eviscerated America's military and intelligence linkages in the region and limited its understanding of the ESAF's internal dynamics.[28] Believing that in El Salvador "the Junta's most immediate threat is a determined and violent challenge from the groups which compose the extreme left," the administration initially focused on strengthening the Junta against "Marxist extremists."[29] Aware that the fragmentation of the National Guard in neighboring Nicaragua had paved the way for a Sandinista victory, the United States provided only limited support to reformers in the ESAF

---

[25] Jose Napoleon Duarte, *Duarte: My Story* (New York: G.P. Putnam's Sons, 1986), p. 104.

[26] Bosch, *The Salvadoran Officer Corps and the Final Offensive*, p. 34; Tommie Sue Montgomery, *Revolution in El Salvador: From Civil Strife to Civil Peace*, 2nd edn. (Boulder, CO: Westview Press, 1994), p. 128. See also Telegram 5, San Salvador to FCO, January 4, 1980, FCO 99/576, NAUK.

[27] Arturo Gandara and Caesar Sereseres, *U.S.–Latin American Relations under the Carter Administration* (Santa Monica, CA: RAND, 1980), p. 4.

[28] Transcript, John D. Waghelstein interviewed by Aaron Lobel, *America Abroad Media*, September 7, 2006, p. 8.

[29] Memorandum, Vance to Carter, December 26, 1979, NSA; Luigi Einaudi, interview, *OHCES*, pp. 4–5. In contrast, the far right was judged to pose "little immediate threat." Telegram 6976, San Salvador to State, December 4, 1979, STATE.

during their power struggle with the hard-liners, for fear of fracturing the Salvadoran military.[30] Consequently, when a large number of reformers misinterpreted American pressure for improved human rights practices as a sign that Washington backed the wholesale restructuring of the high command, they played their hand too early and were purged by Garcia.[31] This crucial outcome set the stage for the next decade. With reformist officers largely sidelined by the end of 1981, the ESAF would be led by a military establishment whose natural tendencies inclined more toward waging a "dirty war" against Salvador's leftists than undertaking U.S.-backed reforms. In coming years, American personnel would lament that "no countervailing force presently exists within the Armed Forces to oppose the propensity of the more conservative officers to tolerate the use of excessive force and violence."[32]

The Farabundo Martí National Liberation Front

While the Junta imploded, the far left consolidated. In December 1979, Cuba's Fidel Castro – the traditional patron of Latin American insurgents – brought together the leaders of five different Salvadoran revolutionary groups in Havana to form the Farabundo Martí National Liberation Front (FMLN).[33] In terms of its ideology and actions, the FMLN's constituent elements spanned the spectrum from orthodox Communists to radicals who were closer in character to Peru's ultraviolent Shining Path.[34] The leadership of the movement was overwhelmingly university-educated members of the urban middle class, while 95 percent of its guerrilla fighters were peasants.[35] Notionally adhering to an ideology blending activist Catholic theology with Marxist revolutionary rhetoric, the majority of the FMLN's fighters were motivated by concrete grievances against

---

[30] Telegram 272443, State to San Salvador, October 18, 1979, STATE.

[31] Telegram 6284, San Salvador to State, September 10, 1980, STATE.

[32] Woerner, "Report," p. 46.

[33] For an extended discussion of Cuban support for the FMLN, see Andrea Oñate, "The Red Affairs: FMLN-Cuban relations during the Salvadoran Civil War, 1981–1992," *Cold War History*, 11, no. 2 (May 2011), pp. 133–54.

[34] Timothy Wickham-Crowley, "Understanding Failed Revolution in El Salvador," *Politics and Society*, 17, no. 4 (1989), p. 519.

[35] Hugh Byrne, *El Salvador's Civil War: A Study of Revolution* (Boulder, CO: Lynne Rienner, 1996), p. 35.

the country's security forces.[36] The movement's political wing, the Revolutionary Democratic Front (FDR), was led by Guillermo Ungo and Rueben Zamora. The former had been Duarte's running mate in 1972 and both were among the civilians who quit the Junta in disgust over human rights abuses. For the first half of the conflict, the FMLN's political and military leaders were based in Managua, Nicaragua; however, the military leaders would eventually decamp for "liberated territory" in El Salvador while the FDR stayed behind.

The insurgents' support network was strongest in the North and East of the country, which bordered Honduras, as well as in the central departments of San Vicente and Usulután. Nationwide, political support for the FMLN was estimated to hover around 20 percent.[37] Within contested zones, where neither the guerrillas nor the government held sway, scholarly study suggests that 25 to 30 percent of the population were active supporters, but "even in highly organized areas, revolution was not the choice of the majority."[38] In the countryside, the FMLN methodically marked the country's ablest politicians, administrators, and their families for death. FMLN fighters often targeted moderates and reformers – rather than supporters of the extreme right – which further polarized political life.

By 1980, the insurgency possessed 4,000 guerrilla fighters backed by a 5,000-man part-time militia and a political wing that could put 200,000 demonstrators on the streets.[39] The FMLN received weapons,

---

[36] Journalist Tom Gibb's survey of 200 ex-FMLN fighters cited in Stanley, *The Protection Racket State*, pp. 222, 302.

[37] The U.S. embassy estimated that the FMLN would win 20 percent of the vote in a free and fair election. Donald R Hamilton, "Strategic Communications in El Salvador 1982–1986: A Personal Perspective," Washington, DC, September 13, 2010. Napoleon Durate similarly believed that the insurgents could win 15 to 20 percent of the vote. Raymond Bonner, "Duarte Is Seeking to Stay in Power, Defying the Right," *New York Times*, April 2, 1982. In 1994, the first elections after the peace accords, FMLN candidates received slightly more than 21 percent of the vote. Shawn Bird and Philip Williams, "El Salvador: Revolt and Negotiated Transition," in Thomas W. Walker and Ariel C. Armony, eds., *Repression, Resistance, and Democratic Transition in Central America* (Wilmington, DE: Scholarly Resources, 2000), p. 32.

[38] Elisabeth Wood, *Insurgent Collective Action and Civil War in El Salvador* (Cambridge: Cambridge University Press, 2003), p. 157; Greentree, *Crossroads of Intervention*, p. 88.

[39] Bosch, *The Salvadoran Officer Corps and the Final Offensive*, p. 61; Montgomery, *Revolution in El Salvador*, p. 116.

military training, and assistance from neighboring Nicaragua and Cuba, as well as the Soviet Union, Bulgaria, East Germany, and even Vietnam.[40] To disguise this external support, arms and ammunition procured from abroad were initially largely of Western origin, supplemented by equipment captured from government forces.[41] Later in the conflict, however, the FMLN would be reequipped by their patrons with Warsaw Pact weaponry.[42]

Conditional Aid Preserves the Junta

The Carter administration's aim in El Salvador was to prevent either the far left or the extreme right from seizing power; support the junta's economic and political reforms, which could reduce popular support for a revolution as well as weaken the power of the oligarchy; and reduce state-linked violence by bringing the security forces under the junta's control. In an effort to preserve some semblance of a centrist government in San Salvador, the United States brokered a deal with Napoleon Duarte's Christian Democrat Party (PDC) to rejoin the Junta. This was hardly an easy bargain to make because the two sides had been bitter enemies for more than two decades: Hard-liners in the military thought that members of the PDC were "crypto-Communists" and Duarte deeply distrusted them in return because widespread electoral fraud engineered by the military denied him victory in the 1972 presidential election.[43] The American envoy, Deputy Assistant Secretary of State James Cheek, made it clear to all parties, however, that U.S. aid was contingent on the Christian Democrats joining the military as partners in government.[44] As Cheek later recounted,

---

[40] Byrne, *El Salvador's Civil War*, p. 210; James LeMoyne, "El Salvador's Forgotten War," *Foreign Affairs*, 68, no. 3 (Summer 1989); Hal Brands, *Latin America's Cold War* (Cambridge, MA: Harvard University Press, 2010), p. 202.

[41] Based on a trace of their serial numbers, the supermajority of M-16s captured from the guerrillas were last recorded in the possession of the South Vietnamese Army in the early 1970s. Hamilton, "Strategic Communications in El Salvador," p. 7.

[42] Telegram 297087, State to Havana, September 15, 1989, DDRS; Brands, *Latin America's Cold War*, p. 205.

[43] Fred Woerner, interview, November 7, 1987, *Oral History of the Conflict in El Salvador*, vol. 2, p. 5, MHI; Duarte, *Duarte*, p. 106.

[44] At the time, Cheek was also functioning as acting ambassador. Telegram 46, San Salvador to State, January 4, 1980 and Telegram 51, San Salvador to State, January 4, 1980, both NSA.

U.S. leverage over the Salvadoran military derived almost solely from "conditional promises of future assistance."[45]

The officer corps tolerated the Christian Democrats as a necessary evil to prevent a leftist takeover and to keep U.S. aid flowing.[46] As American observers noted, however, the coalition was a highly tenuous "marriage of convenience" that was "driven by a sense of mutual need but with important differences of orientation."[47] The military wanted to focus on restoring law and order in the country, which the PDC saw as attempting to solve a political problem with wholesale violence. In contrast, the military feared that the economic and social reforms favored by the Christian Democrats would accelerate the country's decline into economic chaos.[48] As the price of joining the government, the PDC extracted a promise from the military to nationalize the banking sector; control the export of coffee, cotton, and sugar; expropriate 2 million acres of farmland for purchase by sharecroppers and agricultural co-ops; and end repression against the population.[49] The PDC also won an agreement to exclude representatives of El Salvador's business sector from the Junta lest they impede the process of economic reform and democratization.[50] To support these reforms – which would greatly diminish the power of the country's landed oligarchy – the United States pledged $5.7 million in nonlethal military aid and $50 million in economic assistance.[51]

Although the CIA estimated that the FMLN had "a better-than-even chance to seize and hold power" from the fragile Junta, the far left was not the only threat that the Salvadoran government faced.[52] "The right in El Salvador is broad by almost any definition," agency analysts noted, "conservative tendencies run wide and deep in the military,

[45] Quoted in Stanley, *The Protection Racket State*, pp. 183, 296.
[46] Woerner, "Report," pp. 206–7; Greentree, *Crossroads of Intervention*, p. 83.
[47] Telegram 529, San Salvador to State, January 24, 1980, NSA.
[48] Telegram 312, San Salvador to State, January 11, 1980 and Telegram 523, San Salvador to State, February 6, 1980, both STATE.
[49] Bureau of Public Affairs, "El Salvador: U.S. Policy," March 1980, STATE. The British ambassador judged that violent opposition to the reforms by both the far left and the far right "itself indicated that they were on the right level." Telegram 69, San Salvador to FCO, April 1, 1980, FCO 99/576, NAUK.
[50] Duarte, *Duarte*, pp. 108–9.
[51] Telegram 7724, San Salvador to State, November 4, 1980, STATE.
[52] Memorandum, Brzezinski to Carter, "U.S. Policy to El Salvador," January 29, 1980, NSA.

the business community and beyond."[53] El Salvador's large land-owners and segments of the business community objected to aspects of the Junta's reform program, particularly land reform. Giving highly productive agricultural land to illiterate peasants engaged in primitive subsistence farming, they contended, would devastate the country's already brittle economy.[54] With even moderate or progressive elements of the private sector excluded from government by the Christian Democrats, the means by which these reform opponents pressed their objections would be devastating.[55] Supported by wealthy exiles in Guatemala and Miami, the far right took a page from their Communist foes in organizing their own overt political and clandestine military wings.[56]

The overt face of the extreme right was Robert D'Aubuisson, a charismatic former major in the National Guard who had been the deputy director of ANSESAL. When the Junta disbanded the domestic intelligence agency and purged D'Aubuisson from the military, the cunning major took copies of the agency's files with him. Leveraging that information, he led "an anti-Communist crusade" on national television that focused on Christian Democrats and reform-minded military officers, whom he accused of being leftist agents.[57]

Many of those that D'Aubuisson denounced were subsequently murdered by the far right's covert military wing, the so-called death squads. Some of these right-wing paramilitaries were independent of the government, while others consisted of former members of ANSESAL's network of informants; however, most were organized and manned by members of the security corps. The National Police reportedly hosted the most efficient terror cell in the country; the National Guard, the most active; and the Treasury Police, the most brutal.[58] Death squads also existed in the intelligence sections of some

---

[53] CIA, "El Salvador: The Right Wing," April 17, 1981, LOC.

[54] Byrne, El Salvador's Civil War, pp. 43–4

[55] Telegram 312; Telegram 837, San Salvador to State, February 6, 1980, STATE; Duarte, *Duarte*, pp. 110.

[56] Memorandum of Conversation, Keene (Buenos Aires) and [name redacted], January 5, 1981, NSA; Telegram 96, San Salvador to State, January 6, 1981, NSA; "El Salvador: The Role of Roberto D'Aubuisson," March 4, 1981, CIA; "El Salvador: Controlling Rightwing Terrorism," February 1, 1985, p. 3, CIA.

[57] Telegram 1257, San Salvador to State, February 20, 1980, STATE

[58] Telegram 8084, San Salvador to State, November 19, 1980, STATE; Stanley, *The Protection Racket State*, p. 167.

army units, but the regular army generally did not participate in these activities. These right-wing paramilitaries employed active duty and retired members of the security forces and were led by junior officers or senior enlisted men who functioned, the Central Intelligence Agency believed, "with or without the knowledge of immediate superiors."[59]

In 1980 political killings in El Salvador would claim 8,000 to 9,000 lives, 90 percent of which were attributed to the security forces or the death squads. Some of this violence was highly effective in retarding the insurgency: According to the FMLN's top military commander, the group "lost most of its urban network to death squad counter-terrorism in the 1981–1983 period."[60] However, right wing violence extended beyond the insurgents. Among their victims were several members of the *Juventud Militar*; the country's Archbishop, Oscar Romero; the Attorney General; and hundreds of PDC activists.

By early 1980, CIA analysts were reporting that "all of the symptoms associated with impending revolutionary upheaval are present in El Salvador today."[61] Moreover, even with substantial foreign aid, the prospects for the Junta's survival "beyond a period of months" appeared slim. Rumors began to circulate that Defense Minister Garcia was planning to seize control of the "moribund" Junta to head off a far right coup that was in the making, while disaffected reformers in the military plotted their own effort to oust Garcia.[62] To keep the military in their barracks, the United States warned the Salvadoran high command that the recent offer of $50 million in economic aid and $5.7 million in nonlethal military assistance would be canceled if the government was overthrown. The defense attaché and the leader of the U.S. Military Group (MILGROUP) accompanied State Department colleagues to meetings with Defense Minister Garcia to ensure that Salvadoran military leaders understood that stringent anti-Communism alone would not win Washington's

---

[59] "Controlling Rightwing Terrorism," p. 7.
[60] Commandante Joaquin Villalobos, quoted in Telegram 1355, San Salvador to State, February 5, 1992, NSA.
[61] CIA, "El Salvador: The Potential for Violent Revolution," February 20, 1980, p. iii, DDRS.
[62] Memorandum, Situation Room to Brzezinski, January 22, 1980, DDRS; Memorandum, Derian to Acting Secretary, February 19, 1980, STATE; Telegram 1336, San Salvador to State, February 22, 1980, STATE; Duarte, *Duarte*, p. 112.

favor.[63] Robert D'Aubuisson urged the army not to be intimidated by America's threats to withhold aid; however, the need for U.S. assistance carried the day as Garcia publicly pledged support for the Junta and its reform program.[64]

The Helicopter Deal and Leverage Lost

With a military coup temporarily averted, the United States turned its attention to restraining repression by the PSC. If this violence was unchecked, the new U.S. ambassador, Robert White – an experienced Foreign Service officer who was committed to Carter's human rights agenda – feared that Salvadoran society would be polarized to the point where a brutal civil war would be both unavoidable and inevitably won by the FMLN.[65] A debate over how to achieve the influence necessary to bring this about was initiated by a Salvadoran request to lease six surplus Vietnam-era transport helicopters – to compensate for the limited ground mobility of government forces – along with training for twenty pilots and the deployment of three teams of American technicians to maintain the aircraft.[66] Despite their immediate military utility, Ambassador White argued that the helicopters and technicians should be withheld "until the worst of the right-wing violence is brought to an end."[67] Believing that the ESAF's leaders either endorsed or tolerated death-squad activity, he contended that making such a visible American commitment without insisting on reform would bolster the military at the expense of the civilians on the Junta and "strengthen the baleful influence of Colonel Garcia."[68] While sharing Ambassador White's goals, Deputy Assistant Secretary Cheek pushed for an inducement strategy: the United States should quickly lease the

---

[63] Stanley, *The Protection Racket State*, p. 297. The embassy also gave the same message to the business community. *Ibid.*, p. 193.

[64] Telegram 1358, San Salvador to State, February 23, 1980; Telegram 1886, San Salvador to State, March 13, 1980 and Telegram 2611, San Salvador to State, April 12, 1980, all STATE.

[65] Telegram 2038, San Salvador to State, March 19, 1980, STATE.

[66] Telegram 1099, San Salvador to State, February 17, 1980, STATE; Telegram 1116, San Salvador to State, February 19, 1980, STATE; Telegram 50819, State to San Salvador, February 26, 1980, NSA.

[67] Telegram 2038.

[68] Telegram 3598, San Salvador to State, May 21, 1980; Telegram 1886; Memorandum, Bushell to SecState, March 13, 1980; Telegram 2038, all STATE.

helicopters and dispatch the technicians to signal the credibility of the American commitment, which was necessary to develop the influence required to separate the military from its "traditional patrons on the far right."[69] Contrary to White's formulation, Cheek argued that the prestige of U.S. assistance would strengthen reformers relative to the reactionaries, whereas a failure to provide aid would actually be interpreted as a lack of support for the Junta.[70]

White's arguments for conditionality carried the day with President Carter.[71] Washington sought to cultivate a "very high level of influence" with both the ESAF and the Christian Democrats by conditioning economic and military aid "upon meaningful efforts" to reduce institutional violence.[72] To spur the process forward, the United States offered to lease at no cost six helicopters – for which the ESAF was "anxious to the point of desperation" to receive – along with training for the pilots and spare parts. Delivery was conditioned on five specific actions:[73]

1. Issue a directive denouncing the "indiscriminate violence and human rights violations" occurring in the country, including a repudiation of the abduction, torture, and execution of suspected subversives.
2. Improve command and control of counterinsurgency operations to reduce abuses.
3. Replace senior officers and military units in areas where high levels of official violence have been recorded.
4. Demonstrate a commitment to suppress the influence of the far right, particularly within the military.
5. Commit to defend the judiciary from intimidation and violence.

In order for the training of Salvadoran pilots to begin, the government of El Salvador (GoES) had to submit a phased plan outlining how it would achieve all five conditions. Once that plan was accepted, training

---

[69] Bushell to SecState; Alan Riding, "U.S. Aid to Salvador Army," *New York Times*, February 23, 1980.
[70] Bushell to SecState.
[71] Memorandum to Carter, "Helicopters for El Salvador," June 18, 1980, STATE.
[72] Telegram 70429, State to San Salvador, March 15, 1980, STATE.
[73] Memorandum, Bowdler to SecState, "Helicopters for El Salvador," June 23, 1980; Telegram 4575, San Salvador to State, July 3, 1980; Telegram 210613, State to San Salvador, August 9, 1980; and Telegram 5810, San Salvador to State, August 23, 1980, all STATE.

would commence. The Salvadoran government would then have sixty days to implement it, at which point its progress would be assessed, and if it was found acceptable, the helicopters would be provided.

Both the civilian and military members of the Junta reacted poorly to the idea of conditioning the assistance on their performance, proclaiming it "galling" that "reforms were being enforced by another country." Rather than explicit conditions, they suggested a "private gentlemen's agreement" that the aforementioned terms would be implemented if the United States supplied the helicopters and technicians.[74] Few in the Salvadoran military could fathom that the United States would not spare a few surplus helicopters for a nation fighting against Communist subversion, leading some officers to argue that they should simply go it alone like Guatemala, which had rejected the Carter administration's conditions on aid and pursued a brutal counterinsurgency campaign against their own Communist guerrillas.[75] The Salvadorans attempted to pressure Washington by citing the urgent need for helicopters to defend the upcoming coffee harvest from FMLN sabotage, which was critical for sustaining the country's fragile economy. The United States refused to act, however, until it had received the Junta's written reply.[76] In late September 1980, the Junta officially accepted the conditions – cosmetically amended to save face – and provided Washington with a plan for meeting American requirements.[77]

Having submitted a plan, the training of Salvadoran pilots began, as did the sixty-day monitoring period for measurable improvement in the human rights situation. The ESAF had made some progress in meeting U.S. conditions: officially denouncing human rights abuses, preparing of a code of conduct for the ESAF that condemned abuse of civilians, and strengthening the military chain of command to improve accountability.

---

[74] Telegram 5810.
[75] CIA, "El Salvador: Military Prospects," January 2, 1981, NSA; Bosch, *The Salvadoran Officer Corps and the Final Offensive*, p. 70.
[76] Telegram 6675, San Salvador to State, September 25, 1980; Telegram 257594, State to San Salvador, September 27, 1980; Telegram 7225, San Salvador to State, October 19, 1980; Telegram 7226, San Salvador to State, October 19, 1980 and Telegram 7227, San Salvador to State, October 19, 1980, all STATE
[77] Telegram 6574, San Salvador to State, September 23, 1980; Telegram 6675; Telegram 6729, San Salvador to State, September 29, 1980; Telegram 6738, San Salvador to State, September 29, 1980 and Telegram 7110, San Salvador to State, October 14, 1980, all STATE.

Conditionality had compelled Salvadoran military leaders to accept an agreement they did not like. The credibility of the threat to withhold the helicopters, which was necessary to secure follow-through, vanished, however, in early November with Carter's crushing defeat by Ronald Reagan in the November 1980 U.S. presidential election. To many in El Salvador, Carter's defeat signaled the end of conditions on U.S. military aid and the start of a new policy of unconditional support for pro-American regimes.[78]

Consequently, the Salvadoran government took no firm action against officers implicated in either human rights abuses or the death squads. Instead of declining, Ambassador White soon reported that "killings by the security corps had become more open and more frequent during the past two months."[79] In early November, both PDC leader Napoleon Duarte and the leading reformist officer in the Junta narrowly escaped assassination by a pair of coordinated car bombs.[80] This was followed by the brazen daylight kidnapping and murder of six prominent leaders of the FMLN's political wing by a group linked to Robert D'Aubuisson.[81] At the end of the sixty-day monitoring period, Ambassador White advised Washington that "there is no way that any objective observer could state that the Government has complied with the five steps we proposed."[82]

Aid Suspension and Junta Reorganization

During their last months in office, the administration made a final attempt to regain sufficient leverage over the Salvadoran government to assist the Junta's agricultural reforms, curtail the violence of right-wing terrorists, and defeat the Marxist guerrillas.[83] These efforts,

[78] Telegram 8332, San Salvador to State, November 30, 1980, STATE; CIA Cable [no. redacted], San Salvador to Langley, December 1, 1980, NSA.
[79] Telegram 8117, San Salvador to State, November 20, 1980, STATE.
[80] Telegram 7670, San Salvador to State, November 3, 1980, STATE; Duarte, *Duarte*, p. 129.
[81] Telegram 8301, San Salvador to State, November 28, 1980 and Telegram 8321, San Salvador to State, November 28, 1980, both STATE. On D'Aubuisson's links to the group, see Memo, Millspaugh to Dion, December 11, 1980, STATE.
[82] Telegram 8281, San Salvador to State, November 27, 1980, STATE.
[83] *American Foreign Policy Current Documents, 1981* (Washington, DC: Department of State, 1984), p. 1227.

however, were overtaken by a pair of events.[84] On December 2, three American nuns and a lay missionary of the Maryknoll order were raped and killed by a squadron of National Guardsmen in the vicinity of San Salvador airport.[85] Circumstantial evidence suggested that officers in the area attempted to cover up the crime.[86] A month later, acting on the orders of a local businessman, a pair of National Guardsmen gunned down two American land-reform experts and the head of the Salvadoran land-reform agency while they were dining at the Sheraton Hotel in San Salvador.[87]

These actions provoked outrage in the United States – particularly among liberal Democrats in Congress. Following the first set of murders, Carter suspended all aid and dispatched a high-level delegation to San Salvador to undertake a final attempt to compel the Junta to bring the military under civilian control, remove hard-liners from positions of authority, and control the death squads.[88] The aid suspension put El Salvador in a perilous situation: U.S. embassy analysts estimated that military operations would be adversely affected "in a matter of weeks" and that the Salvadoran economy would suffer a total collapse by March 1981.[89]

One of the Junta's main problems was that its civilian members were largely figureheads with little influence or control over the ESAF. To strengthen the position of the Christian Democrats vis-à-vis the military, the U.S. State Department announced that "the U.S. is ready to resume its assistance to El Salvador upon progress" in achieving a "significant restructuring of the Government and shifts in military personnel."[90] Privately, Napoleon Duarte was informed that if he could reach an agreement with the military that improved civilian control over the PSC, reduced indiscriminate killing, and removed several "hard-liners" from command positions, the United States would release $95 million in economic grants and loans, start delivery of the long-sought-after helicopters, and deploy up to fifty military

[84] *Ibid.*; Memorandum, Derian to DepSec, December 4, 1980, STATE.
[85] "Report of the Special Mission to El Salvador," December 12, 1980, STATE.
[86] Telegram 323787, State to Quarry Heights, December 12, 1980, STATE.
[87] Telegram 42, San Salvador to State, January 4, 1981, NSA.
[88] "Evening Reading: El Salvador," December 5, 1980, NSA; Memorandum, Bushnell to Deputy Secretary, December 11, 1980, STATE.
[89] Bushnell to Deputy Secretary.
[90] "Statement on the Special Presidential Mission to El Salvador," December 12, 1980, NSA.

trainers to assist the ESAF.[91] Although Minister of Defense Garcia was widely viewed as a prime impediment to reform, the Carter administration shied away from demanding his removal, content instead with securing the symbolic removal of Vice Defense Minister Nicholas Carranza, who was seen as being "the principal right-winger among active duty officers."[92]

A deal was brokered after several days of intense negotiations that saw Napoleon Duarte appointed president of a reorganized Junta and commitments that Carranza, the head of the Treasury Police Colonel Francisco Moran, and ten middle-ranking officers associated with extremist violence would be removed from office.[93] The Junta made a renewed commitment to hold free elections in 1982 and called on the FMLN to peacefully join the political process. Despite the CIA's skepticism about the prospects of a long-term partnership between the military and the Christian Democrats, as a reward for partial implementation of the desired reforms and the promise to purge hard-line officers, the United States immediately released $67 million in economic aid to bolster Duarte's position.[94] Former Venezuelan Foreign Minister Arístides Calvani, who was an interlocutor between the military and the PDC during the negotiations, reported that the conditions on U.S. aid "had been an important element in the shaping of the new agreement."[95]

The 1981 Final Offensive and the Abandonment of Conditionality

While U.S. economic assistance was fast-tracked, non-lethal military aid to El Salvador was discretely made available on a "phased incremental basis": tranches would be delivered based on tangible progress in investigating the murders of the churchwomen, removing senior officers implicated in significant human rights abuses, and

---

[91] Telegram 329627, State to San Salvador, December 13, 1980, NSA.
[92] Telegram 4575; Memorandum, Tarnoff to Brzezinski, July 17, 1980; "Presidential Evening Reading: El Salvador," December 9, 1980, STATE; Minutes, Special Coordinating Committee, "U.S. Policy to El Salvador," December 11, 1980, NSA.
[93] Telegram 8717, San Salvador to State, December 13, 1980, NSA.
[94] CIA, "El Salvador: Civilian-Military Agreements," December 10, 1980, LOC; Telegram 335609, State to all ARA Posts, December 20, 1980, NSA.
[95] Telegram 11023, Caracas to State, December 14, 1980, STATE.

a reduction in death squad violence.[96] Although acknowledging conditions on military aid provided important leverage over the military, Duarte urged the United States to drop them in light of growing evidence the FMLN was poised for a "final offensive" to overthrow the Junta.[97] Pressure for dropping the conditions on military aid also came from congressional Republicans and the leaders of neighboring Central American countries, who criticized Carter's restraint in assisting El Salvador in the face of an ascendant guerilla army.[98] Within the administration, an interagency split developed as Under Secretary of Defense Robert "Blowtorch Bob" Komer argued forcibly that tying military aid to human rights issues was akin to "fiddling while Rome burns." The former head of rural pacification programs in South Vietnam insisted that forestalling an insurgent victory in El Salvador had to take precedence. Once peace was restored, "we can later use aid [as] leverage to enhance human rights."[99] Secretary of State Edmund Muskie and Ambassador White took the opposite view, counseling Carter that releasing military aid would send "the wrong signal" to the ESAF, which already "misinterpreted" the resumption of economic assistance as a sign that the United States was not serious about pressing it to purge human rights abusers from its ranks.[100] Events on the ground in El Salvador soon superseded the debate.

With revolutionary sentiment in El Salvador corroded by the combination of the Junta's reforms and far-right violence, the FMLN decided to preempt Ronald Reagan's promised confrontation with Communism in Central America by presenting the American president-elect with "an irreversible situation."[101] Assisted by Nicaraguan and Cuban arms and advisors, on January 10, 1981, a force of several thousand guerrilla fighters launched simultaneous attacks on

---

96 Telegram 8721, San Salvador to State, December 15, 1980, STATE; Telegram 333735, Sate to San Salvador, December 18, 1980 and Memorandum, Muskie to Carter, "Security Assistance to El Salvador," January 8, 1981, both NSA.

97 Telegram 8963, San Salvador to State, December 23, 1980, STATE; Telegram 9059, San Salvador to State, December 31, 1980, NSA.

98 Telegram 7544, Tegucigalpa to State, December 5, 1980, STATE; Letter, Lagomarsino and Gilman to Carter, December 11, 1980, NSA.

99 Memorandum, Komer to SecDef, January 8, 1981, NSA.

100 "Evening Reading: Military Assistance to El Salvador," December 29, 1980, STATE.

101 FMLN Comandante Ferman Cienfuegos quoted in Alan Riding, "Salvadoran Rebel Predicts Final Push," *New York Times*, December 27, 1980.

forty-three different locations across El Salvador. Mirroring the Sandinistas' successful strategy, the insurgents sought to bring down the Junta through coordinated attacks on military posts across the country alongside a popular uprising in the cities.

The "final offensive" initially made impressive gains as the FMLN attacked eighty military posts and temporarily captured an equal number of villages and towns, including four departmental capitals.[102] The call for "all the people to rise up as one person" however, went unheeded.[103] Although initially thrown on the defensive, in nine days of hard fighting the ESAF forced the insurgents to surrender most of their gains. In the process, the military suffered 97 killed and 199 wounded and almost totally exhausted its stock of munitions and consumables.[104] Marred by poor coordination among insurgent factions and insufficient urban organization, the operation proved to be a major failure for the FMLN, which lost between 500 and 1,000 guerrilla fighters.[105] In Havana, senior Cuban leaders declared the offensive a "flop" and suggested that negotiations with the Junta were the best way forward.[106]

Although the Salvadoran security forces and the death squads linked to them were allegedly responsible for most of the estimated 8,000 political murders in 1980 – an eightfold increase from the year before – American conditions on military aid were swept aside in the wake of the FMLN offensive.[107] As one of his final acts in office, President

[102] Ignacio Martin-Baro, "La Guerra Civil En El Salvador," *Estudios Centroamericanos*, no. 387/388 (January–February 1981), p. 20.
[103] Bosch, *The Salvadoran Officer Corps and the Final Offensive*, p. 85. For British predictions that this call would be ignored by the masses, see Telegram 234, San Salvador to FCO, November 5, 1979, FCO 99/368, NAUK.
[104] Bosch, *The Salvadoran Officer Corps and the Final Offensive*, p. 90. For example, the army was down to just 1,500 spare rifles. Telegram 340, San Salvador to State, January 16, 1981, NSA.
[105] Bosch, *The Salvadoran Officer Corps and the Final Offensive*, p. 105.
[106] Cuban Vice President Carlos Rafael Rodriguez's conversation with former British prime minister Ted Heath, reported in Telegram 704, Havana to State, January 4, 1981, Box 29, Executive Secretariat, NSC Country File, RRL. For a similar view from the international relations department of the Central Committee of the Cuban Communist Party, see Telegram 1159, Havana to State, February 19, 1981, Box 29, Executive Secretariat, NSC Country File, RRL.
[107] Memorandum, Muskie to Carter; Meeting Notes, Special Coordinating Committee, January 12, 1981, NSA; William LeoGrande, *Our Own Backyard: The United States in Central America, 1977–1993* (Chapel Hill: University of North Carolina Press, 1998), p. 50.

Carter – who previously declared the United States "free of that inordinate fear of communism which once led us to embrace any dictator who joined us in that fear" – used the "unforeseen emergency" provisions of the Foreign Assistance Act to dispatch six helicopters, twenty-eight military trainers, and $5.9 million in lethal military hardware, including new M-16 rifles, M-79 grenade launchers, and millions of rounds of ammunition, to El Salvador without congressional approval.[108] By the time American military supplies began arriving in country, however, the ESAF had already regained the initiative over the insurgents, as Colonel Garcia proudly proclaimed, "without one bullet" from the United States.[109]

Though militarily irrelevant, this emergency aid undercut the administration's conditionality strategy. Carter attempted to justify the aid release by citing Salvadoran compliance with American conditions; however, both the Secretary of State and Ambassador White argued it was "too early to assess progress" in either the murder investigations or the control of institutional violence.[110] By unilaterally abrogating its own conditions on military aid, the Carter administration appeared to confirm the Salvadoran high command's long-held belief that the United States would never risk a break with El Salvador.

PART II THE REAGAN INITIATIVE, 1981–1984

With the ascent of Ronald Reagan, observers in San Salvador and Washington braced themselves for a major reorientation of U.S. policy in El Salvador.[111] Despite the new president's clear antipathy toward Communism, however, in many respects there was significant continuity

---

[108] Quote from Jimmy Carter, "Human Rights and Foreign Policy," Commencement Speech Given at Notre Dame University, June 1977; Telegram 12962, State to San Salvador, January 17, 1981, NSA.

[109] Quoted in Bosch, *The Salvadoran Officer Corps and the Final Offensive*, p. 97.

[110] Telegram 9213, State to San Salvador, January 14, 1981, Memorandum, Muskie to Carter, Telegram 340, San Salvador to State, January 16, 1981, all NSA.

[111] Despite these expectations, Secretary of State Muskie privately apprised Salvadoran leaders that "he was sure that the Reagan administration would not want to shift to the right." Telegram 313007, State to San Salvador, November 24, 1980, STATE. The distinction between Reagan's rhetoric on Central America and his actions is discussed in Russell Crandall, *The Salvador Option: The United States in El Salvador, 1977–1992* (Cambridge: Cambridge University Press, 2016), pp. 201–23.

as the new administration shared its predecessor's belief that "the alternative to the existing Junta today is extremism on either side."[112] Although Reagan and some of his senior advisors saw a Cuban (and by extension Soviet) hand behind the insurgencies breaking out in Central America, that did not blind them to the need to encourage countries like El Salvador to "correct the social inequities which make them ripe for Cuban inspired revolution."[113] As long as the Junta continued its reform program, Duarte and his colleagues were assured of the administration's support.[114] American interests in El Salvador were defined as

1. "Prevention of the takeover of a friendly neighbor of the U.S. by a Communist guerrilla army" while also "avoiding an extreme right coup";
2. "The maintenance in El Salvador of a government which shares our ideal of democracy and of change through reform"; and
3. "[P]revention of further deterioration of the economy of El Salvador."[115]

Although some of the Junta's economic reforms, such as the nationalization of banking and commodity exports as well as the collectivization of agriculture, clashed with the Reagan administration's free-market economic principles – and thus appeared to threaten the third goal – they believed that such measures were succeeding in the political battle

---

[112] Incoming National Security Advisor Richard Allen quoted in Christopher Dickey, "Envoy Assails Reagan Aides on El Salvador," *Washington Post*, December 10, 1980. Despite the skepticism of some of his advisors, President-elect Reagan expressed support for Duarte. Duarte, *Duarte*, p. 159. Reagan himself described the situation as a "three-way civil war" between "a moderate government, a right-wing faction and a left-wing faction." Bob Levin, "El Salvador's Short Fuse," *Newsweek*, January 19, 1981. The administration's support for the Junta and antipathy toward the extreme right was communicated to the Cuban government via interlocutors. Telegram 585, Havana to State, January 28, 1981, Box 29, Executive Secretariat, NSC Country File, RRL.

[113] Diary entry for June 8, 1981. Douglas Brinkley, ed., *The Reagan Diaries* (New York: HarperCollins, 2009), p. 24. The view is repeated in Ronald Reagan, *An American Life* (New York: Simon & Schuster, 1990), p. 474. For a similar view from the Secretary of State, see Alexander M. Haig, *Caveat* (New York: Macmillan, 1984), p. 117.

[114] Telegram 26592, State to San Salvador, February 2, 1981, Box 29, Executive Secretariat, NSC Country File, RRL.

[115] Telegram 4468, San Salvador to State, June 12, 1981, NSA.

against the insurgency.[116] As Deputy Secretary of State Walter Stoessel explained to Duarte, "[A] retreat from reform in El Salvador might have temporary success, but all our lessons from other countries should teach us that down that road lies ultimate failure and complete defeat."[117] Even supposed administration hard-liners, such as Secretary of State Alexander Haig, agreed that Duarte's government was "the best, indeed probably the only, hope for a peaceful, moderate solution to El Salvador's political problems."[118]

Rather than embracing the Salvadoran right, within weeks of taking office Reagan approved a proposal from CIA Director William Casey to provide covert financial and political support to the Christian Democrats and the remaining reform-minded officers in the Junta.[119] The administration also bolstered Duarte's position by bringing him to Washington for a high-profile visit designed to strengthen his position vis-à-vis the Salvadoran military.[120] Sharing the Carter's administration's fear that pushing the Salvadoran military too hard for change too quickly could fracture the institution or trigger a right-wing coup, Reagan's team advised the embassy in San Salvador to be "non-confrontational and sensitive to [Duarte and Garcia's] difficulties in controlling the Treasury Police and other security forces."[121] As a result of these continuities, the head of Latin American policy planning in Carter's State Department, Luigi Einaudi, described the Reagan approach as "Carter plus" – the "plus" being enhanced military aid.[122]

---

[116] One NSC official described the reforms as "manifestly in contradiction to the philosophy and principles of this administration." Memorandum, Bailey to Allen, July 1, 1981, Box 30, Executive Secretariat, NSC Country File, RRL; Juan de Onis, "U.S. Firmly Endorses Salvador Reforms," *New York Times*, February 19, 1981; Luigi Einaudi, interview, *OHCES*, pp. 7–8.

[117] Memorandum, Enders to Stoessel, "Your Luncheon for President José Napoleon Duarte," September 18, 1981, NSA. See also Max G. Manwaring and Court Prisk, *El Salvador at War: An Oral History* (Washington, DC: National Defense University Press, 1988), p. 98.

[118] Memorandum, Haig to Reagan, "Your Meeting at the White House with President José Napoleon Duarte of El Salvador," September 19, 1981, NSA.

[119] This was part of a broader $19.5 million CIA program that also sought to interdict arms supplies for the FMLN from Nicaragua and Honduras. See Bob Woodward, *Veil: The Secret Wars of the CIA, 1981–1987* (New York: Simon & Schuster, 1987), p. 91 and LeoGrande, *Our Own Backyard*, p. 89.

[120] Telegram 7063, San Salvador to State, September 19, 1981, NSA.

[121] Telegram 89363, State to San Salvador, April 9, 1981, NSA.

[122] Quoted in LeoGrande, *Our Own Backyard*, p. 94. This assessment is shared by Greentree, *Crossroads of Intervention*, p. 99.

In February 1981, the United States granted $25 million in military aid to El Salvador – more than it gave to the rest of Latin America combined – as well as $74.4 million in economic and development assistance. Following Carter's lead, Reagan also invoked an "unforeseen emergency" to rush modern rifles, machine guns, mortars, medical equipment, four more transport helicopters, and an additional twenty-six military trainers to El Salvador without waiting for congressional approval. Secretary Haig sold the maneuver to skeptical international audiences as "only carrying out the military assistance program of the Carter administration."[123] To assuage congressional concerns about creeping escalation of American involvement in El Salvador, the administration pledged to cap the number of trainers deployed there at fifty-five.[124] The military assistance being provided was "only enough to give the government a breathing space," one State Department official noted, "the war cannot be won militarily; it must be won politically."[125]

Inducement without Results

The primary point of departure from the Carter administration's dominant approach was Reagan's embrace of an inducement influence strategy. Unconditioned aid and unambiguous statements of support for El Salvador were advised in the belief that dispensing U.S. largesse provided leverage over the local government, particularly the military, that could be used to influence their behavior.[126] Advocates of inducement argued that Carter had demonstrated conditions on aid were "counterproductive" and actually led to a "waning" of American influence over its client.[127] The government in San Salvador could not

---

[123] Telegram 3668, State to London, March 11, 1981, DDRS.
[124] LeoGrande, *Our Own Backyard*, p. 208.
[125] Quoted in Loren Jenkins, "Arms Put U.S. Stamp on Salvadoran War," *Washington Post*, May 7, 1981.
[126] Memorandum, Shultz to Reagan, "Managing Our Central America Strategy," May 25, 1983, RRL; "Summary NSC Paper on El Salvador," attached to Memorandum, Richard Allen, "Paper for NSC Meeting on February 11, 1981," February 10, 1981, box 1, Executive Secretariat, NSC Meeting Files, RRL and Telegram 204069, Abrams to SecState, July 23, 1982, STATE.
[127] Bernard Weinraub, "U.S. Envoy to Salvador Ordered to Stop Criticizing Rights Abuses," *New York Times*, November 10, 1982; Telegram 204069; Schultz to Reagan, "Managing Our Central America Strategy."

count on the United States, Secretary Haig argued, because "assistance was promised one day and turned off the next."[128] Such coercive measures should be used to influence hostile states, not friendly ones.[129] If assistance were withheld, it was feared that the ESAF would abandon all restraint and adopt the "self-defeating brutality" employed in neighboring Guatemala.[130] The Reagan administration would continue to try to convince Salvadoran leaders to reduce human rights abuses by the security forces and sustain the junta's reforms, but it would do so using inducements and friendly persuasion rather than conditions on aid.[131]

The switch to an inducement strategy registered immediate results – none of them positive – as the ESAF reneged on the reform promises made in December 1980. The murder investigations stalled, the pace of extrajudicial killings spiked, hard-line officers – such as the commander of the Treasury Police Colonel Moran – retained their posts, and the land-reform program was soon "in serious danger of failure."[132] In the darker corners of San Salvador, the inducement strategy was interpreted as an endorsement of the extreme right, and plotting against Duarte and his Christian Democrats resumed.[133]

With Robert D'Aubuisson publicly alleging that there was "high-level Washington support" for a military coup, Secretary Haig had to overtly reaffirm American commitments to Duarte and firmly inform the Salvadorans that military aid would be terminated if the

---

[128] Memorandum, Haig to Reagan, January 26, 1981, Box 1, Executive Secretariat, NSC Meeting Files, RRL.

[129] For evidence that senior U.S. officials believed in using conditionality against hostile states, see the discussion at the National Security Council meeting on February 11, 1981, in Jason Saltoun-Ebin, ed., *The Reagan Files: Inside the National Security Council*, vol. 2 (Santa Barbara, CA: Seabec, 2014), pp. 6–9. For a more general discussion of the value of positively engaging with friendly Latin American nations in need of reform rather than sanctioning them, see the National Security Council meeting on February 6, 1981, in *ibid.*, pp. 2–6.

[130] State Department Briefing Paper, "Central America," June 26, 1982, NSA. This worry carried over to the Bush administration. Memorandum, Byron to Director of the Joint Staff, September 25, 1990, NSA.

[131] Crandall, *The Salvador Option*, pp. 219–20.

[132] Telegram 85909, State to San Salvador, April 4, 1981, NSA; Al Kamen, "Salvador Conflict Centers on Army's Role," *Washington Post*, April 21, 1981. The U.S. embassy estimated that 9,118 political murders were carried out in 1981. The University of Central America put the figure at 11,727.

[133] LeoGrande, *Our Own Backyard*, p. 90.

government was overthrown.[134] The far right responded to the threat with a series of drive-by shootings and rocket attacks on the U.S. embassy. The potential loss of military aid once again spurred Defense Minister Garcia into action. Publicly warning partisans of the far right that a coup would "sink" El Salvador, he insisted that "without foreign support, especially that of the United States, there could be no survival."[135] Threats to suspend assistance, rather than grants of aid, also moved the churchwomen case forward. In late April 1981, Haig called Duarte to warn him that growing impatience in the White House and in Congress over the progress of the case "threatens our ability to continue to assist you."[136] Three days later, the six guardsmen suspected of the murders were arrested. When possible, the approach was also employed on the individual unit level: as MILGROUP Commander Colonel Waghelstein recalled, after amassing evidence that a particular signal unit hosted a death squad, he confronted the unit's chief of staff and told him, "I have my hands on the spigot of a $2 million communications package. I'm going to turn off the spigot if . . . [you do] not knock that shit off and disband the unit, and they did."[137]

In July, Thomas Enders – a towering career Foreign Service officer who served as the Assistant Secretary of State for Inter-American Affairs – outlined the administration's political solution for El Salvador: "prompt, free and open" elections for the constituent assembly.[138] Not only would democratization be the best way to ensure that the Salvadoran government broadened its base of support and responded to popular demands for reform, but elections could

---

[134] Telegram 54855, State to San Salvador, March 6, 1981, Box 29, Executive Secretariat, NSC Country File, RRL; Telegram 64402, State to All ARA Post, March 11, 1981, NSA; Juan de Onis, "Haig Opposes Coup by Salvador's Right," *New York Times*, March 5, 1981.

[135] Telegram 2671, San Salvador to State, April 8, 1981; Telegram 64402 and Telegram 89485, State to all ARA posts, April 9, 1981, all NSA.

[136] Telegram 112041, State to San Salvador, April 30, 1981 and Telegram 3279, San Salvador to State, April 30, 1981, both NSA.

[137] Waghelstein, interview, January 31, 1985, *SOOHP*, p. 36; Waghelstein, interview, February 23, 1987, *OHCES* p. 33; Telegram 7437, San Salvador to State, September 9, 1982, STATE.

[138] U.S. Department of State, *American Foreign Policy: Current Documents, 1981* (Washington, DC: GPO, 1982), pp. 1326–30. See also Telegram 204069; and "Insurgent Troops Vie for Village," *Miami Herald*, August 19, 1981.

force the far right to compete for power politically instead of through force. It was also hoped that free elections would potentially drive a wedge between the political activists of the Revolutionary Democratic Front – who turned to violence out of frustration with the country's political system – and the committed guerrillas of the FMLN. The Salvadoran government, Enders proclaimed, "should be and are willing to compete with the insurgents at the polls."[139] If the FMLN renounced violence, it would be welcome to take part in the elections. The Reagan administration's focus on elections and competition for political power contrasted sharply with the guerrilla's position that they should be brought directly into a power-sharing government with the "quota of power based on the correlation of forces."[140] The idea that "an armed minority" could "shoot its way into power" in this manner was, of course, anathema to senior American officials.[141] Although a number of critics questioned the feasibility of holding elections in the midst of a civil war, democracy promotion would be a key aspect of the Reagan administration's approach.

Congress Pushes Conditions

Following the failure of the "final offensive," the insurgents retreated to their rural strongholds in the north and east of the country and regrouped for a protracted fight. For the next several years, 12,000 to 14,000 FMLN guerrillas fought a quasi-conventional war against a Salvadoran military that had expanded from 20,000 in 1980 to 54,000 men by the second half of the decade. Immediately following the 1981 final offensive, the ESAF launched more than two dozen large-scale sweeps to surround and wipe out the insurgents. With only a dozen functioning helicopters, however, government forces were primarily road bound, which made it easy for the guerrillas to avoid them.[142] The FMLN's growing prowess in executing company-sized

---

[139] Thomas Enders, "El Salvador: The Search for Peace," *U.S. Department of State Bulletin* (September 1981), pp. 70–3.

[140] FMLN negotiating proposal quoted in Greentree, *Crossroads of Intervention*, p. 139.

[141] Quotes from Memorandum, Bremer to Clark, March 7, 1983. See also Memorandum, Haig to Reagan, "Elections or Negotiations in El Salvador," February 27, 1981, both in Box 30, Executive Secretariat, NSC Country File, RRL.

[142] Byrne, *El Salvador's Civil War*, p. 81.

(100-man) ambushes that could annihilate even medium-sized army units led the military to largely confine its operations to daylight hours, surrendering the night to the insurgents.[143]

The Salvadoran military's attempts to bring the insurgents to battle incurred a considerable toll: in 1981, government troops suffered an astounding 3,827 casualties, 19.1 percent of the total force.[144] Lacking even rudimentary medical evacuation capabilities, one-third of soldiers wounded in the field died from their injuries.[145] By the middle of the year, the ESAF high command had abandoned offensive action for fear that its forces were on the verge of collapse.[146] The U.S. Defense Attaché in San Salvador judged that "both sides had fought to a draw ... there is no military end in sight for the war of attrition in El Salvador," a view shared by representatives of the FDR, who admitted to American interlocutors that "none of the FMLN commanders thought they could win a military victory."[147]

The stalemate was short-lived. A renewed FMLN offensive in August 1981 forced the government to focus the military on guarding economic infrastructure and government installations.[148] Well equipped with small arms, mortars, and mines, guerrilla units consisting of several hundred fighters temporarily captured smaller towns and mauled the ESAF in numerous attacks on military posts. By September 1981, senior officers at U.S. Southern Command (SOUTHCOM) began to voice concerns that the ESAF was losing the war, a view echoed in the State Department and the National Security Council.[149]

---

[143] Waghelstein, interview, January 31, 1985, *SOOHP*, p. 37.

[144] Edward Cody, "Army's Toll Doubles in El Salvador," *Washington Post*, August 12, 1983.

[145] The comparable figure for the U.S. military in Vietnam was 10 percent. Memorandum from North, Sapia-Bosch, and Fontaine to Clark, "Medical Evacuation Helicopter for El Salvador," September 15, 1983, DDRS.

[146] Loren Jenkins, "Silent Stares of Death Routine in El Salvador," *Washington Post*, May 3, 1981.

[147] Telegram 4455, San Salvador to State, June 12, 1981 and Telegram 3163, Managua to State, July 22, 1981, both NSA.

[148] Telegram 803, San Salvador to State, November 18, 1981, NSA.

[149] "Salvador Junta Seeks More U.S. Aid," *Miami Herald*, September 10, 1981. Memorandum, Allen to Reagan, "Secretary Haig's Recommendations on El Salvador" [n.d.] and Memorandum, Schweitzer and Fontaine to Allen, "Situation in El Salvador," August 19, 1981, both in Box 30, Executive Secretariat, NSC Country File, RRL.

The situation deteriorated further in January 1982, when an FMLN raid on the Ilopango Airbase succeeded in destroying a significant portion of the Salvadoran Air Force on the ground.[150] The insurgents' string of military successes had divergent impacts on perceptions of their popular legitimacy: the Salvadoran Church's hierarchy denounced their violence, proclaiming that the FMLN "has lost its popular support and is dedicated to sowing terror among the population," while the Mexican and French governments jointly recognized the FMLN as a "representative political voice" in El Salvador.[151]

The inducement strategy's failure to reduce human rights abuses by the PSC and death squads emerged as a subject of partisan debate on Capitol Hill. Secretary Haig warned Reagan that in order to approve future military and economic aid, congressional Democrats who controlled the House of Representatives would require concrete evidence that the Junta was actively working to control abuses by the PSC and the death squads.[152] In December 1981, an amendment to the foreign aid bill – passed over the objections of both Reagan and Duarte – required the president to certify every six months that the Salvadoran government was

1. Making a concerted and significant effort to comply with internationally recognized standards of human rights;
2. Achieving substantial control over all elements of its Armed Forces so as to bring to an end the indiscriminate torture and murder of Salvadoran citizens;
3. Making continued progress in implementing essential economic and political reforms, including a land-reform program;
4. Committed to the holding of elections at an early date and to that end has demonstrated good-faith efforts to begin discussions with all major factions in El Salvador that are seeking an equitable political solution to the conflict; and
5. Making a good-faith effort to bring to trial those responsible for the murders of the American missionaries and land-reform experts.

---

[150] Telegram 634, San Salvador to State, January 27, 1982, RRL.
[151] Duarte, *Duarte*, p. 170; "Reacciones Nacionales," *Processo*, no. 33 (August 31–September 6, 1981), p. 5.
[152] Memorandum, Haig to Reagan, September 19, 1981, NSA.

If the president could not make such a certification, Congress would cut off all military assistance to El Salvador.[153] This certification requirement attempted to push the United States back toward a conditionality strategy. The all-or-nothing nature of the certification rendered it a blunt tool, however, that was easily subverted by a White House that did not favor the approach because, in the words of United Nations ambassador Jeane Kirkpatrick, it was "undermining the confidence of vulnerable allies."[154]

Military Reforms Stagnate

During the early 1980s, the ESAF lacked trained officers, standardized equipment, and sufficient soldiers to sustain offensive operations, not to mention adequate communications, intelligence, and maintenance capabilities.[155] U.S. military observers judged that the force was "unprepared, strategically, tactically, organizationally or equipment wise to confront a credible guerrilla force or insurgency."[156] Beyond that, El Salvador lacked a comprehensive strategy for countering the insurgency. At Duarte's request, in November 1981, an American team under the leadership of Brigadier General Fred Woerner, worked with the ESAF general staff to devise a military plan of action.

The Woerner Report outlined a five-year program to suppress the guerrillas at a cost of $300 to $400 million. These efforts focused on expanding the ESAF's force structure and modifying its tactical performance. Woerner sought to increase the army by ten battalions – including the creation of several rapid-reaction battalions that could be used to assault large FMLN formations – as well as modernize the Salvadoran Air Force and improve the military's command-and-control, communications, and intelligence functions. The goal was to transition counterinsurgency operations in the countryside from the abuse-prone National Guard to better-trained army units.[157] In the tactical and operational realm, the Woerner Report called for the army

---

[153] Sections 728(b), (d), and (e) of the International Security and Development Cooperation Act of 1981, Pub. Law 97–113, December 29, 1981.

[154] Crandall, *The Salvador Option*, p. 260.

[155] Telegram 803; Jamie Guiterrez, interview, December 18, 1986, *Oral History of the Conflict in El Salvador*, vol. 4, p. 11, MHI.

[156] Woerner, interview, *OHCES*, p. 37.

[157] Telegram 8963, San Salvador to State, December 23, 1980, STATE.

to abandon its defensive posture and carry out aggressive, small-unit operations by day and by night. Rather than attempting to defend the entire country with its limited forces, Woerner argued that the Salvadoran military should concentrate on protecting key economic and population centers and temporarily ceding control over the resource-poor eastern and northern areas, which would later be squeezed by aggressive military operations once government control over more important zones was secured. In a classic "clear, hold, build" model, civic action and development in these cleared zones would be undertaken to win popular support.[158] As a result, the 55-man U.S. military assistance group in El Salvador had two key goals: (1) to expand and modernize the ESAF so that it could take on the FMLN and (2) to alter the ESAF's operational and tactical approach to counterinsurgency.

Over the course of the civil war, the army nearly tripled in size, its soldiers were issued modern weapons and equipment, and the number of helicopters and counterinsurgency-relevant fixed-wing aircraft in the air force increased sixfold. Altering the ESAF's tactical approach, however, would be stymied by three major impediments: the lack of effective leadership, permissive attitudes toward institutional violence, and the inability to carry out nonmilitary aspects of counterinsurgency.

It is significantly easier to provide an army with advanced weapons and recruit new enlisted personnel than it is to develop the competent leaders required to use them effectively. More concerned with maintaining his power base than enhancing military effectiveness, Defense Minister Garcia ignored American entreaties to appoint capable and aggressive officers to senior posts in lieu of his *tanda*-mates. Consequently, the head of the U.S. MILGROUP estimated that "of the 14 departments there were only two departmental commanders that were worth a damn, the others being notably ineffective."[159] The situation was similar among the ESAF's battalion commanders: According to the U.S. defense attaché, "some of these guys are very, very good, but most of them . . . really are lacking in basic military training."[160] Despite the serious military challenge posed by the FMLN, many officers approached the conflict as a "nine-to-five

---

[158] Byrne, *El Salvador's Civil War*, pp. 78–9.
[159] Waghelstein, interview, January 31, 1985, *SOOHP*, p. 28.
[160] Lyman Duryea, interview, March 4, 1986, Senior Officers Oral History Program, p. 114, MHI.

war," returning to San Salvador to see their families on weekends while their troops remained in the field.[161] Moreover, small-unit operations were hindered by the shortage of junior officers. "You had maybe a lieutenant or a cadet with forty to fifty with no rank at all," the U.S. defense attaché recalled, "it was like a boy scout troop."[162] A subsequent MILGROUP commander, Colonel James Steele, concurred: at the platoon level, "you'd be hard pressed to find anybody you could really describe as an effective leader ... I could talk about ... small unit operations until I was blue in the face, and it wasn't going to happen when you have that kind of leadership quotient."[163]

To quickly expand the number of junior officers and weaken the corrosive influence of Salvadoran military culture, officer candidates were brought to American-run institutions, where they received training in individual leadership, small-unit operations, and counterinsurgency theory. Although more than a thousand cadets were trained in this manner, on returning to El Salvador they came under significant pressure to ignore American training and conform to the ESAF's mode of operations.[164] Despite significant American assistance, as of 1983, the U.S. ambassador thought "it was still in doubt as to whether the Salvadorian Army would ever be an effective field force."[165]

A second major obstacle was the ESAF high command's inability or unwillingness to prevent the institutional abuse that was inflaming the insurgency.[166] Prior to 1983, the ESAF did not take prisoners in the field; captured insurgents were just summarily executed.[167] The ESAF's brutality was not merely confined to its guerrilla opponents: in December 1981, elements of the American-trained Atlacatl rapid-reaction battalion committed the single greatest massacre of the war when they rampaged through the village of El Mozote, torturing and killing 767 men, women, and children over the course of three days.[168]

---

[161] Moyar, *A Question of Command*, p. 174.
[162] Duryea, interview, *OHCES*, p. 131.
[163] James Steele, interview, October 5–10, 1986, in Manwaring and Prisk, *El Salvador at War*, pp. 278–9.
[164] Duryea, interview, *OHCES*, pp. 117–18, 163–4.
[165] Deane Hinton, interview, September 10, 1987, *Oral History of the Conflict in El Salvador*, vol. 1, p. 8, MHI.
[166] Woerner, "Report," p. 17.
[167] Mark Danner, *The Massacre at El Mozote: A Parable of the Cold War* (New York: Vintage, 1994), p. 42.
[168] CIA, "Armed Forces Sweep in Morazan," December 15, 1981, NSA; Greentree, *Crossroads of Intervention*, pp. 101–2.

Even when these problems were recognized, the "tenuous and often non-existent control" that senior officers possessed over units stationed in remote rural areas hindered their ability to rein in a significant source of human rights abuses.[169] American training attempted to emphasize the practical benefits of respecting human rights: a live prisoner with information is more valuable than a dead one, for example, while violations of the laws of war were major obstacles to obtaining aid from the United States and Europe.[170] Despite these efforts, progress on controlling institutional violence was slow.

No amount of civic action or development projects would rally civilians to the government's cause when the armed forces were the primary source of human rights abuses, yet El Salvador's effort also strayed far from the ideal in the nonmilitary aspects of counterinsurgency. As one American diplomat recalled, the implementation of "psychological operations, civil defense, and civic action tended to be paternalistic, manipulative and superficial, while the presence of the ESAF in the countryside was more often a source of fear rather than security."[171] Salvadoran officers charged with carrying out the political and economic aspects of counterinsurgency were not chosen for their prowess in these areas but for their failings as combat commanders, indicating the low priority the military gave to these missions.

1982 Constituent Elections and Land Reform

While attempts to reform the Salvadoran military foundered, political reform was more promising. Elections for a Constituent Assembly that would draft a constitution were scheduled for March 28, 1982. It was hardly a favorable environment: approximately 25 to 33 percent of the country was outside of the government's control, the ruling Junta remained unstable, roughly 30,000 civilians had been killed and another 600,000 displaced since the 1979 coup, and the economy was on the verge of collapse as violence and massive capital flight led

---

[169] Director of Central Intelligence, "El Salvador: Performance on Certification Issues," January 13, 1983, LOC; CIA, "El Salvador: Situation Report 13," March 16, 1983, p. 2, LOC.

[170] John Waghelstein quoted in Manwaring and Prisk, *El Salvador at War*, pp. 278–9.

[171] Greentree, *Crossroads of Intervention*, p. 102.

gross domestic product (GDP) to contract an astonishing 9.5 percent in 1981.[172]

The Reagan administration saw elections as a key means of building support for the Salvadoran government while simultaneously disarming its domestic opponents by enticing the far right into the political process and demonstrating the limited political support for the insurgents.[173] As Deane Hinton – the tough-minded career Foreign Service officer Reagan selected as his first ambassador – quipped, "How are they going to go around the world saying they represent the people of El Salvador if the people of El Salvador are on record supporting somebody else?"[174]

The Christian Democrats and the former party of the oligarchy, the National Conciliation Party (PCN), were joined in the contest by the new Nationalist Republican Alliance (ARENA), headed by Robert D'Aubuisson. Emphasizing free-market economics with a strong religious, nationalist, and anti-Communist element, the party pledged to end the civil war by installing competent leadership in the place of Duarte's Junta that would energetically prosecute the conflict, revitalize the economy by reversing key economic reforms, and eliminate subversives.[175] The Salvadoran Electoral Commission also recognized several of the constituent parties making up the FMLN's political wing – the Revolutionary Democratic Front – as legitimate political voices and offered to facilitate their campaigns from exile via television if security concerns made physically returning to El Salvador too risky a proposition.[176] The insurgents continued to insist on negotiations for an interim power-sharing government, however, and declined to compete for power.

---

[172] Loren Jenkins, "Rebel Rallies Preempted Vote in 'Other El Salvador,'" *Washington Post*, April 5, 1982.

[173] Although the Reagan administration wanted the far right to compete electorally, it was made clear to Salvadoran military leaders and diplomats from neighboring countries that the United States could not support a rightist government. Telegram 1896, Caracas to State, March 10, 1982, STATE.

[174] Quoted in Christopher Dickey, "Left Expected to Ignore Salvador Vote," *Washington Post*, August 31, 1981.

[175] D'Aubuisson also pledged to try Duarte and his colleagues for treason. Telegram 2022, San Salvador to State, March 10, 1982, NSA; Warren Hoge, "'Pathological Killer' Candidate Gains," *New York Times*, February 19, 1982.

[176] Montgomery, *Revolution in El Salvador*, p. 158; Duarte, "Duarte," p. 178.

In a contest that has been judged to be "relatively free, fair and competitive," 85 percent of El Salvador's eligible voters went to the polls in the face of FMLN threats to kill anyone seeking to participate in the election.[177] The Christian Democrats finished first, capturing 40 percent of the vote and twenty-four of the sixty seats in the Assembly, ARENA finished second with nineteen seats, the PCN won fourteen, and the remaining three were taken by two minor centrist parties. International news media provided widespread coverage of the massive turnout and the country's archbishop declared the result a clear "vote in favor of peace, democracy and justice" calling on the FMLN to "accept the judgment of the people and lay down their arms."[178] Free elections were one of the conditions for continued American aid: after five decades of running the country, the Salvadoran military made no attempt to influence the result and even won praise for providing security during the balloting.[179]

In Washington, elation quickly turned to alarm when it became clear that ARENA and the PCN had won enough seats between them to form a right-wing government that sidelined the Christian Democrats and named D'Aubuisson as provisional president. In an attempt to force a coalition including all parties, the United States threatened to cut off aid to a D'Aubuisson-led government.[180] Unfortunately for Washington, past inducement policies reduced the credibility of the warning. As a senior ARENA official told a reporter, "The United States has never cut off aid anywhere for very long or even entirely. Reagan will never let the Communists win here. It's just a complete bluff."[181]

[177] Enrique Baloyra, "The Salvadoran Elections of 1982–1991," *Studies in Comparative International Development*, 28, no 3 (Fall 1993), p. 24. The U.S. embassy reported few complaints of fraud or intimidation. Telegram 2704, San Salvador to State, March 28, 1982, NSA. Although the FMLN sought to disrupt the election, it only managed to prevent voting in approximately twenty of the country's 500 polling stations. Telegram 6485, San Salvador to State, August 4, 1982, NSA; Marta Harnecker, *Pueblos en Armas* (Mexico City: Universidad Autónoma de Guerrero, 1983), p. 103.

[178] Memorandum, Clark to Reagan, "El Salvador's Elections," April 19, 1982, RRL; Christopher Dickey, "Salvadoran Prelate Warns of Return to Violence," *Washington Post*, April 5, 1982.

[179] Telegram 6485, San Salvador to State, August 4, 1982, NSA; Foreign and Commonwealth Office, "Developments in El Salvador," November 1983, FO 973/162, NAUK.

[180] Telegram 84176, State to San Salvador, March 30, 1982, RRL.

[181] Joanne Omang, "As Salvadoran Politics Boil, U.S Envoy Shifts Attention," *Washington Post*, April 24, 1982.

In the face of this intransigence, the United States pressured the Salvadoran military to back a government of national unity. A personal envoy from Secretary Haig to the high command and the heads of the major political parties explicitly specified that continued U.S. support required (1) a national unity government in which the Christian Democrats wielded power in proportion to their poll results, (2) sustained reforms in economics, land, and human rights, and (3) presidential elections by 1983. A D'Aubuisson presidency, however, would result in a suspension of all military aid.[182] Alarmed by the threat coming from a noted anti-Communist in the administration, the military announced that a government without the Christian Democrats was unacceptable. Working from a list of nine candidates provided by the U.S. embassy, the ESAF compelled the formation of a provisional government with Alvaro Magana – a nonpolitical banker with close ties to the military – as provisional president.[183]

Following the election, Washington's attention turned to sustaining land reform ahead of the July 28 deadline when President Reagan would have to certify to Congress that Salvadoran reforms were making progress in order to win $100 million in military aid. The agrarian reform program initiated by the Junta in 1980 had three parts. In phase 1, the country's largest landholdings, those in excess of 500 hectares (two square miles), accounting for approximately 15 percent of farmland, had been seized and given to peasant cooperatives. Phase 2 affected medium-sized estates from 100 to 500 hectares, but its implementation had been delayed. The final component was the "land-to-the-tiller" program, which allowed sharecroppers to purchase up to seven hectares of farmland that they currently leased from their landlords. The Reagan administration viewed land reform as a way to bolster support for the government while undercutting the appeal of the far left; however, with El Salvador's economy stagnating, the right-wing parties dominating the Constituent Assembly attempted to boost the production of export crops by halting the "land-to-the-tiller program" and turning a blind eye as several thousand peasants were forcibly evicted from plots they held

---

[182] Telegram 104143, State to San Salvador, April 18, 1982, STATE.
[183] Telegram 3497, San Salvador to State, April 23, 1982, NSA; Jose Guillermo Garcia, interview, July 2, 1987, *Oral History of the Conflict in El Salvador*, vol. 4, p. 52, MHI.

title to.[184] This violation of aid conditions drew a swift reaction on Capitol Hill, as the Senate Foreign Relations Committee voted to cut military aid for 1983 by 60 percent if the Salvadoran government failed to implement the program.[185] Although the Salvadoran officer corps was split on the importance of land reform, once again, the threat to military aid spurred it into action against the far right. Both Defense Minister Garcia and the Army Chief of Staff publicly endorsed the program, dispatching soldiers to actively return thousands of illegally evicted peasants to their farms.[186] Throughout this period, in moments of crisis, conditions on American military aid and clear threats to suspend it continually proved to be the key to mobilizing the ESAF to support U.S.-backed reforms.[187] In turn, this kind of visible action bought the government some necessary breathing room and fostered a sense that a degree of positive change was possible without revolution.[188]

Denouncing the Death Squads

At Washington's urging, and with the backing of El Salvador's major political parties, President Magana had opened a dialogue with the FMLN about peaceably joining the political process ahead of the 1984 presidential election.[189] The Reagan administration was engaged in

---

[184] Memorandum, Eagleburger to Reagan, June 10, 1983, Box 30, Executive Secretariat, NSC Country File, RRL; Intelligence Community Assessment, "El Salvador: Performance on Certification Issues," July 27, 1982, DDRS.

[185] Bernard Weinraub, "Proposal for Aid to Salvador Cut by Senate Panel," *New York Times*, May 27, 1982.

[186] Christopher Dickey, "El Salvador Gives Farmers Land to Show Progress in Reforms," *Washington Post*, June 5, 1982; Shirley Christian, "Salvadorans Battle Erosion of Land Reform," *Miami Herald*, June 13, 1982; Intelligence Community Assessment, "El Salvador: Performance on Certification Issues," July 27, 1982, LOC.

[187] LeoGrande, *Our Own Backyard*, p. 170.

[188] Pickering, interview, *OHCES*, p. 29.

[189] Memorandum, Enders to SecState, August 9, 1982, STATE; James Nelson Goodsell, "Central America Feels Pressure to Talk with Opposition," *Christian Science Monitor*, October 28, 1982. Assent of all the major parties, including ARENA, to including the FDR in the elections can be found in Telegram 1791, San Salvador to State, March 3, 1983, DDRS; Memorandum, Schultz to Reagan, "Next Steps in the Salvadoran Dialogue," June 20, 1983 and Telegram 6082, San Salvador to State, 10 July 1983, both Box 28, Executive Secretariat, NSC Country File, RRL.

back-channel discussions with the insurgents' political representatives, the FDR – brokered by the Colombian and Costa Rican governments – and there were positive signs that leftist political leaders might be persuaded to participate.[190] This effort was crushed under the boots of the right-wing death squads, however, who responded to this "most vile treason" by murdering a host of politicians and union chiefs with suspected links to the FMLN.[191] The leaders of the far left could never be co-opted into the political process as long as their lives were constantly at risk in El Salvador.

Beyond the aim of splitting the insurgents' political and military wings, both Ambassador Hinton and Assistant Secretary Enders believed that controlling extrajudicial violence was critical to ensure continued U.S. assistance to the fragile national unity government. Salvadoran leaders had achieved a degree of success in suppressing political murders over the past year, but with such violence still occurring at the rate of several hundred deaths a month, Hinton judged that the country's elites required "a sharp whack over the head" to convince them to take the issue seriously. With Enders' blessing, he delivered a blistering speech in October 1982 to the American Chamber of Commerce in San Salvador – a who's who of the country's ruling class. Calling the death squads a "mafia" that was "destroying El Salvador," the ambassador bluntly warned that American aid could be withheld if the kidnappings and murders by members of the security forces were not eliminated.[192]

Hinton's outraged audience accused him of "blackmailing" the country and compared him to an "arrogant, imperious" Roman proconsul.[193] Importantly, the speech eschewed the quiet diplomacy favored by the White House, which sought to employ friendly

---

[190] Transcript, Roger W. Fontaine interviewed by Aaron Lobel and Steve Roberts, *America abroad Media*, September 17, 2006, pp. 16, 45–50; Memorandum, "Senator Stone's Mission to Central America" [n.d.], Box 29, Executive Secretariat, NSC Country File, RRL.

[191] "Salvadorans Reject Rebel Call for Talks," *New York Times*, October 28, 1982.

[192] Telegram 3805, San Salvador to State, March 2, 1983, RRL; Greentree, *Crossroads of Intervention*, p. 99; Hamilton, "Strategic Communications in El Salvador," p. 10.

[193] Edward Cody, "U.S. Warns El Salvador on Rights Abuses," *Washington Post*, October 30, 1982; Edward Cody, "Salvadoran Businessmen Assail U.S. Ambassador as Roman 'Proconsul'," *Washington Post*, November 3, 1982.

persuasion behind closed doors but not to make a public confrontation with the Salvadorans front-page news. Although congressional certification requirements clearly conditioned aid on improvement in the country's human rights situation, National Security Advisor William Clark publicly repudiated Hinton's threat to withhold aid as a "counterproductive" Carter administration strategy.[194]

Enders and Hinton soon became caught up in a tug of war over Central American policy between the CIA, National Security Council, and Department of Defense on the one hand, who wanted a more robust military response to the FMLN, and the State Department on the other, which favored a political solution to the Salvadoran Civil War.[195] The pair also came under fire from conservative commentators in the United States who denounced their approach as a "no-win" policy that took a page from left-wing congressional democrats.[196] Enders' imposing personality – which had rubbed a number of senior officials the wrong way – helped to ensure that both he and Hinton would be replaced by the end of 1983.[197] Nevertheless, the strategy that they had set in motion would continue.[198]

The End of Garcia

Between June 1982 and June 1983, the ESAF suffered a crippling 6,815 killed and wounded out of a force of approximately 30,000 – double

---

[194] Weinraub, "U.S. Envoy to Salvador Ordered to Stop Criticizing Rights Abuses."

[195] On the battle for control over Central America policy, see George P. Shultz, *Turmoil and Triumph* (New York: Charles Scribner, 1993), pp. 297–318 and Robert Kagan, *A Twilight Struggle: American Power and Nicaragua, 1977–1990* (New York: Free Press, 1996), pp. 267–72.

[196] Virginia Prewett and Willliam Mizelle, "Salvadoran Commander Bucks No-Win U.S. Policy," *Washington Times*, January 14, 1983.

[197] Bernard D. Gwertzman, "Shultz Replaced Latin Aides as Part of a Reagan Pact," *New York Times*, June 5, 1983.

[198] Emphasis on the continuity of policy despite personnel changes can be found in Langhorne A. Motley, "Oral History Interview," March 1, 1997, Association for Diplomatic Studies and Training, Arlington, VA (ADST), pp. 10–11, 27–8; Telegram 3868, San Jose to State, June 5, 1983, DDRS; Memorandum, Schultz to Reagan, "Dick Stone's Visit to El Salvador," June 6, 1983, Box 28, Executive Secretariat, NSC Country File, RRL; Memorandum, Michel to Schultz, June 17, 1983, DDRS. In his diary, Reagan says of Hinton, "[H]e's a good man and did a fine job under difficult circumstances." Brinkley, *The Reagan Diaries*, p. 158.

the losses from the previous twelve months.[199] At the same time, the high command continued to favor inefficient, large-scale sweep operations that were easy for the insurgents to avoid and failed to prevent the guerrillas from returning once the troops had withdrawn from "cleared" areas. With most of the departmental commanders fighting the war during bankers' hours and rarely venturing our of their garrisons, aggressive, small-unit patrolling – particularly at night – by Salvadoran troops was minimal.[200]

In an effort to improve the quality of ESAF operations, the United States continued to advocate replacing the departmental commanders – who were largely Defense Minister Garcia's *tanda*-mates – with more competent officers. Instead, Garcia focused on removing a political rival: Lieutenant Colonel Sigifredo Ochoa. The Americans regarded Ochoa as one of the best commanders in the entire military for his embrace of small-unit counterinsurgency tactics and civic action projects, which allowed him to pacify a department that had once been an FMLN hotbed.[201] Refusing to relinquish command, Ochoa mobilized his troops and called for Garcia to resign, citing his gross corruption and incompetence. The crisis appeared ready to fracture the military because Ochoa won the support of a large swath of junior combat officers who respected his action and aggressiveness and despised Garcia for his lack of the same.[202] The contest also had significant political overtones because Ochoa and a number of the most effective and popular field commanders were close to Roberto D'Aubuisson, who personally blamed Garcia for the military's role in denying him the presidency of the provisional government.[203]

At this critical moment, the United States ended its tactical alliance with the controversial Defense Minister. Although, under American pressure, Garcia had defended several of the Junta's socioeconomic

[199] Edward Cody, "Army's Toll Doubles in El Salvador," *Washington Post*, August 12, 1983.

[200] Telegram 437, San Salvador to State, January 15, 1983, STATE; Memorandum, Michel to Schultz, June 17, 1983, DDRS.

[201] Telegram 437.

[202] Telegram 6485, San Salvador to State, August 4, 1982, NSA. It should be noted that these officers also had a vested interest in seeing Garcia and his *tanda* retire so that the path could be cleared for their own advancement.

[203] Telegram 7437; CIA, "El Salvador: Status of Military Discipline," January 12, 1983, DDRS; CIA, "El Salvador: Politics in the Military," January 24, 1983, DDRS.

reforms against the far right's efforts to undo them, as discontent with his leadership grew, his continued presence caused more problems than it solved.[204] When Garcia requested a high-profile visit to Washington to bolster his domestic standing, he was denied.[205] Instead, the United States helped to broker a face-saving compromise that saw Ochoa assigned abroad and Garcia succeeded by Colonel Carlos Eugenio Vides Casanova, an officer Duarte described as "the one natural leader of the armed forces."[206] With a personal reputation for professionalism, integrity, and moderation, he also voiced public support for political and military reform.[207]

In a significant shake-up of the high command, Vides Casanova replaced Garcia's cronies and several known human rights abusers with dynamic younger officers who had proven themselves in the field and were largely selected on merit rather than their *tanda*.[208] To enhance military effectiveness, the new Defense Minister also streamlined the ESAF's command structure – which had been purposefully designed to prevent any one commander from gaining sufficient power to mount a coup – despite the risk this posed to his position. Empowering the most capable field commanders without increasing the influence of the extreme right over the military or provoking a putsch required a careful balancing act.[209]

In visits to troops in the field, the new Defense Minister was vocal in his denunciation of right-wing extremists, which he said were undermining El Salvador's path to democracy and risking a rupture with the United States.[210] Under Vides Casanova's hand-picked Chief of Army Staff, Colonel Adolfo Blandón, the Salvadoran military began to undertake the kind of aggressive operations favored by the United

[204] Telegram 995, San Salvador to State, February 16, 1983, DDRS.
[205] Memorandum, Sapia-Bosch to Clark, "Private Meeting with Salvadoran Defense Minister Garcia," March 15, 1983, DDRS.
[206] Duarte, *Duarte*, p. 187.
[207] Carlos Eugenio Vides Casanova, interview, December 18, 1987, *Oral History of the Conflict in El Salvador*, vol. 4, pp. 62–3, MHI; Bosch, *The Salvadoran Officer Corps and the Final Offensive*, pp. 33–34; Manwaring and Prisk, *El Salvador at War*, p. 217.
[208] State Department Briefing Paper, "El Salvador: Death Squads," November 1983, NSA; Memorandum for the Record, "Briefing of the House Permanent Select Committee on Intelligence Staff on the Central American Finding," January 26, 1984, CIA.
[209] Telegram 4992, San Salvador to State, June 4, 1983, DDRS.
[210] CIA, "El Salvador: Vides and the Death Squads," December 1, 1983, LOC.

States to deny the guerrillas sanctuary. Decentralized authority gave brigade commanders the freedom of action to decide how to carry out missions in their area of responsibility, and Blandón reprimanded commanders who lacked initiative or did not spend sufficient time in the field with their troops.

To support these reforms, the Pentagon relaxed its restrictions on trainers in the field, assigning them to brigade headquarters so that they could exercise more influence over the operational level of the conflict where the Salvadoran commanders were most deficient. At the same time, the Department of Defense began to skirt the fifty-five-man limit on trainers by only counting personnel actively instructing Salvadoran forces in combat tasks. The number of U.S. military personnel in El Salvador soon exceeded 100, with dozens more working there on "temporary duty" from assignments in Honduras and Panama.

National Campaign Plan

In June 1983, the Salvadoran military moved forward with the American-designed National Campaign Plan (NCP), which sought to win popular support by undertaking rural development projects behind a security screen. The army's elite rapid-reaction battalions were to be concentrated in the San Vicente department – a major producer of coffee, cotton, and sugar – to clear out the FMLN presence. The units remained in place to protect a USAID-funded reconstruction campaign that was resettling displaced civilians, as well as building roads, schools, and health clinics in an effort to convince the local population of the material benefits of supporting the government. With locally recruited militias preventing guerrilla reinfiltration, it was envisioned that once San Vicente was secure, the army would repeat the process in a neighboring department, systematically expanding the government's zone of control and squeezing the guerrillas into the periphery of the country.

For the first several months, the NCP made significant progress; however, efforts stagnated due to a lack of resources and enemy action.[211] Although the Salvadoran military largely fulfilled its role, civilian agencies lacked the capacity to provide the necessary public services to rural inhabitants.[212] More important, the FMLN took advantage of the

[211] Bacevich et al., *American Military Policy in Small Wars*, p. 81.
[212] *Ibid.*, p. 44.

concentration of the army's best troops in San Vicente to launch a major offensive in other departments – killing 800 soldiers and capturing another 400 in just two months.[213] This was followed by another major assault that annihilated two army battalions in the space of three weeks and overran the headquarters of the 4th Infantry Brigade, inflicting 300 more casualties. "There were days at the end of 1983," the U.S. ambassador recalled, "when we wondered whether we would make it through the next two or three months."[214] In the judgment of one historian, "According to all indicators – ESAF casualties, arms taken, prisoners captured, terrain controlled, major towns and army positions taken, infrastructure damaged or destroyed, level of enemy morale – the guerrillas were winning the war."[215] To respond to this challenge, the rapid-reaction battalions had to be withdrawn from San Vicente, which allowed the FMLN to destroy the roads, schools, and local militias that the government had established in the department. The Salvadoran government simply lacked sufficient troops to carry out the NCP while also maintaining pressure on the FMLN elsewhere.

Conditionality and the "New Contract"

From the U.S. standpoint, the 1982 elections had been a major success that generated positive political momentum while preventing the Salvadorian government from being captured by the far right. However, it became increasingly clear in Washington that the death squads were undermining efforts to defeat the insurgency and build a democracy. On the battlefield, the military situation was so precarious that the SOUTHCOM Commander personally informed the National Security Advisor that "if we did not step up our effort ... the thing was going to go down the tubes."[216] American public support for the administration's approach to El Salvador was anemic, receiving less than 30 percent approval in dozens of polls, while congressional opposition

---

[213] Lydia Chavez, "Salvador Rebels Make Gains and U.S. Advisors are Glum," *New York Times*, November 4, 1983.

[214] Pickering, interview, *OHCES*, p. 4. For a similar view, see the account of James F. Mack, who was a Foreign Service officer in San Salvador at the time. James F. Mack, "Oral History Interview," March 20, 2004, p. 59, ADST.

[215] Byrne, *El Salvador's Civil War*, p. 104.

[216] Wallace Nutting, interview, January 29, 1987, *Oral History of the Conflict in El Salvador*, vol. 2, p. 11, MHI.

was growing. With progress in the churchwomen murder case "marginal at best," Congress decided to provide the Salvadorans with an incentive to act by conditioning 30 percent of the $64.8 million in military aid appropriated for FY1984 on a trial and verdict in the case.[217] Between the deteriorating military situation in El Salvador and the strong opposition to its policies in the United States, the Reagan administration's approach appeared to be increasingly untenable.

An interagency policy review in July 1983 concluded that U.S. efforts in El Salvador were being hindered by "critical issues of troop motivation, treatment of civilians and military discipline." On the ground in San Salvador, the embassy was reportedly frustrated over the inability to translate dependence on American support into influence over the local government.[218] Ambassador Hinton insisted that the time had come to pressure the Salvadorans to follow American guidance, advising Washington:

> The more the [Salvadoran government] needs our assistance, the more leverage we have. What we need to do is use it in concrete cases ... [otherwise] we will have strengthened the position of those Salvadorans, probably a majority, who believe and assert that no matter what they do or do not do, the U.S. will support and protect them against a Communist takeover...we are a great power. From time to time we should behave like one.[219]

Congressional certification was intended to provide an incentive for the Salvadoran government to alter its grievance-causing behavior; however, the all-or-nothing nature of the conditions gave little room to calibrate aid to the level of Salvadoran compliance. Consequently, four times in the previous two years the Reagan administration had complied with the letter of the law rather than its spirit by certifying progress in order to keep aid flowing despite limited or even nonexistent evidence of the consolidation of civilian authority, a reduction in officially committed human rights abuses, or improvements in military discipline.[220] The State Department argued that this shortcutting of

---

[217] CIA, "El Salvador: Performance on Certification Issues," July 13, 1983, NSA; Cynthia Arnson, *Crossroads: Congress, the President, and Central America, 1976–1992* (State College, PA: Penn State University Press, 1993), p. 140.

[218] Weinraub, "U.S. Envoy to Salvador Ordered to Stop Criticizing Rights Abuses."

[219] Telegram 1543, San Salvador to State, March 6, 1983, DDRS.

[220] Arnson, *Crossroads*, pp. 84–91, 100–5, 119, 136–9.

conditionality was harming American interests because Salvadoran leaders have "not been motivated to take the minimal actions required to help us sustain our support."[221] Embracing real conditionality, the interagency task force recommended forging "a new and reliable contract" with San Salvador that spelled out what the Salvadorans must do to win – with particular attention given to the "elimination of military participation in death squads" – and what assistance the United States will provide in return.[222]

To forge consensus for his Central America policy, President Reagan established a bipartisan commission under the leadership of Henry Kissinger in July 1983. With respect to El Salvador, the Kissinger Commission's report gave a concrete articulation to the ad hoc policy the administration had been pursuing. Arguing that free elections – in which all major groups can take part – are the only way to achieve a lasting political solution, the commission counseled that the focus of American efforts "must be the legitimation of governments by free consent." This required "the rejection of violence and murder as political instruments."[223] Population-centric counterinsurgency measures backed by balanced economic growth were advocated "to give democratic forces there the time and the opportunity to carry out the structural reforms essential for that country's security and well-being."[224] Echoing the interagency task force's conclusion that unconditional inducements had not produced significant influence over Salvadoran behavior, the report argued that military aid should be "conditioned upon demonstrated progress towards free and fair elections; freedom of association; the establishment of the rule of law and an effective judicial system; and the termination of the activities of the so-called death squads, as well as vigorous action against those guilty of crimes and the prosecution to the extent possible of past offenders."[225] Unlike the past approach to congressional certification requirements, the commission emphasized that "these conditions should be seriously enforced."[226]

---

[221] Philip Taubman, "U.S. Said to Weigh 40 percent Increase in Military Funds for Latin Allies," *New York Times*, July 17, 1983.

[222] *Ibid.*

[223] *Report of the Bipartisan Commission on Central America* (Washington, DC: GPO, 1984), pp. 13, 110–1.

[224] *Ibid.*, p. 86.   [225] *Ibid.*, p. 104.   [226] *Ibid.*

On dispatching veteran diplomat Thomas Pickering to replace Hinton in San Salvador in August 1983, Haig's pragmatic successor as Secretary of State, George Schultz, instructed him to "raise hell" on human rights.[227] The death squads had unleashed a wave of violence against union organizers, peasant groups, and Christian Democrats in order to sabotage reform efforts, which Ambassador Pickering saw as a direct challenge to the Salvadoran and American governments.[228] In line with his mandate, Pickering delivered another hard-hitting speech to the Chamber of Commerce the year after Hinton's, denouncing the right-wing paramilitaries as "murderers, torturers and kidnappers" who must be punished for their crimes.[229] Echoing Hinton, Pickering warned of an "extremely serious risk" that military aid would be cut off without drastic action. This time, however, the Reagan administration followed up the threat with an even higher-level messenger.[230]

Less than a month after Pickering's speech, in December 1983, Vice President George H. W. Bush was secretly dispatched to San Salvador to negotiate a new contract with the Salvadoran government. Carrying a letter from Reagan which stressed that it was more important than ever to show dramatic progress in areas such as elections, land reform, and human rights, Bush emphasized that both he and President Reagan believed Pickering's comments were "right on the mark."[231] Forcibly denouncing the death squads as "rightwing fanatics" and "cowardly terrorists," the American vice president warned Salvadoran leaders that "every murderous act they commit poisons the well of friendship between our two countries."[232] In a series of private meetings with President Magana, the Minister of Defense, and

---

[227] Quoted in George S. Vest et al., *Report on the Secretary of State's Panel on El Salvador* (Washington, DC: Department of State, July 1993), p. 26.

[228] CIA, "Central American Monthly Report 3," October 1983, NSA; Telegram 9483, San Salvador to State, October 14, 1983, NSA; Sam Dillion, "El Salvador Give in to U.S. Demands," *Miami Herald*, December 19, 1983.

[229] Quoted in U.S. House of Representatives, *The Situation in El Salvador: Hearings before the Subcommittee on Human Rights* (Washington, DC: GPO, 1984), pp. 248–57.

[230] For similar visits by other senior administration officials, see Montgomery, *Revolution in El Salvador*, p. 203; Woodward, *Veil*, p. 291.

[231] Letter, Reagan to Magana, December 10, 1983, RRL.

[232] Bureau of Public Affairs, *U.S. Condemns Salvadoran Death Squads, Current Policy No. 533* (Washington, DC: Department of State, December 11, 1983).

senior military commanders, Bush concretely laid out the terms of the bargain the United States had in mind:

1. Arrest former National Guard Captain Eduardo Avila for the murder of the American land-reform experts and agree to a timeline for the prosecution of that case, as well as the murders of several other U.S. citizens;
2. Explicitly condemn death-squad violence, send a list of three military officers and three civilians with known links to death squads into exile, and implement due-process procedures for suspects detained by the security corps that require arresting officers to identify themselves, notify the families of detainees, take suspects to official detention facilities, and refrain from the use of torture or force against any person;
3. Publicly commit to support and protect the March 25, 1984, presidential elections; and
4. Complete constitutional action on land reform that will defend the agricultural cooperatives formed by expropriating large landholdings as well as the "land-to-the-tiller program" while moving forward on the expropriation of smaller landholdings.[233]

Emphasizing that these issues "cannot be set aside since our support hinges directly on all of them," the vice president announced a one-month deadline for their execution, to ensure tangible evidence of progress when the U.S. Congress returned from its Christmas recess. "Without actions in these areas there is no point in trying to obtain additional funds for El Salvador," Bush warned, "and to be honest we will not even make the effort because it would be fruitless."[234]

The reward for compliance was sufficient U.S. military aid to field forty-two additional army battalions as well as attack aircraft, helicopters, and an enhancement of El Salvador's airborne medical evacuation capability, the latter of which was critical for boosting troop morale.[235] Behind the scenes, President Magana had advised Bush ahead of time to set tight deadlines for compliance because "our military will agree to

---

[233] Telegram 11567, San Salvador to State, December 14, 1983, NSA.
[234] *Ibid*; Details of the Pickering list comes from Transcript, Thomas Pickering interviewed by Aaron Lobel, *America Abroad Media*, September 6, 2006, p. 18.
[235] Telegram 11567.

anything if there is no time deadline connected with it."[236] Indeed, the Salvadoran leader suggested that the threat of a congressionally mandated aid cutoff was "very important in persuading the commanders to act positively and act soon."[237]

At least one death squad condemned Bush's ultimatum as "extortion" and threatened to retaliate against the "gringos."[238] Within the ESAF, several senior officers vocally denounced American "arm-twisting tactics" at a time when "Salvadoran soldiers are shedding their blood in the fight against Communism so that U.S. soldiers will not have to do the same."[239] Reform-minded officers who wanted the killings to end, however, finally believed that they had high-level allies in the U.S. administration that would no longer overlook abuses in the name of anti-Communism.[240] At the end of the day, the threat of an aid suspension and the promise of sufficient support to defeat the FMLN were too much for the ESAF leadership to pass up. Defense Minister Vides Casanova bluntly admitted that "[w]e know that improving our image is worth millions of dollars of aid for the country."[241]

Due to its previous circumvention of congressional certification requirements and its public commitments to arrest Communist expansion in Central America – which would make "losing" El Salvador a serious blow – the administration faced an uphill battle in its efforts to gain leverage from the conditions on aid.[242] Nevertheless, by linking specific aid to specific actions, it still managed to engender a high degree of compliance.[243] Days after Bush's visit, the ESAF high command

[236] Telegram 11456, San Salvador to State, December 11, 1983, NSA.
[237] *Ibid.*
[238] State Department Briefing Paper, "El Salvador: Death Squads," January 23, 1984, NSA.
[239] CIA Cable, "Military Commanders' Resentment and Opposition to U.S. Government Pressure," January 25, 1984, CIA.
[240] Pickering, interview, *OHCES*, p. 11.
[241] Quoted in Cynthia McClintock, *Revolutionary Movements in Latin America: El Salvador's FMLN and Peru's Shining Path* (Washington, DC: USIP Press, 1998), p. 151.
[242] On the stakes in El Salvador for America's credibility in the world, see Memorandum, Fontaine and Schweitzer to Allen, "Central America: Biting the Bullet," September 12, 1981, Box 30, Executive Secretariat, NSC Country File, RRL and Telegram 1268, San Salvador to State, February 14, 1983, STATE.
[243] CIA, "Recommendations by Salvadoran Army Political Commission on Points Raised during the Visit of the United States Vice President," December 14, 1983, NSA.

circulated a proclamation signed by thirty-one senior officers supporting a crackdown on the death squads. Within a month, extrajudicial
killings fell by more than 75 percent. The three officers on Ambassador
Pickering's list were removed by the ESAF high command, and several
of the named civilians soon lost their jobs as well but General Vides
Casanova could not legally force the latter into exile.[244] In accordance
with the U.S. conditions, the Salvadoran government introduced new
due process requirements for suspects detained by the security forces,
the full weight of the ESAF was put behind the 1984 presidential
election, and the army pressured the Constituent Assembly into extend-
ing the "land-to-the-tiller program." The army also had Captain Avila
arrested for his role in the murders of the American land-reform experts
at the Sheraton Hotel and prevented his uncle, the president of the
Salvadoran Supreme Court, from interfering in the case.[245]

Initial assessments by Central Intelligence Agency analysts suggested
that the Salvadoran government was taking only symbolic steps against
the rightwing paramilitaries; however, death squad activity declined
significantly in the wake of the U.S. ultimatum and remained low for
the next several years.[246] By the first quarter of 1984, the embassy was
reporting that it was unaware of any assassinations of labor leaders,
political activists, or other traditional targets of right-wing violence,
nor had any of the known death squads claimed responsibility for any

[244]   Telegram 11882, San Salvador to State, December 22, 1983, NSA; "El
    Salvador: Crackdown on Death Squads," December 23, 1983, CIA; Excised
    Cable, "Actions Taken by the Minister of Defense against Salvadoran Officials
    Allegedly Involved in Right-Wing Death Squad Activities," December 23,
    1983, CIA.
[245]   Telegram 11707, San Salvador to State, December 17, 1983, NSA;
    Memorandum for the Record, "Briefing of the House Permanent Select
    Committee on Intelligence Staff on the Central American Finding," January 26,
    1984, CIA; Robert McCartney, "U.S. Lauds Drive to Halt Death Squads,"
    Washington Post, January 8, 1984.
[246]   CIA, "El Salvador: Dealing with Death Squads," January 20, 1984, pp. 2, 4–5,
    NSA; "El Salvador: Controlling Rightwing Terrorism," p. iii; Jose Garcia, "El
    Salvador: Legitimizing the Government," *Current History*, 84, no. 500 (March
    1985), pp. 102–3; Montgomery, *Revolution in El Salvador*, p. 178. Even
    organizations sympathetic to the FMLN such as the human rights group *Tutela
    Legal* recorded a sharp decline in official violence. They reported 1,259 death
    squad killings in 1983 and 224 such murders in 1984. Congressional Research
    Service (CRS), "El Salvador, 1979–1989: A Briefing Book on U.S. Aid and the
    Situation in El Salvador" (Washington, DC: Library of Congress, April 28,
    1989), p. 88.

killings since Bush's visit.[247] Moreover, in the political sphere, as the high command continued to back reform, the gap between the military and the ultraright was growing.[248] The improvements were incremental and Salvadoran compliance was grudging and subject to backsliding, but compared with past efforts, the Reagan administration's conditionality approach had achieved a significant success.

1984 Presidential Election

Democratization had become a key pillar of the Reagan administration's El Salvador policy both for normative reasons and as a means to delegitimize the FMLN and the far right.[249] The 1984 presidential election was primarily a contest between Napoleon Duarte and Roberto D'Aubuisson. Well funded by his oligarch patrons, D'Aubuisson held an early lead over Duarte and campaigned promising to achieve "peace through victory" by removing the human rights restrictions that "prohibit the army from winning against the subversives."[250] Fearing that D'Aubuisson would block U.S.-backed reforms – leading Congress to cut aid to El Salvador – Reagan authorized the CIA to give $1.4 million to the Christian Democrats and PCN.[251] The CIA also covertly paid for international journalists to visit El Salvador, where they deliberately received interviews calculated to give the worst possible impression of D'Aubuisson.[252] While Duarte was given high-profile visit to Washington to clearly signal the administration's preference, D'Aubuisson was denied a visa to enter the United States, and the embassy hinted that an ARENA win would jeopardize continued American assistance.[253]

---

[247] Telegram 2447, San Salvador to State, March 8, 1984, STATE.
[248] CIA, "El Salvador: Dealing with Death Squads: Comments," January 20, 1984, LOC.
[249] State Department, "Central America Review," February 17, 1983, NSA.
[250] "Salvador Seeking a Way Out in Vote Today," *New York Times* March 25, 1984.
[251] Robert McCartney, "U.S. Seen Assisting Duarte in Sunday's Salvadoran Vote," *Washington Post*, May 4, 1984.
[252] Philip Taubman, "CIA Said to Aid Salvador Parties," *New York Times*, May 12, 1984.
[253] Telegram 2710, San Salvador to State, March 13, 1984, NSA; Department of State, "El Salvador's Political Situation," May 17, 1984, RRL.

On election day, the FMLN succeeded in disrupting voting in 13 percent of municipalities; however, as in 1982, the image of 1.4 million Salvadorans queuing to exercise their democratic franchise was interpreted as a clear rejection of the insurgents.[254] In a run-off election, Duarte defeated D'Aubuisson 53.6 to 46.4 percent, becoming the first opposition candidate in Salvadorian history to peacefully become president.[255] Marshalling support from a coalition of labor unions and peasant groups, Duarte promised to accelerate land reform, negotiate with the insurgents, and allow nonviolent protest. Judging the elections to be relatively free and fair, France and Mexico upgraded their diplomatic ties with San Salvador while West Germany resumed foreign aid.[256]

In his first weeks in office, Duarte disbanded the intelligence section of the Treasury Police – home to a death squad so brutal that one Salvadoran officer admitted that "even the other soldiers here feared it" – and shut down a similar unit within the National Police.[257] To increase oversight of the paramilitary police forces, he subordinated the three security corps to a newly created Vice Minister of Defense for Public Security and replaced their commanders with respected officers who were close to the U.S. embassy.[258] Several senior army officers and more than 100 members of the public security forces suspected of human rights abuses were also removed from their positions or dismissed.[259] Although these reforms did not completely eradicate the death squads, extrajudicial killings plunged 80 percent, from an average of 105 per month in 1983 to 18 per month in 1984 and fewer than a dozen per month in 1985.[260] Duarte's unprecedented ability to reshape a military establishment that cared about its institutional prerogatives above all else directly resulted from the ESAF's

---

[254] Telegram 3884, San Salvador to State, April 9, 1984 and Telegram 5354, San Salvador to State, May 12, 1984, both NSA; Joanne Omang, "El Salvador Faction Reportedly Split on Election Violence," *Washington Post* February 17, 1984; Montgomery, *Revolution in El Salvador*, p. 180.

[255] Duarte, *Duarte*, p. 19.   [256] Byrne, *El Salvador's Civil War*, p. 94.

[257] James LeMoyne, "A Salvadoran Police Chief Vows to End Rights Abuses," *New York Times*, July 1, 1984.

[258] Lydia Chavez, "Salvador to Restructure Security Forces," *New York Times*, June 14, 1984; CIA, "El Salvador: Durate's First 100 Days," September 14, 1984, LOC.

[259] "El Salvador: Durate's First 100 Days," p. 1 and "El Salvador: Controlling Rightwing Terrorism," p. 10.

[260] CRS, "El Salvador, 1979–1989," p. 88.

recognition that substantial American aid required having a government that could win congressional approval.[261]

Within weeks of Duarte's election, the murderers of the Maryknoll nuns were finally prosecuted. Five guardsmen were convicted of the crimes and sentenced to thirty-five years in prison. With the pressure tactics having achieved their result, the $19.4 million in military aid tied to the outcome could be released.[262]

Although the insurgents had pushed the Salvadoran military to the brink of collapse in late 1983, the increased number of troops, supported by U.S.-supplied transport aircraft, was able to blunt the FMLN's quasi-conventional large-unit operations. The formerly truck-bound rapid-reaction battalions became an air-mobile force that could be anywhere in the country within an hour. The army mauled the FMLN in a series of engagements, with helicopter-borne penetrations into insurgent-controlled territory described by one guerrilla leader as "a very significant turn in the war."[263] In 1984, ESAF losses fell by 50 percent and casualties the following year were smaller still.[264] Although the FMLN was far from defeated, the tide in the conflict had turned, and guerrilla morale plummeted as the prospect of victory ebbed after five years of hard fighting.[265] This achievement was tempered by the fact that since 1979 tens of thousands of civilians had perished, and several times that number had been internally displaced or fled the country.[266]

By mid-1984, U.S. efforts in El Salvador were finally registering visible successes: the country had its first democratically elected president, the far right had been co-opted into the political process but kept out of power, the insurgent's military capacity had been

---

[261] Terry Karl, "After La Palma: Christian Democracy, U.S. Policy, and the Prospects for Democratization in El Salvador," *World Policy Journal* (Winter 1985), p. 318–9. On the ESAF's priorities, see Greentree, *Crossroads of Intervention*, p. 82.

[262] LeoGrande, *Our Own Backyard*, p. 257.

[263] Miguel Castellanos, *The Comandante Speaks: Memoirs of an El Salvadoran Guerrilla Leader* (Boulder, CO: Westview Press, 1991), p. 88.

[264] Tim Golden, "U.S.-Backed Salvadorans Haunt Rebels," *Miami Herald*, July 10, 1985.

[265] Telegram 2104, San Salvador to State, February 19, 1985, NSA; Bacevich et al., *American Military Policy in Small Wars*, pp. 32–3; Byrne, *El Salvador's Civil War*, p. 88; LeoGrande, *Our Own Backyard*, pp. 267–8.

[266] Segundo Montes, "Hambre a Causa Del Armamentismo," *Estudios Centroamericanos*, no. 429–30 (July–August 1984), pp. 491–502.

retarded, extrajudicial killings had fallen significantly, and the murderers of the American churchwomen had finally been brought to justice. Yet this very success would undermine the means by which it had been achieved.

PART III RETURN TO STALEMATE, 1985–1992

In the euphoria following Duarte's win, congressional demands for conditions on aid faded away.[267] Proponents insisted that conditionality was still required "to spur reforms that must occur if a military victory by the left is to be avoided," but these voices were a distinct minority.[268] As Enders' successor, Assistant Secretary of State Tony Motley, testified to Congress, while conditionality "served a useful purpose, the need has passed."[269] In a bipartisan effort to bolster Duarte, Congress increased 1984 military aid nearly two-and-a-half times to $196 million and authorized an additional $123 million for the following year.[270] With the exception of a symbolic $5 million linked to the arrest and prosecution of a second officer involved in the Sheraton Hotel murders – and the proviso that aid would be suspended in case of a coup – U.S. military assistance was no longer conditioned on reforms in El Salvador. Progress had been made through the use of conditionality and credible threats of aid suspension; however, in mid-1984 the pendulum swung back toward inducement as San Salvador was given a blank check.

The impact of this policy change was seen almost instantly as the ARENA/PCN-dominated National Assembly repealed the "land-to-the-tiller" program over Duarte's objection.[271] Despite winning a majority in the 1985 assembly elections, without the "stick" of conditions on U.S. aid supporting their reform proposals, the Christian Democrats could not exert much influence over their political opponents. With military aid freely flowing, the ESAF blocked civilian

---

[267] Bacevich et al., *American Military Policy in Small Wars*, p. 35; LeoGrande, *Our Own Backyard*, pp. 256–9.

[268] Congressman Gerry Studds, quoted in *Congressional Record*, May 10, 1984, H3687.

[269] Tony Motley, quoted in U.S. House of Representatives, *Foreign Assistance Legislation for Fiscal Years 1986–1987*, part 6, pp. 3–4.

[270] LeoGrande, *Our Own Backyard*, pp. 257–8.

[271] James LeMoyne, "Salvadoran Right Blocks Land Plan," *New York Times*, June 30, 1984.

investigations into human rights abuses by officers. The ESAF high command may have come to recognize that a democratic system was more stable than the alternative and that Duarte was key to obtaining U.S. aid, but complete submission to civilian control of the military was not in its interest. The end of conditionality also removed the pressure keeping death-squad activity in check, and by 1988, a modest resurgence in extrajudicial killings was triggering alarm bells in the U.S. embassy.[272]

Under Duarte, the one area where the United States continued to employ conditionality was economics. Despite the improving security and political situation, the Salvadoran economy remained weak: industrial production languished as the Christian Democrat government gave preference to less efficient state-owned enterprises over the private sector, while many of the country's farms suffered from poor care and management. Since 1979, real GDP had declined 23 percent, unemployment was 30 percent – with an equal percentage of the population underemployed – and inflation was above 22 percent. Moreover, the war was consuming half the national budget. The government was running an annual deficit – financed by Washington – of $100 million.[273] In an effort to reduce government spending, combat inflation, and shift the Salvadoran economy away from dependence on commodity exports, the USAID began to attach conditions to its economic aid. In November 1984 it required Duarte to devalue the colón in order to gain $65 million in economic assistance.[274] When that failed to turn around the ailing economy, fourteen months later, USAID again pressured Duarte into devaluing the currency and adopting austerity measures – such as capping wages and raising gas prices by 50 percent – by tying economic assistance to compliance.[275] Despite the significant unpopularity of these measures among the labor unions and peasant cooperatives that had gotten Duarte elected, the Salvadoran government had little choice but to comply with U.S. conditions. As Planning

---

[272] Telegram 8711, San Salvador to State, June 29, 1988, NSA.

[273] Montgomery, *Revolution in El Salvador*, p. 190.

[274] James LeMoyne, "Duarte's Power Seems Eroded as Voting Nears," *New York Times*, February 17, 1985.

[275] Majorie Miller, "Thousands of Salvadorans March to Protest Duarte's Economic Austerity Plan," *Los Angeles Times*, February 22, 1986; Stanley, *The Protection Racket State*, p. 237.

Minister Fidel Chavez Mena bluntly stated, "[W]ithout U.S. aid, we would be absolutely broke and inflation would be totally out of control."[276] This was hardly an exaggeration since American economic assistance accounted for somewhere between a quarter and a third of the money spent by the Salvadoran government.[277]

Resisting Counterinsurgency

American military assistance largely succeeded in meeting the Woerner Report's first objective, expanding the ESAF, which reached 56,000 men by 1987.[278] The FMLN's quasi-conventional strategy increasingly played to the strengths of the Salvadoran military, which could employ artillery and airpower against large guerrilla formations. To build forces rapidly, the insurgents began to rely on forced recruitment, which alienated locals in rebel-held zones.[279] As casualties and desertions mounted, the rebels sought to offset the ESAF's advantages by moving to a more traditional guerrilla war strategy that emphasized small-unit operations, the development of a political base in the civilian population, and a campaign of economic sabotage.

The FMLN's change of strategy put a premium on the Woerner Report's second priority: adapting the ESAF for small-unit counter-insurgency. As the CIA emphasized, however, the Salvadoran military possessed "an institutional reluctance ... to proceed with U.S.-sponsored counterinsurgency programs."[280] Instead, commanders continued to favor the conventional approach that had succeeded in the first half of the conflict: employing air-mobile and road-bound battalion-sized units in operations backed by close air support and heavy artillery.[281] The handful of elite Salvadoran units that did employ small-unit tactics and dispersed operations achieved dispropor-tionate success against the FMLN, but they were the exception rather

---

[276] Quoted in Peter Ford, "Civil War Undermines Efforts to Boost Salvador's Ailing Economy," *Christian Science Monitor*, May 21, 1986.

[277] Congressional Research Service, *El Salvador, 1979–1989* (Washington, DC: Library of Congress, 1989), pp. 43–57.

[278] Bacevich et al., *American Military Policy in Small Wars*, p. 5.

[279] Robert McCartney, "Rebels Use Harsher Methods: Guerrillas Recruit Youths by Force in Salvadoran Towns," *Washington Post*, June 18, 1984.

[280] CIA, "The Salvadoran Military: A Mixed Performance," June 1984, p. 4, CIA.

[281] Bacevich et al., *American Military Policy in Small Wars*, p. 37.

than the rule.[282] The question was not one of capacity: as a frustrated American military trainer noted, "[T]he Salvadoran Army has been thoroughly trained in U.S. counterinsurgency tactics and they can do them well – the problem is getting them to actually use these tactics."[283] Salvadoran officers believed that confronting and defeating the guerrillas would resolve the conflict faster than U.S. counterinsurgency strategies could, yet ironically, doing so was returning the war to a stalemate.[284] At the highest levels of government, however, Washington did not push for a change in the Salvadoran military's approach and the United States did not condition military aid on the ESAF's adoption of its tactical advice. Instead, senior American officials specifically told their counterparts that "our partnership does not require you to adopt any particular doctrine," provided that you "respect the welfare of civilians and [fight] clearly in support of democracy."[285]

In its struggle against the FMLN, the Salvadoran government lacked a strategic plan to coordinate its efforts across departments and paid only lip service to the need to win popular support.[286] Instead, the military focused on "draining the sea" of civilians the insurgents relied on for support. Where possible, civilians were forcibly evacuated by the thousands and resettled into government-run refugee camps. In other areas, however, the Salvadoran Air Force regularly bombed rebel-held villages in the logic that "civilians who don't want to cooperate [with the insurgents will] leave the area and those who remain are collaborating."[287] Although the actual number of casualties from such air strikes was low, they were a propaganda boon for the guerrillas.[288]

---

[282] Department of State, "The Shift in Rebel Tactics, 1985–1986," n.d., STATE; Bacevich et al., *American Military Policy in Small Wars*, p. 37.

[283] U.S. trainer quoted in Michael Childress, *The Effectiveness of U.S. Training Efforts in Internal Defense and Development* (Santa Monica, CA: RAND, 1995), p. 31.

[284] *Ibid.*, p. 31.   [285] Memo, Levitsky to Lord, February 1, 1989, NSA.

[286] CIA, "El Salvador: Government and Insurgent Prospects," February 1989, pp. iii–iv, NSA; James LeMoyne, "The Guns of El Salvador," *The New York Times*, February 5, 1989.

[287] Salvadoran Army commander quoted in Montgomery, *Revolution in El Salvador*, p. 152. See also James LeMoyne, "Salvador Air Role in War Increases," *New York Times*, July 18, 1985.

[288] James S. Corum and Wray R. Johnson, *Airpower in Small Wars: Fighting Insurgents and Terrorists* (Manhattan: University Press of Kansas, 2003), p. 344.

Having transitioned to guerrilla warfare, the FMLN focused on wearing down the armed forces: the ESAF suffered 2,200 to 3,000 (6 to 7 percent) casualties per year, two-thirds of which were caused by the insurgent' use of landmines.[289] The guerrillas also exploited the U.S.-enforced reduction in death-squad activities to reestablish cells in El Salvador's cities – the government's strongholds – where their urban commandos waged a campaign of bombings and assassinations in an effort to provoke the government and the far right into a violent overreaction. By the end of 1985, the FMLN had driven 25 percent of the country's 262 mayors from their offices, a number that would climb to nearly 50 percent by 1989.[290] The real goal, however, as Commandante Joaquin Villalobos admitted, was "to break the capacity of the economy to sustain the war."[291] Not only did a strategy of severing power lines, destroying bridges, and attacking plantations inflict millions of dollars of direct damage and lost production, it forced the army to commit scarce troops to defend critical economic infrastructure instead of hunting down rebel fighters.[292]

As part of its switch to a guerrilla strategy, the FMLN sought to purify its ideological and political core: defections increased as waverers were eliminated in a series of purges.[293] To bolster their numbers, the guerrillas employed child soldiers as young as eleven or twelve.[294] The increasingly radicalized insurgent army stabilized at 6,000 fighters in 1987 – half its strength in 1983. Although the FMLN could deny the government control over one-third of the country, it was unable to harness growing opposition to Duarte and

---

[289] LeoGrande, *Our Own Backyard*, p. 277.

[290] Marlise Simons, "Uprooted Salvador Mayors Carry On," *New York Times*, October 9, 1985; Lindsey Grunson, "Salvador's War Gets Dirtier," *New York Times*, March 5, 1989.

[291] Joaquin Villalobos, *The War in El Salvador* (San Francisco: Solidarity Publications, 1986), p. 17.

[292] CRS, "El Salvador, 1979–1989," p. 6.

[293] Commandante "Miguel Castellanos" (real name Napoleon Garcia) describes his disaffection as a result of the FMLN leadership's use of violence against other leaders. Castellanos, *The Comandante Speaks: Memoirs of an El Salvadoran Guerrilla Leader*, pp. xvii–xix.

[294] IIR [no. redacted], [Name redacted] to DIA, "The FMLN and Human Rights – The Other Side of the Issue," December 26, 1989, DDRS. The FMLN's own estimates put the number of child soldiers in their ranks at 2,000. Beth Verhey, *The Demobilization and Reintegration of Child Soldiers: El Salvador Case Study* (Washington, DC: World Bank, 2001), p. 8.

his U.S.-imposed economic austerity measures to expand its support base.[295] A trio of successful elections had convinced large majorities that the ballot box could bring a degree of change. Moreover, the FMLN's indiscriminate use of landmines in rural areas, its campaign of car bombings and assassinations in the cities, and its increasing violence against uncooperative peasants cost it popular support. Attempts to cripple the Salvadoran economy also won little favor from the 50 to 60 percent of the population that was unemployed or underemployed.[296] Even members of the country's Jesuit community – who had been strong proponents of liberation theology – acknowledged that "the left has alienated the general populace," who now blamed their growing misery on FMLN violence and political intransigence rather than the Salvadoran military or government.[297] The rector of Central American University, Ignacio Ellacuría, who was not unsympathetic to the insurgent cause, judged that the FMLN's leadership was "blind" to the political changes that had occurred in El Salvador as well as in its relative military power.[298]

The Salvadoran military's unwillingness to adapt for counterinsurgency and the insurgents' limited appeal returned the conflict to a stalemate: Neither side could gain the upper hand, yet neither side was at risk of military defeat.[299] One Salvadoran pithily summarized the plight of his fellow *campesinos*: "The army comes and goes. The guerrillas come and go. We hide under our beds."[300]

Change in San Salvador and Washington

El Salvador's political environment saw several major developments in the second half of the 1980s. Amid Washington's continued hostility and electoral defeats in 1984 and 1985, ARENA replaced D'Aubuisson with political neophyte Alfredo Cristiani, a Georgetown-educated

---

[295] Brands, *Latin America's Cold War*, p. 205.
[296] "El Salvador: Guerrilla use of Mine Warfare," June 5, 1987, CIA; LeMoyne, "The Guns of El Salvador."
[297] Chris Hedges, "Salvadorans Reported Angry at Lefists' Push," *Dallas Morning News*, August 23, 1987; "Recrudecimiento De La Violencia En El Salvador," *Estudios Centroamericanos*, no. 480 (October 1988), pp. 874, 876.
[298] Quoted in Telegram 6383, San Salvador to State, May 22, 1985, NSA.
[299] Manwaring and Prisk, *El Salvador at War*, p. 471.
[300] Quoted in Dan Williams, "Signs Positive but Reality Is Still Painful in Salvador," *Los Angeles Times*, May 30, 1985.

coffee grower with no ties to the death squads.[301] As urban entrepreneurs who were not members of the traditional landowning class came to dominate the party's leadership, its politics moderated.[302] ARENA's business-minded leaders spoke of defeating the left with "intelligent reform" and securing economic recovery, both of which were impossible while the war continued.[303] Increased political liberalization led the leaders of the Revolutionary Democratic Front to return to El Salvador in 1987 to openly organize political activity without formally severing their links to the FMLN. The Reagan administration's hopes of splitting the political and military wings of the insurgency appeared to be coming to fruition: if left-wing parties could openly compete for office in El Salvador, what legitimacy did the guerrillas possess?

For Duarte and his Christian Democrats, the military stalemate only deepened their problems: the PDC's administrative ineffectiveness and the unpopularity of American-imposed economic reforms – which saw the Salvadoran economy grow by less than 1 percent between 1984 and 1989 – led their approval ratings to plummet. In the 1989 elections to succeed Duarte, ARENA's Alfredo Cristiani – running on a platform promising economic recovery and openness to negotiations with the FMLN – swept thirteen of fourteen departments.[304] The FMLN's affiliated party won only 3.8 percent of the vote, even less than the oligarchy's traditional standard bearer, the PCN. Once again, insurgents' attempts to disrupt polling – including cutting power to 80 percent of the country on election day – failed as 1 million Salvadorans turned out to vote. In office, Cristiani attacked corruption and instituted economic reforms to jump-start the ailing economy.[305] Duarte had signed on to Costa Rican president Oscar Arias's Central American Peace Accord in 1987, which sought to resolve the various

---

[301] For a discussion of Cristiani's political cohort, see William Jeffras Dieterich, "Oral History Interview," October 19, 1999, pp. 156–7, ADST.

[302] William Stanley, "El Salvador: State-Building before and after Democratization, 1980–95," *Third World Quarterly*, 27, no. 1 (2006), pp. 107–8. For a similar view from Ignacio Ellacuría, see Telegram 4293, San Salvador to State, April 5, 1989, NSA.

[303] Chris Norton, "Salvador Peace: Hard Work Ahead," *Christian Science Monitor*, September 22, 1989; CRS, "El Salvador, 1979–1989," p. 6.

[304] The win marked the first peaceful transition of power from an elected president to a successor from the political opposition in Salvadoran history.

[305] LeoGrande, *Our Own Backyard*, pp. 264, 565–8; Victor Rosello, "Lessons from El Salvador," *Parameters*, 23, no. 4 (Winter 1993–1994), p. 102.

civil wars in El Salvador, Guatemala, and Nicaragua. Cristiani was, however, better positioned to gain the military's support for dialogue with the insurgents, and he called for negotiations two days after winning office.

Within the Salvadoran military, new leadership also came to the fore as the pragmatic Vides-Casanova and his colleagues in the high command – seen as too close to the Christian Democrats to remain in office – retired.[306] In their wake, a group of colonels from the academy class of 1966 – nicknamed the *tandona* due to its large size – came to dominate the high command, the leadership of the security corps, and key brigade positions. Bloodied in the hard fighting of the early 1980s, this new cohort reportedly contained a number of officers who thought Vides-Casanova had been "too soft on the FMLN and too quick to respond to human rights complaints."[307] Although the Minister of Defense, General Rafael Humberto Larios of the class of 1961, possessed titular authority, power actually rested with the *tandona*'s de facto leader, Army Chief of Staff Colonel Rene Emilio Ponce.

The changes in San Salvador were matched by a change in Washington as George H. W. Bush succeeded Ronald Reagan at a time when the adherents of international Communism were being "blown away like leaves from an ancient, lifeless tree."[308] The Bush administration encouraged the Salvadoran government's efforts to engage the FMLN in the political process.[309] These political overtures were conducted from a position of perceived strength because the CIA estimated that "the guerrillas have lost 15 to 19 percent of their force over the last two years, their base areas are less secure, and their attacks on military targets have been less effective."[310] With the Salvadoran government expected to exhaust the insurgents militarily over the next three to five years, "no one," U.S. ambassador Edwin Corr confidently asserted, "believes that the guerrillas have a chance of winning the war."[311]

---

[306] James Lemoyne, "Salvadoran Army Starts a Shake-Up," *New York Times*, July 3, 1988.

[307] Telegram 4071, San Salvador to State, March 31, 1989, STATE.

[308] George H. W. Bush, "Inaugural Address," Washington, DC, January 20, 1989.

[309] Arnson, *Crossroads*, p. 243.

[310] CIA, "El Salvador: Government and Insurgent Prospects," February 1989, pp. iii–iv, NSA.

[311] *Ibid.*, p. iv; Edwin Corr, interview, September 24, 1987, *Oral History of the Conflict in El Salvador*, vol. 1, p. 7, MHI.

The apparent quiescence masked the fact that the FMLN was consolidating its forces for one final military thrust. On November 11, 1989 – two days after the Berlin Wall was torn down – the FMLN launched its largest offensive of the war. Although the insurgents attacked government facilities and military outposts across the country, the primary target was San Salvador. In a coup de main, 2,000 FMLN fighters captured parts of the city ranging from the poorest barrios to upper-class neighborhoods while attempting to assassinate President Cristiani and the military high command.[312] In the months leading up to the 1989 "Final Offensive," guerrilla fighters and weapons had been infiltrated into working-class neighborhoods in the north and east of the city. These efforts were facilitated by the reestablishment of an urban support network, which was able to function thanks to increased liberalization and the reduction in political violence compelled by the United States.

The intensity of the surprise assault sent shockwaves across the country. Nevertheless, as in 1981, the Salvadoran people did not respond to the call for a mass rising. Instead, working-class San Salvadorians were infuriated at the rebels for bringing the war on to their doorstep.[313] The insurgents responded by forcibly conscripting civilians to dig trenches, carry supplies, and join in the battle despite no experience or training.[314] FMLN fighters cynically barricaded themselves in busy neighborhoods in order to neutralize the ESAF's superior firepower or force the government to risk international condemnation by using airpower and artillery in an urban setting. In a three-week campaign, the military fought block by block to recapture the city, at times employing helicopter gunships and fighter aircraft to dislodge the insurgents' strong points.[315] Even with the military's use of heavy firepower in the city, its improved tactics and more advanced weapons meant that the damage inflicted was far less than predicted. During the fighting the security forces detained union members, opposition leaders, and left-wing clergy; however, despite declaring a state of

---

[312] IIR [no. redacted], [Name redacted] to DIA, "FMLN Final Offensive 1989 – A Wrap Up," December 22, 1989, DDRS.

[313] Even very pro-FMLN authors acknowledge the lack of popular appeal; see Saul Landau, *The Guerrilla Wars of Central America* (New York: St. Martin's Press, 1993), pp. 139–41.

[314] "FMLN Final Offensive 1989 – A Wrap Up."

[315] Schwarz, *American Counterinsurgency Doctrine*, p. 21.

emergency, the government did not initiate a systematic campaign of violence against suspected subversives.[316] This relative restraint has been attributed to the ESAF's fear of alienating the United States. The military had only a one-month supply of fuel and ammunition, while operations relied heavily on helicopters that required maintenance and spare parts that only the United States could provide.[317]

The offensive was a military disaster for the FMLN, which sustained 50 percent casualties.[318] More important, as its political leaders forthrightly judged, "[T]he people are not in an insurrectional stage."[319] After the fact, some guerrilla commanders suggested that the real purpose of the offensive was simply to strengthen their negotiating position vis-à-vis the government. This goal may have been partially achieved because the CIA noted that the attack forced the heretofore insulated Salvadoran elite "to question the government's ability to provide for their most basic requirement: security."[320] The insurgent assault shocked Washington, where it was compared to the 1968 Tet Offensive in Vietnam – itself a "dismal military failure and a brilliant political success."[321] Although it took nearly two years to plan and prepare for the operation, in its wake, the Salvadoran and American governments dramatically revaluated the FMLN's military strength.[322] Within weeks, the SOUTHCOM Commander had informed the Senate

---

[316] LeoGrande, *Our Own Backyard*, pp. 569–71; Schwarz, *American Counterinsurgency Doctrine*, p. 65.

[317] Stanley, *The Protection Racket State*, pp. 249–50.

[318] Greentree, *Crossroads of Intervention*, p. 151; Leroy Thompson, *Ragged War: The Story of Unconventional and Counterrevolutionary Warfare* (London: Arms & Armor, 1994), p. 79.

[319] Richard Boudreaux and Majorie Miller, "Offensive Pushed Salvador War to New, Bloodier Level," *Los Angeles Times*, November 30, 1989; CIA, "El Salvador: The FMLN after the November 1989 Offensive," January 26, 1990, CIA.

[320] "The FMLN after the November 1989 Offensive;" Mario Lungo Uclés, *El Salvador in the Eighties: Counterinsurgency and Revolution*, trans. Amelia Shogan (Philadelphia: Temple University Press, 1996), pp. 177–8.

[321] On the comparison to Tet, see Chris Norton, "After Salvador's Rebel Offensive," *Christian Science Monitor*, December 8, 1989. The assessment of the Tet Offensive comes from James Wirtz, *The Tet Offensive* (Ithaca, NY: Cornell University Press, 1994), p. 17.

[322] As Commandante Facundo Guardado admitted, "[I]t was not something we could do every six months, much less every month. It was a question of years." Byrne, *El Salvador's Civil War*, p. 173.

Armed Services Committee that the Salvadoran government could not defeat the rebels.[323]

The Jesuit Murders and the Return of Conditionality

Despite the relative restraint displayed during the fighting, El Salvador's military leaders managed to snatch political defeat from the jaws of military victory. Five days into the fighting, on the early morning of November 16, elements of the Atlacatl rapid reaction battalion – which had been rushed to San Salvador from counterinsurgency operations in the countryside – raided the Jesuit-run Central American University. Acting on the instructions of Colonel Guillermo Benavides – the commander of a special security zone in the capital – members of the unit executed the university rector Ignacio Ellacuría, five priests, and two bystanders. The Jesuits in question were prominent scholars of international standing and a key conduit for the government's dialogue with the FMLN. Many in the ESAF, however, viewed the men as the intellectual architects of the revolution.[324]

The murders shattered the bipartisan consensus in Washington. Even though the FMLN offensive was still under way, some in the Democrat-dominated House of Representatives called for an immediate aid suspension, while other legislators threatened that next year's appropriations would be cut unless the perpetrators were quickly arrested and prosecuted.[325] To underscore this point, the U.S. ambassador and the SOUTHCOM commander bluntly warned the ESAF high command that "if by the end of January 1990 the [government and military] have not done everything humanly possible to find the guilty parties, all security assistance to El Salvador could be halted by Congress as its first order of business in the new year."[326]

---

[323] Michael Gordon, "General Says Salvador Can't Defeat Guerrillas," *New York Times*, February 9, 1990.

[324] Telegram 2104; Telegram 6383. ESAF views of the Jesuits of UCA are discussed in Greentree, *Crossroads of Intervention*, p. 153 and Moyar, *A Question of Command: Counterinsurgency from the Civil War to Iraq*, p. 186. For a similar view from U.S. military trainers, see Arnson, *Crossroads*, p. 247.

[325] Robert Pear, "House Rejects Curb on Salvador Aid," *New York Times*, November 21, 1989.

[326] Telegram 15668, San Salvador to State, December 5, 1989, NSA.

The threat led to fairly rapid results: in early January 1990, President Cristiani announced that nine suspects, including Colonel Benavides and two lieutenants, had been arrested for the murders.[327] Having governed the country for more than fifty years, the Salvadoran military traditionally did not cooperate with civilian courts that were investigating fellow officers.[328] Unlike in previous cases of abuse, however, a senior Salvadoran colonel broke the "code of silence" by passing the names of the killers to an American counterpart.[329] Other Salvadoran officers confided to the American defense attaché that they were shocked by the murders and supported a rapid investigation and prosecution of those responsible.[330] Yet, the following month, while congratulating Cristiani on the progress in the investigation and emphasizing the need to move it forward, President Bush sent the Salvadoran government a conflicting signal by unilaterally pledging to increase El Salvador's $131 million economic aid package by $50 million.[331]

Unsurprisingly, in the ensuing months after this inducement was announced, the Jesuit case stagnated. Despite a host of senior administration officials and members of Congress "forcefully" pressing the Salvadoran Army Chief of Staff for "a thorough and timely investigation," the leadership of the Salvadoran military stonewalled, in the apparent belief that concern about the issue would eventually disappear.[332] As evidence accumulated that members of the high command had attempted to cover up the crime, the embassy received reports that a large number of midlevel Salvadoran officers were openly

[327] "Cristiani Names Colonel, Eight Others as Presumed Culprits in Massacre," Associated Press, January 13, 1990. The effects of U.S. pressure on Cristiani and the pace of the investigation are discussed in CIA message; [no. redacted], "New Developments in the Investigation into the Jesuit Murders," January 12, 1990, LOC.

[328] CIA, "El Salvador: The Issue of Military Impunity," *Latin America Review*, August 24, 1990, LOC.

[329] Memorandum, Thurman to SecDef, January 19, 1990, NSA.

[330] IIR 509, DAO San Salvador to DIA, January 17, 1990, LOC; IIR 525, DAO San Salvador to DIA, January 24, 1989, LOC.

[331] Maureen Dowd, "Bush Seeks a Rise in Aid to Salvador," *New York Times*, February 2, 1990.

[332] Telegram 2787, San Salvador to State, February 27, 1990; Memorandum, Byron to Assistant Secretary of Defense for International Security Affairs, "El Salvador Update," August 15, 1990; Memorandum, Byron to Assistant Secretary of Defense for International Security Affairs, "El Salvador Security Assistance," August 16, 1990, all NSA.

critical of their superiors' failure to get to the bottom of the case and remove those involved.[333]

In Washington, administration officials who had previously been "vehemently opposed" to conditionality began to recognize that "now we have to play hardball ... we're now basically supporting the move to condition or cut military aid."[334] To demonstrate displeasure with the lack of progress in the case, the United States withheld $19.65 million in military assistance.[335] The aid would be released, President Cristiani was informed, only if the military leadership cooperated with the investigating judge by providing him with testimonies of all officers present at a meeting at army headquarters where the murders were allegedly planned, records of who visited Benavides at the military academy the night of the killings, and the testimony of two other colonels who planned the raid on the University of Central America.[336] In conditioning aid, the Bush administration believed it was sending a clear message to the Salvadoran government about the gravity of the situation.[337]

The impact of these conditions on military aid was undercut by the fact that the embargoed items were specifically chosen so that "withholding these materials will not greatly affect the ESAF's basic ability to fight the war, but will cause inconvenience."[338] Unsurprisingly, Salvadoran interlocutors informed the defense attaché that their senior officers were not feeling significant pressure to comply with U.S. demands.[339] Indeed, analysts for the U.S. Joint Chiefs of Staff judged that while the Salvadoran military leadership took "some cosmetic steps" in response to the imposition of conditionality, its "cooperation has been reluctant and without real substance."[340]

The United States further undermined its position when the Pentagon released $250,000 worth of spare parts for Salvadoran helicopters in late September 1990. The aid was notionally granted in

[333] Telegram 10791, San Salvador to State, August 13, 1990, STATE; CIA, "Dissatisfaction in the Officer Corps ...," August 17, 1990, NSA.
[334] Phil Bronstein, "U.S. Officials Reverse View on Salvador Army," *San Francisco Examiner*, May 6, 1990.
[335] Byron, "El Salvador Security Assistance."
[336] Telegram 11127, San Salvador to State, August 18, 1990, NSA.
[337] Byron to ASD/ISA, August 16, 1990.
[338] Telegram 10914, San Salvador to State, August 14, 1990, NSA.
[339] Telegram 13617, DAO San Salvador to DIA, October 5, 1990, NSA.
[340] Memorandum, Byron to Director of the Joint Staff, September 25, 1990, NSA.

return for "positive, though insufficient, progress" in the Jesuit case; however, the parts in question were identified as "critical components" for the Salvadoran Air Force to remain ready against a guerrilla threat.[341] President Cristiani and Salvadoran military leaders were informed that despite the release of the spare parts, military assistance remained conditioned on significant progress in the Jesuit case. Within weeks, however, Salvadoran military commanders were pressing the embassy for the release of additional "vital" aid to maintain the army's armored personnel carriers without having compelled any of the officers identified by the United States to testify to investigators.[342] In San Salvador, the frustrated U.S. ambassador took it as a clear indication of the hollowness with which the Salvadorans perceived the American threat.[343]

Conditions, Negotiations, and Prosecution of the Murders

In the aftermath of the 1989 "Final Offensive," the political positions of the Salvadoran government and the FMLN underwent a transformation. The scope of the offensive appeared to dash any hopes of an imminent government victory. Moreover, the FMLN's introduction of advanced surface-to-air missiles neutralized the Salvadoran Air Force's tactical advantages which, in turn, constrained the aggressiveness of the army's ground operations.[344] At the same time, the insurgents recognized that they were unlikely to trigger a popular insurrection in El Salvador.[345] Their overall diplomatic position was also eroding as reform swept through the Communist countries of Eastern Europe and the FMLN's Nicaraguan patrons – the Sandinistas – were voted out of power in Managua.

---

[341] Telegram [excised], State to San Salvador, "$250,000 to be Released of Remaining FY90 Military Aid," September 1990; Telegram 331044, State to San Salvador, September 29, 1990 and Telegram 13730, San Salvador to State, October 18, 1990, all NSA.

[342] Telegram 13730; Telegram [no. illegible], San Salvador to State, October 15, 1990, NSA.

[343] Letter, CDR USMILGRP El Salvador to CINCSOUTH, February 10, 1991, LOC.

[344] JTIC Advisory 15–90, "The Gremlin Comes to El Salvador," November 29, 1990, NSA.

[345] Byrne, *El Salvador's Civil War*, p. 161.

Within weeks of the end of the 1989 "Final Offensive," both the Salvadoran government and the FMLN had contacted the United Nations to help with mediation. This began a two-year period of "fighting while negotiating." To exert pressure on the Salvadoran government to make a deal – and express outrage over the Jesuit murders – Congress returned to conditionality. It cut military aid for El Salvador by 50 percent. The remaining balance would be withheld if the government failed to negotiate in good faith with the FMLN for a permanent settlement, if it did not thoroughly investigate the Jesuit killings, or if it employed large-scale violence against civilians.[346] As an incentive for the FMLN to reach a compromise, Congress included a provision to reinstate the funds if the insurgents failed to negotiate in good faith or received significant military assistance from abroad. The sharp reduction in military assistance was a wake-up call for those in El Salvador who believed that the United States would sustain them indefinitely.[347] After initially signaling that he would restore the full amount of military aid, President Bush, who was interested in winding down U.S. involvement in El Salvador, embraced conditionality as a means to move the peace process and the Jesuit murder investigation forward.[348]

In response to the pressure from Washington, the Salvadoran government conducted a series of intense negotiations with the FMLN during the fall and winter of 1991. Meanwhile, Colonel Benavides was found guilty of ordering the murders of the Jesuits and, along with an accomplice, was sentenced to thirty years in prison. Three more officers were convicted for their role in attempting to cover up the crime. The case was a demonstration of how far El Salvador had come in the past decade: not only was this the first time a senior officer had been tried for human rights abuses, as William LeoGrande noted, "[F]or the first time in modern Salvadoran history, two officers were convicted for the politically motivated murder of civilians."[349] This success would be incomplete, however; the investigation never extended beyond Benavides to other senior officers who may have ordered the killings.[350]

---

[346] Section 531(d) of the Foreign Operations, Export Financing, and Related Programs Appropriations Act, Pub. Law 101–513, November 5, 1990.
[347] LeoGrande, *Our Own Backyard*, p. 575.   [348] *Ibid.*   [349] *Ibid.*, p. 576.
[350] The Commission on the Truth for El Salvador subsequently alleged that the kill order originated with then Army Chief of Staff René Emilio Ponce and was

Dénouement

On January 16, 1992, representatives of the Salvadoran government and the FMLN signed a UN-brokered peace accord in
Chapultepec, Mexico. It brought to an end a twelve-year insurgency that had taken 75,000 lives and exhausted the country.
In the final settlement, the army and the PSC were permanently
separated, with the former focused exclusively on national defense,
while the latter concentrated on domestic law enforcement.
The army was shrunk by 50 percent, the rapid-reaction battalions
were eliminated, and the military intelligence section – a source of
death-squad activity – was replaced with a civilian intelligence
agency that reported directly to the country's president. More
than a dozen high-ranking officers found guilty of human rights
abuses by an independent tribunal were relieved of duty and new
civil-military arrangements clearly established the principle of
civilian supremacy over the armed forces. Both the Treasury
Police and the National Guard – which had provided the bulk of
death-squad personnel – were replaced by a new civilian National
Police Force that incorporated some former FMLN fighters into its
ranks.[351]

This far-reaching restructuring of the ESAF did not mean that the
peace accord was achieved on the FMLN's terms. The insurgents had to
disarm but were not brought into a power-sharing government as they
had long demanded. Instead, they merely gained the right to compete
for political power in El Salvador – which successive governments had
offered them since 1981. Authority remained vested in the constitutional order that had been forged in 1982, an arrangement that the
FMLN had long decried as illegitimate. Beyond the reforms that had
been implemented during the counterinsurgency campaign, which
broke the power base of the old oligarchy, there were no further
changes in the economic or social order within the country.
The radical vision for El Salvador's future that the FMLN once

given in the presence of several other senior officers. UN Security Council,
From Madness to Hope: The 12-Year War in El Salvador. Report of the
Commission on the Truth for El Salvador, S/25500, 1993, pp. 38–47.
[351] Ian Johnstone, "Rights and Reconciliation in El Salvador," in Michael Doyle,
Ian Jonstone, and Robert Orr, eds., *Keeping the Peace: Multidimensional UN
Operations in Cambodia and El Salvador* (Cambridge: Cambridge University
Press, 1997), pp. 323–5.

advocated was jettisoned as it accepted existing democratic structures, a mixed economy, and an ongoing relationship with the United States.

Assessment

At the outset of U.S. intervention, El Salvador was governed by a weak civil-military Junta that possessed only notional control over elements of the security forces and the far right, who pursued their own dirty war against suspected leftists and government reformers. Repression as well as economic and social grievances drove support for a guerrilla movement that became the most potent in Latin America. In response, the United States tried to encourage a broad counterinsurgency approach that gave attention to building the Salvadoran government's legitimacy by ameliorating grievances and advancing democratization, while developing a military capable of confronting the insurgents in the field.

How much influence was Washington able to wield over the government in San Salvador? The record is mixed: far more success was achieved in the political and economic realm than in the military. Democratization was seen as a way to simultaneously delegitimize the far left and compel the hard right to contest for political power. During the course of the American intervention, both the radical left and the extreme right were denied their objectives, and the conflict terminated with a democratic government that was friendly to Washington. From its autocratic position in the late 1970s, El Salvador crossed the threshold of democracy for the first time in its history with Duarte's 1984 election (Figure 6.1), which was critical for building domestic and international support for the Salvadoran government.[352] Although institutionalization of full civilian control over the military did not approach Western standards until after the conflict ended, it is telling that even noted partisans of the far right, such as Colonel Ochoa, proclaimed that "the armed forces do not want to execute coups d'état or return to the past . . . the democratic system is the best system."[353] Similarly, despite challenges to the government's land-reform efforts by both landowners and segments of the business

---

[352] "Polity IV Project: Political Regime Characteristics and Transitions, 1800–2008," Center for Systemic Peace, Vienna, VA, 2008.

[353] Sigifredo Ochoa, interview, October 14, 1987, *Oral History of the Conflict in El Salvador*, vol. 7, p. 18, MHI.

community, the United States succeeded in pressuring the Salvadoran military – which possessed little innate interest in agricultural restructuring – to break with their patrons in the oligarchy and publicly back the measure. Although even the most widespread land redistribution program could not solve El Salvador's overpopulation problem, an estimated 25 percent of the rural population (87,547 small-farm families) benefited from the transfer of 22 percent of the country's farmland.[354] The development that made much of this possible was the sharp reduction in death-squad violence – which declined from a rate of 750 murders per month during Carter's last year in office to an average of 8 per month by 1990 – that created political space for opposition parties to pursue their agendas within the political system.[355] At the end of the civil war El Salvador was still plagued by a host of problems, yet even critics concede that "it is impossible to imagine any point in the past decade or the future when El Salvador would not be a far more violent and unjust place, but for the American effort."[356]

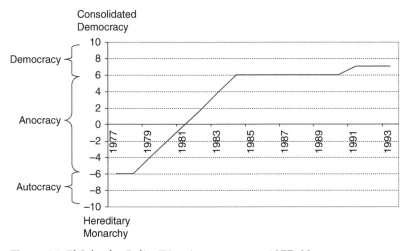

Figure 6.1 El Salvador Polity IV regime type score, 1977–93.

[354] CRS, "El Salvador, 1979–1989," p. 10.
[355] *El Salvador: Military Assistance Has Helped Counter but Not Overcome the Insurgency* (Washington, DC: General Accounting Office, April 23, 1991), p. 31.
[356] Schwarz, *American Counterinsurgency Doctrine*, p. 81.

In the military realm, the United States had significantly greater success in changing the "hardware" of the ESAF (force structure, equipment, and size) than modifying the "software" (organizational culture and attitudes). American aid and support facilitated the transformation of the ESAF from a poorly trained garrison-bound force of 11,000 into a well-equipped 56,000-man military. Once the FMLN resorted to a guerrilla war strategy after 1984, however, the United States was singularly unable to convince the military to adapt for counterinsurgency.[357] The issue was one of will not capacity – and the failure of the ESAF to adapt has been blamed for the stalemate that emerged in the later 1980s.[358]

How do the observed patterns of influence compare to the strategies employed by the United States to shape the behavior of its local ally? In comparison with the Philippines and Vietnam, the United States varied its approach to influencing the Salvadoran government. The Carter administration initially employed conditionality to extract reform from the Salvadoran Junta; however, in the wake of the FMLN's 1981 "Final Offensive," it rushed military aid to El Salvador before reforms occurred. The Reagan administration's initial approach was inducement; however, a combination of congressional pressure and frustration over the lack of influence led it back toward conditionality, which was largely relaxed following Duarte's election. The Bush administration briefly vacillated but ultimately followed Congress' lead in using conditions on aid to pressure San Salvador to negotiate with the FMLN and prosecute the Jesuits' murderers.

On balance, this case provides more evidence to support the effectiveness of the conditionality strategy than it does for the inducement approach. The use of conditions on U.S. aid was associated with Salvadoran compliance, even in areas where reform or policy change had previously been resisted. The Carter administration successfully employed conditionality to broker the Christian Democrats' entry into the Junta and stave off a right-wing coup attempt in 1980. The Reagan administration's threat to suspend military aid spurred the ESAF to defend the "land-to-the-tiller program" and compelled the formation

---

[357] Bacevich et al., *American Military Policy in Small Wars*, p. 38.

[358] Childress, *The Effectiveness of U.S. Training Efforts in Internal Defense and Development*, p. 30; *El Salvador: Military Assistance Has Helped Counter but Not Overcome the Insurgency*, p. 24.

of a coalition government including the Christian Democrats in 1982. Vice President Bush's "New Contract" in 1983 tied aid to suppressing right-wing paramilitary groups, which led to a sharp and lasting decline in death squad murders. Both Congress and the Reagan administration made assistance contingent on democratization. Even scholars disapproving of U.S. involvement in El Salvador acknowledge that "had the United States not insisted on elections as a condition for aid, El Salvador's transition to elected government and the first steps towards transforming the social elite into a political class would have come later, if at all."[359] Similarly, unpopular economic austerity measures that were a death sentence for the Christian Democrats, negotiations with the FMLN, and the prosecution of the Jesuit case were all advanced by conditions on aid.

In contrast, unilateral grants of American aid were not met by reciprocal compliance with American policies or priorities. After Carter rushed military aid to the Salvadorans in 1981, the ESAF subsequently failed to follow through on many of its reform pledges. Similarly, the response to the Reagan administration's initial inducement strategy was to renege on reform pledges while stimulating extrajudicial killings and right-wing coup plots. Following Duarte's win in 1984, U.S. military aid was no longer conditioned on the ESAF's human rights practices, and by 1988, extrajudicial killings had made a modest resurgence.[360] After the Bush administration promised El Salvador an additional $50 million in economic aid as an inducement to advance the Jesuit murder investigation, progress on the investigation stalled, only to pick up pace again after conditions were again attached to military assistance.

The absence of conditionality is also noted in areas where the United States had the least influence. Despite providing significant amounts of aid for more than a decade, the United States had difficulty influencing the ESAF's strategic decision making with respect to the military aspects of the counterinsurgency campaign. Although at times military aid was conditioned on the Salvadoran military's treatment of civilians or its support for reform measures, military aid was never conditioned on changes to the strategy or force structure of the

---

[359] Stanley, *The Protection Racket State*, p. 254. See also Bacevich et al., *American Military Policy in Small Wars*, p. 25.

[360] Telegram 8711, San Salvador to State, June 29, 1988, NSA.

military itself. Even late in the conflict when a failure to adjust to counterinsurgency was leading to a military stalemate, high-level American officials specifically told the ESAF that "the military doctrine the armed forces want to adopt is up to the government and the armed forces to decide."[361] Thus, the fact that the United States achieved more success in influencing the Salvadoran government in the political and economic spheres than in the military sphere is not surprising when we see that conditionality was employed in the former but not in the latter.

This is not to suggest that the use of conditionality resulted in complete compliance with U.S. preferences on every occasion. In some instances, other factors undercut the credibility of U.S. conditions. The 1980 helicopter deal, for example, generated partial compliance by the ESAF, but the credibility of the threat to withhold aid was dissipated by Carter's defeat in the 1980 election before all the terms of the deal were fulfilled. Similarly, the Reagan administration's decision to certify compliance irrespective of the actual level of Salvadoran progress rendered the congressional certification requirements of the early 1980s largely ineffective. At other times, conditionality's credibility was affected by the amount of aid involved. Conditioning 30 percent of the FY1984 military assistance budget – roughly $19.4 million – on the trial and conviction of the five guardsmen accused of the murders of the churchwomen saw results. Withholding a mere $5 million, however, pending the arrest of an officer in the Sheraton Hotel murder case – when more than $100 million in military assistance to San Salvador was unconditioned – came to naught. Similarly, the Bush administration efforts to use conditionality to pressure the Salvadoran military into cooperating with the investigation of the Jesuit murders was undercut by the fact that the suspended aid was specifically chosen so that it would not adversely affect ongoing military operations. The use of conditions on aid was a source of friction between the two governments, and American advisors in the field frequently complained that it hindered their long-term planning and reduced the efficiency of assistance.[362] Nevertheless,

---

[361] "Brief Contingency Press Statement," attached to Memo, Levitsky to Lord, February 1, 1989, NSA.
[362] Bacevich et al., *American Military Policy in Small Wars*, p. 13.

as several former U.S. military trainers noted, "[I]n general, the United States made headway only when it used what one diplomat termed the 'blunt, heavy tools' in its bag, most notably the threat of cutting off security assistance."[363]

The case provides some support for the notion that tranching aid increases compliance. When specific aid was tied to specific reforms, in the case of the Carter administration's helicopter deal or Vice President Bush's human rights ultimatum, client state agreement was achieved. This strategy was not employed consistently enough, however, nor was it followed through in both instances. While the 1983 deal was largely successful, the Carter administration's tranched aid bargain was subsequently derailed by both Ronald Reagan's election and the churchwomen and Sheraton Hotel murders.

Finally, the case also provides only limited insight into the role public commitments to the client state have on influence. Although some senior U.S. officials, such as Secretary of State Al Haig, made sweeping pledges to "draw the line" against "communist aggression" in El Salvador, on the ground, the MILGROUP commander and other officials consistently emphasized to their Salvadoran counterparts the contingent nature of the American commitment, which was facilitated by the extremely small footprint of U.S. personnel.[364] This issue is harder to adjudicate than in prior cases due to the extremely divided nature of the Salvadoran government and military between reformers and reactionaries. Washington's public support for the former (Magana and Duarte) appeared to bolster them in their domestic power struggles with the latter, which subsequently led to a higher degree of compliance with Washington's desired policy outcomes. There was no sustained pattern, however, where commitments made to the Salvadoran government in toto increased or decreased influence.

---

[363] *Ibid.*, p. 25.
[364] LeoGrande, "Splendid Little War," p. 27. When the Chief of Staff of the Salvadorian Army suggested that the United States was "irrevocably committed" to the conflict, Waghelstein retorted, "How long do you think it will take me to put 55 guys on an airplane?" Transcript, Waghelstein interviewed by Lobel, pp. 22–3.

All things considered, the evidence reviewed here suggests that U.S. influence over the Salvadoran government flowed from the use of tight conditions on aid rather than the granting of inducements. As the Chief of Staff of the Salvadoran Army, General Adolfo Blandón, acknowledged, "I'll be frank, though some don't want to admit it: The conditions the U.S. placed on us helped."[365]

---

[365] Quoted in Mark Hatfield et al., *Bankrolling Failure: United States Policy in El Salvador and the Urgent Need for Reform* (Washington, DC: Arms Control and Foreign Policy Caucus, November 1987), p. 26.

7 | Conclusion

At the time of this writing, the United States has ended its large-scale military interventions in Iraq and Afghanistan. History suggests that the intense scholarly and policy interest in counterinsurgency that accompanied these interventions will wane as the United States, in the words of President Barack Obama, "turns the page" on the conflicts of the past decade.[1] History also suggests that this would be a mistake. Despite cries of "never again" following Vietnam, within a decade of the final withdrawal of American combat troops, the United States was supporting counterinsurgency efforts in El Salvador. Similarly, the contemporary counterinsurgency era began within a decade of the end of American involvement in El Salvador. In each instance, policymakers had to relearn past lessons as they repeated past mistakes.

The U.S. military may be restructuring in a manner that would make large-scale direct intervention in counterinsurgency, à la Iraq, unfeasible in the future, but the same is not true for indirect intervention.[2] It would appear that as long as the United States continues to be a global power with global interests, it will be unable to avoid the kinds of foreign entanglements that will, at times, necessitate indirect interventions to assist other nations in counterinsurgency. Indeed, four years after he claimed to have ended the war in Iraq, President Barak Obama has had to reverse course, deploying more than 5,000 American soldiers to train and advise Iraqi forces in their fight against

---

[1] Obama quoted in "U.S. Defence Spending: Closing the Book," *Guardian*, January 5, 2012. For evidence that interest in COIN is already waning, see Michael Hirsh and Jamie Tarabay, "Washington Losing Patience with Counterinsurgency in Afghanistan," *National Journal*, June 25, 2011; Gian Gentile, "A Requiem for American Counterinsurgency," *Orbis*, 57, no. 4 (Autumn 2013), pp. 549–58.

[2] Toward that end, the U.S. Army is creating specialist advisor brigades to train and assist local militaries. Sydney J. Freedberg Jr., "Army Builds Advisor Brigades: Counterinsurgency Is Here to Stay," *Breaking Defense*, February 16, 2017.

the so-called Islamic State.[3] While it is fair to ask, as Benjamin Schwarz does, whether a regime incapable of controlling "its own territory, imposing order among its population, winning popular support when it has been given reasonable assistance to compensate for help given to its own internal enemies" can or should survive, it is unlikely that such considerations will restrain U.S. policymakers from assisting a state if significant national interests are perceived to be at stake.[4] Therefore, if we believe that the United States will continue to support other countries in counterinsurgency, it is imperative to understand the roots of past successes and failures so that patron-client relations can be better managed in the future.[5] This book has taken up this task.

The Dynamics of Patron-Client Relations

The detailed case studies of U.S. indirect intervention in the Philippines, Vietnam, and El Salvador in Chapters 4 through 6 demonstrate that American counterinsurgency doctrine – as outlined in the various editions of the *Counterinsurgency Field Manual* (FM 3–24) and much of the extant counterinsurgency literature it draws on – contain a fundamental error in presuming a unity of interest between the United States and the state it is supporting. These works also understate the difficulties the United States can have in convincing a local government to adopt its preferred approach. In all the episodes examined here, differing interests and priorities between patron and client repeatedly emerged as a source of conflict in the bilateral relationship. The patron's prescriptions – which were intended to enhance the counterinsurgency prowess of the security forces and ameliorate the grievances driving support for the insurgents – were rarely welcomed or willingly implemented by the local government.

In the Philippines, Vietnam, and El Salvador, the military, political, and economic shortcomings of the local government were key factors driving popular support for the insurgents while also alienating non-Communist elites. When assisting a state in counterinsurgency, the United States cannot afford to overlook these failings. Since

---

[3] Paul D. Shinkman, "U.S. to Send 600 More Troops to Iraq," *U.S. News and World Report*, September 28, 2016.

[4] Schwarz, *American Counterinsurgency Doctrine*, p. x.

[5] For a belief in the inevitability of future commitments from a critic of U.S. counterinsurgency policy, see Shafer, *Deadly Paradigms*, p. 276.

contemporary American counterinsurgency doctrine carries with it a strong presumption that the host nation government is the legitimate authority, however, there is good reason to worry that such issues will be downplayed, which could have a seriously debilitating impact on a counterinsurgency campaign. For example, contemporary scholarship suggests that building state capacity to administer peripheral zones of a country is a key element in countering the emergence of an insurgency.[6] Yet, as David Kilcullen wrote of the Karzai government in Afghanistan, "[I]f our strategy is to extend the reach of a government that is corrupt, is oppressing its people and failing them, then the better we do at that strategy, the worse things are going to get."[7]

If the success of a client regime is deemed important to U.S. security interests, then modifying the client's unproductive policies and behavior becomes a necessary component of assisting it in counterinsurgency. Given the trajectory of the conflict, it is hard to see how the Hukbalahap in the Philippines could have been defeated without Washington's concerted effort to reduce abuse by the security forces, suppress electoral fraud, and improve the bleak economic prospects of rural inhabitants, all of which were driving support for the insurgency. Conversely, the failure to compel the Diem government to promote effective military leadership, embrace elements of the political opposition, and forge a broader base of popular support almost guaranteed the failure of its counterinsurgency effort in Vietnam.

Recognizing the flaws of a client is only the first step. Attempting to alter its grievance-producing behaviors and counterinsurgency policies without contributing to its collapse is an extremely challenging undertaking. Not only is it necessary to work through an unenthusiastic local partner, who may view the proposed measures as undesired or even threatening, but bringing about changes to existing political structures in the face of an insurgency creates significant risk of destabilizing the incumbent government. Such an effort is also likely to be time-consuming because there will be few quick fixes for a local ally that is ineffective, corrupt, or abusive enough to have fostered an internal rebellion.

---

[6] Fearon and Laitin, "Ethnicity, Insurgency and Civil War," pp. 88–9.
[7] Kilcullen, *Counterinsurgency*, p. 160. Fearon and Laitin do acknowledge this problem, "Ethnicity, Insurgency and Civil War," p. 89.

If engendering reform and policy change in the client government is critical to the achievement of U.S. goals in counterinsurgency, how does one achieve the necessary influence to bring it about?

Inducement versus Conditionality

In the course of the three interventions studied here, the United States employed two different strategies for using aid to influence clients: inducement and conditionality. Inducement posits a fundamentally cooperative interaction between patron and client in which both sides can achieve their aims without resorting to threats or negative sanctions. The patron's primary means of generating influence is through unilateral grants of assistance, which are expected to be reciprocated by the client's compliance with the patron's preferred policies. Proponents of inducement also suggest that the more extensive and more public the patron's commitment to the client, the more influence the patron will have over the client government. Since inducement seeks to influence a client with proactive gifts of aid, the strategy should be a viable one at any stage of an intervention, regardless of whether any alternative approach preceded it. In the course of the case studies, the success of inducement would have been clearly recognizable if client compliance resulted from the rewards granted to the client *before* it carried out the specified action.

In contrast, conditionality posits a more contested relationship between the patron and client, in which each side attempts to maximize gains over the other. The patron's primary influence-generating mechanism is the promise to provide aid if the client takes specified actions, coupled with the threat to withhold it otherwise. Conditionality also suggests that a more transactional relationship with a client – in which the patron's level of commitment is hedged or ambiguous – will be associated with more influence over that client. Since conditionality requires making credible threats to a client and carefully managing commitments, it is expected that this strategy will be much more difficult to employ if the client has already been the recipient of unconditional aid and extensive political commitments. Evidence in the case studies of a client's reform or policy change resulting from the threat or promise of aid, when the client acts before the patron dispenses its largess, would strengthen the case for conditionality.

Unilateral Grants of Aid versus Conditioned Assistance

The detailed historical studies of U.S. patron-client interaction in the Philippines, Vietnam, and El Salvador (summarized in Table 7.1) offer little support for the claim that the extension of unilateral grants of aid to a client will be met by the implementation of a reform it had previously opposed. Instead, the case studies offer fairly strong evidence that the patron's enforcement of strong conditions on aid is more closely associated with client compliance with the patron's counter-insurgency preferences. The Philippines was the only case in which the United States employed a conditionality strategy throughout the intervention. It was also the case where the client government demonstrated the highest degree of compliance with Washington's policy prescriptions. In both Vietnam and El Salvador, unconditional grants of aid to the client resulted in low levels of compliance. Despite the strenuous appeals of Ambassador Durbrow, both the Eisenhower and the Kennedy administrations were largely unwilling to press Diem hard or attach conditions to military aid to Vietnam. Unsurprisingly, this signaled to Saigon that the United States was not very serious about political liberalization, suppression of the Can Lao Party, or the rationalization of the ARVN's command structure. Subsequently, compliance with American preferences was low. In El Salvador, when inducement was employed, client compliance was also minimal. Every time unilateral grants of aid were extended by the Carter, Reagan, or Bush administration, the Salvadoran military or government failed to follow through on reform. In contrast, the successes that Washington did have in shaping the policies and behaviors of San Salvador – such as the reduction in human rights abuses following Vice President Bush's visit or the adoption of economic austerity measures – were uniformly associated with the use of strict conditions on its aid. There were episodes in El Salvador when conditions were attached to aid, yet the local government did not comply; however, these were the result of situational factors. The circumvention of congressional certification requirements in the early 1980s by the Reagan administration, for example, left it with little coercive power. Similarly, the $5 million in military aid conditioned on progress in the Sheraton murder case was merely a symbolic measure that provided no real incentive for compliance in light of the fact that El Salvador was already receiving more than $100 million annually in unconditioned military assistance.

Table 7.1 *Summary of Patron-Client Influence Episodes*

Case	Date	Event	Strategy	Compliance
Philippines	1949–50	Restructuring of the Philippine Constabulary	Conditionality	High
Philippines	1950–1	Implementation of the Quirino-Foster Agreement	Conditionality	High
Philippines	1950	Appointment of Magsaysay as Secretary of National Defense	Conditionality	High
Philippines	1952	Removal of General Castañeda and Brigadier Ramos	Conditionality	High
Philippines	1952–3	Prevention of backsliding by Liberal Party	Conditionality	High
Vietnam	1957–9	Durbrow's press for political liberalization	Inducement[a]	Low
Vietnam	1961	Counterinsurgency Plan	Inducement	Low
Vietnam	1961	Joint Action Plan	Inducement	Low
Vietnam	1961	Limited partnership	Inducement[b]	Low
Vietnam	1963	Final push for reform	Conditionality	Low[c]
El Salvador	1980	Christian Democrat entry into Junta	Conditionality	High
El Salvador	1980	Prevention of military coup	Conditionality	High
El Salvador	1980	Improving human rights in return for helicopters	Conditionality	Low[d]
El Salvador	1980	Restructuring Junta and purge human rights abusers	Conditionality	High
El Salvador	1980	Controlling human rights abuses and death squads	Inducement[e]	Low
El Salvador	1981	Sustaining Junta reforms and reduce human rights abuses	Inducement	Low
El Salvador	1981–91	Adapting the Salvadoran military for counterinsurgency	Inducement	Low
El Salvador	1981	Prevention of right-wing coup and prosecute churchwomen case	Conditionality	High
El Salvador	1981–4	Congressional certification requirements	Conditionality	Low[f]
El Salvador	1982	Including Christian Democrats in coalition government	Conditionality	High
El Salvador	1982	Defending "land-to-the-tiller" program	Conditionality	High

El Salvador	1983	Vice President Bush's "new contract"	Conditionality	High
El Salvador	1984–5	Implementing economic austerity measures	Conditionality	High
El Salvador	1984–6	Prosecution of additional suspects in land reform murders	Conditionality	Low[g]
El Salvador	1990	Promoting the military's cooperation with Jesuit investigation	Conditionality	Low[b]
El Salvador	1990–2	Prosecution of the Jesuit murders and negotiate with the FMLN	Conditionality	High

[a] Conditions on minor economic aid.
[b] Conditional deal but aid delivered before reforms.
[c] Some compliance before government overthrown.
[d] Partial compliance derailed by Ronald Reagan's election.
[e] Conditions attached, but aid rushed in the wake of 1981 final offensive before Salvadoran government compliance.
[f] Congressional certification requirements subverted by the Reagan administration.
[g] Only $5 million in military aid conditioned on the case.
[h] Conditions attached to equipment specifically chosen to that "withholding these materials will not greatly affect the ESAF's basic ability to fight the war."

Commitments to the Client: Strong versus Weak

With respect to the link between commitments and leverage, the cases studied here do not support the notion that a stronger commitment to a client leads to more leverage over its policies. Indeed, in Vietnam, whenever the United States issued strong statements of support for the client government, American influence diminished. Rather than being part of the solution, strong visible commitments to client states appear to be part of the problem. In contrast, there is modest support for the alternate argument that a weaker or more ambiguous commitment is associated with a greater degree of leverage over the host nation. Despite the symbolic and substantive importance of the Philippines to U.S. interests in Asia, the Truman administration succeeded in keeping Quirino at arm's length and creating enough uncertainty about American intentions that Washington's support was not taken for granted. This suggests that as long as a client government believes that its survival is more important to the patron than any particular policy change being pushed, advice and counsel that run counter to the client's interests will be ignored. Consequently, a patron can enhance its leverage by maintaining a degree of ambiguity about the depth of its willingness to support a client. Ambiguous commitments may also have a secondary effect of stimulating beneficial "self-help" behavior on the part of clients. In this vein, Hilton Root reports that during the Cold War, America's East Asian allies who were the least certain of U.S. support worked to establish the most stable and inclusive governments, while those more assured of American backing did not.[8]

In undertaking an intervention, a patron needs to carefully calibrate its perceived level of commitment to the client state: not enough reassurance and the client may be unwilling to make the hard changes necessary to defeat the insurgents; too much reassurance and the patron risks creating a moral hazard in which the client thinks that it does not need to provide for its own security because the patron will always bail them out of trouble.

Consistent Application Required?

Does inducement or conditionality require consistent application to succeed? Since the cases did not provide any examples of the

---

[8] Root, *Alliance Curse*, p. 65.

successful use of an inducement strategy, it is impossible to test its sensitivity to consistent application. The same is not true for conditionality, where the case studies provide evidence to support the notion that conditionality will have to be employed consistently if it is to prove effective. One implication of this is that a patron state will have difficulty transitioning from an inducement strategy to the use of conditionality. The Kennedy administration's prior use of inducements and its publicly effusive embrace of Diem harmed its subsequent ability to use conditioned aid to generate leverage over his government after the prior approach had clearly failed. Similarly, after previously using inducement and avoiding the enforcement of congressionally mandated conditionality, the Reagan administration had to be extremely forceful in its 1983 "new contract" with the government of El Salvador to convince Salvadoran leaders that aid really would be withheld if substantive action was not forthcoming. If a country has already been the recipient of lavish aid and political commitments, it can be difficult to subsequently threaten to withhold assistance in a manner that makes its leaders believe future aid will actually be conditioned on their action.

A second finding regarding the need for consistency is that conditions on assistance have to be applied to all forms of aid. When the U.S. government decided to get tough with Diem, for example, it attached conditions to economic aid but was unwilling to threaten to withhold military assistance to South Vietnam. Predictably, these efforts generated marginal influence because decision-makers in Saigon had every reason to believe that if the situation was serious enough for the United States to provide unconditional military aid, Washington would eventually provide economic aid rather than let the country's economy collapse. In contrast, in the Philippines, both economic assistance and military aid were conditioned on Quirino's actions, which left no doubt as to the seriousness of American intentions. Moreover, the conditions were actually interconnected such that a failure to follow through on political and economic reform actually held up military aid that had already been "earned" by the Philippine government.

The Utility of Tranching?

Finally, the utility of tranching conditioned aid receives some support here. When overly broad conditions were attached to an entire aid package, the credibility of threats to withdraw assistance was reduced. While Congress occasionally functioned as a bogeyman with which to threaten the Salvadoran military, for example, the certification requirements it imposed on aid to El Salvador in the early 1980s were generally too vague. The U.S. president had to certify every six months that the government of El Salvador was making "progress" or a "concerted and significant effort" to implement specific reforms. These requirements were subject to interpretation and had no room for calibration, fine-tuning, or nuance.[9] What if gains were registered in some areas, but backsliding occurred in another? The blunt and sweeping nature of these conditions had limited credibility as a threat to withhold aid, even if the Reagan administration had not undercut them by choosing to certify results and disperse aid despite the Salvadoran government's lack of compliance.

In contrast, the Truman administration conditioned its economic and military aid on specific actions by the Philippine government, such as the subordination of the Philippine Constabulary to the Department of National Defense, the appointment of Magsaysay as Secretary of National Defense, and the approval of specific tax increases and minimum-wage legislation. Implementation of these reforms was tied to an aid package consisting of several tranches, each tranche associated with a specific reform. Similarly, the "new contract" negotiated by Vice President Bush in 1983 mandated removing particular individuals from office and the issuing of specific public statements by the ESAF high command that condemned right-wing terrorist groups and supported presidential elections and land reform. As with the Philippines, specific blocks of aid were linked to these actions. Compliance was also much higher in the episodes in which Congress linked specific aid to specific actions, such as the military aid linked to prosecuting the Churchwomen murders or negotiations with the FMLN. In both the Philippines and El Salvador, compliance with these specific requirements was higher when aid was tranched and, in the case of the latter, much higher than compliance with the broad and vague congressional certification requirements of the early 1980s.

---

[9] Unsurprisingly, members of the Reagan administration viewed the congressional action more as a way to pass the buck for making tough decisions on a contentious foreign policy issue than a determined effort to shape the Salvadoran government's behavior. Telegram 204069, Assistant Secretary Abrams to SecState, July 23, 1982, STATE.

Assessment

The cases reviewed here do not provide evidence to support any of the observable implications associated with the inducement influence strategy. Neither unilateral grants of aid nor strong public commitments to the client government were associated with its compliance with the patron's preferred counterinsurgency strategy. In contrast, the evidence assembled here provides moderate to strong support for all four of the expected observations associated with conditionality. The use of ex-post conditions on aid and ambiguous commitments to the client government were both associated with a high degree of client compliance with patron preferences. Furthermore, the effectiveness of this approach appears to be enhanced when it is applied consistently and the aid is broken into specific tranches. As a result, in these instances, conditionality can be deemed to be a relatively superior strategy for influencing wayward client states.

This does not mean that the American government's use of conditionality resulted in complete compliance with its preferences in all instances and at all times. Nor can conditions attached to aid bring about unlimited change in another country. Even in the Philippines – the most successful intervention studied here – political reform did not result in true democracy, nor were the problems of corruption or land tenure addressed in a meaningful and lasting manner. Merely possessing the ability to influence a client's counterinsurgency choices is certainly no guarantee that an assistance effort will succeed or that the costs involved will be proportional to the objectives sought. Nevertheless, when American influence was successfully exercised in these cases, it was the result of conditioning aid on specific actions.

Constraints on Conditionality in Counterinsurgency?

Although the findings drawn from the case studies of the Philippines, Vietnam, and El Salvador generally support the efficacy of conditionality as a tool of influence, it is worth pondering whether or not there are situations in which this approach might be less effective due to structural factors in the patron-client relationship that are different from those examined in this book. Two factors are considered here: the polarity of the international system and the self-sufficiency of the client state.

Since the presence of more than one potential patron state might reduce a client's dependence on a particular patron, the first variable to consider is the configuration of the international system. A classic client strategy to deflect patron pressure is the threat to defect to a rival. However, the effectiveness of this maneuver depends on the prevailing geopolitical circumstances. In a unipolar system, there is simply no opposing camp to desert to, therefore less opportunity to exercise reverse leverage against the patron. In contrast, during the bipolar Cold War, it was generally presumed that the two superpowers competed for allies, which gave small states potential leverage against them. In the context of assisting counterinsurgency, however, the effectiveness of a client's threats to realign depended on the nature of the insurgency they faced. It would have been hard, for example, for a U.S. client government fighting against a Communist-linked guerrilla movement to credibly threaten to defect to the Soviet or Chinese camp. That may not be the case, however, in a more multipolar environment. There is no guarantee that a major power rival would have the means and desire to involve itself in a particular conflict as a competing patron; however, a full-blown defection may not be necessary. Simply reducing its dependence on a single patron by courting multiple powers may be enough for a client to improve its bargaining position. In the context of a multilateral effort to support a client government, such as the NATO intervention in Afghanistan, the presence of multiple major powers might undermine conditionality if the parties fail to synchronize their policies. Even if the intervening powers all desire the same basic outcome, the client government can exploit the presence of multiple uncoordinated patrons to subvert pressure by playing one off another. The presence of multiple powers, either hostile or benign, does not render conditionality ineffective per se; it just increases the client's relative leverage. This, in turn, means a patron may have to expend more effort to influence a local government, but it is not a barrier to the use of conditions on aid.

The second factor that could weaken the effectiveness of conditions on aid would be the client state's ability to independently develop its own capabilities as an alternative to the patron's assistance. The less dependent a local government is on external military equipment, economic aid, or diplomatic support, the less influence conditionality is likely to generate. This situation could come about as a result of the client's endowment in valuable natural resources or its possession of

Table 7.2 *Completed Counterinsurgency Campaigns Supported by U.S. Indirect Intervention, 1944–2010*

Country	Initial year	% USA CINC	Resource endowment
Greece	1947	1.07	Poor
Philippines	1946	0.95	Poor
Vietnam	1957	1.12	Poor
Laos	1959	0.19	Poor
Guatemala	1960	0.21	Poor
Cambodia	1967	0.21	Poor
Morocco	1975	1.88	Poor
Nicaragua	1978	0.21	Poor
El Salvador	1979	0.35	Poor
Croatia	1992	0.85	Poor

Note: The list of externally supported insurgencies comes from Christopher Paul et al., *Paths to Victory: Lessons from Modern Insurgencies* (Santa Monica, CA: RAND Corporation, 2013), pp. 77–8. The Composite Index of National Capability (CINC) comes from Singer, "Reconstructing the Correlates of War Dataset on Material Capabilities of States, 1816–1985," pp. 115–32. Resource endowment measures the amount of oil and/or diamonds in a country and comes from Girod, "Foreign Aid and Post-Conflict Reconstruction," p. 39.

substantial unrealized material power. Although compelling in theory, such situations are unlikely to arise when assisting counterinsurgency. It is difficult to predict where the United States will intervene in the future, but from a historical standpoint, the countries that have received aid and support in counterinsurgency from the United States, short of the intervention of combat troops, were overwhelmingly small, resource-poor states whose material capabilities (as measured by the Composite Index of National Capability) were a bare fraction of those of their patron (see Table 7.2).

These were certainly not countries that were able to forego external assistance and rely on their own resources to contend with an insurgency. Although it is possible that these historical patterns won't hold in the future, one must wonder if a local government had the means to respond to an insurgency on their own, would U.S. policymakers feel the need to intervene to assist them?

The three cases examined in this book all occurred during a period in which the international system was bipolar and involved relatively poor client states. It is possible that altering these two characteristics could affect the difficulty of generating influence via conditionality in the future; however, the utility of this approach in situations beyond those studied here cannot be dismissed prima facie.

The Trouble with Allies Redux: Influencing Modern Client States

It would be nice to think that the dilemmas posed in this book are Cold War relics of no contemporary consequence, however, this is not the case.[10] In pursuit of its aims in the "War on Terror," the United States came to rely on partnerships with several corrupt, inefficient, or abusive regimes – distinguished by their notional opposition to Islamic extremism – whose principles, interests, and aims were often quite different from its own.[11] As with their Cold War counterparts, it was erroneous for American policymakers to believe that the governments of contemporary client states, such as Iraq, Afghanistan, and Pakistan, necessarily shared their desire to defeat radical Islamic insurgents by adhering to the prescriptions of U.S. counterinsurgency doctrine. American exhortations to eliminate the corruption, oppression, inadequate governance, and economic stagnation driving support for militancy by embracing minority populations, strengthening state institutions, enhancing the capacity of local security forces, and encouraging political and economic liberalization are as equally likely to fall on deaf ears today as they were in the past.

There is no question that one of the major factors contributing to the difficulties the United States experienced in Iraq and Afghanistan was the behavior of the local governments. In both countries, the pursuit of

---

[10] While some may suggest that the experience of Cold War–era insurgencies are of little contemporary relevance, Stathis Kalyvas and Laia Balcells argue that the dynamics of the Cold War actually made these groups significantly more robust and threatening to state authorities in their time than either Islamic radicals or "sons of the soil" insurgencies are today. Stathis Kalyvas and Laia Balcells, "International System and Technologies of Rebellion: How the Cold War Shaped Internal Conflict," *American Political Science Review*, 104, no. 3 (2010).

[11] Daniel Byman, "The Intelligence War on Terrorism," *Intelligence and National Security*, 29, no. 6 (2014), pp. 850, 859–60.

patronage politics and sectarian agendas by Nouri Maliki and Hamid Karzai alienated segments of society and fueled armed opposition to the very government authority the United States was attempting to bolster and expand. In both cases, inducement influence strategies coupled with personal commitments to specific leaders – and in the case of Karzai, direct cash payments – rendered the local regimes largely unreceptive to subsequent American exhortations to reduce corruption, address the lack of government capacity, hold free elections, and engage in political reconciliation.[12] As a result, America's ability to translate the gains from military operations into political outcomes suffered.

In both these episodes, the United States had significant ground forces committed to the conflict, which resulted in a different dynamic than the cases studied here. Even more illustrative of the patron-client dynamics studied here is the recent U.S. experience with Pakistan. An American treaty ally, Pakistan was also a sanctuary for insurgent groups attacking NATO forces in Afghanistan and undermining attempts to bring stability to the country.[13] Although the United States has provided inducements in the form of more than $30 billion in military and economic aid since 2001, Washington has had little success in persuading the Pakistani government and military to sever their long-standing ties to the Afghan Taliban.[14] Instead, successive Pakistani governments have provided a safe haven for the leaders of the Taliban's Quetta Shura, not to mention Osama bin Laden. Although the United States pays for 20 percent of Pakistan's defense expenditures, when undertaking counterinsurgency operations, the political and military leaders in Islamabad and Rawalpindi only target the jihadists who wage war against the Pakistani state, ignoring "friendly" extremist groups such as the Haqqani Network and the Lashkar-e-Taiba that focus their efforts against Afghanistan or India.

In 2009, Congress attempted to redirect the U.S. influence strategy from inducement toward conditionality by making some economic and

---

[12] On payments to Karzai, see Matthew Rosenberg, "With Bags of Cash, C.I.A. Seeks Influence in Afghanistan," *New York Times*, April 28, 2013.

[13] *Report on Progress toward Security and Stability in Afghanistan* (Washington, DC: Department of Defense, October 2014), p. 95.

[14] Aid figure comes from K. Alan Kronstadt, *Pakistan-U.S. Relations: Issues for the 114th Congress* (Washington DC: Congressional Research Service, May 14, 2015), p. 13.

military assistance dependent on certification of the Pakistani government's "sustained commitment" to combat terrorist groups – as demonstrated by making "progress" in ending government support for groups
attacking U.S. and NATO troops in Afghanistan as well as preventing Al
Qaeda, the Taliban, Lashkar-e-Taiba, and Jaish-e-Mohammed from
enjoying sanctuary in the country – a determination that the Pakistani
military is not "materially or substantially subverting" the political process within the country, and evidence that the Pakistani government was
"continuing to cooperate" with the United States in efforts to dismantle
Pakistan-linked nuclear supplier networks.[15] This initial attempt at conditionality generated little result because the supermajority of American
assistance to Pakistan remained unconditioned: only $296 million in
military aid out of total annual aid package of $3 billion (10 percent)
was subject to these certification requirements.[16] Moreover, like the congressional certification requirements imposed by Congress on aid to El
Salvador, these conditions on aid to Pakistan were sufficiently broad to
make a determination of "progress" a subjective undertaking. Possessing
the same all-or-nothing structure as in El Salvador, the Obama administration faced the same pressure to assert progress regardless of the facts on
the ground as the Reagan administration did thirty years before. The most
notable example of this occurred in March 2011, when Secretary of State
Clinton certified to Congress that progress was being made in meeting
American conditions even though the United States was aware that
Osama bin Laden was hiding in an affluent suburb near Islamabad.

In 2011, Congress extended conditions to all military assistance and
select economic aid. As in the past, however, the legislation contained
vague conditions requiring a certification that Pakistani authorities
were "taking demonstrable steps" to support counterterrorism operations, prevent cross-border attacks on Afghanistan from Pakistani
territory, and assist in countering the threat of improvised explosive
devices, in addition to the previously noted counter-proliferation cooperation. Moreover, the law allowed the Secretary of State to wave the
conditions if it was in U.S. national security interests to do so.

---

[15] All quotes taken from Hillary Clinton, "Certification Relating to Pakistan under
     Section 203 of the Enhanced Partnership with Pakistan Act of 2009," March 18,
     2011.
[16] *Pakistan Assistance*, GAO-11-786R (Washington, DC: GAO, July 19, 2011),
     pp. 5–6.

Consequently, since 2011, the Obama administration repeatedly invoked "national security interests" to waive all congressionally imposed conditions on aid to Pakistan, with the expected deleterious effect on U.S. influence over Islamabad.[17]

In 2015 the Republican-controlled Congress succeeded in attaching further conditions on U.S. reimbursements to the Pakistani military for operations it conducts against militants on its soil. The move was opposed by the Obama administration on the grounds that enhanced conditions will "complicate progress" in bilateral ties.[18] Of an authorized $900 million in support funds, $300 million (33 percent) was contingent on the Secretary of Defense's certification that the Pakistani government was taking specific actions to disrupt the sanctuaries of the Haqqani network in Pakistan, arrest and prosecute their senior leaders, and coordinate border security operations with the Afghan government. Secretary of Defense Ashton Carter's refusal to provide such a certification in August 2016, in the face of clear evidence that the Pakistani government had not met the stated requirements, suggests the Obama administration may have finally learned its lesson. With 45% of reimbursements to Pakistan for 2017 ($400 million) conditioned on action against the Haqqani network, the history reviewed here suggests the Trump administration would be wise to embrace and expand this approach.[19]

Policy Implications

Although this book is principally an exercise in academic scholarship, its conclusions can inform policy as well.[20] In daring to provide counsel to policymakers, however, scholars must be circumspect, recognizing Hans Morgenthau's maxim that "the first lesson the student of international politics must learn and never forget is that the complexities of international affairs make simple solutions and trustworthy prophecies impossible. Here the scholar and the charlatan part

---

[17] Kronstadt, *Pakistan-U.S. Relations*, p. i.
[18] "Obama Administration Opposes Congressional Move to Condition Aid to Pakistan," *Indian Express*, May 17, 2016.
[19] "U.S. Congress Conditions $400 million of $900 million Aid to Pakistan," *Times of India*, December 9, 2016.
[20] Alexander L. George, "Knowledge for Statecraft: The Challenge for Political Science and History," *International Security*, 22, no. 1 (Summer 1997), p. 45.

company."[21] With this injunction in mind, this study offers several suggestions for managing patron-client relations in future interventions.

By demonstrating that conditionality is associated with a higher level of influence over the client's counterinsurgency strategy, this book corroborates the seemingly paradoxical notion suggested by agency theory that the establishment and enforcement of strict conditions on aid to a partner government will be a necessary component of any successful counterinsurgency assistance effort. What specific actions can a patron take to enhance the effectiveness of conditionality and therefore its potential leverage over a client? Five recommendations follow on from the theoretical literature and historical cases examined here.

1. Expect Tense Relations with the Client

In contemporary and historical interventions to assist counterinsurgency, the United States has repeatedly found that its local partners were significant obstacles to success. A shared interest in defeating an insurgency does not guarantee that a patron and its client government will prefer the same policies for carrying out that task. In theory, U.S. policymakers should assist only those countries with which their interests and priorities clearly align. In practice, however, the problem of adverse selection means that the types of governments most in need of counterinsurgency assistance are largely those that are least likely to heed U.S. guidance. Consequently, policymakers planning to assist counterinsurgency will be best served by expecting a contested relationship with the client from the outset.

The divergent preferences of local allies (or powerful elements within their regimes) can lead them to resist U.S. recommendations for responding to internal violence and instead pursue policies or behaviors that are antithetical to U.S. counterinsurgency doctrine. Under such circumstances, the patron's advice and material support will not necessarily enhance the client's counterinsurgency prowess. Therefore, a key focus of attention should be on bringing the client's behavior into line with the requirements of the patron.

---

[21] Hans Morgenthau, *Politics Among Nations: The Struggle for Power and Peace* (New York: Knopf, 1967), p. 19.

2. Do Not Fear Coercing Allies in Crisis

Although the reflexive response of most policymakers would be to prop up a failing partner, if shaping the counterinsurgency behavior of a client state is a priority, then pressing it to make changes when it is weak, rather than strengthening it, is the way to succeed. The imperatives of responding to the deteriorating security situation in a client state can lead some officials in the patron government to push for the expedited delivery of assistance rather than condition aid on reform as a bargaining tactic. However, the client is most susceptible to the patron's pressure when it is feeling most vulnerable. The more directly the insurgents threaten the ruling elites in the client state, the greater the client's incentive to cooperate with the patron.[22] Conversely, the client has no incentive to undertake reform when the situation is stable. In all three cases, the United States succeeded in extracting agreements from the local government – the Quirino-Foster Agreement of 1950, the limited partnership with Diem in 1961, and Vice President Bush's 1983 "new contract" with the Salvadoran government – when it conditioned aid on reforms at a time when the respective insurgents were in the ascendancy, and the client had reason to doubt the depth of American willingness to support and defend it. The very moment when the local regime is feeling most vulnerable, due to a combination of internal instability and uncertainty about the patron's steadfastness, is the ideal time to compel that government to adopt reform and policy changes in return for aid. In contrast, attempting to reassure a client by telling the world that you are willing to "pay any price, bear any burden, [or] meet any hardship" on its behalf simply reduces the local government's incentives for reform.[23]

Conditionality is the optimal influence strategy to employ at the outset of an intervention because it is always possible to abandon it for inducement if the client readily complies with the patron's desired policies. Once the client has become accustomed to unconditioned aid, however, going in the opposite direction from inducement to conditionality may be much harder to do effectively. If the patron has previously signaled to the client that it is so important as to merit

[22] Steven R. David, *Choosing Sides: Alignment and Realignment in the Third World* (Baltimore: Johns Hopkins University Press, 1991), p. 6.
[23] Kennedy, "Inaugural Address."

unqualified support, subsequent threats to suspend vital aid may not have sufficient credibility in the eyes of the client to merit compliance.

In light of the sometimes sluggish pace of reform in developing countries, the case studies suggest that even after an initial reform or policy change occurs, it may be necessary to maintain pressure on the client regime to ensure they don't seek to backslide. The protracted effort to implement and defend reorganization of the PC in the Philippines or land-reform programs in El Salvador, for example, not only raises questions about the durability of foreign-imposed policy changes, it also suggests that the patron may have to continue conditions on aid for a significant period of time to ensure that reforms remain in place long enough to have their desired effect.

3. Make Conditions Clear, Measurable, and Realistic

When employing a conditionality-based influence strategy, the conditions and their desired policy outcomes should be as unambiguous as possible. Precise objectives that can be easily measured and recognized facilitate the enforcement of conditionality. In contrast, vague requirements that tie aid to demonstrations of "effort" or "progress" introduce a high degree of subjectivity into a process that is already potentially subject to internal political pressures for weak enforcement. Models for the structure of conditions can be found in the Truman administration's approach to the Philippine government or Vice President Bush's "new contract" with the Salvadorans. For the most part, the conditions were very specific, compliance was easily measureable, and a clear deadline was set for meeting the requirements. By identifying the specific actions it wants the client government to take and the specific blocks of aid associated with compliance, the patron can remove much of the subjectivity from the process and reduce the pressure to release aid in the face of noncompliance.

In setting conditions on aid it will be essential to prioritize the specific military, political, and economic measures a patron wants to see implemented. The broader the scope of policy changes desired, the more difficult it will be to effectively focus the leverage provided by conditionality. Attempting to do too much at once could dissipate influence with minimal results. Establishing a hierarchy of objectives will also be necessary because it is highly likely that some of the patron's policy goals will have consequences or second-order effects that conflict with one other. In El Salvador, for example, many of the aggressive junior officers who were most amenable to American counterinsurgency practices were also staunch supporters of D'Aubuisson and the far right, which was actively seeking to bring down the ruling Christian Democrats.[24] Thus, empowering these young officers to capitalize on their much-needed initiative and leadership to achieve military objectives on the battlefield risked undermining efforts to curtail death-squad violence and potentially threatened the fledgling civilian government's weak grip on the reins of office. Conversely, successful U.S. efforts to promote political liberalization and reduce death-squad violence fostered an environment where the FMLN could reestablish its urban support network, which facilitated the 1989 "Final Offensive."

Finally, in setting conditionality requirements, it is critical to have a realistic appreciation of what can actually be accomplished. The goal of a conditional aid strategy is to press the client to ameliorate the worst of its grievance-causing behavior while also sufficiently strengthening the regime vis-à-vis the insurgents. External aid, support, and pressure can help with these tasks, but they cannot bring about a fundamental transformation of the client state's society. Even in the Philippines, the most successful intervention reviewed here, many of the underlying economic and political conditions that drove peasant farmers to support the Huks remained unaddressed. Under the best circumstances, the degree and scope of change that external influence can bring out in another nation's policies is limited.

4. *Prepare for Internal Opposition*

The client government may not be the only party opposed to a conditionality strategy. The patron can also face internal pressure not to enforce its own conditions. On a strategic level, some policymakers may believe that the local government is simply too important to threaten it by denying aid. Such views are largely unfounded. Examining the list of countries that have been historically assisted in counterinsurgency by the United States (Table 7.2), it is clear that these were not countries that were too important to fail; the loss of any one of these minor client states would have had a minimal impact on the standing or alliances of a superpower such as the United

---

[24] "El Salvador: Controlling Rightwing Terrorism," February 1, 1985, p. 7, CIA.

States.[25] Of course, irrespective of their validity, geopolitical considerations, reputational concerns, or the fear of falling dominos could
lead U.S. policymakers to conclude that a state is vital to U.S. security
even if its material endowments are minimal.[26] Yet this perception of
both importance and vulnerability did not prevent U.S. administrations
from bringing pressure to bear on the Philippine and Salvadoran
governments via conditions on aid. Moreover, the withholding of aid
pending compliance does not pose an existential threat to the client's
survival. Except in the most extreme cases, it is unlikely that the local
government will immediately collapse from a single instance of aid
suspension. If that appears legitimately imminent, the patron can
always temporarily reverse its policy

On a programmatic level, the uncertainty surrounding aid disbursement inherent with conditionality can hinder the effectiveness of assistance efforts. Programs such as military training and economic
development are typically medium- or long-term processes that are
not necessarily structured or organized to respond well to inconsistent
aid flows. If aid actually must be withheld due to a failure of client
compliance, these support efforts could suffer a serious disruption.
Thus, elements within the bureaucracy of the patron state whose
programs would be affected by an aid suspension could actually have
a vested interest in not having the conditions implemented.

In turn, the credibility of threats to condition aid on client action can
be harmed by the perception of internal disagreements within the
government of the patron state. Local allies are likely to interpret
evidence of bureaucratic disagreements over conditionality as a clear
sign that the patron is not serious about the need for change or that
threats to withhold aid can be circumvented by appealing to "friendly"
agencies. In Vietnam, evidence of significant disagreement within the
U.S. government with respect to the ideal response to the insurgency led
the Saigon government to conclude that Washington's demands could
be placated with superficial reforms or simply waited out. Thus
Ambassador Durbrow's repeated attempts to pressure Diem into

---

[25] Waltz, *Theory of International Politics*, p. 169.

[26] Historically, great powers have repeatedly overestimated the threat that
disorder in peripheral states poses to their core interests. See Jack Snyder,
"Imperial Myths and Threat Inflation," in A. Trevor Thrall and Jane K. Cramer,
eds., *Politics of Fear: Threat Inflation since 9/11* (New York: Routledge, 2009),
p. 41.

broadening his government, ending Can Lao corruption, and sending Nhu out of the country were undercut by General Williams' assurances of unconditional support.

In sharp contrast, in the Philippines, the military and the political wings of the U.S. bureaucracy were unified both in their assessment of the "root causes" of the Huk insurgency and in their prescriptions for military action to serve as a temporary expedient while reforms ameliorated major grievances in the population. The notable unity among the various U.S. agencies involved, both on the ground in Manila and back in Washington, undoubtedly strengthened the Truman administration's position when it sought to translate conditions on aid into influence over the Quirino government. Forging this kind of solid interagency consensus on both the problem and the solution will significantly enhance the bargaining power of the U.S. government vis-à-vis its client, whereas evidence of a bureaucratic rift can weaken the American position as a local ally attempts to play "friendly" agencies or actors against "unfriendly" ones.

5. *Cultivate Ties with Local Reformers*

Although it was not theorized in Chapter 3, the case studies suggest a positive interaction between the use of conditionality by the patron state and the ability of domestic reformers in the host nation to bring about desired policy changes. The issue is an important one because any lasting solution to a local problem ultimately requires local legitimacy. In all three cases, key government figures or opposition leaders supported the policy changes and reforms the United States was pressing the client government to make. Although unconditioned aid can strengthen the hand of hard-liners in the government by providing them with additional resources to repress or co-opt the political opposition, it appears that conditions on aid can strengthen reform-minded local officials or members of the political opposition, particularly in regimes in which power or authority is fragmented, such as El Salvador and the Philippines. Indeed, in El Salvador, President Magana specifically told American interlocutors that he "welcomed" conditions on aid because "they would help him enormously in dealing with the military."[27] Similarly, in the Philippines, the perception that

---

[27] Telegram 11456, San Salvador to State, December 11, 1983, NSA.

Magsaysay held the keys to unlocking American largess facilitated his rapid implementation of a number of reforms. Yet later as president, without the threat or promise of American aid to use as a tool, he was far less successful in addressing the grievances that helped to provoke the Huk Rebellion.

This finding, in turn, suggests that it is imperative that the United States does not "personalize" its relationship with the client government. The bilateral relationship should be between two governments, not between a government and a single leader or a single party. This error was made in Vietnam, where the Kennedy administration effectively treated Diem as if he was "the government" to the point where Ambassador Nolting was accused of not even cultivating ties with opposition figures or maintaining a position independent of Diem.[28] Conversely, in the Philippines, the United States did not tie its policy to a single leader. Indeed, given the covert support for political liberalization and fair elections – which weakened Quirino politically and ultimately led to his defeat – the U.S. government could be said to have actively subverted an American ally in the process of supporting the government in counterinsurgency.

Cultivating ties with the opposition, while maintaining a working relationship with the incumbent government, requires skilled diplomacy. If handled poorly, such a maneuver may be interpreted as undermining the regime. The ideal position is to remain close enough to sustain influence over the local government yet sufficiently distant that the regime's incentives to reform are not undermined, and the political opposition is not alienated by support for the incumbent government. Admittedly, executing such a maneuver is easier said than done, but it remains a necessary aim for diplomatic interaction. Policymakers would be well served to remember Richard Nixon's guidance that fellow democracies merit "a warm embrace," while less liberal partners should only receive "a firm handshake."[29]

Final Thoughts

Counterinsurgency is a challenging undertaking, the difficulties of which are only magnified when one state attempts to assist another

---

[28] FRUS 1963/1, pp. 49–62.
[29] Richard Nixon, *Six Crises* (New York: Doubleday, 1962), pp. 191–2.

state in its counterinsurgency effort. Policymakers facing this challenge must recognize that the prevalent assumption in both counterinsurgency scholarship and U.S. doctrine – that patron-client preferences will closely align – is wrong. Although it is tempting to think that significant amounts of assistance will easily shape a client's behavior and policies, influence is more likely to flow from tight conditions on aid than from boundless generosity. These conditions must be carefully structured so that the requirements are measurable and achievable, and that the aid the client desires most – in all likelihood military aid – is offered as the reward. To enhance its leverage, a patron may need to press its client government hard to make reforms, even when it is at its weakest, rather than take immediate measures to strengthen it against the insurgents. These recommendations to condition aid to a friendly government, to bargain hard with it, and to exploit its vulnerability may run counter to the instincts of many policymakers. But sometimes being a good ally means being a stern friend.

Bibliography

Archival Sources

Alderman Library, University of Virginia
   Fredrick Nolting Papers
The Association for Diplomatic Studies and Training, Arlington, Virginia
   William Jeffras Dieterich Oral History
   James F. Mack Oral History
   Langhorne A. Motley Oral History
Center for Army Lessons Learned, Fort Leavenworth, Kansas
   MAAG Memos, Lessons Learned
Central Intelligence Agency Declassified Document Collection
   Human Rights in Latin America
Declassified Documents Reference Service, Farmington Hills, Michigan
Dwight D. Eisenhower Presidential Library, Abilene, Kansas
   Joseph M. Dodge Papers
Filipinas Heritage Library, Manila, Philippines
   Elpidio R. Quirino Papers
Hoover Institution Archive, Stanford University
   Charles Bohannan Papers
   Elbridge Durbrow Papers
   Edward Lansdale Papers
   Samuel T. Williams Papers
John F. Kennedy Presidential Library, Boston, Massachusetts
   National Security Files
   Presidential Papers
   Presidential Recordings
Library of Congress, Hispanic Reading Room, Washington, DC
   El Salvador Human Rights Collection

Lyndon B. Johnson Presidential Library, Austin, Texas
  William E. Colby Oral History
  Elbridge Durbrow Oral History
  Fredrick Nolting Oral History
  Rufus Phillips Oral History
  William Trueheart Oral History
  Samuel T. Williams Oral History
MacArthur Memorial Library and Archives, Norfolk, Virginia
  Records of General Headquarters, Supreme Commander for the
    Allied Powers, 1945–1951 (RG 5)
  General Douglas MacArthur's Private Correspondence,
    1848–1964 (RG 10)
National Archives of the United Kingdom, Kew, United Kingdom
  Records of the Foreign and Commonwealth Office
National Security Archive, George Washington University
  El Salvador: The Making of U.S. Policy, 1977–1984
  El Salvador: War, Peace, and Human Rights, 1980–1994
Harry S. Truman Presidential Library, Independence, Missouri
  Dean G. Acheson Papers
  Myron M. Cowen Papers
  John F. Melby Oral History
  John F. Melby Papers
  Official File
  Philippine General File
  President's Secretary's Files
  Theodore Tannenwold, Jr. Papers
Ramon Magsaysay Award Foundation, Manila, Philippines
  Charles Bohannan Oral History
  Jacinto Gavino Oral History
  Ramon Magsaysay Papers
  Osmundo Mondeñedo Oral History
Ronald W. Reagan Presidential Library, Simi Valley, California
  Country Files, NSC
  Roger Fontaine Files
  Latin American Affairs Directorate, NSC
  Office of the Assistant to the President for National Security
    Affairs
  Oliver L. North Files

University of the Philippines Diliman, Quezon City, Philippines
    Manuel A. Roxas Papers
U.S. Air Force Historical Research Agency, Maxwell, Alabama
    Edward Lansdale Oral History
U.S. Army Center for Military History, Washington, DC
    Samuel Myers Oral History
    John Ruggles Oral History
    Eugene Stein Oral History
U.S. Army Military History Institute, Carlisle, Pennsylvania
    Oral History of the Conflict in El Salvador
        Carlos Vides Casanova
        Edwin Corr
        Lyman Duryea
        Luigi Einaudi
        Jose Guillermo Garcia
        Jamie Guiterrez
        Deane Hinton
        Alvaro Magana
        Wallace Nutting
        Sigifredo Ochoa
        Thomas Pickering
        John D. Waghelstein
        Fred Woerner
    Senior Officer Debriefing Reports: Vietnam War 1962–1972
        Bryce Denno
        Hal McCowen
        George Morton
        Edward Rowny
    Samuel T. Williams Papers
    Wilbur Wilson Papers
U.S. National Archive at College Park, Maryland
    Records of the U.S. Department of State (RG 59)
    Records of the U.S. Joint Chiefs of Staff (RG 218)
    Records of the U.S. Secretary of Defense (RG 330)
    Records of Interservice Agencies (RG 334)
    Records of the U.S. Forces in Southeast Asia (RG 472)
U.S. State Department Declassified Document Collection
    El Salvador Churchwomen Documents
The Virtual Vietnam Archive, Texas Tech University
    Central Intelligence Agency Collection

Government Documents

Ahern, Thomas L., Jr., *CIA and the House of NGO: Covert Action in South Vietnam, 1954–1963* (Washington, DC: Center for the Study of Intelligence, 2000).

Bureau for Legislative and Public Affairs, "U.S. Overseas Loans and Grants: Obligations and Loan Authorizations, July 1, 1945–September 30, 2008," U.S. Agency for International Development, Washington, DC, 2008.

Bureau of Public Affairs, *U.S. Condemns Salvadoran Death Squads* (Washington, DC: Department of State, December 11, 1983).

Congressional Research Service, "El Salvador, 1979–1989," Library of Congress, Washington, DC, 1989.

El Salvador: Military Assistance Has Helped Counter but Not Overcome the Insurgency (Washington, DC: General Accounting Office, April 23, 1991).

Enders, Thomas, "El Salvador: The Search for Peace," *U.S. Department of State Bulletin* (September 1981).

Field Manual 3–24, *Insurgencies and Countering Insurgencies* (Washington, DC: Department of the Army, 2014).

"Foreign Assistance Program: FY1986 and 1985 Supplemental Request," U.S. Department of State, Washington, DC, May 1985.

Foreign Relations of the United States 1948, vol. I, part 2: *General*.

Foreign Relations of the United States 1950, vol. VI: *East Asia and the Pacific*.

Foreign Relations of the United States 1951, vol. VI: *East Asia and the Pacific*.

Foreign Relations of the United States 1952–1954, vol. XIII: *Indochina*, part 2.

Foreign Relations of the United States 1955–1957, vol. I: *Vietnam*.

Foreign Relations of the United States 1958–1960, vol. I: *Vietnam*.

Foreign Relations of the United States 1961–1963, vol. I: *Vietnam, 1961*.

Foreign Relations of the United States 1961–1963, vol. II: *Vietnam, 1962*.

Foreign Relations of the United States 1961–1963, vol. III: *Vietnam, January–August 1963*.

Foreign Relations of the United States 1961–1963, vol. IV: *Vietnam, August–December 1963*.

Foreign Relations of the United States 1964–1968, vol. I: *Vietnam, 1964*.

Hatfield, Mark, Jim Leach, and George Miller, *Bankrolling Failure: United States Policy in El Salvador and the Urgent Need for Reform* (Washington, DC: Arms Control and Foreign Policy Caucus, November 1987).

Kronstadt, K. Alan, *Pakistan-U.S. Relations: Issues for the 114th Congress* (Washington DC: Congressional Research Service, May 14, 2015).

Pakistan Assistance, GAO-11-786 R (Washington, DC: GAO, July 19, 2011).

The Pentagon Papers, Gravel Edition (Boston: Beacon Press, 1971).

Report of the Bipartisan Commission on Central America (Washington, DC: U.S. Government Printing Office, 1984).

Report to the President of the United States by the U.S. Economic Survey Mission to the Philippines (Washington, DC: U.S. Government Printing Office, October 1950).

Sustaining U.S. Global Leadership: Priorities for 21st Century Defense (Washington, DC: Department of Defense, 2012).

UN Security Council, *From Madness to Hope: The 12-year War in El Salvador*. Report of the Commission on the Truth for El Salvador, S/25500 (New York: UN, 1993).

U.S. Army/Marine Corps, *Counterinsurgency Field Manual* (Chicago: University of Chicago Press, 2007).

U.S. Department of State, *U.S. Government Counterinsurgency Guide* (Washington, DC: Bureau of Political-Military Affairs, January 2009).

U.S. Department of State, *American Foreign Policy: Current Documents, 1981* (Washington, DC: U.S. Government Printing Office, 1982).

U.S. Department of State, *American Foreign Policy: Current Documents, 1983* (Washington, DC: U.S. Government Printing Office, 1984).

U.S. House of Representatives, *Foreign Assistance Legislation for Fiscal Years 1986–1987, Part 6*.

U.S. House of Representatives, *Presidential Certification on El Salvador* (Washington, DC: U.S. Government Printing Office, 1982).

U.S. House of Representatives, *The Situation in El Salvador: Hearings before the Subcommittee on Human Rights* (Washington, DC: U.S. Government Printing Office, 1984).

United States–Vietnam Relations, 1945–1967: A Study Prepared by the Department of Defense (Washington, DC: U.S. Government Printing Office, 1971).

Vest, George S., Richard Murphy, and I. M. Destler, *Report on the Secretary of State's Panel on El Salvador* (Washington, DC: Department of State, July 1993).

Secondary Sources

Abaya, Hernando, *Betrayal in the Philippines* (New York: A.A. Wyn, 1946).

Abueva, Jose Veloso, *Ramon Magsaysay* (Manila: Solidaridad Publishing House, 1971).

Acheson, Dean, *Present at the Creation* (New York: W.W. Norton, 1969).

Almond, Gabriel, *The Appeals of Communism* (Princeton, NJ: Princeton University Press, 1954).

Armstrong, Adrienne, "The Political Consequences of Economic Dependence," *Journal of Conflict Resolution*, 25, no. 3 (1981), pp. 401–28.

Arnson, Cynthia, *Crossroads: Congress, the President, and Central America, 1976–1992* (State College, PA: Pennsylvania State University Press, 1993).

Arreguin-Toft, Ivan, "How the Weak Win Wars: A Theory of Asymmetric Conflict," *International Security*, 26, no. 1 (Summer 2001), pp. 93–128.

Axelrod, Robert, *The Evolution of Cooperation* (New York: Basic Books, 1984).

Bacevich, Andrew J., James Hallums, Richard White, and Thomas Young, *American Military Policy in Small Wars: The Case of El Salvador* (Boston: Potomac Books, 1988).

Baldwin, David A., *Economic Statecraft* (Princeton, NJ: Princeton University Press, 1985).

Baldwin, David A., "The Power of Positive Sanctions," *World Politics*, 24, no. 1 (1971), pp. 19–38.

Baloyra, Enrique, "The Salvadoran Elections of 1982–1991," *Studies in Comparative International Development*, 28, no. 3 (Fall 1993), pp. 3–30.

Barnett, Michael N., and Jack S. Levy, "Domestic Sources of Alliances and Alignments: The Case of Egypt, 1962–73," *International Organization*, 45, no. 3 (Summer 1991), pp. 369–95.

Bauer, P. T., *Equality, the Third World, and Economic Delusion* (Cambridge, MA: Harvard University Press, 1981).

Beckett, Ian, *The Roots of Counter-Insurgency: Armies and Guerrilla Warfare 1900–1945* (London: Blandford, 1988).

Beckett, Ian, and John Pimlott, *Armed Forces and Modern Counter-Insurgency* (London: Croom Helm, 1985).

Beede, Benjamin R., *Intervention and Counterinsurgency* (New York: Garland, 1985).

Beinart, Peter, "The Surge Fallacy," *The Atlantic*, September 2015.

Ben-Zvi, Abraham, *The United States and Israel: The Limits of the Special Relationship* (New York: Columbia University Press, 1994).

Bercovitch, Jacob, "Superpowers and Client States: Analyzing Relations and Patterns of Influence," in Moshe Efrat and Jacob Bercovitch, eds., *Superpowers and Client States in the Middle East: The Imbalance of Influence* (London: Routledge, 1991).

Bergerud, Eric, *Dynamics of Defeat: The Vietnam War in Hau Nghia Province* (Boulder, CO: Westview Press, 1993).

Berlin, Donald, "Prelude to Martial Law: An Examination of Pre-1972 Philippine Civil-Military Relations," Ph.D. dissertation, University of Southern Carolina, 1974.

Betts, Richard, "The Tragicomedy of Arms Trade Control," *International Security*, 5, no. 1 (Summer 1980), pp. 80–110.

Biddle, Stephen, "The New U.S. Army/Marine Corps Counterinsurgency Field Manual as Political Science and Political Praxis," *Perspectives on Politics*, 6, no. 2 (June 2008), pp. 347–50.

Biddle, Stephen, Jeffrey Friedman, and Jacob Shapiro, "Testing the Surge, Why Did Violence Decline in Iraq in 2007?" *International Security*, 37, no. 1 (Summer 2012), pp. 7–40.

Bird, Shawn, and Philip Williams, "El Salvador: Revolt and Negotiated Transition," in Thomas W. Walker and Ariel C. Armony, eds., *Repression, Resistance, and Democratic Transition in Central America* (Wilmington, DE: Scholarly Resources, 2000).

Birtle, Andrew, *U.S. Army Counterinsurgency and Contingency Operations Doctrine, 1942–1976* (Washington, DC: Center of Military History, 2007).

Blaufarb, Douglas S., *The Counterinsurgency Era: U.S. Doctrine and Performance, 1950 to the Present* (New York: Free Press, 1977).

Blechman, Barry M., Janne E. Nolan, and Alan Platt, "Negotiated Limitations on Arms Transfers: First Steps towards Crisis Prevention?" in Alexander L. George, ed., *Managing U.S.-Soviet Rivalry: Problems of Crisis Prevention* (Boulder, CO: Westview Press, 1983).

Blessing, James A., "The Suspension of Foreign Aid: A Macro-Analysis," *Polity*, 13, no. 3 (Spring 1981), pp. 524–35.

Bohannan, Charles T., "Antiguerrilla Operations," *Annals of the American Academy of Political and Social Sciences*, 341 (May 1962), pp. 19–29.

Bosch, Brian, *The Salvadoran Officer Corps and the Final Offensive* (London: McFarland, 1999).

Boyce, James, *Investing in Peace* (Oxford: Oxford University Press, 2002).

Brady, Henry, and David Collier, *Rethinking Social Inquiry: Diverse Tools, Shared Standards* (Oxford: Rowman & Littlefield, 2004).

Brands, Hal, *Latin America's Cold War* (Cambridge, MA: Harvard University Press, 2010).

Brinkley, Douglas, ed., *The Reagan Diaries* (New York: HarperCollins, 2009).

Brown, Stephen, "Donors' Dilemmas in Democratization: Foreign Aid and Political Reform in Africa," Ph.D. dissertation, New York University, 2000.

Buchanan, James M., "The Samaritan's Dilemma," in Edmund S. Phelps, ed., *Altruism, Morality and Economic Theory* (New York: Sage, 1975).

Bueno de Mesquita, Bruce, *Principles of International Politics* (Washington, DC: CQ Press, 2009).

Bueno de Mesquita, Bruce, Alastair Smith, Randolph Siverson, and James Morrow, *The Logic of Political Survival* (Cambridge, MA: MIT Press, 2003).

Bueno de Mesquita, Bruce, James Morrow, and Alastair Smith, "Foreign Aid and Policy Concessions," *Journal of Conflict Resolution*, 51, no. 2 (2007), pp. 251–84.

Bueno de Mesquita, Bruce, James Morrow, Randolph Siverson, and Alastair Smith, "An Institutional Explanation of the Democratic Peace," *American Political Science Review*, 93, no. 4 (December 1999), pp. 791–807.

Bull, Bartle Breese, "The Wrong Force for the 'Right War,'" *New York Times*, August 14, 2008.

Buss, Arnold, *The Psychology of Aggression* (New York: Wiley, 1961).

Byman, Daniel L., "Friends Like These: Counterinsurgency and the War on Terrorism," *International Security*, 31, no. 2 (Fall 2006), pp. 79–115.

Byman, Daniel L., "Going to War with the Allies You Have: Allies, Counterinsurgency and the War on Terrorism," Strategic Studies Institute, Carlisle, PA, 2006.

Byman, Daniel L., "The Intelligence War on Terrorism," *Intelligence and National Security*, 29, no. 6 (2014), pp. 850, 859–60.

Byman, Daniel L., and Matthew Waxman, *The Dynamics of Coercion: American Foreign Policy and the Limits of Military Might* (New York: Cambridge University Press, 2002).

Byrne, Hugh, *El Salvador's Civil War: A Study of Revolution* (Boulder, CO: Lynne Rienner, 1996).

Cable, Larry E., *Conflict of Myths: The Development of American Counterinsurgency Doctrine during the Vietnam War* (New York: New York University Press, 1986).

Carney, Christopher, "International Patron-Client Relationships: A Conceptual Framework," *Studies in Comparative International Development*, 24, no. 2 (1989), pp. 42–55.

Cassidy, Robert M., "Back to the Street without Joy: Counterinsurgency Lessons from Vietnam and Other Small Wars," *Parameters*, XXXIV, no. 2 (Summer 2004), pp. 73–83.

Castellanos, Miguel, *The Comandante Speaks: Memoirs of an El Salvadoran Guerrilla Leader* (Boulder, CO: Westview Press, 1991).

Catrina, Christian, *Arms Transfers and Dependence* (New York: Taylor & Francis, 1988).

Catton, Philip, *Diem's Final Failure: Prelude to America's War in Vietnam* (Lawrence: University Press of Kansas, 2003).

Chau, Tran Ngoc, "From Ho Chi Minh to Ngo Dinh Diem," in Harvey C. Neese and John O'Donnell, eds., *Prelude to Tragedy: Vietnam, 1960–1965* (Annapolis, MD: Naval Institute Press, 2001).

Childress, Michael, *The Effectiveness of U.S. Training Efforts in Internal Defense and Development* (Santa Monica, CA: RAND, 1995).

Ciorciari, John D., "A Chinese Model for Patron-Client Relations? The Sino-Cambodian Partnership," *International Relations of the Asia-Pacific*, 15, no. 2 (May 2015), pp. 245–78.

Clancy, James, and Chuck Crossett, "Measuring Effectiveness in Irregular Warfare," *Parameters*, 37, no. 2 (Summer 2007), pp. 88–100.

Cohen, Craig, and Derek Chollet, "When $10 Billion Is Not Enough: Rethinking U.S. Strategy towards Pakistan," *Washington Quarterly*, 30, no. 2 (Spring 2007), pp. 7–19.

Colby, William, *Lost Victory: A Firsthand Account of America's Sixteen-Year Involvement in Vietnam* (Chicago: Contemporary Books, 1989).

Collier, David, and James Mahoney, "Insights and Pitfalls: Selection Bias in Qualitative Research," *World Politics*, 49, no. 1 (1996), pp. 56–91.

Collier, Paul, Patrick Guillaumont, Sylviane Guillaumont, and Jan Willem Gunning, "Redesigning Conditionality," *World Development*, 25, no. 9 (1997), pp. 1399–407.

Collins, James L., *The Development and Training of the South Vietnamese Army, 1950–1972* (Washington, DC: Center of Military History, 1975).

The Constabulary Story (Quezon City: Public Information Office, 1982).

Cortright, David, *The Price of Peace: Incentives and International Conflict Prevention* (Lanham, MD: Rowman & Littlefield, 1997).

Corum, James S., and Wray R. Johnson, *Airpower in Small Wars: Fighting Insurgents and Terrorists* (Manhattan: University Press of Kansas, 2003).

Cosmas, Graham, *MACV: The Joint Command in the Years of Escalation, 1962–1967* (Washington, DC: Center for Military History, 2005).

Cottam, Richard W., *Competitive Interference and Twentieth Century Diplomacy* (Pittsburgh: University of Pittsburgh Press, 1967).

Crandall, Russell, *The Salvador Option: The United States in El Salvador, 1977–1992* (Cambridge: Cambridge University Press, 2016).

Crawford, Gordon, *Foreign Aid and Political Reform: A Comparative Analysis of Democracy Assistance and Political Conditionality* (New York: Palgrave, 2001).

Cross, James E., *Conflict in the Shadows: The Nature and Politics of Guerrilla War* (New York: Doubleday, 1963).

Crozier, Brian, *The Rebels* (Boston: Beacon Press, 1960).

Currey, Cecil, *Edward Lansdale, the Unquiet American* (Washington, DC: Brassey's, 1998).

Dacy, Douglas C., *Foreign Aid, War and Economic Development: South Vietnam, 1955–1975* (Cambridge: Cambridge University Press, 1986).

Danner, Mark, *The Massacre at El Mozote: A Parable of the Cold War* (New York: Vintage, 1994).

David, Steven R., *Choosing Sides: Alignment and Realignment in the Third World* (Baltimore: Johns Hopkins University Press, 1991).

Davidson, Janine, *Lifting the Fog of Peace* (Ann Arbor: University of Michigan Press, 2010).

Djankov, Simeon, José Garcia Montalvo, and Marta Reynal-Querol, "The Curse of Aid," *Economics Working Papers 870* (Department of Economics and Business, Universitat Pompeu Fabra, 2005).

Dockery, Martin, *Lost in Translation: A Combat Advisor's Story* (New York: Ballantine, 2003).

Dollar, Dave, and Lant Pritchett, *Assessing Aid: What Works, What Doesn't and Why* (New York: Oxford University Press, 1998).

Don, Tran Van, *Our Endless War* (San Rafael, CA: Presidio Press, 1978).

Doohovskoy, Andrei, "Soviet Counterinsurgency in the Soviet Afghan War Revisited," Master's thesis, Harvard University, September, 2009.

Downes, Alexander, "Draining the Sea by Filling the Graves: Investigating the Effectiveness of Indiscriminate Violence as a Counterinsurgency Strategy," *Civil Wars*, 9, no. 4 (December 2007), pp. 420–44.

Drazen, Allan, *Political Economy in Macroeconomics* (Princeton, NJ: Princeton University Press, 2000).

Drazen, Allan, "What Is Gained by Selectively Withholding Foreign Aid?" working paper, University of Maryland and NBER, April 1999.

Drezner, Daniel, "Are Carrots and Sticks Good for You? The Utility of Economic Statecraft," Ph.D. dissertation, Stanford University, 1996.

Drezner, Daniel, *The Sanctions Paradox: Economic Statecraft and International Relations* (Cambridge: Cambridge University Press, 1999).

Duarte, José Napoleon, *Duarte: My Story* (New York: G.P. Putnam's Sons, 1986).

Duiker, William, *The Communist Road to Power in Vietnam* (Boulder, CO: Westview Press, 1981).

Duncanson, Dennis, *Government and Revolution in Vietnam* (London: Oxford University Press, 1968).

Dwyer, F. Robert, and Orville C. Walker, "Bargaining in an Asymmetric Power Structure," *Journal of Marketing*, 55, no. 1 (Winter 1981), pp. 104–15.

Fair, C. Christine, "Time for Sober Realism: Renegotiating U.S. Relations with Pakistan," *Washington Quarterly*, 32, no. 2 (April 2009), pp. 149–72.

Fair, C. Christine, and Sumit Ganguly, "An Unworthy Ally," *Foreign Affairs*, 94, no. 5 (September–October 2015), pp. 160–70.

Fall, Bernard, *The Two Viet-Nams: A Political and Military Analysis* (London: Praeger, 1963).

Fearon, James, "Domestic Political Audiences and the Escalation of International Disputes," *American Political Science Review*, 88, no. 3 (September 1994), pp. 577–92.

Fearon, James, "Rationalist Explanations for War," *International Organization*, 49, no. 3 (1995), pp. 379–414.

Fearon, James, and David Laitin, "Ethnicity, Insurgency and Civil War," *American Political Science Review*, 97, no. 1 (February 2003), pp. 75–90.

Felter, Joseph H., "Taking Guns to a Knife Fight: A Case for Empirical Study of Counterinsurgency," Ph.D. dissertation, Stanford University, 2005.

Feng, Yi, "Political Freedom, Political Instability and Policy Uncertainty: A Study of Political Institutions and Private Investments in Developing Countries," *International Studies Quarterly*, 45, no. 2 (June 2001), pp. 271–94.

Fernandez-Arias, Eduardo, "Crisis, Foreign Aid, and Macroeconomic Reform," paper presented at the Fifteenth Meeting of the Latin American Econometric Society, Santiago, Chile, March 1997.

Finel, Bernard, "A Substitute for Victory," *Foreign Affairs*, April 8, 2010, available at www.foreignaffairs.com/articles/66189/bernard-finel/a-substitute-for-victory.

Fishel, John T., and Max G. Manwaring, *Uncomfortable Wars Revisited* (Norman: University of Oklahoma Press, 2006).

Fisher, Roger, *International Conflict for Beginners* (New York: Harper & Row, 1969).

Fisher, Ross A., "The Kennedy Administration and the Overthrow of Ngo Dinh Diem," in Ross A. Fisher, John Norton Moore, and Robert F. Turner, eds., *To Oppose Any Foe: The Legacy of U.S. Intervention in Vietnam* (Durham, NC: Carolina Academic Press, 2006).

Forbes, Elise, "Our Man in Kinshasa: U.S. Relations with Mobutu 1970–1983," Ph.D. dissertation, Johns Hopkins University, 1987.

Fox, Annette Baker, "The Power of Small States: Diplomacy in World War II," in Christine Ingebritsen, Iver Neumann, Sieglinde Gstohl, and Jessica Beyer, eds., *Small States in International Relations* (Seattle: University of Washington Press, 2006).

Freedman, Lawrence, *Kennedy's Wars: Berlin, Cuba, Laos, and Vietnam* (Oxford: Oxford University Press, 2000).

Gaddis, John Lewis, "On Starting All over Again: A Naive Approach to the Study of the Cold War," in O. A. Westad, ed., *Reviewing the Cold War: Approaches, Interpretations, Theory* (London: Frank Cass, 2000).

Galtung, Johan, "A Structural Theory of Imperialism," *Journal of Peace Research*, 8, no. 2 (1971), pp. 81–117.

Galula, David, *Counter-Insurgency Warfare: Theory and Practice* (London: Pall Mall Press, 1964).

Gandara, Arturo, and Caesar Sereseres, *U.S.-Latin American Relations under the Carter Administration* (Santa Monica, CA: RAND, 1980).

Garcia, José, "El Salvador: Legitimizing the Government," *Current History*, 84, no. 500 (March 1985), pp. 101–36.

Gelb, Leslie, "Vietnam: The System Worked," *Foreign Policy*, no. 3 (Summer 1971), pp. 141–4.

Gentile, Gian, "A Requiem for American Counterinsurgency," *Orbis*, 57, no. 4 (Autumn 2013), pp. 549–58.

George, Alexander L., *Presidential Decision Making in Foreign Policy* (Boulder, CO: Westview Press, 1980).

George, Alexander L., *Bridging the Gap* (Washington, DC: U.S. Institute of Peace, 1993).

George, Alexander L., "Knowledge for Statecraft: The Challenge for Political Science and History," *International Security*, 22, no. 1 (Summer 1997), pp. 44–52.

George, Alexander L., and Andrew Bennett, *Case Studies and Theory Development in the Social Sciences* (London: MIT Press, 2005).

George, Alexander L., and Richard Smoke, *Deterrence in American Foreign Policy: Theory and Practice* (New York: Columbia University Press, 1974).

Gerring, John, "What Is a Case Study and What Is It Good For?" *American Political Science Review*, 98, no. 2 (May 2004), pp. 341–54.

Gibbons, William, *The U.S. Government and the Vietnam War* (Princeton, NJ: Princeton University Press, 1986).

Gilpin, Robert, *U.S. Power and the Multinational Corporation: The Political Economy of Foreign Direct Investment* (New York: Basic Books, 1975).

Girod, Desha, "Foreign Aid and Post-Conflict Reconstruction," Ph.D. dissertation, Stanford University, 2008.

Gleditsch, Kristian, "Expanded Trade and GDP Data," *Journal of Conflict Resolution*, 46 (2002), pp. 712–24.

Golay, Frank, *The Philippines: Public Policy and National Economic Development* (Ithaca, NY: Cornell University Press, 1961).

Goldberg, Jeffrey, and Marc Ambinder, "The Ally from Hell," *The Atlantic*, December 2011.

Goldstone, Jack A., "An Analytical Framework," in Jack A. Goldstone, ed., *Revolutions of the Late Twentieth Century* (Boulder, CO: Westview Press, 1991).

Gordon, D. F., "Conditionality in Policy-Based Lending in Africa: USAID Experience," in Paul Mosley, ed., *Development Finance and Policy Reform* (London: Macmillan, 1992).

Grant, Thomas, "Government, Politics, and Low-Intensity Conflict," in Edwin Corr and Stephen Sloan, eds., *Low-Intensity Conflict: Old Threats in a New World* (Boulder, CO: Westview Press, 1992).

Greenberg, Lawrence, *The Hukbalahap Insurrection* (Washington, DC: U.S. Army Center of Military History, 1987).

Greene, Thomas, *Comparative Revolutionary Movements: Search for Theory and Justice* (London: Prentice-Hall International, 1990).

Greentree, Todd, *Crossroads of Intervention: Insurgency and Counterinsurgency Lessons from Central America* (Westport, CT: Praeger, 2008).

Guevara, Ernesto, *On Guerrilla Warfare* (New York: Praeger, 1962).

Gurr, Ted, *Why Men Rebel* (Princeton, NJ: Princeton University Press, 1974).

Hackworth, David, and Julie Sherman, *About Face* (New York: Simon & Schuster, 1989).

Haig, Alexander M., *Caveat* (New York: Macmillan, 1984).

Hamilton, Donald R., "Strategic Communications in El Salvador 1982–1986: A Personal Perspective," Center for Hemispheric Defense, Santiago, Chile, 2003.

Hamilton, Donald R., "Strategic Communications in El Salvador 1982–1986: A Personal Perspective," Washington, DC, September 13, 2010.

Hammer, Ellen, *A Death in November: America in Vietnam 1963* (New York: Dutton, 1987).

Handel, Michael, "Does the Dog Wag the Tail or Vice Versa? Patron-Client Relations," *Jerusalem Journal of International Relations*, 6, no. 2 (1982), pp. 24–35.

Handel, Michael, *Weak States in the International System* (London: Frank Cass, 1990).

Harford, Tim, and Michael Klein, "Aid and the Resource Curse," *View Points 291* (Washington, DC: World Bank, 2005).

Harkavy, Robert, *Arms Trade and International Systems* (Cambridge, MA: Ballinger, 1975).

Harnecker, Marta, *Pueblos En Armas* (Mexico City: Universidad Autónoma de Guerrero, 1983).

Harris, Louis, *The Anguish of Change* (New York: W.W. Norton, 1973).

Hart, Donn, "Magsaysay: Philippine Candidate," *Far Eastern Survey*, 22, no. 6 (May 1953), pp. 67–70.

Hartendorp, A. V. H., *History of Industry and Trade of the Philippines* (Manila: ACCP, 1958).

Hellmann, John, *American Myth and the Legacy of Vietnam* (New York: Columbia University Press, 1986).

Helman, Joseph, "The Politics of Patron-Client State Relationships: The United States and Israel, 1948–1992," Ph.D. dissertation, George Washington University, 2002.

Henderson, William, "South Viet Nam Finds Itself," *Foreign Affairs*, 35, no. 2 (January 1957), pp. 283–94.

Herring, George C., *America's Longest War: The United States and Vietnam, 1950–1975* (Philadelphia: Temple University Press, 1986).

Hibbs, Douglas A., *Mass Political Violence: A Cross-National Causal Analysis* (New York: Wiley, 1973).

Hilsman, Roger, "Internal War: The New Communist Tactic," in Thomas Greene, ed., *The Guerrilla and How to Fight Him* (New York: Praeger: 1962).

Hilsman, Roger, *To Move a Nation: The Politics of Foreign Policy in the Administration of John F. Kennedy* (Garden City, NJ: Doubleday, 1967).

Hoffmann, Stanley, "Restraints and Choices in American Foreign Policy," *Daedelus*, 91 (Fall 1962), pp. 668–704.

Hoffmann, Stanley, *Gulliver's Troubles: The Setting of American Foreign Policy* (New York: McGraw-Hill, 1968).

Holsti, K. J., *International Politics: A Framework for Analysis* (Englewood Cliffs, NJ: Prentice-Hall, 1977).

Holsti, Ole, *Public Opinion and American Foreign Policy* (Ann Arbor: University of Michigan Press, 2004).

Hoyt, Timothy D., "Pakistan, an Ally by Any Other Name," *U.S. Naval Institute Proceedings*, 137/7/1,301 (July 2011).

Huntington, Samuel P., and Joan M. Nelson, *No Easy Choice: Political Participation in Developing Countries* (Cambridge, MA: Harvard University Press, 1976).

Huth, Paul, "Deterrence and International Conflict," *Annual Review of Political Science*, 2 (1999), pp. 25–48.

Huth, Paul, and Bruce Russett, "Deterrence Failure and Crisis Escalation," *International Studies Quarterly*, 32, no. 1 (1988), pp. 29–45.

Isham, Jonathan, Daniel Kaufmann, and Lant Pritchett, "Civil Liberties, Democracy and the Performance of Government Projects," *World Bank Economic Review*, 11, no. 2 (1997), pp. 219–42.

Jensen, Lloyd, "Negotiating Strategic Arms Control, 1969–1979," *Journal of Conflict Resolution*, 28, no. 3 (September 1984), pp. 535–59.

Jensen, Michael, and William Meckling, "Theory of the Firm: Managerial Behavior, Agency Costs and Ownership Structure," *Journal of Financial Economics*, 3, no. 4 (October 1976), pp. 305–60.

Jentleson, Bruce, "American Commitments in the Third World: Theory vs. Practice," *International Organization*, 41, no. 4 (Autumn 1987), pp. 667–704.

Jervis, Robert, *The Logic of Images in International Relations* (Princeton, NJ: Princeton University Press, 1970).

Jervis, Robert, "Deterrence Theory Revisited," *World Politics*, 31, no. 2 (January 1979), pp. 289–324.

Joes, Anthony James, *America and Guerrilla Warfare* (Lexington: University Press of Kentucky, 2000).

Joes, Anthony James, *Resisting Rebellion: The History and Politics of Counterinsurgency* (Lexington: University Press of Kentucky, 2004).

Johnson, Chalmers A., "Civilian Loyalties and Guerrilla Conflict," *World Politics*, 14, no. 4 (July 1962), pp. 646–61.

Johnstone, Ian, "Rights and Reconciliation in El Salvador," in Michael Doyle, Ian Jonstone, and Robert Orr, eds., *Keeping the Peace: Multidimensional UN Operations in Cambodia and El Salvador* (Cambridge: Cambridge University Press, 1997).

Jones, Howard, *Death of a Generation* (Oxford: Oxford University Press, 2003).

Kagan, Robert, *A Twilight Struggle: American Power and Nicaragua, 1977–1990* (New York: Free Press, 1996).

Kahin, George McTurnan, *Intervention: How America Became Involved in Vietnam* (New York: Knopf, 1986).

Kalyvas, Stathis, "New and Old Civil Wars: A Valid Distinction?" *World Politics*, 54, no. 1 (October 2001), pp. 99–118.

Kalyvas, Stathis, *The Logic of Violence in Civil War* (Cambridge: Cambridge University Press, 2006).

Kalyvas, Stathis, and Laia Balcells, "International System and Technologies of Rebellion: How the Cold War Shaped Internal Conflict," *American Political Science Review*, 104, no. 3 (2010), pp. 415–29.

Kaplan, Jacob J., *The Challenge of Foreign Aid* (New York: Praeger, 1967).

Karl, Terry, "After La Palma: Christian Democracy, U.S. Policy, and the Prospects for Democratization in El Salvador," *World Policy Journal* (Winter 1985), pp. 305–30.

Karl, Terry, "The Perils of the Petro-State: Reflections on the Paradox of Plenty," *Journal of International Affairs*, 53, no. 1 (Fall 1999), pp. 31–48.

Karnow, Stanley, *Vietnam: A History* (London: Pimlico, 1994).

Kennan, George, *Realities of American Foreign Policy* (New York: W.W. Norton, 1966).

Kennedy, John F., "Inaugural Address," Washington, DC, January 20, 1961.

Kennedy, John F., "America's Stake in Vietnam," in Wesley Fishel, ed., *Vietnam: Anatomy of a Conflict* (Itasca, IL: F.E. Peacock, 1968).

Keohane, Robert, "Political Influence in the General Assembly," *International Conciliation*, no. 557 (1966), pp. 1–64.

Keohane, Robert, "The Big Influence of Small Allies," *Foreign Policy*, no. 2 (Spring 1971), pp. 161–82.

Keohane, Robert, "Theory of World Politics: Structural Realism and Beyond," in Robert O. Keohane, ed., *Neorealism and Its Critics* (New York: Columbia University Press, 1986), pp. 158–203.

Kerkvliet, Benedict, *The Huk Rebellion: A Study of Peasant Revolt in the Philippines* (Los Angeles: University of California Press, 1977).

Kiewiet, Roderick, and Matthew McCubbins, *The Logic of Delegation: Congressional Parties and the Appropriation Process* (Chicago: University of Chicago Press, 1991).

Kilcullen, David, *The Accidental Guerrilla: Fighting Small Wars in the Midst of a Big One* (Oxford: Oxford University Press, 2009).

Kilcullen, David, *Counterinsurgency* (Oxford: Oxford University Press, 2010).

Kilcullen, David, "Two Schools of Classical Counterinsurgency," *Small Wars Journal*, January 27, 2007, available at http://smallwarsjournal .com/printpdf/6415.

King, Gary, Robert O. Keohane, and Sidney Verba, *Designing Social Inquiry* (Princeton, NJ: Princeton University Press, 1994).

Kirkpatrick, Jeane, "Dictatorships and Double Standards," *Commentary*, 68, no. 5 (November 1979), pp. 34–45.

Kitson, Frank, *Low Intensity Operations: Subversion, Insurgency, Peacekeeping* (London: Faber & Faber, 1971).

Klare, Michael, *American Arms Supermarket* (Austin: University of Texas Press, 1984).

Klare, Michael, "The Deadly Connection: Paramilitary Bands, Small Arms Diffusion and State Failure," in Robert Rotberg, ed., *When States Fail: Causes and Consequences* (Princeton, NJ: Princeton University Press, 2003).

Klare, Michael, and Peter Kornbluh, *Low Intensity Warfare: Counterinsurgency, Proinsurgency, and Antiterrorism in the Eighties* (New York: Pantheon Books, 1988).

Knorr, Klaus, *On the Uses of Military Power in the Nuclear Age* (Princeton, NJ: Princeton University Press, 1966).

Knorr, Klaus, *The Power of Nations: The Political Economy of International Relations* (New York: Basic Books, 1975).

Knorr, Klaus, "International Economic Leverage and Its Uses," in Klaus Knorr and Frank Trager, eds., *Economic Issues and National Security* (Lawrence: University of Kansas Press, 1977).

Kolko, Gabriel, *Vietnam: Anatomy of a War, 1940–75* (New York: HarperCollins, 1986).

Kotowitz, Yehuda, "Moral Hazard," in John Eatwell, Murray Milgate, and Peter Newman, eds., *The New Palgrave: A Dictionary of Economics* (New York: W.W. Norton, 1987).

Krause, Keith, "Military Statecraft: Power and Influence in Soviet and American Arms Transfer Relationships," *International Studies Quarterly*, 35, no. 3 (1991), pp. 313–36.

Krepinevich, Andrew F., *The Army and Vietnam* (Baltimore: Johns Hopkins University Press, 1986).

Lachica, Eduardo, *The Huks: Philippine Agrarian Society in Revolt* (London: Praeger, 1971).

Ladwig, Walter C., III, "Managing Counterinsurgency: Lessons from Malaya," *Military Review*, 87, no. 3 (May–June 2007), pp. 56–66.

Ladwig, Walter C., III, "When the Police Are the Problem: The Philippine Constabulary and the Hukbalahap Rebellion," in C. Christine Fair and Sumit Ganguly, eds., *Policing Insurgencies: Cops as Counterinsurgents* (Oxford: Oxford University Press, 2014), pp. 19–45.

Ladwig, Walter C., III, "Influencing Clients in Counterinsurgency: U.S. Involvement in El Salvador's Civil War, 1979–92," *International Security*, 41, no. 1 (Summer 2016), pp. 99–146.

Laffont, Jean-Jacques, and David Martimort, *The Theory of Incentives: The Principal-Agent Model* (Princeton, NJ: Princeton University Press, 2002).

Lall, Arthur, *Modern International Negotiation: Principles and Practice* (New York: Columbia University Press, 1966).

Landau, Saul, *The Guerrilla Wars of Central America* (New York: St. Martin's Press, 1993).

Lande, Carl, "The Dyadic Basis of Clientelism," in Steffen W. Schmidt, Laura Guasti, Carl Lande, and James Scott, eds. (Berkeley: University of California Press, 1977).

Lansdale, Edward G., *In the Midst of Wars: An American's Mission to Southeast Asia* (New York: Harper & Row, 1972).

Laqueur, Walter, *Guerrilla: A Historical and Critical Study* (Boston: Little Brown, 1976).

Laqueur, Walter, *Guerrilla Warfare: A Historical and Critical Study* (New Brunswick, NJ: Transaction, 1998).

Larson, Deborah Welch, "Crisis Prevention and the Austrian State Treaty," *International Organization*, 41, no. 1 (Winter 1987), pp. 27–60.

Lawrence, T. E., *Seven Pillars of Wisdom* (Garden City, NY: Doubleday, 1935).

Lebow, Richard Ned, *The Art of Bargaining* (Baltimore: Johns Hopkins University Press, 1996).

Ledeen, Michael, and Michael Lewis, *Debacle: The American Failure in Iran* (New York: Knopf, 1981).

Leites, Nathan, and Charles Wolf, *Rebellion and Authority: An Analytic Essay on Insurgent Conflicts* (Santa Monica, CA: RAND, 1970).

LeMoyne, James, "El Salvador's Forgotten War," *Foreign Affairs*, 68, no. 3 (Summer 1989), pp. 105–25.

LeoGrande, William, "A Splendid Little War: Drawing the Line in El Salvador," *International Security*, 6, no. 1 (Summer 1981), pp. 27–52.

LeoGrande, William, *Our Own Backyard: The United States in Central America, 1977–1993* (Chapel Hill: University of North Carolina Press, 1998).

Lewis, William, "Political Influence: The Diminished Capacity," in Stephanie Neuman and Robert Harkavy, eds., *Arms Transfers in the Modern World* (New York: Praeger, 1979).

Lewy, Guenter, *America in Vietnam* (New York: Oxford University Press, 1978).

Lichbach, Mark I., *The Rebel's Dilemma* (Ann Arbor: University of Michigan Press, 1995).

Licklider, Roy E., "How Civil Wars End: Questions and Methods," in Roy E. Licklider, ed., *Stopping the Killing: How Civil Wars End* (London: New York University Press, 1993).

Licklider, Roy E., "The Consequences of Negotiated Settlements in Civil Wars, 1945–1993," *American Political Science Review*, 89, no. 3 (1995), pp. 681–90.

Lindell, Ulf, and Stefan Persson, "The Paradox of Weak State Power," in *International Relations: Contemporary Theory and Practice* (Washington, DC: CQ Press, 1989).

Long, William, *Economic Incentives and Bilateral Cooperation* (Ann Arbor: University of Michigan Press, 1996).

Lowi, Theodore, "Making Democracy Safe for the World: On Fighting the Next War," in John Ikenberry, ed., *American Foreign Policy: Theoretical Essays* (New York: HarperCollins, 1989).

Luckham, Robin, "Security and Disarmament in Africa," *Alternatives*, 9, no. 2 (Fall 1983), pp. 203–28.

Luttwak, Edward N., "Dead End: Counterinsurgency Warfare as Military Malpractice," *Harper's*, February 2007.

Lyall, Jason, "Does Indiscriminate Violence Incite Insurgent Attacks? Evidence from Chechnya." *Journal of Conflict Resolution*, 53, no. 3 (June 2009), pp. 331–62.

Macdonald, Douglas J., *Adventures in Chaos: American Intervention for Reform in the Third World* (Cambridge, MA: Harvard University Press, 1992).

Mahoney, James, and Dietrich Rueschemeyer, "Comparative Historical Analysis: Achievements and Agendas," in James Mahoney and Dietrich Rueschemeyer, eds., *Comparative Historical Analysis in the Social Sciences* (Cambridge: Cambridge University Press, 2003).

Manwaring, Max G., and Court Prisk, *El Salvador at War: An Oral History* (Washington, DC: National Defense University Press, 1988).

Martin-Baro, Ignacio, "La Guerra Civil En El Salvador," *Estudios Centroamericanos*, nos. 387–388 (January–February 1981).

McClintock, Cynthia, *Revolutionary Movements in Latin America: El Salvador's FMLN and Peru's Shining Path* (Washington, DC: USIP Press, 1998).

McCubbins, Matthew, Roger Noll, and Barry Weingast, "Administrative Procedures as Instruments of Political Control," *Journal of Law, Economics and Organization*, 3, no. 2 (Autumn 1987), pp. 243–77.

McCubbins, Matthew, and Thomas Schwartz, "Congressional Oversight Overlooked: Police Patrols versus Fire Alarms," *American Journal of Political Science*, 28, no. 1 (February 1984), pp. 165–79.

Meara, William, *Contra Cross: Insurgency and Tyranny in Central America, 1979–1989* (Annapolis, MD: Naval Institute Press, 2006).

Metz, Steven, "Rethinking Insurgency," Strategic Studies Institute, Carlisle, PA, 2007.

Miller, Edward, *Misalliance: Ngo Dinh Diem, the United States, and the Fate of South Vietnam* (Cambridge, MA: Harvard University Press, 2013).

Millman, Joel, "El Salvador's Army: A Force unto Itself," *New York Times Magazine*, December 10, 1989.

Moaz, Zeev, "Power Capabilities and Paradoxical Conflict Outcomes," *World Politics*, 46, no. 2 (January 1989), pp. 239–66.

Moe, Terry, "The New Economics of Organization," *American Journal of Political Science*, 28, no. 4 (November 1984), pp. 739–77.

Montes, Segundo, "Hambre a Causa Del Armamentismo," *Estudios Centroamericanos*, nos. 429–430 (July–August 1984).

Montgomery, Tommie Sue, *Revolution in El Salvador: From Civil Strife to Civil Peace* (Boulder, CO: Westview Press, 1994).

Morgenthau, Hans, "Alliances in Theory and Practice," in Arnold Wolfers, ed., *Alliance Policy in the Cold War* (Baltimore: Johns Hopkins University Press, 1959).

Morgenthau, Hans, "A Political Theory of Foreign Aid," *American Political Science Review*, 56 (June 1962), pp. 287–305.

Morgenthau, Hans, *Politics Among Nations: The Struggle for Power and Peace* (New York: Knopf, 1967).

Mott, William, *United States Military Assistance: An Empirical Perspective* (Westport, CT: Greenwood Press, 2002).

Mouritsen, David Jeffrey, "The United States in El Salvador, 1979–1992: Success through the Eyes of the Diplomats," Master's thesis, Brigham Young University, June 2003.

Moyar, Mark, *Triumph Forsaken: The Vietnam War, 1954–1965* (New York: Cambridge University Press, 2006).

Moyar, Mark, *A Question of Command: Counterinsurgency from the Civil War to Iraq* (New Haven, CT: Yale University Press, 2009).

Muller, Edward, and Mitchell Seligson, "Inequality and Insurgency," *American Political Science Review*, 81, no. 2 (June 1987), pp. 435–52.

Murphy, Kevin, Andrei Schleifer, and Robert Vishny, "Why Is Rent-Seeking So Costly to Growth," *American Economic Review*, 83, no. 2 (May 1993), pp. 409–14.

Nachimas, Nitza, *Transfer of Arms, Leverage and Peace in the Middle East* (Westport, CT: Greenwood Press, 1988).

Nagl, John A., *Learning to Eat Soup with a Knife: Counterinsurgency Lessons from Malaya and Vietnam* (London: Praeger, 2002).

Nelson, Joan, *Aid, Influence and Foreign Policy* (New York: Macmillan, 1968).

Nelson, Joan, and Stephanie Eglinton, *Global Goals, Contentious Means* (Washington, DC: Overseas Development Council, 1993).

Nincic, Miroslav, "The Logic of Positive Engagement: Dealing with Renegade Regimes," *International Studies Perspectives*, 7, no. 4 (November 2006), pp. 321–41.

Nincic, Miroslav, "Getting What You Want: Positive Inducements in International Relations," *International Security*, 35, no. 1 (Summer 2010), pp. 138–83.

Nixon, Richard, *Six Crises* (New York: Doubleday, 1962).

North, Douglas, John Wallis, and Barry Weingast, *Violence and Social Orders: A Conceptual Framework for Interpreting Recorded Human History* (Cambridge: Cambridge University Press, 2009).

O'Neill, Bard E., *Insurgency and Terrorism: Inside Modern Revolutionary Warfare* (Washington, DC: Potomac Books, 2005).

Odom, William E., *On Internal War: American and Soviet Approaches to Third World Clients and Insurgents* (London: Duke University Press, 1992).

Olson, Mancur, "Dictatorship, Democracy and Development," *American Political Science Review*, 87 (September 1993), pp. 567–76.

Olson, William J., "The New World Disorder," in Max G. Manwaring, ed., *Gray Area Phenomena: Confronting the New World Disorder* (Boulder, CO: Westview Press, 1993).

Olson, William J., "U.S. Objectives and Constraints," in Richard Shultz, Robert Pfaltzgraff, Uri Ra'anan, William Olson, and Igor Lukes, eds., *Guerrilla Warfare and Counterinsurgency* (Lexington, MA: Lexington Books, 1993).

Operations Evaluation Department, "Higher Impact Adjustment Lending: Initial Evaluation," World Bank, Washington, DC, June 1999.

Owens, William, *Eye-Deep in Hell: A Memoir of the Liberation of the Philippines* (Dallas: SMU Press, 1989).

Park, Chang Jin, "The Influence of Small States upon the Superpowers: The United States-South Korean Relations as a Case Study, 1950–1953," *World Politics*, 28 (1975), pp. 97–117.

Patchen, Martin, *Resolving Disputes Between Nations: Coercion or Conciliation?* (Durham, NC: Duke University Press, 1988).

Pauker, Guy J., *Notes on Non-Military Measures in Control of Insurgency* (Santa Monica, CA: RAND, 1962).

Paul, Roland A., *American Military Commitments Abroad* (New Brunswick, NJ: Rutgers University Press, 1973).

Paul, T. V., "Influence through Arms Transfers: Lessons from the U.S.-Pakistani Relationship," *Asian Survey*, 32, no. 12 (December 1992), pp. 1078–92.

Pfeffer, Richard M., ed., *No More Vietnams? The War and the Future of American Foreign Policy* (New York: Harper & Row, 1968).

Phillips, Rufus, "Before We Lost in Vietnam," in Harvey C. Neese and John O'Donnell, eds., *Prelude to Tragedy: Vietnam, 1960–1965* (Annapolis, MD: Naval Institute Press, 2001).

Plascov, Avi, *Modernization, Political Development and Stability* (London: Gower, 1982).

Podhoretz, Norman, *Why We Were in Vietnam* (New York: Simon & Schuster, 1984).

"Polity IV Project: Political Regime Characteristics and Transitions, 1800–2008," Center for Systemic Peace, George Mason University, Arlington, VA.

Pomeroy, William, "The Philippine Peasantry and the Huk Revolt," *Journal of Peasant Studies*, 5, no. 4 (1978), pp. 497–517.

Porter, Gareth, *Perils of Dominance: Imbalance of Power and the Road to War in Vietnam* (Los Angeles: University of California Press, 2005).

Pratt, John, and Richard Zeckhauser, "Principals and Agents: An Overview," in John Pratt and Richard Zeckhauser, eds., *Principals and Agents: The Structure of Business* (Cambridge, MA: Harvard Business School Press, 1985).

Pribbenow, Merle L., *Victory in Vietnam: The Official History of the People's Army of Vietnam, 1954–1975* (Lawrence: University Press of Kansas, 2002).

Pye, Lucian, "Roots of Insurgency," in Harry Eckstein, ed., *Internal War* (New York: Free Press, 1964).

Pye, Lucian, *Aspects of Political Development: An Analytic Study* (Boston: Little Brown, 1966).

Quinlivan, James T., "Coup-Proofing: Its Practice and Consequences in the Middle East," *International Security*, 24, no. 2 (Fall 1999), pp. 131–65.

Quirino, Elpidio, "Initial Views on the Huk Problem," in *The New Philippine Ideology* (Manila: Bureau of Printing, 1949).

Race, Jeffrey, *War Comes to Long An* (Berkeley: University of California Press, 1972).

Ramazani, Rouhollah, *The United States and Iran: The Patterns of Influence* (New York: Praeger, 1982).

Ramsey, Robert, *Advising Indigenous Forces: American Advisors in Korea, Vietnam and El Salvador* (Ft Leavenworth, KS: Combat Studies Institute, 2006).

Rashid, Ahmed, "How Obama Lost Karzai," *Foreign Policy* (March–April 2011).

"Reacciones Nacionales," *Processo*, no. 33 (August 31–September 6, 1981).

Reagan, Ronald, *An American Life* (New York: Simon & Schuster, 1990).

"Recrudecimiento De La Violencia En El Salvador," *Estudios Centroamericanos*, no. 480 (October 1988).

Rees, Ray, "The Theory of Principal and Agent: Part 1," *Bulletin of Economic Research*, 37, no. 1 (1985), pp. 3–26.

Reeves, Richard, *President Kennedy: Profile in Power* (New York: Simon & Schuster, 1993).

Remmer, Karen, "Does Foreign Aid Promote the Expansion of Government?" *American Journal of Political Science*, 48, no. 1 (2004), pp. 77–92.

Resenick, Evan N. "Strange Bedfellows: U.S. Bargaining Behavior with Allies of Convenience," *International Security*, 35, no. 3 (Winter 2010–2011), pp. 144–84.

Reynolds, Celia L., and Wilfred T. Wan, "Empirical Trends in Sanctions and Positive Inducements in Nonproliferation," in Etel Solingen, ed., *Sanctions, Statecraft, and Nuclear Proliferation* (Cambridge: Cambridge University Press, 2012).

Risse-Kappen, Thomas, "Public Opinion, Domestic Structure and Foreign Policy in Liberal Democracies," *World Politics*, 43, no. 4 (July 1991), pp. 479–512.

Romulo, Carlos, *Crusade in Asia* (New York: John Day, 1955).

Romulo, Carlos, and Marvin Gray, *The Magsaysay Story* (New York: Pocket Books, 1957).

Root, Hilton L., *Alliance Curse: How America Lost the Third World* (Washington, DC: Brookings Institution Press, 2008).

Rosecrance, Richard, "Reward, Punishment and Interdependence," *Journal of Conflict Resolution*, 25, no. 1 (1981).

Rosello, Victor, "Lessons from El Salvador," *Parameters*, 23, no. 4 (Winter 1993–1994), pp. 100–8.

Ross, Stephen, "The Economic Theory of Agency: The Principal's Problem," *American Economic Review*, 63, no. 2 (May 1973), pp. 134–9.

Rosson, William, "Four Periods of American Involvement in Vietnam," Ph.D. dissertation, University of Oxford, 1978.

Rostow, Walt, *The Diffusion of Power: An Essay in Recent History* (New York: Macmillan, 1972).

Rothschild, Michael, and Joseph Stiglitz, "Equilibrium in Competitive Insurance Markets," *Quarterly Journal of Economics*, 90, no. 4 (November 1976), pp. 629–49.

Rothstein, Robert, *Alliances and Small Powers* (New York: Columbia University Press, 1968).

Rubin, Jeffrey, and Bert Brown, *The Social Psychology of Bargaining and Negotiation* (New York: Academic Press, 1975).

Satoshi, Nakano, "Gabriel L. Kaplan and U.S. Involvement in Philippine Electoral Democracy: A Tale of Two Democracies," *Philippine Studies*, 52, no. 2 (2004), pp. 149–78.

Scaff, Alvin, *The Philippine Answer to Communism* (Palo Alto, CA: Stanford University Press, 1955).

Schelling, Thomas C., *The Strategy of Conflict* (Cambridge, MA: Harvard University Press, 1960).

Schelling, Thomas C., *Arms and Influence* (New Haven, CT: Yale University Press, 1966).

Schelling, Thomas C., *Strategies of Commitment and Other Essays* (Cambridge, MA: Harvard University Press, 2006).

Schlesinger, Arthur M., *A Thousand Days* (London: Deutsch, 1965).

Schwarz, Benjamin C., *American Counterinsurgency Doctrine and El Salvador: The Frustrations of Reform and the Illusions of Nation Building* (Santa Monica, CA: RAND, 1991).

Sciolino, Elaine, "Panama's Chief Defies U.S. Powers of Persuasion," *New York Times*, January 17, 1988.

Sepp, Kalev, "The Evolution of United States Military Strategy in Central America, 1979–1991," Ph.D. dissertation, Harvard University, 2002.

Shafer, D. Michael, *Deadly Paradigms: The Failure of U.S. Counterinsurgency Policy* (Princeton, NJ: Princeton University Press, 1988).

Shalom, Stephen, "Counter-Insurgency in the Philippines," *Journal of Contemporary Asia*, 7, no. 2 (1977), pp. 153–77.

Sheehan, Michael, "Comparative Counterinsurgency Strategies: Guatemala and El Salvador," *Conflict*, 9, no. 2 (1989), pp. 127–54.

Sheehan, Neil, *A Bright Shining Lie: John Paul Vann and America in Vietnam* (New York: Random House, 1988).

Shoemaker, Christopher, and John Spanier, *Patron-Client State Relationships: Multilateral Crises in the Nuclear Age* (New York: Praeger, 1984).

Shultz, George P., *Turmoil and Triumph* (New York: Charles Scribner, 1993).

Shultz, Richard, "Strategy Lessons from an Unconventional War: The U.S. Experience in Vietnam," in Sam Sarkesian, ed., *Nonnuclear Conflicts in the Nuclear Age* (New York: Praeger, 1980).

Singer, J. David, "Inter-Nation Influence: A Formal Model," *American Political Science Review*, 57, no. 2 (June 1963), pp. 420–30.

Singer, J. David, "Reconstructing the Correlates of War Dataset on Material Capabilities of States, 1816–1985," *International Interactions*, 14, no. 2 (April 1987), pp. 115–32.

Skocpol, Theda, *States and Social Revolutions: A Comparative Analysis of France, Russia, and China* (Cambridge: Cambridge University Press, 1979).

Slater, Jerome, *Intervention and Negotiation* (New York: Harper & Row, 1970).

Smith, Alastair, "International Crises and Domestic Politics," *American Political Science Review*, 92, no. 3 (September 1998), pp. 623–38.

Smith, Joseph, *Portrait of a Cold Warrior* (New York: G.P. Putnam and Sons, 1976).

Smith, Robert, *Philippine Freedom, 1946–1958* (New York: Columbia University Press, 1958).

Smith, Robert, *The Hukbalahap Insurgency: Economic, Political and Military Factors* (Washington, DC: Office of the Chief of Military History, 1963).

Smith, Tony, "New Bottles for New Wine: A Pericentric Framework for the Study of the Cold War," *Diplomatic History*, 24, no. 4 (Fall 2000), pp. 567–91.

Snyder, David, and Charles Tilly, "Hardship and Collective Violence in France, 1830 to 1960," *American Sociological Review*, 37, no. 5 (October 1972).

Snyder, Glenn, and Paul Diesing, *Conflict among Nations: Bargaining, Decision Making, and System Structure in International Crises* (Princeton, NJ: Princeton University Press, 1977).

Spector, Ronald H., *Advice and Support: The Early Years, 1941–1960* (Washington, DC: Center of Military History, 1985).

Spencer, John H., *Ethiopia at Bay: A Personal Account of the Selassie Years* (Algonac, MI: Reference Publications, 1984).

Stanley, William, *The Protection Racket State: Elite Politics, Military Extortion, and Civil War in El Salvador* (Philadelphia: Temple University Press, 1996).

Stanley, William, "El Salvador: State-Building before and after Democratization, 1980–95," *Third World Quarterly*, 27, no. 1 (2006), pp. 101–14.

Starner, Frances, *Magsaysay and the Philippine Peasantry* (Los Angeles: University of California Press, 1961).

Statler, Kathryn, *Replacing France: The Origins of American Intervention in Vietnam* (Lexington: University Press of Kentucky, 2007).

Stiglitz, Joseph, "Principal and Agent (II)," in *A Dictionary of Economics* (Basingstoke: Palgrave, 2002) pp. 185–90.

Strachan, Hew, "British Counter-Insurgency from Malaya to Iraq," *The RUSI Journal*, 152, no. 6 (2007), pp. 8–11.

Summers, Harry, "A War Is a War Is a War Is a War," in Loren B. Thompson, ed., *Low-Intensity Conflict* (Lexington, MA: Lexington Books, 1989).

Svensson, Jakob, and David Dollar, "What Explains the Success or Failure of Structural Adjustment Programmes?" *Economic Journal*, 110, no. 466 (October 2000).

Talmadge, Caitlin, "Different Threats, Different Militaries: Explaining Organizational Practices in Authoritarian Armies," *Security Studies*, 25, no. 1 (February 2016), pp. 111–141.

Tanham, George, *Communist Revolutionary Warfare: From the Vietminh to the Viet Cong* (New York: Praeger, 1967).

Tanham, George, and Dennis Duncanson, "Some Dilemmas of Counterinsurgency," *Foreign Affairs*, 48, no. 1 (October 1969), pp. 113–22.

Taruc, Luis, *Born of the People* (Bombay: People's Publishing House, 1953).

Taruc, Luis, *He Who Rides the Tiger: The Story of an Asian Guerrilla Leader* (New York: Praeger, 1967).

Taylor, Maxwell, *Swords and Plowshares* (New York: W.W. Norton, 1972).

Thayer, Carlyle, "Southern Vietnamese Revolutionary Organizations," in Joseph Zasloff and MacAlister Brown, eds., *Communism in Indochina* (Lexington, MA: Lexington Books, 1975).

Thomas, *Comparative Revolutionary Movements: Search for Theory and Justice* (London: Prentice-Hall International, 1990).

Thompson, Leroy, *Ragged War: The Story of Unconventional and Counterrevolutionary Warfare* (London: Arms & Armor, 1994).

Thompson, Robert, *Defeating Communist Insurgency: The Lessons of Malaya and Vietnam* (London: Praeger, 1966).

Thompson, Robert, "Civic Action in Low-Intensity Warfare," *Proceedings of the Low Intensity Warfare Conference* (Washington, DC: Department of Defense, 1986).

Thorpe, William, "Huk Hunting in the Philippines, 1946–1953," *The Airpower Historian* (April 1962), pp. 95–100.

Tirona, Tomas, "The Philippine Anti-Communist Campaign," *Air University Quarterly Review* (Summer 1954), pp. 42–55.

Trachtenberg, Marc, "Audience Costs: An Historical Analysis," *Security Studies*, 21, no. 1 (March 2012), pp. 3–42.

Trinquier, Robert, *Modern Warfare: A French View of Counterinsurgency* (New York: Praeger, 1964).

Uclés, Mario Lungo, *El Salvador in the Eighties: Counterinsurgency and Revolution* (Philadelphia: Temple University Press, 1996).

Valeriano, Napoleon D., and Charles T. Bohannan, *Counter-Guerrilla Operations: The Philippine Experience* (London: Pall Mall Press, 1962).

Valeriano, Napoleon D., and Charles T. Bohannan, *Counter-Guerrilla Operations: The Philippine Experience* (Westport, CT: Praeger, 2006).

Van de Walle, Nicolas, *African Economies and the Politics of Permanent Crisis, 1979–1999* (New York: Cambridge University Press, 2001).

Vien, Cao Van, *The U.S. Advisor* (Washington, DC: U.S. Army Center of Military History, 1980).

Villalobos, Joaquin, *The War in El Salvador* (San Francisco: Solidarity Publications, 1986).

Waldner, David, *State Building and Late Development* (Ithaca, NY: Cornell University Press, 1999).

Walt, Stephen, *The Origins of Alliances* (Ithaca, NY: Cornell University Press, 1987).

Waltz, Kenneth N., *Theory of International Politics* (London: Addison-Wesley, 1979).

Warner, Denis, "Fighting the Viet Cong," *Army*, 12, no. 2 (September 1961).

Weber, Max, "Politics as a Vocation," in H. H. Gerth and C. Wright Mills, eds., *From Max Weber: Essays in Sociology* (Oxford: Oxford University Press, 1958).

Weder, Alberto, and Beatrice Alesina, "Do Corrupt Governments Receive Less Foreign Aid?" *American Economic Review*, 92, no. 4 (September 2002), pp. 1126–37.

Weinstein, Franklin, "The Concept of a Commitment in International Relations," *Journal of Conflict Resolution*, 13, no. 1 (March 1969), pp. 39–56.

Weinstein, Jeremy, "Resources and the Information Problem in Rebel Recruitment," *Journal of Conflict Resolution*, 49, no. 4 (2005), pp. 598–624.

Wendt, Alexander, "Anarchy Is What States Make of It: The Social Construction of Power Politics," *International Organization*, 46, no. 2 (Spring 1992), 391–425.

Whitcomb, Darrel, "Farm Gate," *Air Force Magazine*, 88, no. 12 (December 2005), pp. 82–7.

White, Theodore, ed., *The Stilwell Papers* (New York: W. Sloane Associates, 1948).

Wickham-Crowley, Timothy, "Understanding Failed Revolution in El Salvador," *Politics and Society*, 17, no. 4 (1989), pp. 511–30.

Wickham-Crowley, Timothy, *Guerrillas and Revolution in Latin America: A Comparative Study of Insurgents and Regimes since 1956* (Princeton, NJ: Princeton University Press, 1992).

Williams, Fredrick, "Guerrilla Warfare," in Franklin Osanka, ed., *Modern Guerrilla Warfare: Fighting Communist Guerrilla Movements, 1941–1961* (New York: Free Press, 1962).

Williamson, Oliver, *The Economic Institutions of Capitalism* (New York: Free Press, 1985).

Wirtz, James, *The Tet Offensive* (Ithaca, NY: Cornell University Press, 1994).

Wolfers, Arnold, *Discord and Collaboration: Essays in International Politics* (Baltimore: Johns Hopkins University Press, 1962).

Wood, Elisabeth, *Insurgent Collective Action and Civil War in El Salvador* (Cambridge: Cambridge University Press, 2003).

Woodward, Bob, *Veil: The Secret Wars of the CIA 1981–1987* (New York: Simon & Schuster, 1987).

Wriggins, W. Howard, and Gunnar Adler-Karlsson, *Reducing Global Inequities* (New York: McGraw-Hill, 1978).

Wurfel, David, "Philippine Agrarian Reform under Magsaysay, Part I," *Far Eastern Survey*, 27, no. 1 (January 1958), pp. 13, 23–30.

Wurfel, David, "Foreign Aid and Social Reform in Political Development: A Philippine Case Study," *American Political Science Review*, 53, no. 2 (June 1959), pp. 456–82.

Yin, Robert K., *Case Study Research: Design and Methods* (Thousand Oaks, CA: Sage, 2003).

Yoon, Mi Yung, "Explaining U.S. Intervention in Third World Internal Wars, 1945–1989," *Journal of Conflict Resolution*, 41, no. 4 (1997), pp. 580–602.

Young, Marilyn, John Fitzgerald, and Tom Grunfeld, *The Vietnam War: A History in Documents* (Oxford: Oxford University Press, 2003).

Zasloff, Joseph, *Origins of the Insurgency in South Vietnam, 1954–1960: The Role of the Southern Vietminh Cadres* (Santa Monica, CA: RAND, 1968).

Index